GREAT ATHLETES

FOOTBALL

GREAT ATHLETES

FOOTBALL

Volume 1

Herb Adderley–Peyton Manning

Edited by

The Editors of Salem Press

Special Consultant

Rafer Johnson

SALEM PRESS

Pasadena, California   Hackensack, New Jersey

Editor in Chief: Dawn P. Dawson

Editorial Director: Christina J. Moose   *Photo Editor:* Cynthia Breslin Beres
Managing Editor: R. Kent Rasmussen   *Acquisitions Editor:* Mark Rehn
Manuscript Editor: Christopher Rager   *Page Design and Layout:* James Hutson
Research Supervisor: Jeffry Jensen   *Additional Layout:* Frank Montaño and Mary Overell
Production Editor: Andrea Miller   *Editorial Assistant:* Brett Weisberg

Cover photo: Rebecca Cook/Reuters/Landov

Library of Congress Cataloging-in-Publication Data

Great athletes / edited by The Editors of Salem Press ; special consultant Rafer Johnson.
   p. cm.
Includes bibliographical references and index.
   ISBN 978-1-58765-473-2 (set : alk. paper) — ISBN 978-1-58765-474-9 (vol. 1 football : alk. paper) — ISBN 978-1-58765-475-6 (vol. 2 football : alk. paper) — ISBN 978-1-58765-476-3 (set football : alk. paper)
   1. Athletes—Biography—Dictionaries. I. Johnson, Rafer, 1935-   II. Salem Press.
   GV697.A1G68 2009
   796.0922—dc22
   [B]
   2009021905

First Printing

Contents

Publisher's Note vii
Introduction xi
Contributors xvii
Complete List of Contents xxv

Herb Adderley 1
Troy Aikman 4
Shaun Alexander 7
Damon Allen 9
Marcus Allen 12
Mike Alstott 15
Lance Alworth 17
Lyle Alzado 20
Morten Andersen 22
Doug Atkins 25
Champ Bailey 27
Sammy Baugh 29
Chuck Bednarik 32
Raymond Berry 35
Jerome Bettis 38
Fred Biletnikoff 41
Doc Blanchard 44
George Blanda 46
Drew Bledsoe 49
Tony Boselli 52
Terry Bradshaw 54
Tom Brady 57
Bob Brown 60
Jim Brown 62
Tim Brown 65
Tedy Bruschi 68
Buck Buchanan 70
Nick Buoniconti 72
Reggie Bush 74
Dick Butkus 77
Earl Campbell 80
John Carney 83
Cris Carter 85
Dutch Clark 88
Larry Csonka 91
Randall Cunningham 94
Ernie Davis 97
Glenn Davis 100
Terrell Davis 103
Len Dawson 106

Eric Dickerson 109
Dan Dierdorf 112
Mike Ditka 114
Clint Dolezel 117
Tony Dorsett 119
Warrick Dunn 122
Kenny Easley 125
Carl Eller 127
John Elway 130
Boomer Esiason 133
Marshall Faulk 135
Brett Favre 138
Doug Flutie 141
Dan Fouts 144
Benny Friedman 147
Rich Gannon 149
Antonio Gates 152
Eddie George 154
Frank Gifford 156
George Gipp 159
Tony Gonzalez 162
Otto Graham 164
Red Grange 167
Hugh Green 170
Joe Greene 172
Forrest Gregg 174
Bob Griese 176
Archie Griffin 179
Lou Groza 182
Ray Guy 185
Jack Ham 188
John Hannah 190
Tom Harmon 192
Franco Harris 194
Marvin Harrison 197
Ted Hendricks 199
Gene Hickerson 201
Elroy "Crazylegs" Hirsch 204
Priest Holmes 207
Paul Hornung 209
Ken Houston 212
Sam Huff 214
Don Hutson 216
Michael Irvin 219
Bo Jackson 222

Keith Jackson. 225
Edgerrin James. 227
Jimmy Johnson. 230
John Henry Johnson. 232
Deacon Jones. 235
Lee Roy Jordan. 238
Sonny Jurgensen 240
Jim Kelly 243
Nile Kinnick 246
Jerry Kramer 249
Jack Lambert 251
Dick "Night Train" Lane. 253
Steve Largent. 256
Bobby Layne 259
Jamal Lewis. 261
Ray Lewis 264

Bob Lilly 266
Floyd Little 268
Howie Long 271
Ronnie Lott 273
Sid Luckman 275
Johnny Lujack 278
John Lynch 280
Hugh McElhenny 283
Reggie McKenzie. 286
Jim McMahon 288
Donovan McNabb 291
Steve McNair 294
Archie Manning 297
Eli Manning 299
Peyton Manning 302

Publisher's Note

The two volumes of *Great Athletes: Football* are part of Salem Press's greatly expanded and redesigned *Great Athletes* series, which also includes self-contained volumes on baseball, basketball, boxing and soccer, golf and tennis, Olympic sports, and racing and individual sports. The full 13-volume series presents articles on the lives, sports careers, and unique achievements of 1,470 outstanding competitors and champions in the world of sports. These athletes—many of whom have achieved world renown—represent more than 75 different nations and territories and more than 80 different sports. Their stories are told in succinct, 1,000-word-long profiles accessible in tone and style to readers in grades 7 and up.

The 13 *Great Athletes* volumes, which include a cumulative index volume, are built on the work of three earlier Salem Press publications designed for middle and high school readers—the 20 slender volumes of *The Twentieth Century: Great Athletes* (1992), their 3-volume supplement (1994), and the 8 stouter volumes of *Great Athletes, Revised* (2002). This new 13-volume edition retains articles on every athlete covered in those earlier editions and adds more than 415 entirely new articles—a 40 percent increase—to bring the overall total to 1,470 articles.

These football volumes add 71 new articles to the 146 in the previous edition to cover a total of 217 football players. The content of other articles has been reviewed and updated as necessary, with many articles substantially revised, expanded, or replaced, and the bibliographical citations for virtually all articles have been updated. Information in every article is current through the end of the 2008-2009 football season.

Criteria for Inclusion

In selecting new names to add to *Great Athletes: Football*, first consideration was given to players whose extraordinary achievements have made their names household words. These include such undeniable stars as Tom Brady, Tony Gonzalez, Donovan McNabb, and the Canadian Football League's extraordinary Damon Allen, the brother of the NFL's Marcus Allen. Consideration was next given to accomplished young players who during the early twenty-first century appeared destined for even more greatness, such as Reggie Bush, Eli Manning, Adrian Peterson, and Ben Roethlisberger.

Organization

Each article covers the life and career of a single football player, and all names are arranged in one alphabetical stream. Every article is accompanied by at least one boxed table, summarizing the career statistics, honors and awards, records, and other milestones that set apart each great player. Most articles are also accompanied by photographs of their subjects. Every article also lists up-to-date bibliographical notes under the heading "Additional Sources." These sections list from three to five readily available books and articles containing information pertinent to the athlete and sport covered in the article. Appendixes in volume 2 contain additional sources in published books and Web sites.

Averaging three pages in length, each article is written in clear language and presented in a uniform, easily readable format. All articles are divided into four subheaded sections that cover the athlete's life and achievements chronologically.

- *Early Life* presents such basic biographical information as vital dates, parentage, siblings, and early education. It also sketches the social milieu in which the football player grew up and discusses other formative experiences.

- *The Road to Excellence* picks up where the player's earliest serious involvement in sports began. This section describes experiences and influences that shaped the player's athletic prowess and propelled him toward football greatness. These sections also often discuss obstacles—such as poverty, discrimination, and physical disabilities—that many great athletes have had to overcome.

- *The Emerging Champion* traces the player's advance from the threshold of football stardom to higher levels of achievement. This section explains the characteristics and circumstances that combined to make him among the best in the world in football.

- *Continuing the Story* tracks the player's subsequent career, examining how he may have set new goals and had achievements that inspired others. This section also offers insights into the player's life away from sports. Readers will also learn about the innovations and contributions that athletes have made to their sports and, in many cases, to society at large.

- *Summary* recapitulates the football player's story, paying special attention to honors that he has won and to the human qualities that have made him special in the world of sports.

Appendixes

At the back of volume 2, readers will find 12 appendixes, most of which are entirely new to this edition. The appendixes are arranged under these three headings:

- *Resources* contains a bibliography of recently published books on football and a detailed, categorized listing of sites on the World Wide Web that provide football information. The section also includes a Glossary defining most of the specialized terms used in essays and a Time Line that lists all the players covered in essays in order of their birth dates.

- *All-Time Great Players* contains 2 lists of all-time great football players and a list of Pro Football Hall of Fame Members.

- *Annual Awards and Honors* has 5 appendixes listing Heisman Trophy winners and NFL top draft picks and 3 annual honors.

The *Cumulative Indexes* volume, which accompanies the full *Great Athletes* series, includes every appendix found in this and other volumes on specific sports, *plus* additional appendixes containing information that pertains to all sports. These appendixes include a general bibliography, a comprehensive Web site list, a Time Line integrating the names of all 1,470 athletes in *Great Athletes*, 2 lists of the greatest athletes of the twentieth century, 3 multisport halls of fame, and 10 different athlete-of-the-year awards.

Indexes

Following the Appendixes in *Great Athletes: Football*, readers will find three indexes listing players by their names, positions played, and college and pro teams. The position and team indexes are completely new to this edition of *Great Athletes*. As all but a handful of the football players covered here are Americans, there is no need for a country index. Some athletes have competed in more than one sport, so readers may wish also to consult the *Cumulative Indexes* volume. Its sport, country, and name indexes list all the athletes covered in the full *Great Athletes* series.

Acknowledgments

Once again, Salem Press takes great pleasure in thanking the 383 scholars and experts who wrote and updated the articles making *Great Athletes* possible. Their names can be found at the ends of the articles they have written and in the list of contributors that follows the "Introduction." We also take immense pleasure in again thanking our special consultant, Rafer Johnson, for bringing his unique insights to this project. As an Olympic champion and world record-holder in track and field's demanding decathlon, he has experienced an extraordinarily broad range of physical and mental challenges at the highest levels of competition. Moreover, he has a lifetime of experience working with, and closely observing, athletes at every level—from five-year-old soccer players to Olympic and professional champions. He truly understands what constitutes athletic greatness and what is required to achieve it. For this reason, readers will not want to overlook his "Introduction."

Acronyms Used in Articles

Salem's general practice is to use acronyms only after they have been explained within each essay. Because of the frequency with which many terms appear in *Great Athletes: Football,* that practice is partly suspended for the acronyms listed here:

AFC American Football Conference

AFL American Football League; Arena Football League

CFL Canadian Football League

ESPN Entertainment and Sports Programming Network

NCAA National Collegiate Athletic Association

NFC National Football Conference

NFL National Football League

Introduction

Five decades after reaching my own pinnacle of success in sports, I still get a thrill watching other athletes perform. I have competed with and against some of the greatest athletes in the world, watched others up close and from a distance, and read about still others. I admire the accomplishments of all of them, for I know something of what it takes to achieve greatness in sports, and I especially admire those who inspire others.

This revised edition of *Great Athletes* provides a wonderful opportunity for young readers to learn about the finest athletes of the modern era of sports. Reading the stories of the men and women in these pages carries me back to my own youth, when I first began playing games and became interested in sports heroes. Almost all sports interested me, but I gravitated to baseball, basketball, football, and track and field. Eventually, I dedicated most of my young adult years to track and field's decathlon, which I loved because its ten events allowed me to use many different skills.

Throughout those years, one thing remained constant: I wanted to *win*. To do that meant being the best that I could be. I wondered what I could learn from the lives of great athletes. From an early age I enjoyed reading about sports champions and wondered how they did as well as they did. What traits and talents did the greatest of them have? I gradually came to understand that the essence of greatness in sports lies in competition. In fact, the very word *athlete* itself goes back to a Greek word for "competitor." Being competitive is the single most important attribute any athlete can have, but other traits are important, too. Readers may gain insights into the athletes covered in these volumes by considering the ten events of the decathlon as symbols of ten traits that contribute to athletic greatness. All champions have at least a few of these traits; truly great champions have most of them.

Speed and Quickness

Decathlon events are spread over two days, with five events staged on each day. The first event is always the 100-meter dash—one of the most glamorous events in track and field. Men and women—such as Usain Bolt and Florence Griffith-Joyner—who capture its world records are considered the fastest humans on earth. In a race that lasts only a few seconds, speed is everything, and there is no room for mistakes.

Appropriately, speed is the first of the three standards of athletic excellence expressed in the Olympic motto, *Citius, altius, fortius* (faster, higher, stronger). Its importance in racing sports such as cycling, rowing, running, speed skating, swimming, and the triathlon is obvious: Athletes who reach the finish line soonest win; those who arrive later lose. Speed is also important in every sport that requires moving around a lot, such as baseball, basketball, boxing, football, handball, soccer, tennis, volleyball, water polo, and virtually all the events of track and field. The best athletes in these sports are usually fast.

Athletes who lack speed generally make up for it in other kinds of quickness. For example, while running speed has helped make some football quarterbacks—such as Vince Young—great, some quarterbacks who are slow afoot have achieved greatness with other forms of quickness. Joe Namath is an example. Although he was embarrassingly slow on his feet, he read opposing teams' defenses so fast that he could make lightning-quick decisions and release his passes faster than almost any other quarterback who played the game.

As important as speed is, there are a few sports in which it means little. Billiards, bowling, and golf, for example, all permit competitors to take considerable time responding to opponents' moves. Even so, speed can be important where one may least expect it. For example, major chess competitions are clocked, and making moves too slowly can cost players games.

Courage

The decathlon's second event, the long jump, represents one of the purest contests in sports: Competitors simply run up to a mark and jump as far as they can. Each jumper gets several tries, and only the best marks matter. While it sounds simple, it involves critical little things that can go wrong and ruin one's chance of winning. When the great Jesse Owens jumped in the 1936 Olympics in Berlin, for example, he missed his takeoff mark so many times that he risked disqualification. What saved him was the encouragement of a rival German jumper, who advised him to start his jump from well behind the regular takeoff mark. It takes courage to overcome the fear of making mistakes and concentrate on jumping. It also takes courage to overcome the fear of injury.

A great athlete may have abundant courage but rarely need to call upon it. However, most truly great athletes eventually face moments when they would fail if their courage abandoned them. In fact, courage is often what separates being good from being great. True courage should not be confused with the absence of fear, for it is the ability to overcome fear, including the very natural fears of injury and pain. A wonderful example is gymnast Kerri Strug's amazing spirit in the 1996 Olympics. Ignoring the pain of torn ligaments and a serious ankle sprain, she helped the U.S. women win a team gold medal by performing her final vault at great personal risk.

Some sports challenge athletes with real and persistent threats of serious injuries and even death. Among the most dangerous are alpine skiing, auto racing, boxing, football, horse racing, mountaineering, and rodeo—all of which have killed and disabled many fine athletes. No one can achieve greatness in such sports without exceptional courage.

Consider also the courage required to step up to bat against a baseball pitcher who throws hardballs mere inches away from your head at speeds of more than ninety miles an hour. Or, imagine preparing to dive from atop a 10-meter platform, resting only on your toes, with your heels projecting over the edge, knowing that your head will pass within inches of the rock-hard edge of the platform. Greg Louganis once cut his head open on such a dive. After he had his scalp stitched up, he returned to continue diving into a pool of water colored pink by his own blood. He won the competition.

Another kind of courage is needed to perform in the face of adversity that may have nothing to do with sport itself. The best known example of that kind of courage is the immortal Jackie Robinson, who broke the color line in baseball in 1947. As the first African American player in the modern major leagues, Jackie faced criticism, verbal harassment, and even physical abuse almost everywhere he played. He not only persevered but also had a career that would have been regarded as exceptional even if his color had never been an issue.

Strength

The shot put, the decathlon's third event, requires many special traits, but the most obvious is strength. The metal ball male shot putters heave weighs 16 pounds—more than an average bowling ball. Agility, balance, and speed are all important to the event, but together they can accomplish nothing without great strength. Strength is also the third standard expressed in the Olympic motto, *Citius, altius, fortius.*

Strength is especially valuable in sports that put competitors in direct physical contact with each other—sports such as basketball, boxing, football, and wrestling. Whenever athletes push and pull against each other, the stronger generally prevail. Strength is also crucial in sports requiring lifting, pulling, pushing, paddling, or propelling objects, or controlling vehicles or animals. Such sports include auto racing, baseball and softball, bodybuilding and weightlifting, canoeing and kayaking, golf, horse racing, rowing, and all track and field throwing events.

One sport in which the role of strength has never been underestimated is wrestling. One of the most impressive demonstrations of strength in the sport occurred at the 2000 Olympic Games at Sydney when Rulon Gardner, in a performance of a lifetime, defeated former Olympic champion Aleksandr Karelin in the super-heavyweight class of Greco-Roman wrestling.

Visualization

Visualization is the ability to see what one needs to do before actually doing it. Perhaps no sport better exemplifies its importance than the high jump—the decathlon's fourth event. In contrast to the long jump and throwing events—in which competitors strive to maximize distance in every effort, the high jump (like the pole vault) sets a bar at a fixed height that competitors must clear. Before jumping, they take time to study the bar and visualize what they must do to clear it. If the bar is set at 7 feet, a jump of 6 feet 11¾ inches fails; a jump of 8 feet succeeds, but counts only for 7 feet. To conserve strength for later jumps, jumpers must carefully calculate how much effort to exert at each height, and to do this, they must be able to visualize.

Great baseball and softball batters also visualize well. Before pitches even reach the plate, batters see the balls coming and visualize their bats hitting them. Likewise, great golfers see their balls landing on the greens before they even swing. Soccer players, such as Ronaldo, see the balls going into the goal before they even kick them. Billiard players, such as Jeanette Lee, see all the balls moving on the table before they even touch the cue balls. Bowlers, like Lisa Wagner, see the pins tumbling down before they release their balls.

Visualization is especially important to shooters, such as Lones Wigger, and archers, such as Denise Parker and Jay Barrs, who know exactly what their targets look like, as well as the spots from where they will fire, before they even take aim. In contrast to most other sports, they can practice in conditions almost identical to those in which they compete. However, the athletes against whom they compete have the same advantage, so the edge usually goes to those who visualize better.

Players in games such as basketball, hockey, soccer, and water polo fire upon fixed targets from constantly changing positions—often in the face of opponents doing everything they can to make them miss. Nevertheless, visualization is important to them as well. In basketball, players are said to be in a "groove," or a "zone," when they visualize shots so well they seem unable to miss. Kobe Bryant and Lisa Leslie are among the greatest visualizers in their sport, just as Babe Ruth, Hank Aaron, and Albert Pujols have been great at visualizing home runs in baseball. In tennis, I always admired Arthur Ashe's knack for planning matches in his mind, then systematically dismantling his opponents.

At another level, boxer Muhammad Ali was great at visualizing his entire future. Big, strong, and quick and able to move with the best of them, he had it all. I had the great pleasure of touring college campuses with him after we both won gold medals at the Rome Olympics in 1960. Muhammad (then known as Cassius Clay) had visualized his Olympic victory before it happened, and when I first knew him he was already reciting poetry and predicting what the future held for him. He saw it all in advance and called every move—something he became famous for later, when he taunted opponents by predicting the rounds in which he would knock them out.

Determination and Resilience

The final event of the first day of decathlon competition is the 400-meter run. Almost exactly a quarter mile, this race stands at the point that divides sprints from middle-distances. Should runners go all out, as in a sprint, or pace themselves, as middle-distance runners do? Coming as it does, as the last event of the exhausting first day of decathlon competition, the 400-meter race tests the mettle of decathletes by extracting one last great effort from them before they can rest up for the next day's grueling events. How they choose to run the race has to do with how determined they are to win the entire decathlon.

Every great athlete who wants to be a champion must have the determination to do whatever it takes to achieve that goal. Even so, determination alone is not enough. This was proven dramatically when basketball's Michael Jordan—whom journalists later voted the greatest athlete of the twentieth century—quit basketball in 1994 to fulfill his lifelong dream to play professional baseball. Despite working hard, he spent a frustrating season and a half in the minor leagues and merely proved two things: that determination alone cannot guarantee success, and that baseball is a more difficult sport than many people had realized.

Resilience, an extension of determination, is the ability to overcome adversity, or apparently hopeless situations, and to bounce back from outright defeat. Some might argue that no one can be greater than an athlete who never loses; however, athletes who continually win are never required to change what they do or do any soul searching. By contrast, athletes who lose must examine themselves closely and consider making changes. I have always felt that true greatness in sports is exemplified by the ability to come back from defeat, as heavyweight boxer Floyd Patterson did after losing his world title to Ingemar Johansson in a humiliating 3-round knockout in 1959. Only those athletes who face adversity and defeat can prove they have resilience.

Among athletes who have impressed me the most with their determination and resilience is speed skater Eric Heiden, who was not only the first American to win world speed-skating championships, but the first speed skater ever to win all five events in the Winter Olympics. Another amazingly determined athlete is Jim Abbott, who refused to allow the fact that he was born with only one hand stop him from becoming a Major League Baseball pitcher—one who even pitched a no-hit game. Who could not admire Bo Jackson? An all-star in both professional football and Major League Baseball, he suffered what appeared to be a career-ending football injury. After undergoing hip-joint replacement surgery, he defied all logic by returning to play several more seasons of baseball. Cyclist Lance Armstrong also falls into this category. He won multiple Tour de France championships after recovering from cancer.

Execution

Day two of the decathlon opens with the technically challenging 110-meter high hurdles. A brutally demanding event, it requires speed, leaping ability, and perfect timing. In short, it is an event that requires careful execution—the ability to perform precisely when it matters. Sports differ greatly in the precision of execution they demand. Getting off great throws in the discus, shot put, and javelin, for example, requires superb execution, but the direction in which the objects go is not critical. By contrast, archers, shooters, and golfers must hit precise targets. Some sports not only demand that execution be precise but also that it be repeated. A baseball pitcher who throws two perfect strikes fails if the opposing batter hits the third pitch over the fence. Likewise, a quarterback who leads his team down the field with five consecutive perfect passes fails if his next pass is intercepted.

Consider the differences between the kind of execution demanded by diving and pole vaulting. Divers lose points if their toes are not straight the moment they enter the water. By contrast, pole vaulters can land any way they want, so long as they clear the bar. Moreover, a diver gets only one chance on each dive, while pole vaulters get three chances at each height they attempt—and they can even skip certain heights to save energy for later jumps at greater heights. On the other hand, a diver who executes a dive badly will merely get a poor score, while a pole vaulter who misses too many jumps will get no score at all—which is exactly what hap-

pened to decathlete Dan O'Brien in the 1992 U.S. Olympic Trials. Although Dan was the world's top decathlete at that time, his failure to clear a height in the pole vault kept him off the Olympic team. (To his credit, he came back to win a gold medal in 1996.)

Figure skating and gymnastics are other sports that measure execution with a microscope. In gymnastics, the standard of perfection is a score of ten—which was first achieved in the Olympics by Nadia Comăneci in 1976. However, scores in those sports are not based on objective measures but on the evaluations of judges, whose own standards can and do change. By contrast, archery, shooting, and bowling are unusual in being sports that offer objective standards of perfection. In bowling, that standard is the 300 points awarded to players who bowl all strikes.

Among all athletes noted for their execution, one in particular stands out in my estimation: golf's Tiger Woods. After Tiger had played professionally for only a few years, he established himself as one of the greatest golfers ever. He has beaten the best that golf has had to offer by record margins in major competitions, and wherever he plays, he is the favorite to win. Most impressive is his seeming ability to do whatever he needs to win, regardless of the situation. Few athletes in any sport, or in any era, have come close to matching Tiger's versatile and consistent execution.

Focus

After the high hurdles, the decathlon's discus event is a comparative relief. Nevertheless, it presents its own special demands, one of which is focus—the ability to maintain uninterrupted concentration. Like shot putters, discus throwers work within a tiny circle, within which they must concentrate all their attention and all their energy into throwing the heavy disk as far as they can.

Not surprisingly, one of the greatest discus throwers in history, Al Oerter, was also one of the greatest examples of focus in sports. His four gold medals between 1956 and 1968 made him the first track and field athlete in Olympic history to win any event four times in a row. In addition to beating out the best discus throwers in the world four consecutive times, he improved his own performance at each Olympiad and even won with a serious rib injury in 1964. Eight years after retiring from competition, he returned at age forty to throw the discus farther than ever and earn a spot as an alternate on the 1980 U.S. Olympic team.

Important in all sports, focus is especially important in those in which a single lapse in concentration may result in instant defeat. In boxing, a knockout can suddenly end a bout. Focus may be even more crucial in wrestling. Wrestlers grapple each other continuously, probing for openings that will allow them to pin their opponents. Few sports match wrestling in nonstop intensity; a single split-second lapse on the part of a wrestler can spell disaster. Great wrestlers, such as Cael Sanderson and Aleksandr Karelin, must therefore rank among the most focused athletes in history.

Balance and Coordination

Of all the decathlon events, the most difficult to perform is the pole vault. Think of what it entails: Holding long skinny poles, vaulters run at full speed down a narrow path toward a pit; then, without breaking stride, push the tips of their poles into a tiny slot, propel their bodies upward, and use the poles to flip themselves over bars more than two or three times their height above the ground, finally to drop down on the opposite side. Success in the pole vault demands many traits, but the most important are balance and coordination. Vaulters use their hands, feet, and bodies, all at the same time, and do everything at breakneck speed, with almost no margin for error. There are no uncoordinated champion pole vaulters.

Despite its difficulty, pole vaulting is an event in which some decathletes have performed especially well—perhaps because they, as a group, have versatile skills. I have long taken pride in the fact that my close friend, college teammate, and Olympic rival, C. K. Yang, once set a world record in the pole vault during a decathlon. C. K.'s record was all the more impressive because he achieved it midway through the second day of an intense competition. Imagine what balance and coordination he must have had to propel his body over the record-breaking height after having subjected it to the wear and tear of seven other events.

I cannot think of any athlete, in any sport, who demonstrated more versatility in coordination and balance than Michael Jordan, who could seemingly score from any spot on the floor, at any time, and under any conditions. Not only did he always have his offensive game together, he was also one of the greatest defensive players in the game. Moreover, his mere presence brought balance to his entire team.

Preparation

The ninth event of the decathlon is the javelin—a throwing event that goes back to ancient times. A more difficult event than it may appear to be, it requires more than its share of special preparation. This may be why we rarely see athletes who compete in both the javelin and other events, though the versatile Babe Didrikson Zaharias was an exception.

Along with determination—to which it is closely allied—preparation is a vital trait of great athletes, especially in modern competition. It is no longer possible for even the greatest natural athletes to win against top competition without extensive preparation, which means practice, training for strength and stamina, proper diet and rest, and studying opponents diligently. Football players, especially quarterbacks and defensive backs, spend hours before every game studying films of opponents.

I was fortunate to grow up with an athlete who exemplifies preparation: my younger brother, Jimmy Johnson, who would become defensive back for the San Francisco 49ers for seventeen years and later be elected to the Pro Football Hall of Fame. Every week, Jimmy had to face a completely different set of pass receivers, but he was always ready because he studied their moves and trained himself to run backward fast enough to keep offenses in front of him so he could see every move they made. Coach Tom Landry of the Dallas Cowboys once told me that he always had the Cowboys attack on the side opposite from Jimmy.

Another exceptionally well prepared athlete was Magic Johnson, the great Lakers basketball guard, who played every position on the floor in more than one game. During his rookie season he had one of the greatest performances in playoff history during the NBA Finals. When a health problem prevented the Lakers' great center, Kareem Abdul-Jabbar, from playing in the sixth game against Philadelphia, Magic stunned everyone by filling in for him at center and scoring 44 points. He went on to become one of the great point guards in basketball history because he always knew where every player on the court should be at every moment.

Stamina

If there is one event that most decathletes dread, it is the grueling 1,500-meter race that concludes the two-day competition. While C. K. Yang once set a world-record in the pole vault during a decathlon, no decathlete has ever come close to anything even resembling a world-class mark in the 1,500 meters. On the other hand, it is probable that no world-class middle-distance runner has ever run a 1,500-meter race immediately after competing in nine other events. To win a decathlon, the trick is not to come in first in this final race, but simply to survive it. For decathletes, it is not so much a race as a test of stamina.

When I competed in the decathlon in the Rome Olympics of 1960, I had to go head-to-head against my friend C. K. Yang through nine events, all the while knowing that the gold medal would be decided in the last event—the 1,500 meters. C. K. was one of the toughest and most durable athletes I have ever known, and I realized I could not beat him in that race. However, after the javelin, I led by enough points so that all I had to do was stay close to him. I managed to do it and win the gold medal, but running that race was not an experience I would care to repeat.

Stamina is not really a skill, but a measure of the strength to withstand or overcome exhaustion. Rare is the sport that does not demand some stamina. Stamina can be measured in a single performance—such as a long-distance race—in a tournament, or in the course of a long season.

The classic models of stamina are marathon runners, whose 26-plus-mile race keeps them moving continuously for more than two hours. Soccer is one of the most demanding of stamina among team sports. Its players move almost constantly and may run as far as 5 miles in a 90-minute game that allows few substitutions. Basketball players run nearly as much as soccer players, but their games are shorter and allow more substitutions and rest periods. However, the sport can be even more tiring than soccer because its teams play more frequently and play more games overall. Baseball players provide yet another contrast. They spend a great deal of time during their games sitting on the bench, and when they are on the field, players other than the pitcher and catcher rarely need to exert themselves more than a few seconds at a time. However, their season has the most games of all, and their constant travel is draining. All these sports and others demand great stamina from their players, and their greatest players are usually those who hold up the best.

To most people, chess seems like a physically undemanding game. However, its greatest players must be in top physical condition to withstand the unrelenting mental pressure of tournament and match competitions, which can last for weeks. Bobby Fisher, one of the game's greatest—and most eccentric—champions, exercised heavily when he competed in order to stay in shape. Even sprinters who spend only 10 or 11 seconds on the track in each race, need stamina. In order to reach the finals of major competitions, they must endure the physical and mental strains of several days of preliminary heats.

In reducing what makes athletes great to just ten traits, I realize that I have oversimplified things, but that matters little, as my purpose here is merely to introduce readers to what makes the athletes in these volumes great. Within these pages you will find stories exemplifying many other traits, and that is good, as among the things that make athletes endlessly fascinating are their diversity and complexity.

Rafer Johnson

Contributors

Randy L. Abbott
University of Evansville

Tony Abbott
Trumbull, Connecticut

Michael Adams
*City College of New York
Graduate Center*

Patrick Adcock
Henderson State University

Amy Adelstein
Toluca Lake, California

Richard Adler
University of Michigan, Dearborn

Paul C. Alexander II
Southern Illinois University

Elizabeth Jeanne Alford
*Southern Illinois University,
Carbondale*

Eleanor B. Amico
Whitewater, Wisconsin

Ronald L. Ammons
University of Findlay

Earl Andresen
University of Texas, Arlington

David L. Andrews
*University of Illinois, Urbana-
Champaign*

Frank Ardolino
University of Hawaii

Vikki M. Armstrong
Fayetteville State University

Bryan Aubrey
Maharishi International University

Patti Auer
United States Gymnastics Federation

Philip Bader
Pasadena, California

Sylvia P. Baeza
Applied Ballet Theater

Amanda J. Bahr-Evola
*Southern Illinois University,
Edwardsville*

Alan Bairner
Loughborough University

JoAnn Balingit
University of Delaware

Susan J. Bandy
United States International University

Jessie F. Banks
University of Southern Colorado

Linda Bannister
Loyola Marymount University

C. Robert Barnett
Marshall University

David Barratt
Montreat College

Maryanne Barsotti
Warren, Michigan

Bijan Bayne
*Association for Professional Basketball
Research*

Barbara C. Beattie
Sarasota, Florida

Suzanne M. Beaudet
University of Maine, Presque Isle

Joseph Beerman
*Borough of Manhattan Community
College, CUNY*

Keith J. Bell
Western Carolina University

Stephen T. Bell
Independent Scholar

Alvin K. Benson
Utah Valley University

Chuck Berg
University of Kansas

S. Carol Berg
College of St. Benedict

Milton Berman
University of Rochester

Terry D. Bilhartz
Sam Houston State University

Cynthia A. Bily
Adrian College

Nicholas Birns
New School University

Joe Blankenbaker
Georgia Southern University

Carol Blassingame
Texas A&M University

Elaine M. Blinde
*Southern Illinois University,
Carbondale*

Harold R. Blythe, Jr.
Eastern Kentucky University

Jo-Ellen Lipman Boon
Independent Scholar

Trevor D. Bopp
Texas A&M University

Stephen Borelli
USA Today

John Boyd
Appalachian State University

Marlene Bradford
Texas A&M University

Michael R. Bradley
Motlow College

Carmi Brandis
Fort Collins, Colorado

Kevin L. Brennan
Ouachita Baptist University

Matt Brillinger
Carleton University

John A. Britton
Francis Marion University

Norbert Brockman
St. Mary's University of San Antonio

Howard Bromberg
University of Michigan Law School

Valerie Brooke
Riverside Community College

Dana D. Brooks
West Virginia University

Alan Brown
Livingston University

Valerie Brown
*Northwest Kansas Educational
    Service Center*

Thomas W. Buchanan
Ancilla Domini College

Fred Buchstein
John Carroll University

David Buehrer
Valdosta State University

Cathy M. Buell
San Jose State University

Michael H. Burchett
Limestone College

Edmund J. Campion
University of Tennessee, Knoxville

Peter Carino
Indiana State University

Lewis H. Carlson
Western Michigan University

Russell N. Carney
Missouri State University

Bob Carroll
*Professional Football Researchers
    Association*

Culley C. Carson
University of North Carolina

Craig Causer
Pompton Lakes, New Jersey

David Chapman
*North American Society of
    Sports Historians*

Paul J. Chara, Jr.
Northwestern College

Frederick B. Chary
Indiana University Northwest

Jerry E. Clark
Creighton University

Rhonda L. Clements
Hofstra University

Douglas Clouatre
MidPlains Community College

Kathryn A. Cochran
University of Kansas

Susan Coleman
West Texas A&M University

Caroline Collins
Quincy University

Brett Conway
Namseoul University

Carol Cooper
University of Northern Iowa

Richard Hauer Costa
Texas A&M University

Michael Coulter
Grove City College

David A. Crain
South Dakota State University

Louise Crain
South Dakota State University

Scott A. G. M. Crawford
Eastern Illinois University

Lee B. Croft
Arizona State University

Ronald L. Crosbie
Marshall University

Thomas S. Cross
Texas A&M University

Brian Culp
Indiana University

Michael D. Cummings, Jr.
Madonna University

Joanna Davenport
Auburn University

Kathy Davis
North Carolina State University

Mary Virginia Davis
California State University, Sacramento

Buck Dawson
International Swimming Hall of Fame

Dawn P. Dawson
Pasadena, California

Margaret Debicki
Los Angeles, California

Bill Delaney
San Diego, California

Paul Dellinger
Wytheville, Virginia

Andy DeRoche
Front Range Community College

James I. Deutsch
Smithsonian Institution

Contributors

Joseph Dewey
University of Pittsburgh, Johnstown

M. Casey Diana
Arizona State University

Randy J. Dietz
South Carolina State University

Jonathan E. Dinneen
VeriSign, Inc.

Marcia B. Dinneen
Bridgewater State College

Dennis M. Docheff
Whitworth College

Cecilia Donohue
Madonna University

Pamela D. Doughty
Texas A&M University

Thomas Drucker
University of Wisconsin, Whitewater

Jill Dupont
University of Chicago

William G. Durick
Blue Valley School District

W. P. Edelstein
Los Angeles, California

Bruce L. Edwards
Bowling Green State University

William U. Eiland
University of Georgia

Henry A. Eisenhart
University of Oklahoma

Kenneth Ellingwood
Los Angeles, California

Julie Elliott
Indiana University South Bend

Mark R. Ellis
University of Nebraska, Kearney

Robert P. Ellis
Northboro, Massachusetts

Don Emmons
Glendale News-Press

Robert T. Epling
*North American Society of
Sports Historians*

Thomas L. Erskine
Salisbury University

Steven G. Estes
California State University, Fullerton

Don Evans
The College of New Jersey

Jack Ewing
Boise, Idaho

Kevin Eyster
Madonna University

Norman B. Ferris
Middle Tennessee State University

John W. Fiero
University of Southwestern Louisiana

Paul Finkelman
Brooklyn Law School

Paul Finnicum
Arkansas State University

Jane Brodsky Fitzpatrick
*Graduate Center, City University
of New York*

Michael J. Fratzke
Indiana Wesleyan University

Tom Frazier
Cumberland College

A. Bruce Frederick
*International Gymnastics Hall of Fame
and Museum*

Daniel J. Fuller
Kent State University

Jean C. Fulton
Maharishi International University

Carter Gaddis
Tampa Tribune

Thomas R. Garrett
Society for American Baseball Research

Jan Giel
Drexel University

Daniel R. Gilbert
Moravian College

Duane A. Gill
Mississippi State University

Vincent F. A. Golphin
The Writing Company

Bruce Gordon
Auburn University, Montgomery

Margaret Bozenna Goscilo
University of Pittsburgh

John Gould
Independent Scholar

Karen Gould
Austin, Texas

Lewis L. Gould
University of Texas, Austin

Larry Gragg
University of Missouri, Rolla

Lloyd J. Graybar
Eastern Kentucky University

Wanda Green
University of Northern Iowa

William C. Griffin
Appalachian State University

Irwin Halfond
McKendree College

Jan Hall
Columbus, Ohio

Roger D. Hardaway
*Northwestern Oklahoma State
University*

William Harper
Purdue University

Great Athletes: Football

Robert Harrison
University of Arkansas Community College

P. Graham Hatcher
Shelton State Community College

Karen Hayslett-McCall
University of Texas, Dallas

Leslie Heaphy
Kent State University, Stark

Bernadette Zbicki Heiney
Lock Haven University of Pennsylvania

Timothy C. Hemmis
Edinboro University of Pennsylvania

Steve Hewitt
University of Birmingham

Carol L. Higy
Methodist College

Randall W. Hines
Susquehanna University

Joseph W. Hinton
Portland, Oregon

Arthur D. Hlavaty
Yonkers, New York

Carl W. Hoagstrom
Ohio Northern University

William H. Hoffman
Fort Meyers, Florida

Kimberley M. Holloway
King College

John R. Holmes
Franciscan University of Steubenville

Joseph Horrigan
Pro Football Hall of Fame

William L. Howard
Chicago State University

Shane L. Hudson
Texas A&M University

Mary Hurd
East Tennessee State University

Raymond Pierre Hylton
Virginia Union University

Shirley Ito
Amateur Athletic Foundation of Los Angeles

Frederick Ivor-Campbell
North American Society of Sports Historians

Shakuntala Jayaswal
University of New Haven

Doresa A. Jennings
Shorter College

Albert C. Jensen
Central Florida Community College

Jeffry Jensen
Altadena, California

Bruce E. Johansen
University of Nebraska, Omaha

Lloyd Johnson
Campbell University

Mary Johnson
University of South Florida

Alexander Jordan
Boston University

David Kasserman
Rowan University

Robert B. Kebric
University of Louisville

Rodney D. Keller
Ricks College

Barbara J. Kelly
University of Delaware

Kimberley H. Kidd
*East Tennessee State University
King College*

Leigh Husband Kimmel
Indianapolis, Indiana

Tom Kinder
Bridgewater College

Joe King
Alameda Journal

Jane Kirkpatrick
Auburn University, Montgomery

Paul M. Klenowski
Thiel College

Darlene A. Kluka
University of Alabama, Birmingham

Lynne Klyse
California State University, Sacramento

Bill Knight
Western Illinois University

Francis M. Kozub
College at Brockport, State University of New York

Lynn C. Kronzek
University of Judaism

Shawn Ladda
Manhattan College

P. Huston Ladner
University of Mississippi

Philip E. Lampe
University of the Incarnate Word

Tom Lansford
University of Southern Mississippi

Eugene Larson
Los Angeles Pierce College

Rustin Larson
Maharishi International University

Kevin R. Lasley
Eastern Illinois University

Mary Lou LeCompte
University of Texas, Austin

Denyse Lemaire
Rowan University

Contributors

Victor Lindsey
East Central University

Alar Lipping
Northern Kentucky University

Janet Long
Pasadena, California

M. Philip Lucas
Cornell College

Leonard K. Lucenko
Montclair State College

R. C. Lutz
Madison Advisors

Robert McClenaghan
Pasadena, California

Arthur F. McClure
Central Missouri State University

Roxanne McDonald
New London, New Hampshire

Alan McDougall
University of Guelph

Mary McElroy
Kansas State University

Thomas D. McGrath
Baylor University

Marcia J. Mackey
Central Michigan University

Michelle C. K. McKowen
New York, New York

John McNamara
Beltsville, Maryland

Joe McPherson
East Tennessee State University

Paul Madden
Hardin Simmons University

Mark J. Madigan
University of Vermont

Philip Magnier
Maharishi International University

H. R. Mahood
Memphis State University

Barry Mann
Atlanta, Georgia

Nancy Farm Mannikko
*Centers for Disease Control &
    Prevention*

Robert R. Mathisen
Western Baptist College

Russell Medbery
Colby-Sawyer College

Joella H. Mehrhof
Emporia State University

Julia M. Meyers
Duquesne University

Ken Millen-Penn
Fairmont State College

Glenn A. Miller
Texas A&M University

Lauren Mitchell
St. Louis, Missouri

Christian H. Moe
*Southern Illinois University,
    Carbondale*

Mario Morelli
Western Illinois University

Caitlin Moriarity
Brisbane, California

Elizabeth C. E. Morrish
State University of New York, Oneonta

Todd Moye
Atlanta, Georgia

Tinker D. Murray
Southwest Texas State University

Alex Mwakikoti
University of Texas, Arlington

Alice Myers
Bard College at Simon's Rock

Michael V. Namorato
University of Mississippi

Jerome L. Neapolitan
Tennessee Technological University

Alicia Neumann
San Francisco, California

Caryn E. Neumann
Miami University of Ohio, Middletown

Mark A. Newman
University of Virginia

Betsy L. Nichols
Reynoldsburg, Ohio

James W. Oberly
University of Wisconsin, Eau Claire

George O'Brien
Georgetown University

Wendy Cobb Orrison
Washington and Lee University

Sheril A. Palermo
Cupertino, California

R. K. L. Panjabi
Memorial University of Newfoundland

Robert J. Paradowski
Rochester Institute of Technology

Thomas R. Park
Florida State University

Robert Passaro
Tucson, Arizona

Cheryl Pawlowski
University of Northern Colorado

Leslie A. Pearl
San Diego, California

Judy C. Peel
*University of North Carolina,
    Wilmington*

Martha E. Pemberton
Galesville, Wisconsin

William E. Pemberton
University of Wisconsin, La Crosse

Lori A. Petersen
Minot, North Dakota

Nis Petersen
Jersey City State College

Douglas A. Phillips
Sierra Vista, Arizona

Debra L. Picker
Long Beach, California

Betty L. Plummer
Dillard University

Bill Plummer III
*Amateur Softball Association
of America*

Michael Polley
Columbia College

Francis Poole
University of Delaware

Jon R. Poole
*Virginia Polytechnic Institute and State
University*

David L. Porter
William Penn University

John G. Powell
Greenville, South Carolina

Victoria Price
Lamar University

Maureen J. Puffer-Rothenberg
Valdosta State University

Christopher Rager
San Dimas, California

Steven J. Ramold
Eastern Michigan University

C. Mervyn Rasmussen
Renton, Washington

John David Rausch, Jr.
West Texas A&M University

Abe C. Ravitz
*California State University,
Dominguez Hills*

Nancy Raymond
International Gymnast Magazine

Shirley H. M. Reekie
San Jose State University

Christel Reges
Grand Valley State University

Victoria Reynolds
Mandeville High School

Betty Richardson
*Southern Illinois University,
Edwardsville*

Alice C. Richer
Spaulding Rehabilitation Center

David R. Rider
Bloomsburg University

Robert B. Ridinger
Northern Illinois University

Edward A. Riedinger
Ohio State University Libraries

Edward J. Rielly
Saint Joseph's College of Maine

Jan Rintala
Northern Illinois University

Thurman W. Robins
Texas Southern University

Vicki K. Robinson
*State University of New York,
Farmingdale*

Mark Rogers
University of Chicago

Wynn Rogers
San Dimas, California

Carl F. Rothfuss
Central Michigan University

William B. Roy
United States Air Force Academy

A. K. Ruffin
George Washington University

Todd Runestad
American Ski Association

J. Edmund Rush
Boise, Idaho

Michael Salmon
*Amateur Athletic Foundation of
Los Angeles*

Rebecca J. Sankner
*Southern Illinois University,
Carbondale*

Timothy M. Sawicki
Canisius College

Ronald C. Sawyer
*State University of New York,
Binghamton*

Ann M. Scanlon
*State University of New York, College at
Cortland*

Daniel C. Scavone
University of Southern Indiana

Elizabeth D. Schafer
Loachapoka, Alabama

Lamia Nuseibeh Scherzinger
Indiana University

Walter R. Schneider
Central Michigan University

J. Christopher Schnell
Southeast Missouri State University

Kathleen Schongar
The May School

Stephen Schwartz
Buffalo State College

Deborah Service
Los Angeles, California

Chrissa Shamberger
Ohio State University

Contributors

Tom Shieber
Mt. Wilson, California

Theodore Shields
Surfside Beach, South Carolina

Peter W. Shoun
East Tennessee State University

R. Baird Shuman
*University of Illinois, Urbana-
Champaign*

Thomas J. Sienkewicz
Monmouth College

Richard Slapsys
University of Massachusetts, Lowell

Elizabeth Ferry Slocum
Pasadena, California

John Slocum
Pasadena, California

Gary Scott Smith
Grove City College

Harold L. Smith
University of Houston, Victoria

Ira Smolensky
Monmouth College

A. J. Sobczak
Santa Barbara, California

Ray Sobczak
Salem, Wisconsin

Mark Stanbrough
Emporia State University

Alison Stankrauff
Indiana University South Bend

Michael Stellefson
Texas A&M University

Glenn Ellen Starr Stilling
Appalachian State University

Gerald H. Strauss
Bloomsburg University

Deborah Stroman
University of North Carolina

James Sullivan
California State University, Los Angeles

Cynthia J. W. Svoboda
Bridgewater State College

William R. Swanson
South Carolina State College

J. K. Sweeney
South Dakota State University

Charles A. Sweet, Jr.
Eastern Kentucky University

Glenn L. Swygart
Tennessee Temple University

James Tackach
Roger Williams University

Felicia Friendly Thomas
*California State Polytechnic University,
Pomona*

Jennifer L. Titanski
Lock Haven University of Pennsylvania

Evelyn Toft
Fort Hays State University

Alecia C. Townsend Beckie
New York, New York

Anh Tran
Wichita State University

Marcella Bush Trevino
Texas A&M University, Kingsville

Kathleen Tritschler
Guilford College

Brad Tufts
Bucknell University

Karen M. Turner
Temple University

Sara Vidar
Los Angeles, California

Hal J. Walker
University of Connecticut

Spencer Weber Waller
Loyola University Chicago

Annita Marie Ward
Salem-Teikyo University

Shawncey Webb
Taylor University

Chuck Weis
American Canoe Association

Michael J. Welch
Guilford College

Paula D. Welch
University of Florida

Allen Wells
Bowdoin College

Winifred Whelan
St. Bonaventure University

Nan White
Maharishi International University

Nicholas White
Maharishi International University

Rita S. Wiggs
Methodist College

Ryan K. Williams
University of Illinois, Springfield

Brook Wilson
Independent Scholar

John Wilson
Wheaton, Illinois

Rusty Wilson
Ohio State University

Wayne Wilson
*Amateur Athletic Foundation of
Los Angeles*

John D. Windhausen
St. Anselm College

Michael Witkoski
University of South Carolina

Philip Wong
Pasadena, California

Greg Woo
Independent Scholar

Sheri Woodburn
Cupertino, California

Jerry Jaye Wright
Pennsylvania State University, Altoona

Scott Wright
University of St. Thomas

Lisa A. Wroble
Redford Township District Library

Frank Wu
University of Wisconsin, Madison

Brooke K. Zibel
University of North Texas

Complete List of Contents

Volume 1

Publisher's Note. vii
Introduction xi
Contributors xvii

Herb Adderley 1
Troy Aikman 4
Shaun Alexander 7
Damon Allen 9
Marcus Allen. 12
Mike Alstott 15
Lance Alworth. 17
Lyle Alzado 20
Morten Andersen 22
Doug Atkins 25
Champ Bailey 27
Sammy Baugh 29
Chuck Bednarik. 32
Raymond Berry 35
Jerome Bettis 38
Fred Biletnikoff 41
Doc Blanchard 44
George Blanda 46
Drew Bledsoe 49
Tony Boselli 52
Terry Bradshaw 54
Tom Brady. 57
Bob Brown 60
Jim Brown 62
Tim Brown 65
Tedy Bruschi. 68
Buck Buchanan 70
Nick Buoniconti. 72
Reggie Bush 74
Dick Butkus 77
Earl Campbell 80
John Carney. 83
Cris Carter. 85
Dutch Clark 88
Larry Csonka 91
Randall Cunningham 94
Ernie Davis 97
Glenn Davis 100
Terrell Davis 103
Len Dawson 106

Eric Dickerson 109
Dan Dierdorf. 112
Mike Ditka 114
Clint Dolezel 117
Tony Dorsett 119
Warrick Dunn 122
Kenny Easley 125
Carl Eller 127
John Elway 130
Boomer Esiason 133
Marshall Faulk 135
Brett Favre 138
Doug Flutie. 141
Dan Fouts. 144
Benny Friedman 147
Rich Gannon 149
Antonio Gates 152
Eddie George 154
Frank Gifford 156
George Gipp 159
Tony Gonzalez 162
Otto Graham 164
Red Grange 167
Hugh Green 170
Joe Greene 172
Forrest Gregg 174
Bob Griese 176
Archie Griffin 179
Lou Groza 182
Ray Guy. 185
Jack Ham 188
John Hannah. 190
Tom Harmon 192
Franco Harris 194
Marvin Harrison 197
Ted Hendricks 199
Gene Hickerson 201
Elroy "Crazylegs" Hirsch. 204
Priest Holmes 207
Paul Hornung 209
Ken Houston. 212
Sam Huff 214
Don Hutson 216
Michael Irvin. 219
Bo Jackson 222

Keith Jackson. 225
Edgerrin James. 227
Jimmy Johnson. 230
John Henry Johnson. 232
Deacon Jones. 235
Lee Roy Jordan. 238
Sonny Jurgensen 240
Jim Kelly 243
Nile Kinnick 246
Jerry Kramer 249
Jack Lambert. 251
Dick "Night Train" Lane. 253
Steve Largent. 256
Bobby Layne 259
Jamal Lewis. 261
Ray Lewis 264
Bob Lilly 266
Floyd Little 268
Howie Long 271
Ronnie Lott 273
Sid Luckman 275
Johnny Lujack 278
John Lynch 280
Hugh McElhenny 283
Reggie McKenzie. 286
Jim McMahon 288
Donovan McNabb 291
Steve McNair 294
Archie Manning 297
Eli Manning 299
Peyton Manning 302

Volume 2

Gino Marchetti. 305
Dan Marino 307
Jim Marshall 310
Bruce Matthews 313
Don Maynard. 315
Ron Mix 318
Joe Montana 320
Warren Moon 323
Lenny Moore. 326
Randy Moss. 329
Marion Motley 332
Brick Muller 335
Bronko Nagurski. 338
Joe Namath. 341
Ernie Nevers 344
Ray Nitschke 346

Tommy Nobis 348
Chad Ocho Cinco 350
Merlin Olsen 352
Bennie Oosterbaan 354
Jim Otto 356
Orlando Pace. 359
Alan Page. 361
Carson Palmer 364
Jim Parker 367
Walter Payton 369
Adrian L. Peterson 372
Fritz Pollard 375
Jerry Rice. 377
John Riggins 380
Dave Rimington 383
Jim Ringo. 385
Paul Robeson. 387
Andy Robustelli 390
Johnny Rodgers 392
Ben Roethlisberger 394
Barry Sanders 397
Charlie Sanders 400
Deion Sanders 402
Warren Sapp 405
Gale Sayers 408
Joe Schmidt 410
Junior Seau. 413
Lee Roy Selmon 416
Shannon Sharpe 418
Billy Shaw. 421
Art Shell 423
Jeremy Shockey 426
O. J. Simpson. 429
Mike Singletary 432
Jackie Slater 435
Bruce Smith 437
Bubba Smith 440
Emmitt Smith 442
Chris Spielman 445
Ken Stabler 447
John Stallworth. 450
Bart Starr 453
Roger Staubach 456
Lynn Swann 459
Fran Tarkenton 462
Charley Taylor 465
Jim Taylor 468
Lawrence Taylor 470
Vinny Testaverde. 473
Derrick Thomas 476

Thurman Thomas 479
Zach Thomas. 482
Pat Tillman. 484
Y. A. Tittle 486
LaDainian Tomlinson 489
Charley Trippi 492
Emlen Tunnell 495
Osi Umenyiora 497
Johnny Unitas 499
Gene Upshaw 502
Brian Urlacher 505
Norm Van Brocklin 507
Steve Van Buren 510
Adam Vinatieri 512
Doak Walker 515
Herschel Walker 517
Hines Ward. 520
Paul Warfield 523
Kurt Warner 525
Bob Waterfield 529
Byron "Whizzer" White 531
Charles White 533
Randy White 535
Reggie White 537
Dave Wilcox 540
Ricky Williams 542
Larry Wilson 545
Willie Wood 547

Charles Woodson 549
Rod Woodson 552
Rayfield Wright. 554
Ron Yary 556
Steve Young 558
Vince Young 561
Jack Youngblood 564

Bibliography 569
Football Resources on the
    World Wide Web 571
Glossary 574
Football Players Time Line 581
The Sporting News 100 Greatest
    Football Players 589
ABC Sports Top 25
    College Football Players 590
Pro Football Hall of Fame 591
Heisman Trophy Winners 595
NFL Top Draft Picks 597
NFL Rookies of the Year. 599
NFL Most Valuable Players 601
Walter Payton Man of the Year Award 606

Name Index 609
Position Index 611
Team Index 614

GREAT ATHLETES
FOOTBALL

Herb Adderley

Born: June 8, 1939
Philadelphia, Pennsylvania
Also known as: Herbert A. Adderley (full name)

Early Life

Herbert A. Adderley was born in Philadelphia, Pennsylvania, on June 8, 1939. His parents, Charles, a machinist, and Rene were keen sports enthusiasts who encouraged Herb to engage in many athletic events. Even in grade school, Herb's diverse sporting talents were widely known in north Philadelphia, where he grew up.

When Herb entered Northeast High School in 1953, he joined four athletic teams, eventually gaining all-city honors in football, basketball, and baseball. Although Herb was barely more than 6 feet tall, his superior leaping ability enabled him to be a center on the basketball team. Twice he guarded a 6-foot 11-inch center from Overbrook High School named Wilt Chamberlain. The fact that Herb held Chamberlain, who went on to become one of the greatest scorers in basketball history, to a total of 100 points for the two contests was something of an achievement.

The Road to Excellence

When Herb graduated from high school in 1957, he had matured to his playing weight of nearly 200 pounds. After considering numerous scholarship offers to play football, he chose to attend Michigan State University, whose team he had followed for many years. At Michigan State, under the tutelage of Hugh "Duffy" Daugherty, Herb became a standout offensive threat. He led the Spartans in rushing yardage in 1959, and was the team leader in pass receptions that year and again in 1960. In his senior year Herb was cocaptain of the squad.

Although he was not chosen as a football all-American, Herb made the all-Big Ten Conference team in 1960, and played with the all-stars in the East-West Shrine, the coaches' all-American, and the college all-star games. In Herb's senior year, his Michigan State team lost only to Big Ten rivals Iowa and Ohio State. Before graduating with a degree in education in 1961, Herb was a first-round draft choice of the Green Bay Packers of the NFL.

The Emerging Champion

Herb began his professional career as a running back but was converted to defense by Coach Vince

Cornerback Herb Adderley, who played in four Super Bowls. (Courtesy of Amateur Athletic Foundation of Los Angeles)

1

Lombardi, since the team was already rich in runners like Paul Hornung, Jim Taylor, and Tommie Moore. Even so, in his first season with Green Bay, Herb ran back 18 kickoffs for 478 yards, an average of 27 yards per return. On Thanksgiving Day, in a game against the Detriot Lions, Herb first played defense; he had never played defense while in college. When two regular defensive backs were injured, Lombardi told Herb to go into the game as a cornerback because "you're the best athlete I've got." Playing before a friendly crowd in Detriot, where he had played many of his college games, Herb made the first of his 48 career NFL interceptions.

Lombardi was excited by Herb's play on defense, and Herb never returned to the offensive team, except for kickoffs. In fact, Herb adapted so quickly to defense that he was selected to the all-pro team in his second professional season, when he intercepted seven passes and scored two touchdowns, one on a kickoff return. Herb was chosen for the Pro Bowl five times and became an enthusiastic student of the defensive game. He roomed with fellow cornerback star Willie Wood, and they often sat until late in the morning discussing defensive tactics. When Herb scored a touchdown on an intercepted pass against the Philadelphia Eagles on October 31, 1967, he set an NFL record for most touchdowns, six, scored after interceptions. In 1969, he raised the record—since surpassed—to seven.

Continuing the Story

Herb spent nine years with Lombardi's Green Bay team, which won NFL titles in 1961 and 1965, and Super Bowls I and II in 1967 and 1968. In the latter contest, Herb made history by racing for the first Super Bowl touchdown on an intercepted pass. After picking off the pass by Oakland Raiders quarterback Daryl Lamonica, Herb ran 60 yards for the score.

Herb was still at the peak of his career when he was suddenly traded by Green Bay to Coach Tom Landry and the Dallas Cowboys; Lombardi had departed to Washington by then. In Dallas, Herb played on a pair of National Football Conference (NFC) championship teams, in 1970 and 1971, and on the Dallas Super Bowl championship squad in the latter year. Herb had played in four of the first six Super Bowls, three times on the winning side.

Honors, Awards, and Records

1960	All-Big Ten Conference Team
1961	Chicago College All-Star Team
	East-West All-Star Team
1962-66, 1969	All-NFL Team
1964-68	NFL Pro Bowl Team
1965, 1969	Tied NFL record for the most seasons leading in interception return yards, 2
1968	Tied NFL record for the most interception touchdowns in a Super Bowl game, 1
1970	NFL All-Pro Team of the 1960's
1980	Inducted into Pro Football Hall of Fame
1985	AFL-NFL 1960-1984 All-Star Team

In the summer of 1973, Herb was traded again, this time to the Los Angeles Rams, but rather than report to the Rams he decided to retire. He was disappointed by the trades; at a reunion of the Green Bay Packers in 1984, he announced that he never wore his Dallas Super Bowl ring and preferred to forget that he had played for Dallas.

During his career, Herb led the NFL in touchdowns by interceptions and yards gained by interceptions. He led the Packers in kickoff returns from 1961 to 1964, and in interceptions from 1963 to 1965, and set the Packers record for most scores on interceptions with three in a single season. An all-NFL defensive back in 1963, 1965, 1966, and 1969, Herb played in five Pro Bowls and seven college all-star games. He recorded 48 career interceptions, which he returned for 1,046 yards and an average run of 21.8 yards. His 120 kickoff returns went for 3,080 yards.

After his retirement Herb returned to his home in Philadelphia, where he broadcast football games for Temple University and the Philadelphia Eagles. For a short time he entered the coaching ranks, first as an assistant for Temple and later for the Philadelphia Bell of the World Football League. In 1970, Herb was chosen to the all-Michigan State University team. On August 2, 1980, he was inducted into the Pro Football Hall of Fame, the sixth Green Bay Packer to be so honored. He was chosen also to the American Football League (AFL)-NFL 1960-1984 all-star teams.

Herb went into the cable construction business in 1987. Adderley Industries specialized in the installation of underground and aerial cables. His daughter, Dr. Toni Adderley, graduated from dental school at Howard University. Herb settled in Blackwood, New Jersey, between Atlantic City and Philadelphia.

Summary

Herb Adderley, who might have been a star player in basketball or baseball, not only chose football but also learned a new position—defensive cornerback—as a professional. In so doing, he sacrificed the greater publicity he would have received as a runner or receiver. Herb was the epitome of a team player, and he attributed much of his life's success to Green Bay Coach Lombardi, who taught him that "the harder you work, the harder it is to surrender."

John D. Windhausen

Additional Sources

Barber, Phil. "NFL: Football's One Hundred Greatest Players—The Hit Men." *The Sporting News* 223 (November 1, 1999): 12-16.

Carroll, Bob. *Total Football: The Official Encyclopedia of the National Football League.* New York: HarperCollins, 1999.

Frostino, Nino. *Right on the Numbers.* Victoria, B.C.: Trafford, 2004.

Green, Jerry. "Adderley: From MSU to Hall." *The Detroit News*, May 12, 1996.

Troy Aikman

Born: November 21, 1966
      West Covina, California
Also known as: Troy Kenneth Aikman (full
    name)

Early Life

Troy Kenneth Aikman was born on November 21, 1966, in the Southern California community of West Covina, to Ken Aikman, a pipeline construction worker and rancher, and Charlyn Aikman. Troy, the youngest of three children, was born with deformed feet. Before he was old enough to walk, he had to wear casts on both legs. Once Troy could walk, at about fourteen months of age, the casts

were removed, and he had to wear orthopedic shoes. Troy was able to discard the special shoes when he reached three years of age.

By the time he was nine, Troy was already imagining life as a professional football player. In 1979, the Aikman family moved from California to the small Oklahoma town of Henryetta and took up residence on a 172-acre ranch.

The Road to Excellence

After spending his first twelve years in Southern California, Troy had a difficult time adjusting to life in small-town Oklahoma. He learned from his father how to be tough and how to make the best of any situation. Troy grew to appreciate life in Henryetta. Troy attended the local high school, where he played football and dreamed of playing quarterback for the nearby University of Oklahoma.

The coach of the Oklahoma Sooners was the legendary Barry Switzer, under whose direction the Sooners had consistently been one of the top teams in college football. In 1984, Troy's freshman year, the Sooners were a top-ten team, and in 1985, finished the season as the top-ranked college team in the country according to both the Associated Press (AP) and the United Press International (UPI) polls. Though off to a promising start, Troy's career as quarterback for the Sooners only lasted two years. After playing at Oklahoma for the 1984 and 1985 seasons, his desire to pass the ball more led him to transfer to the University of California at Los Angeles (UCLA).

At UCLA, Troy found an offensive game plan that suited his style of play. Under Coach Terry Donohue, Troy was able to mature as a quarterback. As a transfer student, he was not allowed to play football during the 1986 season, but he contributed immensely to the Bruins' success in 1987 and 1988. At 6 feet 4 inches and 215 pounds, Troy was a sturdy, durable quarterback. In addition to his size, Troy had a strong right arm, was a tough competitor, made intelligent decisions in pressure situations, and

Troy Aikman eyeing a receiver during a game against the Raiders. (Courtesy of Dallas Cowboys)

NFL Statistics

Season	GP	PA	PC	Pct.	Yds.	Avg.	TD	Int.
1989	11	293	155	52.9	1,749	5.97	9	18
1990	15	399	226	56.6	2,579	6.46	11	18
1991	12	363	237	65.3	2,754	7.59	11	10
1992	16	473	302	63.8	3,445	7.28	23	14
1993	14	392	271	69.1	3,100	7.91	15	6
1994	14	361	233	64.5	2,676	7.41	13	12
1995	16	432	280	64.8	3,304	7.65	16	7
1996	15	465	296	63.7	3,126	6.72	12	13
1997	16	518	292	56.4	3,283	6.34	19	12
1998	11	315	187	59.4	2,330	7.40	12	5
1999	14	442	263	59.5	2,964	6.71	17	12
2000	11	262	156	59.5	1,632	6.23	7	14
Totals	165	4,715	2,898	61.5	32,942	6.99	165	141

Notes: GP = games played; PA = passes attempted; PC = passes completed; Pct. = percent completed; Yds. = yards; Avg. = average yards per attempt; TD = touchdowns; Int. = interceptions

was a team leader. He was also a down-to-earth person who earned the respect of his teammates through his honesty and competitive spirit.

The Emerging Champion

Troy helped to lead the Bruins to the 1987 Aloha Bowl, where UCLA defeated the University of Florida by a score of 20-16. The following year, he led UCLA to the Cotton Bowl, where the Bruins defeated the University of Arkansas. Troy was voted the most valuable player in both bowl-game victories. Troy won the 1988 Davey O'Brien National Quarterback Award and was named quarterback on *The Sporting News* all-American team for 1988. Troy finished his college career having thrown for 5,436 yards and 40 touchdowns. With his size and athletic prowess, Troy was definitely qualified to play professional football.

In the 1989 NFL draft, Troy was the first pick overall and the first choice of the Dallas Cowboys, with whom he signed a six-year deal worth more than $11 million. The Cowboys were in the process of rebuilding after several poor seasons and the organization believed that Troy would prove to be one of the primary ingredients of a winning team. Historically, under legendary coach Tom Landry, the Cowboys had been one of the NFL's most successful teams. In 1989, however, the Cowboys had a new coach from the University of Miami, Jimmy Johnson. Troy's rookie season was a nightmare. The team finished the season 1-15, and he missed five

games due to injury. There were bright spots however: Troy threw for 379 yards, setting an NFL rookie record, in a game versus the Phoenix (now Arizona) Cardinals. He was frustrated with losing and hoped that the rebuilding would not take long.

In 1990, the Cowboys went 7-9 and traded away quarterback Steve Walsh, Troy's chief rival for the starting job, to the New Orleans Saints. Late in the season, Troy led the Cowboys to 4 wins in a row, but suffered a separated shoulder and was forced to miss the remainder of the season. In 1991, the Cowboys finally turned the corner and became a quality team. With Troy at quarterback and Emmitt Smith at running back, the Cowboys had a balanced offense that was a threat to score from anywhere on the field. The Cowboys finished the season 11-5 and made the playoffs. Troy was named to the 1991 National Football Conference (NFC) Pro Bowl team.

Continuing the Story

In 1991, the Cowboys served notice as a contender for the Super Bowl. The Dallas fans were finally beginning to believe that the new coach and the new quarterback could win. In 1992, the Cowboys arrived. Troy showed great poise throughout the season, but especially in the playoffs. Troy broke Joe Montana's 1989 NFL playoff record of 83 passes without an interception by throwing 89 passes without an interception. The Cowboys played the Buffalo Bills in Super Bowl XXVII, and the Bills, who

Honors and Awards

1988	College All-American
	Davey O'Brien National Quarterback Award
1991-96	NFL Pro Bowl Team
1993	NFL Super Bowl most valuable player
1997	Received Walter Payton Man of the Year
2005	Inducted into Dallas Cowboys Ring of Honor
2006	Inducted into Pro Football Hall of Fame
2008	Inducted into College Football Hall of Fame

had lost the previous two Super Bowls, proved to be no match for the powerful Cowboys. Dallas won 52-17, and Troy was named the game's most valuable player. He had a remarkable game, completing 22 of 30 passes for 273 yards and 4 touchdowns.

In 1993, the Cowboys played like Super Bowl champions and met the Bills once again, in Super Bowl XXVIII. The championship game was close for the first half, but the Cowboys dominated the second, winning 30-13. The Cowboys had become the best in the NFL, and experts pointed to the Troy's maturity as one of the major factors in the team's success.

During the 1994 season NFC Championship game, Troy broke team records by throwing for 380 yards against San Francisco. After the 1995 season, Troy was selected to his sixth consecutive Pro Bowl, tying Roger Staubach for the most consecutive appearances by a Dallas quarterback. In Super Bowl XXX on January 29, 1996, Troy broke another club record by connecting on 10 straight passes and also tied a club record by throwing for a touchdown in his fifth consecutive postseason game. The Cowboys were once again champions, defeating the Steelers 27-17. In 1997, his sixth consecutive year as a finalist for the honor, Troy received the NFL's Walter Payton Man of the Year award for his work with The Troy Aikman Foundation.

Through twelve NFL seasons, Troy became one of the game's great quarterbacks. As only the third player in NFL history to lead a team to three Super Bowl victories, Troy rewrote virtually every passing record in Cowboys history. By posting 90 regular season wins, he closed out the 1990's as the winningest starting quarterback of any decade in NFL history at that time, topping Joe Montana's previous best of 86 wins in the 1980's. Troy also finished his career with the fourth highest all-time completion percentage, 61.5, among quarterbacks with at least 1,500 attempts.

After Troy was knocked out by four concussions during his last two seasons, he announced his retirement in early 2001. However, it did not take him long to find a new job. Later in 2001, Troy entered the broadcast booth for Fox Sports as an analyst and commentator alongside play-by-play announcer Dick Stockton and former teammate Darryl "Moose" Johnston. The threesome was an instant success becoming Fox's number two team

behind Pat Summerall and John Madden. Afterward, Troy teamed with Joe Buck to become Fox's lead broadcast team.

On September 19, 2005, Troy was inducted into the Cowboys Ring of Honor, alongside Emmitt Smith and Michael Irvin. Almost a year later, on August 5, 2006, Troy was inducted into the Pro Football Hall of Fame in his first year of eligibility. In true team-first fashion, Troy praised the players, coaches, fans, friends, and family that helped and supported him throughout his football endeavors. In 2008, Troy added to his impressive list of accolades with induction into the National Football Foundation's College Football Hall of Fame.

Summary

Troy Aikman combined physical prowess with toughness and leadership skills to become one of the best quarterbacks in the game. He made six consecutive trips to the Pro Bowl, from 1991 to 1996, and three appearances on the all-pro team, 1993 to 1995. He was a key contributor to the resurrection of the Cowboys, leading Dallas to dominance of the NFL during the 1990's. From 1992 to 1998, Troy and the Cowboys won six NFC East titles, four NFC Championship games and three Super Bowls, making them one of the NFL's all-time great teams.

Jeffry Jensen, updated by Trevor D. Bopp

Additional Sources

Aikman, Troy. "Memo to QBs: Stay in Touch." *Sporting News* 230, no. 48 (December 1, 2006): 42.

Aikman, Troy, and Greg Brown. *Things Change.* Dallas, Tex.: Taylor, 1995.

Aikman, Troy, and Marc Serota. *Troy Aikman: Mind, Body, and Soul.* Hollywood, Fla.: EGI Productions, 1998.

Buckley, James, Jr. *Troy Aikman.* New York: Dorling Kindersley, 2000.

Farmer, Sam. "He Wore a Star with Distinction . . . and Sometimes Saw Them." *Los Angeles Times,* August 5, 2006, p. D1.

King, Peter. "The Class of 2006." *Sports Illustrated* (July 26, 2006): 10-13.

_____. *Greatest Quarterbacks.* Des Moines, Iowa: Sports Illustrated Books, 1999.

Monk, Cody. *Legends of the Dallas Cowboys.* Champaign, Ill.: Sports, 2004.

Shaun Alexander

Born: August 30, 1977
 Florence, Kentucky
Also known as: Shaun Edward Alexander (full
 name)

Early Life

Shaun Edward Alexander was born in Florence, Kentucky, and raised there by his father, Curtis, and mother, Carol. He and his older brother Durran, who was a star athlete, shared a bedroom in the family's small apartment. As a child, Shaun cheered for the Cincinnati Bengals and often attended games because his father had season tickets. He became a football star at Boone County High School. During his senior year, he was the Gatorade Circle of Champions Kentucky player of the year and a *Parade* magazine and *USA Today* all-American. During his senior year, he rushed for 3,166 yards and 54 touchdowns. Based on Shaun's performance in high school, many college football programs recruited him.

NFL Record

Most touchdowns in an NFL season, 28

Seattle Seahawks Records

Most rushing attempts in a career, 1,717
Most rushing yards gained in a career, 7,817
Most seasons with at least 1,000 rushing yards, 5
Most rushing yards gained in one season, 1,880
Most rushing yards gained in one game, 266
Most games in a season with at least 100 rushing yards, 11
Most consecutive games with at least 100 rushing yards, 4
Most touchdowns in a career, 89
Most consecutive games with a rushing touchdown, 9

Honors and Awards

1994	Kentucky's Mr. Football Award
2003-05	NFL Pro Bowl
2004-05	NFL All-Pro
2005	Associated Press NFL most valuable player
	Associated Press NFL offensive player of the year
	Bert Bell Award

The Road to Excellence

Shaun decided to attend the University of Alabama. During his freshman year, he carried the ball only 77 times in eleven games, but he did gain 589 yards with those carries, an impressive 7.6 yards per carry. He also scored 6 touchdowns that year. In his sophomore year, he continued as a reserve and played in only nine games. He rushed for 415 yards on 90 carries scoring 3 touchdowns.

Shaun had a breakout season his junior year at Alabama. He rushed for 1,178 yards on 258 carries, for an average of 107 yards per game. In the game against Vanderbilt University that year, he rushed for 206 yards. He also scored 13 touchdowns that season. For his performance, he was selected to the all-Southeastern Conference (SEC) team. In his senior year, he had another extremely strong season. He rushed for 1,383 yards on 302 attempts and scored 19 touchdowns, which was a conference record. One of those touchdowns was scored during one of his two 90-yard kickoff returns. For his performance, he made the all-SEC team again and was a finalist for the Doak Walker Award.

Shaun finished his collegiate career as Alabama's all-time leading rusher with 3,565 yards. He also set records with 727 rushing attempts, fifteen 100-yard games, 41 rushing touchdowns, and 50 total touchdowns.

The Seattle Seahawks chose Shaun as the nineteenth pick in the first round of the 2000 NFL draft. Shaun played sparingly during his first year. He appeared in all sixteen regular-season games and started one, but he rushed for only 313 yards on 64 carries. He was primarily used as a short-yardage back in the early part in his career.

The Emerging Champion

In 2001, Shaun had a breakout season. He played in all sixteen games and started twelve, earning the starting spot after Ricky Watters suffered an injury. Watters came back to the starting lineup later that season, but in his return game, he suffered another injury. That season Shaun rushed for 1,318 yards, which was the sixth most in the NFL that year. He also led the NFL with 14 rushing touchdowns. Fur-

NFL Statistics

Season	GP	Rushing Car.	Yds.	Avg.	TD	Receiving Rec.	Yds.	Avg.	TD
2000	16	64	313	4.9	2	5	41	8.2	0
2001	16	309	1,318	4.3	14	44	343	7.8	2
2002	16	295	1,175	4.0	16	59	460	7.8	2
2003	16	326	1,435	4.4	14	42	295	7.0	2
2004	16	353	1,696	4.8	16	23	170	7.4	4
2005	16	370	1,880	5.1	27	15	78	5.2	1
2006	10	252	896	3.6	7	12	48	4.0	0
2007	13	207	716	3.5	4	14	76	5.4	1
Totals	119	2,176	9,429	4.3	100	214	1,511	7.1	12

Notes: GP = games played; Car. = carries; Yds. = yards; Avg. = average yards per carry or average yards per reception; TD = touchdowns; Rec. = receptions

thermore, he had 44 receptions for 343 yards; 2 of those receptions resulted in touchdowns.

In 2002, Shaun started all sixteen games and led the National Football Conference (NFC) with 16 touchdowns. He rushed for 1,175 yards on 295 carries. He also had a career-high 59 receptions. In one game he scored 5 touchdowns, which set a franchise record. In 2003, he earned his first trip to the NFL's Pro Bowl after rushing for a career high 1,435 yards and scoring 16 touchdowns. That year, he had seven 100-yard games.

In 2004, Shaun had his second-consecutive Pro Bowl season, scoring a career-high 20 touchdowns. He rushed for 1,696 yards, which was second in the NFL and first in the NFC, and had a 4.8 yards-per-carry average. Furthermore, he became Seattle's all-time leading touchdown scorer and established a franchise season record for rushing.

Continuing the Story

In 2005, Shaun had one of the best seasons in NFL history. He rushed for a league-leading 1,880 yards on only 370 carries, a 5.1 yards-per-carry average. At the time, his yardage total was the ninth highest in a single season in NFL history. He set an NFL record with 28 touchdowns and scored 168 points, which was the second most in NFL history. During this season, he became the Seahawks' all-time leader in rushing yards, rushing attempts, and 100-yard

games. He also became the first player in NFL history to score 15 or more touchdowns in five consecutive seasons. He carried his team to the Super Bowl that year and, in that game, rushed for 95 yards on 20 carries as his team lost to the Pittsburgh Steelers.

The next year, Shaun suffered through injuries, including a broken foot, which led him to miss six games. Nonetheless, he rushed for 896 yards. In one game that season he had 201 rushing yards on a club-record 40 carries. In 2007, he struggled slightly, as injuries affected the overall play of the Seahawks' offense. However, he scored the 100th touchdown of his career, joining an elite group of running backs. Somewhat surprisingly, the Seahawks released Shaun after the 2007 season. He signed with the Washington Redskins as a free agent. After he played in only four games during the 2008 season, he was released by the Redskins.

Summary

In his career, Shaun Alexander demonstrated tenacity and perseverance. He achieved excellence in high school athletics and worked for his opportunity in a college program with a storied history. He entered the NFL and initially served as a reserve. However, once he was given the opportunity to play, he became the greatest running back in Seahawks history. For his abilities to carry the ball and to score touchdowns, he will be remembered as one of best players in Seattle history.

Michael Coulter

Additional Sources

Alexander, Shaun, and Cecil B. Murphey. *Touchdown Alexander: My Story of Faith, Football, and Pursuing the Dream.* Eugene, Oreg.: Harvest House, 2007.

Smithwick, John. *Meet Shaun Alexander: Football's Top Running Back.* New York: PowerKids, 2007.

Damon Allen

Born: July 29, 1963
San Diego, California

Early Life

Damon Allen was born to Harold, a carpenter, and his wife Gwen, in San Diego, California, and was raised in an athletic family. His older brother is Marcus Allen, a Pro Football Hall of Fame member. Damon credits his family for his development. "It start[ed] with my parents and my brothers and sisters who instilled in me that I [could] do whatever I want[ed] to do," he told the Canadian Broadcasting Company. He excelled in sports at Lincoln High School, where he was a stellar quarterback during his junior and senior years.

The Road to Excellence

Damon starred in football and baseball at California State University at Fullerton. He finished sixteenth in voting for the Heisman Trophy, an award for college football's player of the year. He was invited to a postseason college football all-star game and had a strong performance. His football team won two Pacific Coast Athletic Association (now Big West Conference) division titles. Furthermore, he was a starting pitcher on his college baseball team, which won the College World Series in 1984.

No NFL team drafted Damon, so he decided to sign with the Edmonton Eskimoes of the Canadian Football League (CFL) in 1985. He knew that Warren Moon, a top quarterback in the NFL in the 1980's and 1990's, had also been initially overlooked by the NFL and achieved success in the CFL. In his first two seasons in the CFL, Damon saw limited action.

Some of the CFL's rules are significantly different from the NFL rules. The CFL uses a wider field, twelve players on each side, and three downs rather than four. In general, the CFL game favors mobile quarterbacks and passing.

The Emerging Champion

In 1987, Damon emerged as a significant player in the CFL. He threw 17 touchdowns, although he was a starter for only a part of the season. However, he led his team to a 38-36 victory over the Toronto Argonauts in the league championship game. Because the previously injured quarterback returned to action in 1988, Damon's role was reduced.

Canadian Football League quarterback Damon Allen. (Christinne Muschi/Reuters/Landov)

In 1989, he signed with the Ottawa Rough Riders and went on to have three successful seasons with the team. In 1991, he earned a CFL East Division all-star nomination after compiling 4,275 passing yards, 24 touchdown passes, 1,036 rushing yards, and 8 rushing touchdowns. The next season he signed with the Hamilton Tiger-Cats and had another great season, tallying 3,858 passing yards and 19 touchdown passes. After the 1992 season, Damon was traded to Edmonton, and his success continued. In 1993, he passed for 3,394 yards and 25 touchdowns and was named the most valuable player (MVP) in the Grey Cup, the CFL championship game.

In 1994, Damon played with Edmonton again. However, after that season, he became a free agent and signed with the Memphis Mad Dogs, a team based in Memphis, Tennessee, participating in the CFL. That club folded after the 1995 season, and Damon signed with the British Columbia Lions. He had seven impressive seasons with that team. In 2000, he broke a CFL career record with more than 50,000 passing yards. In 2001, he became the first CFL quarterback to rush for more than 10,000 yards.

Continuing the Story

Prior to the 2003 season, when Damon was thirty-nine years old, he was traded to the Toronto Argonauts and had a strong season, passing for nearly

Canadian Football League Statistics

Season	PA	PC	Pct.	Yds.	Avg.	TD	Int.
1985	98	48	49.0	661	49.0	3	3
1986	87	49	56.3	878	56.3	8	3
1987	287	150	52.3	2,670	52.3	17	13
1988	218	94	43.1	1,309	43.1	4	12
1989	434	209	48.2	3,093	48.2	17	16
1990	528	276	52.3	3,883	52.3	34	23
1991	546	282	51.6	4,275	51.6	24	31
1992	523	266	50.9	3,858	50.9	19	14
1993	400	214	53.5	3,394	53.5	25	10
1994	493	254	51.5	3,554	51.5	19	15
1995	390	228	58.5	3,211	58.5	11	13
1996	368	219	59.5	2,772	59.5	13	10
1997	583	378	64.8	4,653	64.8	21	11
1998	476	282	58.9	3,519	58.9	16	16
1999	521	315	60.5	4,219	60.5	22	13
2000	525	324	61.7	4,840	61.7	24	11
2001	471	251	53.3	3,631	53.3	18	14
2002	474	268	56.5	3,987	56.5	22	10
2003	450	267	59.3	3,395	59.3	17	10
2004	312	189	60.6	2,438	60.6	12	4
2005	549	352	64.1	5,082	64.1	33	15
2006	335	198	59.1	2,567	59.1	12	11
2007	67	45	67.2	492	67.2	3	0
Totals	9,138	5,158	56.4	72,381	56.4	394	278

Notes: GP = games played; PA = passes attempted; PC = passes completed; Pct. = percent completed; Yds. = yards; Avg. = average yards per attempt; TD = touchdowns; Int. = interceptions

3,400 yards and rushing for more than 500 yards. In 2004, Damon began well, but was limited by injury. Nonetheless, he threw for more than 2,400 yards. Furthermore, he came back for the final game of the regular season and then led his team to playoff victories and a Grey Cup championship. He was the MVP in that game.

In 2005, though Damon was forty-two years old, he had one of the best seasons of his career. He passed for more than 5,000 yards for the first time and had 33 touchdown passes. He had 549 passing attempts and completed 352 of them. He also rushed for nearly 500 yards. Also in 2005, he started the Damon Allen Quarterback Challenge, in which quarterbacks participated in a skills competition; the event raised money for charities.

While playing in 2006, Damon passed Warren Moon's combined CFL/NFL passing-yards record; he finished his career with 72,381 career passing yards. In November 2006, the Canadian Sports Network named him one of the fifty greatest

Record

Most passing yards in professional football history, 72,381

Honors and Awards

1984	Pacific Coast Athletic Association First Team All-Star
1987, 1993, 2004	Grey Cup most valuable player
2005	Canadian Football League All-Star Team
	Canadian Football League most outstanding player
2006	Canadian Sports Network 50 greatest players of modern CFL

players in the CFL's modern era. In 2007, he signed a one-year contract with Toronto but lost the job of starting quarterback. In May, 2008, he announced his retirement.

Summary

While Damon Allen did not get an opportunity in the NFL, he became the all-time leading passer in CFL history. Over his lengthy career, he set many passing and rushing records, earned many league honors, and won three league championships. He ranks as one of the greatest players in CFL history.

Michael Coulter

Additional Sources

"Allen of CFL Sets a Record." *The New York Times,* September 6, 2006, p. D2.

O'Brien, Steve. *The Canadian Football League: The Phoenix of Professional Sports Leagues.* Rev. ed. Morrisville, N.C.: Lulu Press, 2005.

Marcus Allen

Born: March 26, 1960
       San Diego, California
Also known as: Marcus LeMarr Allen (full name)

Early Life

Marcus LeMarr Allen was born on March 26, 1960, in San Diego, California, to Harold Allen, a general contractor, and Gwen Allen, a registered nurse. Marcus was the second of six children; from an early age, Marcus proved to be the most athletic of the children. When he was about ten years old, Marcus started playing organized football. In addition, Marcus learned to play baseball and basketball. His parents, though, made it clear to Marcus and their other children that a good education was of primary importance.

At Lincoln High School in San Diego, Marcus excelled at both basketball and football. Scholastically, he maintained a "B" average. Always a hard worker, Marcus stopped playing basketball during his sophomore year because his fellow teammates did not believe in working as hard as he did. On the school's football team, Marcus was a versatile player. As a defensive safety, he once made thrity unassisted tackles in a single game. During his junior year, Marcus took over as quarterback, and he led Lincoln High School to the city championship in his senior year. He was named California's high school athlete of the year and received the Hertz Number One award. He also became the first Lincoln player to have his football number retired.

The Road to Excellence

Marcus was a heavily recruited athlete out of high school, and he chose to attend the University of Southern California (USC), where his boyhood idol O. J. Simpson had been a star running back in the 1960's. Coach John Robinson recruited Marcus as a defensive back, but soon after Marcus started practicing with the team, Robinson shifted him to tailback. Because USC's starting tailback Charles White was a star, Marcus had to work hard to prove himself.

In 1979, during his sophomore year, Marcus was moved to fullback, where he was primarily called upon to block for White, who won the Heisman Trophy as the outstanding college football player of 1979, then graduated and moved to the NFL. Marcus got his chance as the starting tailback the following year.

During the 1980 season, Marcus came into his own, proving that he was as good as anyone who had ever played tailback for USC. Marcus gained 1,563 yards and scored 14 touchdowns in his junior year. He was more than merely a running back; he could block, and he was a reliable receiver. As a senior, he had a record-breaking season. No college running back had ever rushed for more than 2,000 yards in a season, but Marcus believed that he could not only break Tony Dorsett's single-season rushing record of 1,948 yards but also go over 2,000 yards.

Los Angeles Raiders running back Marcus Allen carrying the ball in a 1985 playoff game. (Courtesy of Los Angeles Raiders)

NFL Statistics

Season	GP	Rushing Car.	Yds.	Avg.	TD	Receiving Rec.	Yds.	Avg.	TD
1982	9	160	697	4.4	11	38	401	10.6	3
1983	15	266	1,014	3.8	9	68	590	8.7	2
1984	16	275	1,168	4.2	13	64	758	11.8	5
1985	16	380	1,759	4.6	11	67	555	8.3	3
1986	13	208	759	3.6	5	46	453	9.8	2
1987	12	200	754	3.8	5	51	410	8.0	0
1988	15	223	831	3.7	7	34	303	8.9	1
1989	8	69	293	4.2	2	20	191	9.6	0
1990	16	179	682	3.8	12	15	189	12.6	1
1991	8	63	287	4.6	2	15	131	8.7	0
1992	16	67	301	4.5	2	28	277	9.9	1
1993	16	206	764	3.7	12	34	238	7.0	3
1994	13	189	764	3.7	7	42	349	7.0	3
1995	16	207	890	4.2	5	27	210	8.3	0
1996	16	206	830	4.0	9	27	270	10.0	0
1997	16	124	505	4.0	11	11	86	7.8	0
Totals	221	3,022	12,298	4.1	123	587	5,411	9.2	24

Notes: GP = games played; Car. = carries; Yds. = yards; Avg. = average yards per carry *or* average yards per reception; TD = touchdowns; Rec. = receptions

Marcus worked hard during the off-season to polish his running skills, and he finished the 1981 season with a total of 2,342 yards. In addition to the single-season rushing mark, Marcus's 212.9 yards per-game rushing average, eight 200-yard games, and 2,559 all-purpose yards were all National Collegiate Athletic Association (NCAA) records. For his record-breaking year, Marcus received a number of awards, including the Heisman Trophy.

The Emerging Champion

The Los Angeles Raiders chose Marcus in the first round of the 1982 NFL draft, the tenth pick overall. At 6 feet 2 inches and 210 pounds, Marcus was not large for an NFL running back; he also did not have blistering speed. He did, however, possess excellent field vision and the ability to change direction when running at full speed. In his rookie season, Marcus did not disappoint the Raiders. The 1982 season was shortened by a player strike, but Marcus helped to lead the Raiders into the playoffs. He gained 697 yards rushing and led the NFL in scoring with 84 points on 14 touchdowns. He also led American Football Conference (AFC) running backs with 38 pass receptions. Marcus was named the *Sporting News* rookie of the year and was selected to play in the Pro Bowl.

The Raiders' offensive strategy, as envisioned by Coach Tom Flores and owner Al Davis, was one of diversification. They did not believe in making any one player the workhorse of the offense. In the 1983 season, Marcus became somewhat frustrated that he was not running the ball at least twenty times a game. At USC, the tailback could run the ball as many as forty times in a game, but that was not the way things were done with the Raiders. Marcus gained 1,014 yards on the season and scored 11 touchdowns, but his yards-per-carry average slipped from 4.4 in 1982 to 3.8 in 1983. He still helped the Raiders to gain a berth in Super Bowl XVIII against the reigning champions, the Washington Redskins. Everything went right for the Raiders and Marcus in the championship game. The Raiders won by the lopsided score of 38-9, and Marcus had the

Honors and Awards

1981	College All-American
	Heisman Trophy
	Maxwell Award
	Sporting News College Football Player of the Year
1982	*Sporting News* NFL Rookie of the Year
	United Press International AFC Rookie of the Year
1982, 1984-87, 1993	NFL Pro Bowl Team
1984	NFL Super Bowl most valuable player
1985	Associated Press NFL Player of the Year
	Professional Football Writers Association Player of the Year
	Sporting News NFL Player of the Year
	United Press International AFC Player of the Year
1993	*Pro Football Weekly* Comeback Player of the Year
1994	Muscular Dystrophy Association Lifetime Achievement Award
1998	Uniform number 32 retired by Kansas City Chiefs
1999	Named one of the *Sporting News* 100 Greatest Football Players
2000	Inducted into College Football Hall of Fame
2003	Inducted into Pro Football Hall of Fame

game of a lifetime. He scored 2 touchdowns and rushed for a Super Bowl-record 191 yards. On one unforgettable play, Marcus turned a potential loss of yardage into a 74-yard touchdown run. He won the Pete Rozelle Award as the game's most valuable player.

For the 1984 season, Marcus hoped that the Raiders would increase the number of times that he touched the ball. He had a stellar year: He rushed for 1,168 yards, caught 64 passes for 758 yards, and led the league with 18 touchdowns, 13 rushing and 5 receiving. The season ended abruptly for the Raiders, however, when the team lost to the Seattle Seahawks in the first round of the playoffs.

In 1985, Marcus's number of carries finally increased, and he rose to the occasion. He became the first Raider running back to lead the NFL in rushing yardage, gaining 1,759 yards rushing and 555 yards receiving for a total of 2,314 all-purpose yards, setting an NFL record. The Raiders lost to the New England Patriots in the AFC Championship game, but Marcus was named NFL player of the year by *Sporting News*, the Professional Football Writers Association, and the Associated Press.

Continuing the Story

Marcus continued to perform well for the Raiders, earning Pro Bowl berths and setting records. In 1987, though, star rookie Bo Jackson joined Marcus in the Raiders' backfield, and Marcus was suddenly no longer the Raiders' primary running back. Marcus also missed eight games of the 1989 season because of a knee injury, and though he had done a remarkable job for the Raiders, he was becoming the forgotten man. He voiced his displeasure with the turn of events, but he still gave his best when given the chance.

After the 1992 season, the Raiders granted Marcus unconditional free agency, and he signed with the Kansas City Chiefs. In his first year with Kansas City, Marcus joined another free agent, Joe Montana, in leading the Chiefs to the AFC championship game. Although the season ended in a loss to the Buffalo Bills, Marcus proved he was still one of the NFL's best, gaining 764 yards and leading the league with 12 rushing touchdowns. Marcus announced his retirement from pro football in April, 1998, with more career rushing yards than his hero O. J. Simpson. The Kansas City Chiefs retired his jersey on November 16, 1998. A standout player as both an amateur and a professional, Marcus was elected to both the National Football Foundation's College Hall of Fame in 2000 and the Pro Football Hall of Fame in 2003.

Summary

Marcus Allen proved throughout his illustrious football career to be an intelligent and versatile running back. A true professional, Marcus carried himself with dignity both on and off the field.

Jeffry Jensen

Additional Sources

Allen, Marcus, and Matt Fulks. *Road to Canton*. Champaign, Ill.: Sports, 2003.

Allen, Marcus, and Carlton Stowers. *Marcus: The Autobiography of Marcus Allen*. New York: St. Martin's Press, 1997.

Deutsch, Richard. "The Longest Yard." *Sports Illustrated* 87, no. 15 (October 13, 1997): 102.

Murphy, Austin, Michael Silver, Tom Verducci, and Stephen Cannella. "Scorecard: Unappreciated Raider." *Sports Illustrated* 86, no. 16 (April 20, 1998): 22.

Mike Alstott

Born: December 21, 1973
   Joliet, Illinois
Also known as: Michael Joseph Alstott (full
   name); A-Train

Early Life

Michael Joseph Alstott was born on December 21,
1973, in the town of Joliet, Illinois, on the outskirts
of Chicago. Mike's parents, Dennis and Jeanne,
provided him and his brother, Mark, a middle-class
upbringing rooted in blue-collar, midwestern values. Mike's pragmatic personality, a trait he carried
with him into adulthood, was shaped by his young
life. Mike played baseball and football at Joliet
Catholic High School, but football was his priority.
As a running back, in his junior year, Mike led the
Hilltoppers to the 1990 Class 4A state championship, the seventh state title for a school that began
its football program in 1920. In Mike's senior year,
his team lost in the Class 5A state semifinals, but
Mike became the school's first 2,000-yard rusher,
compiling 2,026 yards in fourteen games. He was
named the *Chicago Sun-Times* player of the year and
a *Parade* magazine all-American and earned a
scholarship to Purdue University.

The Road to Excellence

As he pursued a business degree at Purdue, Mike
began to develop a reputation for inflicting pain
on football opponents in the Big Ten Conference.
He used his quick feet to elude larger defensive
linemen and used his great size—6 feet, 240
pounds—to run over linebackers and defensive
backs. He suffered a broken leg against Michigan

State University late in his freshman season but
came back to be named Purdue's most valuable
player in each of his final three seasons. He was the
first Boilermakers football player so honored.

After his senior season, in which he became
Purdue's all-time leader in rushing yards and
touchdowns, Mike prepared for the 1996 NFL
draft. His unorthodox training techniques began
to receive national attention. Mike, hoping to improve his speed during predraft workouts for
scouts, shifted his Jeep into neutral and pulled it
with a chain 100 yards across a parking lot. He also
tied two truck tires to his midsection and dragged
them behind him as he jogged.

Mike was projected as a potential first-round
draft pick but fell to the second round. He was chosen by the Tampa Bay Buccaneers with the thirty-
fifth overall pick. The Buccaneers drafted him as a
fullback, which remained his official position
throughout his NFL career. However, Coach Tony
Dungy planned to use Mike as much more than a
traditional blocking back.

The Emerging Champion

The Buccaneers, long considered one of the worst
franchises in the NFL, had not given fans much to
cheer since the early 1980's, during the era of quarterback Doug Williams and hall-of-fame defensive
end Lee Roy Selmon. Dungy's first season was also
Mike's; the team's fortunes began to turn in 1996.
The Buccaneers lost the first five games of Mike's
rookie year but won five of the last seven games,
providing a glimpse of championship potential.
With his parents traveling to see every Buccaneers
game on the road and in Tampa, Mike led all
National Football Conference rookies with 65
receptions and was named a Pro Bowl alternate.

In 1997, Mike was paired with running back
Warrick Dunn to create the "Thunder and
Lightning" backfield that became Tampa Bay's
trademark on offense. The team began to
emerge as a Super Bowl contender. Mike provided the thunder, Dunn the lightning, as the
Buccaneers won the first five games that year

Honors and Awards

1993-95	University of Purdue most valuable player
1995	All-Big Ten Conference
1996	NFL All-Rookie Team
	NFL Players Association NFC Offensive Rookie of the Year
1997-99	NFL All-Pro
1997-2002	NFL Pro Bowl

and made the playoffs for the first time since the 1982 season. In addition to helping clear the way for Dunn, Mike carried the ball with authority, often dragging several tacklers behind him. His greatest run came on a one-yard touchdown, on September 14, 1997, against the Minnesota Vikings, when he was knocked backward three yards before driving backward with his legs and carrying three Vikings defenders into the end zone. Mike earned the first of his six consecutive Pro Bowl berths and was named an all-pro for the first time.

Buccaneers fans began to blow handheld train whistles in support of the "A-Train" every time Mike ran the football. In addition to redefining the fullback position, Mike was helping to eradicate the Buccaneers' laughingstock image.

Continuing the Story

The Buccaneers' rise to prominence mirrored Mike's personal growth. He and his wife, Nicole, had a son, Griffin, and two daughters, Hannah and Lexie. Dungy was fired and Dunn departed for the Atlanta Falcons after the 2001 season, while Jon Gruden became Tampa Bay's coach in 2002. Mike remained the starter at fullback and was named to the Pro Bowl for a final time; however, his role began to diminish even as the Buccaneers completed the organizational turnaround by winning Super Bowl XXXVII in San Diego. Mike scored Tampa Bay's first touchdown in the game, a 48-21 victory against the Oakland Raiders.

A severe neck injury ended Mike's 2003 season after only four games. For the first time, Mike began to contemplate retirement. He worked his way back for the 2004 season, but he no longer was the central focus of the offense. He nearly retired after the 2005 and 2006 seasons but chose to come back each time on a one-year contract. Another neck injury, suffered during training camp, ended his 2007 season before it began. Despite the injury, Mike was on the sideline for every game of what turned out to be his final season.

On January 24, 2008, Mike announced his retirement after twelve seasons with the Buccaneers. He departed as the franchise's all-time leader in touchdowns with 71. At the age of thirty-four, he turned his attention to philanthropic efforts by founding the Mike Alstott Family Foundation. Mike, an avid fisherman and golfer, settled into retirement as an integral part of the Tampa Bay community, with the promise from Buccaneers owner Malcolm Glazer of a future role within the organization.

Summary

Mike Alstott was a running back in a fullback's body, a hybrid back whose combination of punishing power, surprising agility, and pass-catching ability made him one of the most versatile and effective offensive players of his era. He endeared himself to the Tampa Bay region with his hard-running style, his authentic personality, and his charity work in the community. When he retired, he was arguably the most popular player in the history of the Tampa Bay Buccaneers.

Carter Gaddis

Additional Sources

Goodman, Michael E. *The History of the Tampa Bay Buccaneers*. Mankato, Minn.: Creative Education, 2005.

Gruden, Jon, and Vic Carucci. *Do You Love Football?! Winning with Heart, Passion, and Not Much Sleep*. New York: Perennial, 2004.

Harry, Chris, and Joey Johnston. *Tales from the Bucs Sideline*. Champaign, Ill.: Sports, 2004.

NFL Statistics

| Season | GP | Rushing | | | | | Receiving | | | |
		Car.	Yds.	Avg.	TD	Rec.	Yds.	Avg.	TD
1996	16	96	377	3.9	3	65	557	4.0	3
1997	15	176	665	3.8	7	23	178	8.9	3
1998	16	215	846	3.9	8	22	152	7.0	1
1999	16	242	949	3.9	7	27	239	8.3	2
2000	13	131	465	3.5	5	13	93	6.9	0
2001	16	165	680	4.1	10	35	231	6.6	1
2002	16	146	548	3.8	5	35	242	7.2	2
2003	4	27	77	2.9	2	10	83	8.9	0
2004	14	67	230	3.4	2	29	202	6.9	0
2005	16	34	80	2.4	6	25	222	7.7	1
2006	16	60	171	2.9	3	21	85	8.6	0
Totals	158	1,359	5,088	3.7	58	305	2,284	7.5	13

Notes: GP = games played; Car. = carries; Yds. = yards; Avg. = average yards per carry or average yards per reception; TD = touchdowns; Rec. = receptions

Lance Alworth

Born: August 3, 1940
      Houston, Texas
Also known as: Lance Dwight Alworth
    (full name); Bambi; Lancer

Early Life

Born on August 3, 1940, in Houston, Texas, Lance Dwight Alworth grew up in Brookhaven, Mississippi, where he attended the local high school. Lance showed his athletic skills early in life, and the question was not whether he would excel in sports, but rather in which ones. Competing in football, basketball, baseball, and track, Lance earned fifteen sports letters in high school. He was not the only athlete in his family, however. His sister Ann was so fast at 50- and 75-yard sprints that she received an invitation to the Olympic Games trials, a bid she refused.

Lance was such a good center fielder that he was offered attractive contracts by both the New York Yankees and the Pittsburgh Pirates. He listened instead to his father, who advised him that hc should get a college education. The best way for Lance to do that was through a football scholarship. Married at seventeen to his hometown sweetheart, Lance found out that his first choice for college, the University of Mississippi in Oxford, had a rule against married players on the squad. The Rebels revoked that rule quickly in order to attract Lance, but he had already opted for the University of Arkansas.

The Road to Excellence

Lance played for the Arkansas Razorbacks as a flanker. He distinguished himself as a consistent performer and finished his college career as one of the most heralded players in many years. For the University of Arkansas, Lance played in the Cotton, Sugar, Gator, and Hula Bowls as well as in the college all-star game in Chicago. He was named the outstanding back in both the 1961 Cotton Bowl and the 1962 Hula Bowl. He was voted by the

Wide receiver Lance Alworth, who played in seven consecutive Pro Bowls. (Courtesy of Amateur Athletic Foundation of Los Angeles)

college all-star coaches the "single best athlete" among the forty-nine collegiate players assembled for the game.

"Lancer," as he was called at the University of Arkansas, also lettered in baseball and in track and held the Razorbacks freshman 100-yard and 200-yard sprint marks of 9.6 and 21.2 seconds, respectively. His football coach, Frank Broyles, who recognized Lance's potential as a freshman, described him as the "most fluid player" he had ever seen. Broyles added that, at 6 feet and 182 pounds, Lance was an "even-and-leavin'" man, "because when he's even with you, he's left you." Other coaches agreed with Broyles's assessment of Lance's elusiveness as a receiver. Some remarked after his all-star game in 1962 that no one in football could cover him man-to-man.

Lance also excelled in the classroom. He was a three-year academic all-American, finishing college with a degree in marketing as a prelaw student. His degree in business benefited him once his football days were over. In 1962, Lance was named to the *Look* magazine, Associated Press, United Press International, and coaches' all-American teams. Although he had certainly distinguished himself as a player in college, Lance's glory days lay ahead.

The Emerging Champion

In 1962, the Oakland Raiders drafted Lance in the second round of the American Football League (AFL) draft. The Raiders chose Lance to negotiate a trade with Coach Sid Gillman of the San Diego Chargers, who grasped Lance's potential as a receiver. The San Francisco 49ers also drafted Lance for the more powerful NFL, but the Chargers' Don Klosterman persuaded Lance to accept the challenge of growing with the weaker, newer league. Lance moved to San Diego and, through his play, proved that the AFL was one of the "big leagues."

In 1962, Charlie Flowers, a fullback for the Chargers, was watching Lance practice with the team. He was so impressed with the rookie's grace and agility, with his slim upper torso and heavily muscled legs, that he remarked that Lance looked like a thoroughbred. He began calling Lance "Bambi"—an appropriate nickname. Lance seemed to have a fawn-like fragility but in reality possessed all the wiry strength and explosive speed of a full-grown deer. "Bambi" stepped lightly and soared mightily to grab balls out of the air.

The San Diego staff was not so sure that the young man with the easy smile and the all-Ameri-

AFL and NFL Statistics

Season	GP	Rec.	Yds.	Avg.	TD
1962	4	10	226	22.6	3
1963	14	61	1,205	19.8	11
1964	14	61	1,235	20.2	13
1965	14	69	1,602	23.2	14
1966	14	73	1,383	18.9	13
1967	11	52	1,010	19.4	9
1968	14	68	1,312	19.3	10
1969	14	64	1,003	15.7	4
1970	14	35	608	17.4	4
1971	12	34	487	14.3	2
1972	14	15	195	13.0	2
Totals	139	542	10,266	18.9	85

Notes: GP = games played; Rec. = receptions; Yds. = yards; Avg. = average yards per reception; TD = touchdowns

can looks would live up to expectations. Their concerns about whether he could withstand the pounding of professional football came to a head when Lance suffered a muscle tear above his right knee while horsing around at practice one afternoon. The injury required surgery, and Lance's career seemed to be in jeopardy.

In 1963, Lance came back in sound physical condition and proved correct Coach Gillman's contention that he should play as a flanker. Fears that Lance would spend his career on the disabled list proved groundless. Lance did occasionally get hurt, but he missed only six regular-season games and the 1964 AFL title game in the remaining nine years of his stay in professional football. One reason for Lance's steady presence in the lineup was that he played hurt. In 1966, he played until mid-season before letting anyone know that he had sustained fractures to both hands earlier in the year.

Continuing the Story

Lance was known for the characteristic leap, twist, and grab with which he caught passes. In early 1963, he astounded the Kansas City Chiefs by catching 9 passes for 232 yards and 2 touchdowns. The Chargers won the AFL title that year, and Lance was on his way to seven straight years as an all-AFL offensive player. He played in seven AFL all-star games from 1963 to 1969.

Catching at least one pass in every AFL game in which he played, including a then-record string of ninety-six straight regular-season games, Lance was truly the premier receiver of the 1960's and the

NFL Record

Most games with at least 200 receiving yards, 5

Honors and Awards

1961	Cotton Bowl Game Outstanding Back
1962	Hula Bowl All-Star Game Outstanding Back
	Hula Bowl All-Star Team
	College All-Star Team in Chicago
	Associated Press All-American
	United Press International All-American
1963	AFL All-League Team
	United Press International AFL Player of the Year
1963-69	AFL All-Star Team
	Sporting News AFL All-Star Team
1964-68	Associated Press All-League Team
1964-69	United Press International All-League Team
1969	All-Time AFL Team
1978	Inducted into Pro Football Hall of Fame
1984	Inducted into College Football Hall of Fame

first star player in the AFL. In his eleven seasons as a professional, he caught 542 passes for 10,266 yards and scored 85 touchdowns. He won the AFL receiving crown for most yards gained three times, in 1966, 1968, and 1969. For a man most people in the sport thought too slight for the game, it was a remarkable record.

The following year, 1970, however, was not a good year for Lance. His 96-game receiving streak ended, and at season's end, he was traded to the Dallas Cowboys, whose coach, Tom Landry, decided to use him primarily as a blocker. Though Lance performed well in that role, the new earthbound position did not sit well with a man used to soaring. Nevertheless, he caught a pass for a touchdown in the championship game against the Miami Dolphins. Lance finally had a Super Bowl ring. Still, he was not happy with the Cowboys and retired in 1972.

After his retirement, Lance returned to his business interests in San Diego with his wife Marilynn and their four children, Lance, Jr., Gregory, Kelly Ann, and Bradley. In 1978, after the required five-year waiting period, Lance became the first origi-nal AFL player elected to the Pro Football Hall of Fame.

Summary

Lance Alworth, the man known as Bambi, proved that speed and agility sometimes count more than size. He also helped sustain the fledgling AFL. For an entire decade, he dominated the league, a performance that earned him his sport's highest honor, a place in the Pro Football Hall of Fame.

William U. Eiland

Additional Sources

Barber, Phil. "NFL: Football's One Hundred Greatest Players—The Hit Men." *The Sporting News* 223 (November 1, 1999): 12-16.

National Football League. *The Official NFL 2001 Record and Fact Book.* New York: Workman, 2001.

Robinson, Grady Jim. *Where Have You Gone, Lance Alworth? Stories About Growing Up in Arkansas.* Fayetteville, Ark.: Diamond Gem, 2001.

Tobias, Todd. *Charging Through the AFL: Los Angeles and San Diego Chargers' Football in the 1960's.* Paducah, Ky.: Turner, 2004.

Lyle Alzado

Born: April 3, 1949
      Brooklyn, New York
Died: May 14, 1992
      Portland, Oregon
Also known as: Lyle Martin Alzado (full name)

Early Life

Lyle Martin Alzado was born on April 3, 1949, in the crime-ridden Brownsville section of Brooklyn, New York. He was the son of a rough, alcoholic Spanish-Italian father and a loving Jewish mother. He was reared on the poor side of affluent Cedarhurst, Long Island. Lyle grew up tough; he did not believe that he was as good as other children. He was involved in many fights, and local police were well aware of him before he turned fifteen. Football saved him and redirected the course of his life. Lyle was a star football player at Lawrence High School on Long Island, where he became known for his speed and aggressive attitude. Lyle was named a high school all-American in football, but he was not quite big enough, nor was he a good enough student, to be recruited to play in college.

Lyle decided to attend Kilgore College, a junior college in Texas, to get away from home and to try to improve his football ability. The story at Kilgore was much the same as it had been in high school: Because of his size and grades, only Yankton College in South Dakota took a chance on him. At Yankton, Lyle's life changed for the better, and for the worse.

The Road to Excellence

Lyle had considered going into the Marines when he was offered a scholarship to Yankton. There, he began to get the physical size and strength to go along with his football talent, and he became a dominant small-college player. He channeled his aggressiveness into football; at the same time, he learned that he had a soft spot in his heart for children.

One day at Yankton, Lyle was approached in the gym by a mentally disabled girl, who cried and asked him why other children did not play with her. From then on, Lyle realized that there was more to life than sacking a quarterback. He went on to earn his degree in special education;

later, he won many community-service awards for his work with children.

At Yankton, Lyle grew as a person and as a football player, but it seemed that he was two different people going in two different directions. On the football field, he was mean and aggressive. Off the field, he could be very sensitive and helpful. He also began to realize that a professional football career was a possibility.

The Emerging Champion

In 1971, Lyle was drafted by the Denver Broncos. He was so determined to make the team that he pushed himself to outrun and outhit everybody else on the team. When a veteran player got hurt in a preseason game against the Chicago Bears, Lyle took his place on the roster and made the team. Lyle became a standout on the defensive line for the Broncos that first year. He combined desire, quickness,

Lyle Alzado celebrating after the Los Angeles Raiders defeated the Pittsburgh Steelers in a 1984 playoff game. (AP/Wide World Photos)

Honors and Awards

1977-78	*Sporting News* AFC All-Star Team
	NFL Pro Bowl Team
1982	*Pro Football Weekly* Comeback Player of the Year

strength, and intricate moves to become one of the best defensive ends in the NFL. Lyle was named NFL defensive player of the year in 1977, and he played in the Pro Bowl in 1977 and 1978. For three years, he led the Broncos in quarterback sacks. The Broncos' aggressive defense, led by Lyle, propelled the team to the Super Bowl in 1977. The loss to the Dallas Cowboys in that Super Bowl only made Lyle want to work harder to get another chance.

By 1979, however, Lyle had become too intense for his Bronco teammates. His aggressive nature began to carry over from the games to off the field. His antics wore thin with the team. When he threatened to pursue a boxing career if the Broncos would not renegotiate his contract, Lyle was traded to the Cleveland Browns.

Lyle was with the Browns from 1979 through 1981, but he was plagued by a series of injuries in Cleveland, and he never seemed to perform at the level he had achieved in Denver. Many observers thought his playing career was winding down. The Browns reached the same conclusion and traded Lyle to the Oakland Raiders for an eighth-round draft choice. Lyle was insulted because he was traded for a low-round draft choice; therefore, he dedicated himself to becoming a star with the Raiders. His first season with the team was so successful that he was voted the NFL's comeback player of the year in 1982.

Continuing the Story

Lyle's years with the Raiders were marked by an increase in his aggressive behavior. Lyle was often seen pointing fingers and flying all over the field for the Raiders. Off the field, too, Lyle was having trouble controlling his temper. His marriage to his first wife, Cindy, ended, although he remained close to his son, Justin. Lyle provoked fights to settle even minor disagreements in public, and during games, he sometimes pulled the helmet off an opposing blocker in a fit of rage. However, toward the end of the Raiders' rout of the Washington Redskins in the 1984 Super Bowl, when the television cameras focused on hulking number 77, the audience saw tears streaming down his cheeks. Perhaps he knew that the price he had paid to reach his goal was a high one.

Lyle retired from football the next year and tried acting, but after four years, he decided to try to return to the violence of professional football. In 1989, he made a valiant bid for a spot on the Raiders' roster at the age of forty-one. His skills had eroded with age, however, and he was released on the final roster cut of the preseason. Not long after that, Lyle married his second wife, Kathy. He also began to have health problems. Eventually he was forced to see a doctor, who told Lyle that he had a severe brain tumor.

After his diagnosis, Lyle revealed that he had taken the body-building drugs known as steroids to increase his muscle mass. Steroids are known to cause aggression in users, and Lyle's disclosure helped to explain his wild behavior. Moreover, steroids have been linked with serious health side effects, and Lyle blamed his illness on his drug use. He spent his last months warning the public of the dangers of taking such muscle-building drugs. Lyle died May 14, 1992, at the age of forty-three.

Summary

Lyle Alzado was a fierce NFL defensive lineman for fourteen seasons. His untimely death was a shocking reminder of the dangers of performance-enhancing drugs. He wanted everyone to know that the price he paid to be a star athlete was too high.

Kevin R. Lasley

Additional Sources

Alzado, Lyle, and Paul Zimmerman. *Mile High: The Story of Lyle Alzado and the Amazing Denver Broncos.* New York: Atheneum, 1978.

Denham, Bryan E. "Building the Agenda and Adjusting the Frame: How the Dramatic Revelations of Lyle Alzado Impacted Mainstream Press Coverage of Anabolic Steroid Use." *Sociology of Sport Journal* 16, no. 1 (1999): 1.

Edwards, Wayne. "Fourth Down and Long: Fighting for His Life, Ex-Football Terror Lyle Alzado Battles Brain Cancer." *People Weekly* 36, no. 3 (July 29, 1991): 52-54.

Newhouse, Dave. *The Ultimate Oakland Raiders Trivia Book.* Rochester, N.Y.: American Sports Media, 2001.

Morten Andersen

Born: August 19, 1960
Copenhagen, Denmark

Early Life

Morten Andersen was born in Copenhagen, Denmark, on August 19, 1960, to Erik and Hanne Andersen. He grew up in the fishing village of Struer on the Danish peninsula. His father was a psychologist for disabled children, and his mother was a Danish language teacher and school librarian.

As a child, Morten was loud and rambunctious, contrasting with his twin, Jakob, who was quiet and shy. Morten began playing soccer at an early age, and as a teenager he just missed making the Danish junior national soccer team. He excelled in the floor exercises in gymnastics and was made an instructor at a local gymnastics club. While Morten was in high school, he studied French, German, English, Latin, and Norwegian.

The Road to Excellence

After Morten graduated from the tenth grade, the final grade in Denmark, his father arranged for him to study as a cultural exchange student in the United States. He arrived in the United States on his seventeenth birthday and was assigned to Ben Davis High School in Indianapolis, Indiana, living with Jean and Dale Baker and their four children.

Baker took Morten to a football jamboree involving six high schools, and Morten became captivated by American football.

The next day Morten went with Baker and his son to the Ben Davis High School football practice, wearing his soccer shoes. Morten got a chance to kick the football at the 20-yard line and booted the ball through the uprights. Dale moved the ball back in increments of 5 yards to the 50-yard line, and Morten easily made field goals at each distance. The coach, Bob Wilbur, immediately issued Morten a uniform. Morten made 5 of his 7 field-goal attempts that season.

At the end of his first year abroad, Morten faced a difficult decision of remaining in the United States or returning to Denmark. He decided to attend Michigan State University on a football scholarship. As a senior at Michigan State, Andersen kicked a 63-yarder against Ohio State University and was named to several all-America teams. During his four years at college, Morten set the school's career scoring record of 261 points. He was also an ambitious student, with a double major in communications and German and a double minor in marketing and French.

The Emerging Champion

In 1982 Morten was selected by the New Orleans Saints in the fourth round, the eighty-sixth pick overall, of the 1982 NFL draft. He

Playing for the New York Giants, Morten Andersen kicking a game-winning field goal against the Dallas Cowboys in 2001. (Larry French/Getty Images)

spent fourteen seasons with the New Orleans Saints, and during that time, he compiled an outstanding record. His last-minute field goals enabled the Saints to win games against the Eagles, the Browns, the Cowboys, the Rams, and the Falcons. Morten left the Saints as the team's all-time scoring leader with 1,318 total points, which included 302 field goals. He also scored in 174 consecutive games.

Continuing the Story

In 1995, during his first season with the Atlanta Falcons, Morten set NFL records for the most 50-yard field goals in a game; he even made 3 against his former team, the Saints. Morten also set Falcons records for points, 123—sixth best in the NFL—and 31 field goals, the second most in the league. Furthermore, he scored the longest field goal in the NFL that year, a 59-yarder against San Francisco. In 1996, Morten scored in every game, maintaining his NFL record for the number of consecutive games scored. He also became the fifth player in NFL history to reach 1,500 career points and only the third player with 350 field goals.

Morten continued to be a consistent kicker for the Falcons through the 2000 season. In 1997, he kicked game-wining field goals against Philadelphia and St. Louis as time expired. In 1998, Morten sent Atlanta to Super Bowl XXXIII, connecting on a 38-yarder in overtime to seal a victory over Minnesota in the National Football Conference (NFC) Championship game. In the Falcons Super Bowl loss to Denver, Morten hit field goals of 28 and 32 yards. In 2000, during a game against Philadelphia, Morten booted a 48-yard field goal, giving him 561 points with the Falcons. Morten had broken the Falcons' career scoring record held by Mick Luckhurst, who had 558 points.

Morten spent the next few seasons among three different teams: the Giants in 2001; the Chiefs in 2002 and 2003; and the Vikings in 2004, before returning to the Falcons for the 2006 season. In 2001, Morten passed George Blanda on the NFL's all-time scoring list, moving into second place with a total of 2,003 points, after a 47-field goal and a point after touchdown (PAT) against Oakland. Two seasons later, with the Chiefs, Morten again spurned rival Oakland by hitting his 500th career field goal with 4 seconds remaining to give Kansas City a 27-24 victory. That same season, Morten hit

NFL Statistics

Season	GP	FGA	FGM	XP	TP
1982	8	5	2	6	12
1983	16	24	18	37	91
1984	16	27	20	34	94
1985	16	35	31	27	120
1986	16	30	26	30	108
1987	12	36	28	37	121
1988	16	36	26	32	110
1989	16	29	20	44	104
1990	16	27	21	29	92
1991	16	32	25	38	113
1992	16	34	29	33	120
1993	16	35	28	33	117
1994	16	39	28	32	116
1995	16	37	31	30	123
1996	16	29	22	31	97
1997	16	27	23	35	104
1998	16	28	23	51	120
1999	16	21	15	34	79
2000	16	25	31	23	98
2001	16	28	23	29	98
2002	14	26	22	51	117
2003	16	20	16	58	106
2004	16	22	18	45	99
2006	14	23	20	27	87
2007	14	28	25	24	99
Totals	**382**	**709**	**565**	**849**	**2,544**

Notes: GP = games played; FGA = field goals attempted; FGM = field goals made; XP = extra points; TP = total points

his thirtieth career game-wining field goal with a 30-yard kick in a victory over Cleveland. In 2004, with Minnesota, Morten broke another of George Blanda's NFL records, playing in his 341st game.

In the 2006 and 2007, while playing with the Falcons, Morten increased his record for most games played. In 2006, Morten added two more NFL career records to his resume, surpassing kicker Gary Anderson to become the NFL's all-time leading scorer with 2,435 points and connecting on his 539th career field goal. Also in 2007, Morten was named the NFC special teams player of the week—the ninth time in his career he was awarded the honor—for his role in the Falcons 20-13 win over the division rival Carolina Panthers. Morten became an unrestricted free agent in 2008. In December, he announced his retirement.

Morten settled in New Orleans, where he became involved in numerous community charities. He was named the New Orleans Sports Foundation's outstanding sports citizen of the year in recognition of his work with local children's hospitals. Morten's Kicks for Kids program raised hundreds of thousands of dollars for hospitals in New Orleans. Able to speak four languages fluently, he served as a television analyst in Denmark. After his career in the NFL, he hoped to pursue a career in broadcasting.

Summary

Morten Andersen set four NFL career records with 2,544 points scored, 565 field goals made, 709 field goals attempted, and 382 games played. He was second in career extra points made with 849.

Lloyd Johnson, updated by Trevor D. Bopp

Additional Sources

Duncan, Jeff. *Tales from the Saints Sideline.* Sports, 2004.

Glier, Ray. "Andersen Gets a Big Kick and Extra Money." *The Washington Post,* January 23, 1999, p. D8.

King, Peter. "Game of the Week." *Sports Illustrated,* October 20, 1993, 64.

Lieber, Jill. "Great Dane in Town." *Sports Illustrated,* December 21, 1987, 73-77.

Stallard, Mark. *Kansas City Chiefs Encyclopedia.* 2d ed. Champaign, Ill.: Sports, 2004.

Doug Atkins

Born: May 8, 1930
        Humboldt, Tennessee
Also known as: Douglas Leon Atkins (full name)

Early Life

Douglas Leon Atkins was born on May 8, 1930, in Humboldt, Tennessee. The future hall-of-fame lineman was primarily interested in sports other than football when he was a young man. At Humboldt High School, Doug played on the school basketball team and was a high jumper on the track squad. When he enrolled at the University of Tennessee in 1949, he did so on a basketball scholarship. Early in his college days, Doug recognized that his physical demeanor was best suited for football. Although he stood 6 feet 8 inches, his weight, which increased to

270 pounds, made him rather heavy for a high jumper or even for a deft forward or center in basketball.

The Road to Excellence

Doug soon became a varsity football player for Tennessee's celebrated coach Robert Neyland in the strong Southeastern Conference (SEC). Neyland saw Doug's potential as a lineman, and Doug was satisfied with his position at tackle. In 1950, Tennessee won 11 of 12 games, including a 20-14 Cotton Bowl victory over Texas. In 1951, Tennessee, the eventual national champion, went undefeated before losing its postseason Sugar Bowl game to Maryland, 28-13. That same season, Doug was chosen to the all-conference team as a defensive tackle along with his all-American teammate, guard John Michels.

As a defensive tackle, Doug was hard to fake out of position and difficult to trap with a side block. He learned to hesitate before charging toward the runner for fear that he might be a victim of a trap play. After his senior year at Tennessee in 1952-1953, Doug was named to several all-American teams. Doug's college teams won twenty-nine games, lost four, and tied one in his three years of varsity play. In 1953, he was selected by Coach Paul Brown of the Cleveland Browns in the first round of the NFL draft.

The Emerging Champion

Brown converted Doug from a tackle to a defensive end. Doug spent two seasons in Cleveland and played in two NFL title games. The Browns, directed by quarterback Otto Graham, lost the 1953 championship to Detroit, 17-16, and won the 1954 championship by defeating Detroit, 56-10. In both years Doug's defensive squads allowed the fewest points in the NFL. After the 1954 season, Doug married Joyce Gay Floyd.

Doug was traded to the Chicago Bears

Defensive end Doug Atkins. (NFL/Getty Images)

and Coach George Halas in 1955. Halas kept Doug at the end position. In Chicago, Doug achieved his greatest fame. He played for the Bears for twelve years, from 1955 through 1966, and, as he had with Cleveland, played in two championship games. In 1956, Doug's Chicago team won the Western Conference title before losing the NFL championship to the New York Giants, 47-7.

In 1958, Doug was chosen to play in the annual NFL Pro Bowl game. He was chosen seven more times over the course of his career. He was also named NFL lineman of the year in 1958. Halas once remarked that Doug was the best defensive player he ever saw, and his line coach George Allen—later the famed coach of the Washington Redskins—remarked that Doug was so big and awesome that he frightened the opponents. Allen ranked Doug with the greatest defensive players in football history.

Continuing the Story

The United Press International (UPI) selected Doug to its all-NFL team as defensive end in 1960; UPI and the Associated Press (AP) selected him to their all-NFL teams in 1963. That year Doug's defensive team allowed the fewest points of any NFL squad, as the Bears won the league title by defeating the New York Giants, 14-10. Doug was later selected to the all-pro team of the 1960's, and to the second team of the American Football League (AFL)-NFL all-stars of the era 1960-1984.

In 1966, Doug publicly expressed displeasure with Halas. The following year, after a contract dispute, Halas traded Doug to a new franchise in New Orleans, the Saints. Doug played his last three years with the Saints. Following the 1969 season, Doug left professional football after seventeen years of competition. At the age of thirty he had played in 205 NFL games, which at that time was second only to hall-of-fame kicker and lineman Lou Groza, his former teammate with the Cleveland Browns. During his professional career, Doug had three pass interceptions and scored two points on a safety, all with Chicago.

In 1982, Doug was selected to the Pro Football Hall of Fame in Canton, Ohio, and, three years later, to the College Football Hall of Fame. After his

Honors and Awards

1952	College All-American
	All-Southeastern Conference Team
1958	NFL Lineman of the Year
1958-64, 1966	NFL Pro Bowl Team
1959	NFL Pro Bowl Coplayer of the Game
1960, 1963	United Press International All-NFL Team
1963	Associated Press All-Pro Team
1970	NFL All-Pro Team of the 1960's
1982	Inducted into Pro Football Hall of Fame
1985	AFL-NFL 1960-1984 All-Star Team
	Inducted into College Football Hall of Fame
	Uniform number 81 retired by New Orleans Saints
2005	University of Tennessee retires his jersey

retirement, Doug moved his family to Knoxville, Tennessee, where he assumed a position as a sales representative. In 2005, the University of Tennessee retired Doug's jersey.

Summary

As a defensive end, Doug Atkins was renowned for closing off the end-around running play to his side of the field, even after the New York Giants introduced the man-in-motion device designed to neutralize the defensive end. Allen had taught Doug the art of pass rushing, and Doug often leaped over the offensive blockers en route to the passer. Also, Doug was remarkably durable. Rarely out of a game because of an injury, he followed the professional football maxim: The one who hits hardest is the one who does not get injured.

John D. Windhausen

Additional Sources

Conner, Floyd. *Football's Most Wanted: The Top Ten Book of the Great Game's Outrageous Characters, Fortunate Fumbles, and Other Oddities.* Washington, D.C.: Brassey's, 2000.

Duncan, Jeff. *Tales from the Saints Sideline.* Champaign, Ill.: Sports, 2004.

Freedman, Lew. *Game of My Life: Memorable Stories of Bears Football.* Champaign, Ill.: Sports, 2006.

Gorr, Beth. *Bear Memories: The Chicago-Green Bay Rivalry.* Chicago: Arcadia, 2005.

West, Marvin. *Legends of the Tennessee Vols.* Champaign, Ill.: Sports, 2005.

Champp Bailey

Born: June 22, 1978
      Folkston, Georgia
Also known as: Roland Bailey (full name)

Early Life

Roland "Champ" Bailey was born and raised in Folkston, Georgia, where he attended Charlton County High School. When Roland was a small boy, his mother nicknamed him "Champ," a moniker that followed him into his professional life. Champ was a standout athlete in high school: He was an all-state selection in football and was a *USA Today* honorable-mention all-American. In his high school career he rushed for 3,573 yards and scored 58 touchdowns. He also passed for 1,200 yards and was a standout defensive player as well.

Champ did not play football only. He was an all-state honorable mention in basketball and the state high-jump champion as a junior. He was a member of an athletic family. His younger brother Boss was an all-American at the University of Georgia and played in the NFL.

The Road To Excellence

Champ had a remarkable career at the University of Georgia and was used on offense, defense, and special teams in the three seasons that he played for the Bulldogs. In his collegiate career, he played in thirty-three games, starting twenty-four. He recorded 147 tackles and had 2 fumble recoveries, 1 forced fumble, and 8 interceptions. As a sophomore, he started every game at cornerback and one at wide receiver, and he was an all-Southeastern Conference (SEC) first-team selection. During his junior season, which was his final year at Georgia, he had 52 tackles, 3 interceptions, and 47 catches for 744 yards. He also returned punts and kicks. Altogether, he averaged more than 100 yards per game in all-purpose yardage.

In 1998, during his junior season, Champ won the Bronko Nagurski Award as the top collegiate defensive player in the United States. He was also an all-American selection and a member of the all-SEC first team.

Champ also competed in indoor track while at Georgia, setting a school record in the long jump with a mark of 25 feet 10¾ inches, which gave him third place at the SEC Indoor Track and Field Championships.

Champ entered the NFL draft after his junior season and was selected in the first round by the Washington Redskins. He was the seventh overall pick.

The Emerging Champion

Champ quickly became an impact player in the NFL during his rookie season in 1999. He started at cornerback in all sixteen games. He had 5 interceptions, which was the second most on his team. He returned 1 of those interceptions for 59 yards and a touchdown, the first of 4 in his NFL career. He also had 61 tackles, 19 pass breakups, and 1 sack. In addition to his defensive duties, he was an active player on special teams and had 14 tackles on special-teams plays. After a 3-interception game in October, he was named NFL defensive player of the week and was rookie defensive player of the month for October.

In 2000, Champ had another stellar season. Once again, he started all sixteen regular-season games and was named a starting cornerback for the National Football Conference Pro Bowl team. He was a key player on the second-best pass defense in the NFL, and he led the team with 5 interceptions.

NFL Statistics

Season	GP	Tac.	Sacks	FF	FR	Int.
1999	16	61	1	0	0	5
2000	16	52	0	0	1	5
2001	16	50	0	1	1	3
2002	16	68	0	0	1	3
2003	16	71	0	1	2	2
2004	16	81	0	0	0	3
2005	14	64	0	1	0	8
2006	16	85	0	0	1	10
2007	15	84	0	0	0	3
2008	9	44	1	0	0	1
Totals	**150**	**660**	**2**	**3**	**6**	**43**

Notes: GP = games played; Tac. = tackles; FF = forced fumbles; FR = fumble recoveries; Int. = interceptions

Honors and Awards

1998	Nagurski Award
	First-Team All-American
	First-Team All-Southeastern Conference
	University of Georgia defensive most valuable player
2000-07	NFL Pro Bowl
2004-07	NFL All-Pro
2005	Most interceptions in NFL (tied)
	Sporting News All-Defensive Team

He was also named the Redskins Quarterback Club player of the year. He returned punts and kicks and logged some playing time at the wide-receiver position.

In 2001, Champ started all sixteen games again and was named a first alternate for the NFC Pro Bowl. He played in the game because another player withdrew with an injury. He recorded 50 tackles and 3 interceptions that season. In 2002, he was again among the top cornerbacks in the NFL and was invited to participate in the Pro Bowl. He had 68 tackles that season and another 3 interceptions. In 2003, he earned a fourth-consecutive trip to the Pro Bowl with another standout season, finishing with 71 tackles and 2 interceptions.

Continuing the Story

After the 2003 season, Champ was part of a significant trade between Washington and the Denver Broncos that involved several players. For the Broncos, Champ started all sixteen regular-season games and returned to the Pro Bowl for the fifth year in a row, this time representing the American Football Conference. He had 81 tackles, 3 interceptions, and 13 pass breakups. He even appeared on offense in three games.

In 2005, he continued with Denver, but could not play a full season for the first time in his professional career because of injuries. Even though he missed two games, he still earned Associated Press first-team honors. He had 64 total tackles and a career-high 8 interceptions; he returned 2 of those interceptions for touchdowns.

In 2006, Champ started all sixteen games and won first-team Associated Press all-pro honors for the third year in a row. He was also selected to play in the Pro Bowl for a seventh time. He had 10 interceptions, sharing the league lead, and 1 fumble recovery. Another Pro Bowl selection came after the 2007 season. He missed one game because of injury but started the fifteen other regular-season games. He had 84 tackles and 3 interceptions. During the 2008 season, he played in only nine games and recorded 44 tackles.

Summary

Champ Bailey was born with great athletic ability but worked hard to develop his talent. He also demonstrated a versatility rarely seen in modern football, playing on offense, defense, and special teams. He became one of the most feared defensive players of his era.

Michael Coulter

Additional Sources

Dater, Adrian. *The Good, the Bad, and the Ugly Denver Broncos: Heart-Pounding, Jaw-Dropping, and Gut-Wrenching Moments from Denver Broncos History.* Chicago: Triumph Books, 2007.

Garbin, Patrick. *About Them Dawgs! Georgia Football's Memorable Teams and Players.* Lanham, Md.: Scarecrow Press, 2008.

Snow, D. C. *Champ Bailey.* Philadelphia: Mason Crest, 2008.

Sammy Baugh

Born: March 17, 1914
    Temple, Texas
Died: December 17, 2008
    Rotan, Texas
Also known as: Samuel Adrian Baugh (full
    name); Slingin' Sammy

Early Life

Samuel Adrian "Slingin' Sammy" Baugh was born
in Temple, Texas, on March 17, 1914. His father,
J. V. Baugh, worked for a railroad. Sammy said that
he began playing football as early as the third
grade. Football was so popular in the farming community of Temple that Sammy's grammar school
had an organized team. Sammy played end when

Sammy Baugh. (AP/Wide World Photos)

he first went to high school, but his coach played
him at many positions. Every day after school
Sammy practiced throwing the football through a
tire he tied to a backyard tree. After Sammy's first
year of high school the Baughs moved to Sweetwater, Texas, where Sammy finished high school.

The Road to Excellence

During his last three years of high school, Sammy
played on the baseball, basketball, and football
teams. Although baseball was his favorite sport,
young Sammy went to the football field to practice
his punting for about one hour each day in the
summer. He kicked the ball out of bounds within
the ten-yard line, walked to the other end of the
field, and kicked the ball back. Usually a
tailback for the Sweetwater High football
squad, during his senior year, he became
a fine blocking back.

In 1933, Sammy entered Texas Christian University (TCU) and joined the
freshman football team under coach Leo
"Dutch" Meyer, who recruited Sammy after watching him play baseball. Meyer
promised Sammy that he could play football and basketball as well. Sammy went
to TCU on a scholarship and played all
three sports for the varsity teams. Meyer
was the first to spot Sammy's unusually
powerful wrists and the exceptional accuracy of his football tosses. The next
year, when Meyer assumed head-coach-
ing duties, Sammy became the passing
tailback for the varsity team.

The Emerging Champion

As a sophomore Sammy led TCU to an 8-
4 record, but the year was a learning experience. The team lost to rivals Texas,
Southern Methodist University (SMU),
Arkansas, and Centenary. Sammy's most
disappointing performance came against
SMU on November 3, 1935, in a game for
the national championship. Unbeaten
SMU won, 20-14, as Sammy completed

only 17 of 45 passes; his bullet tosses were difficult for the receivers to catch. Sammy learned from his mistakes, and under his three-year leadership the TCU Horned Frogs' record was 29-7-2. In 1936, TCU won the Sugar Bowl against Louisiana State. In 1937, TCU beat Marquette University in the Cotton Bowl.

Sammy's passing skills alone made him a football legend, but he was a complete player as well. In the 1936 Sugar Bowl, TCU defeated LSU, 3-2, in a severe rainstorm, as Sammy displayed his uncanny kicking abilities. He punted a slippery, soaked football fourteen times for a 48-yard average. Playing safety on defense, he twice intercepted passes deep in TCU territory, and he once made a game-saving tackle at the TCU two-yard line. Sammy even carried the ball on the day's longest run for 42 yards. He capped his collegiate career by throwing a touchdown pass as the 1937 college all-stars upset the NFL champion Green Bay Packers 6-0 in Chicago.

Continuing the Story

Washington Redskins' owner George Preston Marshall signed Sammy to a hefty contract. Sammy fulfilled Marshall's hopes, leading the team to the NFL championship in his first year. Named all-pro six times, Sammy led the Redskins to five Eastern Division titles and two NFL championships, in 1937 and 1942.

Sammy's biggest football thrill was the 1937 championship game against the Chicago Bears at Wrigley Field. A combination of rain and frost turned the field into balls of mud as sharp as rocks. Slowed by a leg injury and plagued by frozen fingers, Sammy could not get his rhythm, and his team trailed 14-7 at halftime. In the third period, though, Sammy threw three touchdowns, completing 18 of 33 passes, as his team won the title, 28-21.

Sammy regarded the 1940 team as his best, although the team lost to Chicago for the title by the record score of 73-0. The Redskins had beaten Chicago weeks earlier, but on that day every gamble backfired. Eight of Sammy's passes were intercepted. Two years later, Sammy and the Redskins gained their revenge, defeating Chicago in the NFL Championship game 14-6. In the title game in 1943, Sammy suffered an early concussion, and Chicago won 41-21.

When football strategy changed from the single wing to the t-formation in 1944, Sammy became quarterback. Sammy liked the change because it reduced the beatings he was taking as a tailback and lengthened his career. During sixteen seasons with the Redskins from 1937 to 1952, Sammy topped NFL passers six times. His best single-game performances included making 29 completions against Los Angeles in 1949, throwing for 446 yards against Boston in 1948, and tossing 6 touchdown passes in two different games.

In 1947, Washington fans honored Sammy with a special "day." He rewarded the fans with a superb performance against the Chicago Cardinals, completing 25 of 33 passes for 355 yards and 6 touchdowns, but Washington's 45-21 victory did not prevent the Cardinals from winning the 1947 championship. During his last few years, Sammy tutored quarterbacks Harry Gilmer and Eddie LeBaron. A broken hand sidelined Sammy for most of 1952, but he returned to lead the team to victories in the last two games before his retirement.

Sammy was one of the greatest punters in NFL history, retiring with a 45.1-yard career average; in 1940, he once had a 51.3-yard season aver-

NFL Statistics

Season	GP	PA	PC	Pct.	Yds.	Avg.	TD	Int.
1937	11	171	81	.473	1,127	6.59	8	14
1938	10	128	63	.492	853	6.66	5	11
1939	8	96	53	.552	518	5.39	6	9
1940	11	177	111	.627	1,367	7.72	12	10
1941	11	193	106	.549	1,236	6.40	10	19
1942	11	225	132	.586	1,524	6.77	16	11
1943	10	239	133	.556	1,754	7.33	23	19
1944	8	146	82	.561	849	5.81	4	8
1945	10	182	128	.703	1,669	9.17	11	4
1946	9	161	87	.540	1,163	7.22	8	17
1947	12	354	210	.593	2,938	8.29	25	15
1948	12	315	185	.587	2,599	8.25	22	23
1949	12	255	145	.568	1,903	7.46	18	14
1950	9	166	90	.542	1,130	6.80	10	11
1951	11	154	67	.435	1,104	7.16	7	17
1952	4	33	20	.606	152	4.61	2	1
Totals	159	2,995	1,693	.565	21,886	7.31	187	203

Notes: GP = games played; PA = passes attempted; PC = passes completed; Pct. = percent completed; Yds. = yards; Avg. = average yards per attempt; TD = touchdowns; Int. = interceptions

age, and he led the NFL in punting for four consecutive years, from 1940 to 1943. One of Sammy's feats may never be duplicated: One season, he led the NFL in passing, punting, and interceptions. His 4 pass interceptions in one game, against Detroit, was also a record.

In 1941, Sammy built a 6,300-acre ranch near Rotan, Texas, where he became a successful rancher. He married his high school sweetheart, Edmonia Smith, with whom he had five sons: Todd, David, Bruce, Stephen, and Francis. Sammy later coached at Hardin-Simmons University in Abilene before returning to the professionals to coach the New York Titans and Houston Oilers of the American Football League.

Sammy was inducted into the National Football Foundation's College Football Hall of Fame in 1951 and into the Pro Football Hall of Fame in 1963 as one of seventeen charter members. In 1999, the Associated Press voted Sammy the third greatest NFL player of the twentieth century. The famous sportswriter Grantland Rice once named Sammy the finest quarterback of all time in both college and pro football, and *Sports Illustrated* chose Sammy as all-century quarterback to celebrate the hundredth anniversary of football in 1969. He died December 17, 2008, at the age of ninety-four.

NFL Records

Highest average in punting yards, 45.1
Highest average in punting yards, one season, 51.4 (1940)
Highest average in yards per pass, one game, 18.6 (1948)
Most interceptions in a game, 4 (1943) (record shared)

Honors and Awards

1935-36	College All-American
1936	Citizens Savings College Football Player of the Year
1937	Chicago College All-Star Team
1939-40, 1942 (two games), 1952	NFL Pro Bowl Team
1951	Inducted into College Football Hall of Fame
1963	NFL All-Pro Team of the 1940's
	Inducted into Pro Football Hall of Fame
1969	*Sports Illustrated* All-Century NFL Team
	Uniform number 33 retired by Washington Redskins

transition from single wing to t-formation. The 6-foot 2-inch passer remained cool under defensive pressure, was amazingly accurate, and helped to make the professional game into a more exciting, pass-oriented contest.

John D. Windhausen

Summary

Black-haired, blue-eyed Sammy Baugh became the nation's most celebrated collegiate passer. As an all-American tailback at TCU and as a quarterback star with the Washington Redskins of the NFL, Sammy helped to revolutionize football during the

Additional Sources

Canning, Whit. *Sammy Baugh: Best There Ever Was.* Indianapolis, Ind.: Master Press, 1997.

King, Peter. *Greatest Quarterbacks.* Des Moines, Iowa: Sports Illustrated Books, 1999.

Loverro, Thom. *Hail Victory: An Oral History of the Washington Redskins.* New York: John Wiley and Sons, 2006.

Whittingham, Richard. *Hail Redskins: A Celebration of the Greatest Players, Teams, and Coaches.* Chicago: Triumph Books, 2004.

_____. *What a Game They Played: An Inside Look at the Golden Era of Pro Football.* Lincoln: University of Nebraska Press, 2001.

Chuck Bednarik

Born: May 1, 1925
          Bethlehem, Pennsylvania
Also known as: Charles Philip Bednarik (full
   name)

Early Life

Charles Philip "Chuck" Bednarik was born on May 1, 1925, in Bethlehem, Pennsylvania. A town with an economy based on steel mills, Bethlehem was a harsh environment in which to grow up, especially during the years of the Depression. Chuck's parents were immigrants from Czechoslovakia who did not speak English. When Chuck first went to school, he did not speak much English either, and when he came home from school he could not ask his parents for help with his schoolwork. Money was scarce, and Chuck was given his first football after his family saved up twenty-five "Nu-Joy" coffee wrappers to send away for one.

Chuck's first contact with organized sports came when, at the age of ten, he joined the local Boys Club. At the age of fifteen, Chuck decided to follow his friends by dropping out of school to work in a local steel mill. After playing hooky from school for two weeks, though, Chuck ran into Paul Troxell, one of his football coaches. In what proved to be a turning point in Chuck's life, Troxell grabbed him by the shirt and said:

> You dumb kid. Do you want to be like your father the rest of your life and work in these mills? Or do you want to take advantage of your God-given talent in athletics and make something of yourself?

Chuck decided to return to school and concentrate on football. His tough childhood probably contributed to his desire to win. This determination enabled Chuck to leave the poverty of his early life behind to become the last of football's "sixty-minute" men.

The Road to Excellence

Chuck's football career started at Liberty High School in Bethlehem. Originally a fullback, Chuck was offered a starting position as a center. Chuck was so intent on perfection that he practiced hour after hour snapping footballs into peach baskets he had set up in his backyard. Both coaches and players commented that they never saw Chuck make a bad snap from center.

In his junior year in high school, Chuck was already attracting the attention of college coaches. Instead of staying for his senior year, however, Chuck took what was known as the Dalton Plan test, a proficiency examination used to receive a high school diploma. The year was 1943, and the United States was deeply involved in World War II. Most of Chuck's friends had enlisted, and thinking that he was joining them in the camaraderie of war, Chuck entered the Army. The 6-foot, 180-pound boy who went off to war in 1943, came back two years later as a 6-foot 2-inch, 216-pound man with thirty aerial missions under his belt.

On October 11, 1945, Chuck was discharged from the Army as a highly decorated aerial gunner,

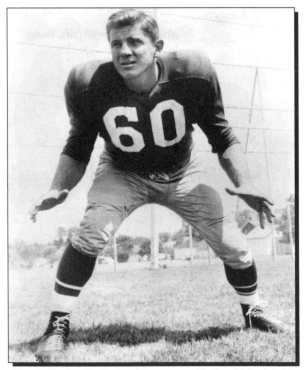

Chuck Bednarik during his years with the Philadelphia Eagles. (NFL/Getty Images)

Honors and Awards

1946	Blue-Gray All-Star Team
1946-48	All-East Coast Athletic Conference Team
1947	Rockne Award
1947-48	College All-American
1948	Maxwell Award
	Citizens Savings College Football Player of the Year
	Chicago College All-Star Team
	North-South All-Star Team
1949	Overall first choice in the NFL draft
1950-56, 1960	NFL All-Pro Team
1951-55, 1957-58, 1961	NFL Pro Bowl Team
1954	NFL Pro Bowl Player of the Game
1960	Twenty-five-year (1925-1950) All-American Team
	Sport magazine All-Time All-American Team
	Wanamaker Award
1962	Hickok Award
1963	NFL All-Pro Team of the 1950's
1967	Inducted into Pro Football Hall of Fame
1969	Inducted into College Football Hall of Fame
	All-Time Fifty-Year NFL Team
	East Coast Athletic Conference All-Time All-American Team
1987	Uniform number 60 retired by Philadelphia Eagles
2007	Elected to Philadelphia Eagles seventy-fifth anniversary team

---

but he felt lost in postwar society. He went to his high school coach, Johnny Butler, for guidance. Butler made a phone call to George Monger, the head football coach at the University of Pennsylvania. Armed with the GI Bill, which assisted war veterans in getting a college education, Chuck headed out to Philadelphia.

The Emerging Champion

Upon arriving in Pennsylvania, Chuck found that—like other returning servicemen—he was a man among boys. Older than most college students in his academic year, Chuck was both bigger and more mature than most of his peers. He started as a linebacker, and his team won the Ivy League title. In his sophomore and junior years, Chuck began to be an all-around performer, playing center and linebacker as well as kicking for extra points and kickoffs. In his junior year, Chuck increased his intensity; he led his team to an undefeated season and was voted all-American.

As a senior in 1948, Chuck was recognized for his on-field excellence. He won the Maxwell Award as the top player in the nation and was runner-up in the Heisman Trophy race. He was again voted all-American and accounted for more than 50 percent of all his team's tackles, an unprecedented sta-

tistic. In 1949, Chuck was the number one draft pick for the Philadelphia Eagles of the NFL. His contract was for $10,000 a year plus a $3,000 signing bonus. After sitting on the bench in his first professional game, Chuck confronted the coach and told him that he wanted to be traded if he was not good enough to play for the Eagles. He started as a linebacker the next week, and the Eagles went on to win the NFL championship in 1949, his rookie year. At the end of the year he married Emma Margetich.

The Eagles' coach was fired the next year, and the team slipped into mediocrity. Even so, Chuck was a Pro Bowl and all-pro selection eight times from 1950 to 1961. After playing only center in 1959, Chuck announced his retirement at the end of the year. He stayed in retirement for only two months, though. In February of 1960, his fifth daughter was born, and Chuck decided to return to work. He signed again with the Eagles, for considerably more than he had been offered in his first Philadelphia contract.

The 1960 season proved to be Chuck's most memorable. Chuck had made his mark playing both offense and defense as one of the so-called "sixty-minute" men—those who played all sixty minutes of the game. By 1960, however, football had progressed to a degree of specialization that prevented any player from playing both offense and defense, even a player as determined as Chuck. Four games into the season, Philadelphia's middle linebacker was injured on the first play. Chuck was asked to become the last of the sixty-minute men.

That season, the NFL Eastern Conference championship came down to a race between the Eagles and the New York Giants. Chuck was again asked to play sixty minutes as the two teams clashed for the conference title. Preserving the game for the Eagles, Chuck knocked Giants' halfback Frank Gifford unconscious as Gifford caught a pass over the middle. Chuck immediately raised his arms in victory as the Eagles recovered Gifford's fumble. Chuck's gesture of victory was mistaken for jubilance over an act of violence, and the incident tainted Chuck's reputation. Chuck and the Eagles finished the 1960 season by beating the Green Bay Packers in the NFL Championship game. That game marked the end of an era: never again did a player participate in all sixty minutes of an NFL game.

Continuing the Story

Upon retiring from football after the 1962 season, Chuck was showered with every honor a football player could receive. In 1962, he accepted the Hickok Award as the greatest professional lineman of the decade. In 1967, he was elected to the Pro Football Hall of Fame and, in 1969, to the National Football Foundation's College Football Hall of Fame. Also, in 1969, he was named the center on the all-time fifty-year NFL team.

After his retirement from football, Chuck took his intense competitiveness to both the business world and the golf course. He became the leading salesman for the Warner Concrete Company, and when the Eagles moved to a new stadium in 1971, it was no surprise that Chuck was involved in the deal to supply the concrete for that stadium. Chuck also focused his fierce competitiveness on the golf course. Leaving behind a trail of broken and bent golf clubs, Chuck became the champion of the Whitemarsh Country Club in 1975.

Still, Chuck longed for the football field. After the Eagles' management twice rejected his request for a coaching position, Chuck gave up on the idea. In 1976, Dick Vermeil took over as the head coach of the Eagles. Vermeil decided that he needed a "motivator" for his team. Although Vermeil had never met Chuck, he knew that he wanted him on the sidelines. Coaching with the same intensity he had played with, Chuck was on the sidelines as the Eagles became Super Bowl contenders. Chuck's number was retired by the Eagles, but his relationship with his former team was rocky throughout the years. He was outspoken about Eagles' personnel. In his retirement, Chuck did not leave his intense attitude on the field, but carried it with him as he walked through life.

Summary

Chuck Bednarik has gone down in history as the last of the sixty-minute men. His retirement in 1962 marked the end of an era. His ability to sustain a high level of intensity while playing both offense and defense has not been matched on the football field since the era of the sixty-minute man ended.

John Gould and Jo-Ellen Lipman Boon

Additional Sources

Anderson, Dave. *Great Defensive Players of the NFL*. New York: Random House, 1967.

Kilduff, Mike. "Thawing the Ice Between Gifford and Bednarik." *Sporting News* 227, no. 34 (August 25, 2003): 8.

McCallum, Jack. *Bednarik, Last of the Sixty-Minute Men*. Englewood Cliffs, N.J.: Prentice-Hall, 1977.

Macnow, Glen, and Big Daddy Graham. *The Great Book of Philadelphia Sports Lists*. Philadelphia: Running Press, 2006.

Rys, Richard. "Interview: Chuck Bednarik." *Philadelphia Magazine* 96, no. 1 (January, 2005): 102.

Raymond Berry

Born: February 27, 1933
 Corpus Christi, Texas
Also known as: Raymond Emmett Berry (full
 name)

Early Life
Beth Berry gave birth to her only child, Raymond
Emmett, on February 27, 1933, in the Texas gulf
port city of Corpus Christi. Ray's father, Mike, who
later became head football coach at several Texas
high schools, was an assistant football and basketball coach at Corpus Christi High School. Raymond often accompanied his father to practices
and games. He developed an early love of football
and dreamed of a career as a professional player.
While Raymond was growing up, his father
and his father's players taught him about
the game. In later years, Raymond credited
the encouragement and support of his father with much of the success he achieved.
Raymond's father was head coach at a high
school in Paris, a small town in east Texas,
when Raymond entered high school.

The Road to Excellence
Raymond started at end for his father's
team at Paris for four years, earning all-
district honors in his senior year. When no
major college offered him a scholarship for
football, he refused to be discouraged. He
enrolled at Schreiner Institute, a junior college, in Kerrville, Texas, for one year. In
1951, he transferred to Southern Methodist
University (SMU) in Dallas. Raymond enrolled at SMU without a scholarship and
walked on to the football team. Although
he was not blessed with superior physical
talent, his persistence and desire impressed
the SMU coaches enough that they offered
him a full scholarship.
 Raymond played sparingly his first two
years at SMU but was popular enough with
the other players that they elected him team
captain for the 1954 season, even though he
had never started a game. During his senior

year, he was selected to the all-Southwest Conference team and earned academic all-American honors as well. The Shrine all-star committee selected
Raymond to play in its annual East-West game.
 After his senior season at SMU, Raymond was
disappointed when he was not chosen until the
twentieth round of the NFL draft. He was picked by
the Baltimore Colts. Twentieth-round draft picks
were seldom able to make the restricted NFL ros-
ters, much less become starting players. Nevertheless, Raymond was determined to overcome his
own lack of physical ability and star in the NFL. He
planned to do it by sheer hard work. In addition to
his lack of ability, Raymond also suffered from poor
eyesight and chronic back problems. He overcame

Wide receiver Raymond Berry. (NFL/Getty Images)

the first problem by becoming the first NFL player to wear contact lenses. He overcame the second by ignoring the pain. Through hard work and extra hours on the practice field he made the Colts' roster.

The Emerging Champion

All of Raymond's persistence paid off. In 1958, he started at wide receiver for the Colts, alongside several outstanding players who led the team to the NFL West Division Championship. Raymond contributed heavily to the Colts' success in the regular season by catching 56 passes for 794 yards and 9 touchdowns. This set the stage for one of the greatest professional football games of all time, a game in which Raymond had his finest hour.

By halftime in the championship game the Colts had built a 14-3 lead over the NFL East champion New York Giants. Ray had scored one of the Colts' touchdowns on a 15-yard pass from quarterback Johnny Unitas. In the second half the Giants came back to take a 17-14 lead. With less than three minutes left, the Colts had the ball on their own 14-yard line. Unitas marched the Colts into position for a game-tying field goal. Raymond had caught three passes for 62 yards on the drive. The Colts won the dramatic game on their first possession in overtime. Raymond caught two more passes during the winning drive. For the day, Raymond had twelve catches for 178 yards and one touchdown.

Continuing the Story

Raymond continued to have productive seasons for the Colts as a pass receiver until his retirement after the 1967 season. During his career he caught 631 passes for 9,275 yards and 68 touchdowns,

NFL Statistics

Season	GP	Rec.	Yds.	Avg.	TD
1955	8	13	205	15.8	0
1956	10	37	601	16.2	2
1957	12	47	800	17.0	6
1958	11	56	794	14.2	9
1959	12	66	959	14.5	14
1960	12	74	1,298	17.5	10
1961	12	75	873	11.6	0
1962	14	51	687	13.5	3
1963	9	44	703	16.0	3
1964	12	43	663	15.4	6
1965	13	58	739	12.7	7
1966	14	56	786	14.0	7
1967	7	11	167	15.2	1
Totals	146	631	9,275	14.7	68

Notes: GP = games played; Rec. = receptions; Yds. = yards; Avg. = average yards per reception; TD = touchdowns

ranking him high on the NFL career receiving charts. He played in three NFL Championship games and in five Pro Bowls. He was inducted into the Pro Football Hall of Fame in 1973, and into the Texas Sports Hall of Fame in 1974. The Pro Football Hall of Fame selected him to the AFL-NFL 1960-1984 all-star team. His career proved that hard work and determination can overcome physical limitations in championship sports.

At the conclusion of his playing career, Raymond began a second, and equally successful, career as a coach. He served as assistant coach with the Dallas Cowboys from 1968 to 1969, the University of Arkansas from 1970 to 1973, the Cleveland Browns from 1976 to 1977, and the New England Patriots from 1979-1981. In October, 1984, he replaced Ron Meyer as head coach of the New England Patriots. In 1985, sportswriters named Raymond AFC coach of the year after his Patriots finished with an 11-5 record, the team's best ever at the time, and made it to the Super Bowl before losing to the Chicago Bears. Raymond's coaching career ended with a 26-14-0 record.

In addition to his activities as a player and a coach in the NFL, Raymond also wrote a very successful book, *Ray Berry's Complete Guide for Pass Receivers.* Raymond also served on the boards of directors of the Fellowship of Christian Athletes, the Alan Ameche Memorial Foundation, Telemissions International, and Bill Glass Ministries.

Honors and Awards

1955	East-West Shrine All-Star Team
	All-Southwest Conference Team
	Academic All-American
1958-60	NFL All-Pro Team
1959-60, 1962, 1964-65	NFL Pro Bowl Team
1963	NFL All-Pro Team of the 1950's
1973	Inducted into Pro Football Hall of Fame
1974	Inducted into Texas Sports Hall of Fame
1985	United Press International AFC Coach of the Year
	Uniform number 82 retired by Indianapolis Colts

Summary

Raymond Berry epitomizes the individual with limited athletic skills who excels through hard work and determination. He made himself into one of the premier pass catchers of all time, but his inability to understand the lack of those qualities in his players made his coaching career shorter than it might have been. His performance in the 1958 NFL Championship game assured him an honored place in football history.

Paul Madden

Additional Sources

Barber, Phil. "NFL: Football's One Hundred Greatest Players—The Hit Men." *The Sporting News* 223 (November 1, 1999): 12-16.

McCullough, Bob. *My Greatest Day in Football: The Legends of Football Recount Their Greatest Moments.* New York: Thomas Dunne Books/St. Martin's Press, 2001.

Patterson, Ted. *Football in Baltimore: History and Memorabilia.* Baltimore: Johns Hopkins University Press, 2000.

Jerome Bettis

Born: February 16, 1972
     Detroit, Michigan
Also known as: Jerome Abram Bettis (full name);
    the Bus; Bussy

Early Life

Jerome Abram Bettis was born February 16, 1972, to John and Gladys Bettis of Detroit, Michigan. Jerome was the youngest of three children. He became one of Michigan's finest athletes, but academics and bowling took precedence over football in Jerome's early childhood. At the age of fourteen, he suffered a severe asthma-related attack and was hospitalized. Instead of quitting sports and allow-

Pittsburgh Steelers running back Jerome Bettis carrying the ball against the Seattle Seahawks in Super Bowl XL. (Jimmy Cribb/NFL/Getty Images)

ing the condition to dictate his life, Jerome persevered. His passion for school superseded his need for sports, but his athleticism did not go unnoticed. As a member of the MacKenzie High School national honor society and as a scholastic award winner, Jerome gained his ticket out of Detroit and into stardom through football but was assisted by his academic performance. At the age of eighteen, Jerome was selected Michigan's number-one high school talent and awarded the Gatorade player of the year award for high school athletes. His football skills combined with his academic achievements allowed Jerome to select the University of Notre Dame—one of the most prestigious schools in the United States—in nearby South Bend, Indiana, to further his career.

The Road to Excellence

Ranked as one of the top offensive talents in the country, Jerome lived up to his expectations. Wearing number six for the Fighting Irish, Jerome often "bulled over" his opponents like a Mack truck or bus, earning him the nickname "The Bus." His spot in Fighting Irish football history was established after several successful seasons at Notre Dame. Although signed as a fullback, Jerome also played tailback, ending his career with a 5.69 average yards per carry and rushing for almost 2,000 yards (1,912). He was used as an inside power runner to punish opposing defenses, allowing the outside running game and the passing game to open up. Jerome starred at Notre Dame until 1992 and, upon leaving, was the single-season points leader with 120. He was the tenth selection in the first found of the 1993 NFL draft, taken by the Los Angeles Rams.

The Emerging Champion

In 1993, Jerome emerged as the prototype for power runners in the NFL. His rookie season far exceeded the expectations of the Rams organization and NFL fans. Jerome was the first Ram to rush for more than 1,000 yards since the great Pro Football Hall of Fame inductee Eric Dickerson. Jerome also rushed for more than 200 yards in a game and

NFL Statistics

Season	GP	Rushing				Receiving			
		Car.	Yds.	Avg.	TD	Rec.	Yds.	Avg.	TD
1993	16	294	1,429	4.9	7	26	244	9.4	0
1994	16	319	1,025	3.2	3	31	293	9.5	1
1995	15	183	637	3.5	3	18	106	5.9	0
1996	16	320	1,431	4.5	11	22	122	5.5	0
1997	15	375	1,665	4.4	7	15	110	7.3	2
1998	15	316	1,185	3.8	3	16	90	5.6	0
1999	16	299	1,091	3.6	7	21	110	5.2	0
2000	16	355	1,341	3.8	8	13	97	7.5	0
2001	11	225	1,072	4.7	4	8	48	6.0	0
2002	13	187	666	3.6	9	7	57	8.1	0
2003	16	246	811	3.3	7	13	86	6.6	0
2004	15	250	941	3.8	13	6	46	7.7	0
2005	12	110	368	3.3	9	4	40	10.0	0
Totals	192	3,479	13,662	3.9	91	200	1,449	7.2	3

Notes: GP = games played; Car. = carries; Yds. = yards; Avg. = average yards per carry or average yards per reception; TD = touchdowns; Rec. = receptions

was named corookie of the year. After two successful seasons, Jerome did not perform as well in his third year. The decrease in production, associated with the organization's relocation to St. Louis and a coaching change to a pass-oriented style of offense, meant Jerome became expendable. He was traded on draft day to the Pittsburgh Steelers.

In his first year with the Steelers, Jerome rushed for more than 1,000 yards and appeared in his third career Pro Bowl. A milestone of his inaugural season with the Steelers was when he ran for more than 200 yards against his former team. Beginning in 1996, Jerome ran for more than 1,000 yards in his first six seasons for the Steelers. His popularity in Pittsburgh propelled him into the national spotlight. He had his own television show and appeared in several commercials, including a parody of the famous Joe Green Coca-Cola commercial of the 1970's. Fan support for Jerome was overwhelming, but Pro Bowls, divisional championships, and statistical accolades did little to quell the desire to win a Super Bowl trophy.

Continuing the Story

In 2001, Jerome's playing time was reduced because of the additions of Amos Zereoue and, later, Deuce Staley, and nagging injuries. From 2001 until mid-2004, Jerome's carries decreased. However, after an injury to Pittsburgh's starting running back, the rested Jerome compiled six-straight 100-yard games as the starter to end the season. In his career, he was a six-time Pro Bowl selection, a three-time all pro, the 1996 comeback player of the year, and the 2001 Walter Payton Award winner. He ended his career fifth all time with 13,662 yards rushing.

Finally, in January, 2006, in front of his hometown fans in Detroit, Michigan, Jerome capped a remarkable season: The Steelers secured a 21-10 Super Bowl XL victory over the Seattle Seahawks. The win almost did not occur as, two weeks prior against the heavily favored Indianapolis Colts, Jerome fumbled as the Steelers tried to run out the clock. A game-saving, shoestring tackle by quarterback Ben Roethlisberger preserved the win and earned the Steelers its first Super Bowl appearance in nearly a decade. The win gave Jerome his first and only Super Bowl ring. Following the victory and subsequent parades, Jerome retired from the NFL as a champion.

Summary

At the time of his retirement, Jerome Bettis ranked near the top in many statistical categories in NFL history. His significance to the game came in two

Honors and Awards

1993	NFL Offensive Rookie of the Year
	Rams Rookie of the Year
	Rams most valuable player
	Sporting News Rookie of the Year
1993-94, 1996-97, 2001, 2004	NFL Pro Bowl
1993, 1996-97	NFL All-Pro
1996	NFL Comeback Player of the Year
1996-97, 2000	Pittsburgh Steelers' most valuable player
2001	Walter Payton Man of the Year Award
2002	Citizenship Through Sports Alliance Good Sportsmanship Award
2006	H. J. Heinz Company Foundation Community Service Award

key areas. First, his bruising style of running, in which he punished opposing defensive players, caused the pass-oriented offensives of the NFL to revert to the rushing, hard hitting, pounding offensives of the past. Second, his off-field contributions were numberless. He publicized his illnesses and asthma, thus showing youth how to deal with hardship and still be successful. He also used his star power to aid inner-city youth with his "The Bus Stops Here" foundation. He continued to show his passion for football as a broadcaster for both NBC and the NFL Network.

Keith J. Bell

Additional Sources

Bendel, Joe. *Tough as Steel: Pittsburgh Steelers—2006 Super Bowl Champions.* Champaign, Ill.: Sports, 2006.

Bettis, Jerome, and Teresa Varley. *Driving Home: My Unforgettable Super Bowl Run.* Chicago: Triumph Books, 2006.

Bettis, Jerome, and Gene Wojciechowski. *The Bus: My Life in and out of the Helmet.* New York: Doubleday, 2007.

Chadiha, Jeffri. "The Steelers Hope to Avenge Their Loss to the Colts." *Sports Illustrated* 104, no. 2 (2006).

Fred Biletnikoff

Born: February 23, 1943
    Erie, Pennsylvania
Also known as: Frederick S. Biletnikoff (full
name)

Early Life

Frederick S. Biletnikoff was born on February 23, 1943, in Erie, Pennsylvania, the son of Ephraim and Natalie Biletnikoff. Ephraim was a boxing champion in his youth but worked all of his life as a welder. Fred excelled in four sports—football,

Oakland Raiders wide receiver Fred Biletnikoff, who was inducted into the Pro Football Hall of Fame in 1988, running a passing route. (Courtesy of Amateur Athletic Foundation of Los Angeles)

basketball, baseball, and track—at the Technical Memorial High School in Erie. Ephraim was an authoritarian father who, according to his son, instilled in Fred disciplined work habits and a determination to excel. Fred's high school sports career brought him offers for scholarships from colleges and universities in several sports. On the advice of his father, Fred decided to concentrate on football.

The Road to Excellence

Fred chose to attend Florida State University (FSU), primarily to escape the harsh winters of his native Pennsylvania. He enrolled at FSU in 1961, but played only sparingly as a sophomore—freshmen were ineligible for varsity competition at the time. During his junior year, Fred began to show the skills that eventually allowed him to excel in the NFL in subsequent years.

During his junior year at FSU, Fred led his team in pass receptions, and entered into the Seminole record book with a 99-yard return of an intercepted pass against the University of Miami. In 1964, his final college season, Fred was elected cocaptain by his teammates. That year he caught 57 passes for 987 yards and 11 touchdowns, fourth best in the nation. Those statistics won Fred consensus all-American honors. His finest game as a collegian came in the 1965 Gator Bowl against the University of Oklahoma Sooners, when he caught 13 passes from quarterback Steve Tinsi for 192 yards and 4 touchdowns. Fred finished his college playing days with 87 catches for 1,463 yards and 16 touchdowns, not counting his performance in the 1965 college all-star game. Shortly after the 1965 Gator Bowl, he wed Jerrylin O'Connor, and together they had two children.

The Emerging Champion

Fred's collegiate career convinced the Oakland Raiders of the American Football League (AFL) to pick him in the fourth round of the 1965 draft. During his first two years in the AFL, Fred was used as a reserve. Fred never had the blazing speed many considered a requisite for success in professional football, so he concentrated on running precise pass routes and refining the hands that many coaches say were the best of his era.

By 1968, Fred had become a starting wide receiver for the Raiders, and he responded by catching 61 passes for 1,037 yards, including a career-best 82-yard reception. In a playoff game against the New York Jets that year, he caught 7 passes for 190 yards, his career high. By Fred's own admission, his success was due primarily to the precision of the routes he ran, which forced many coaches to abandon their standard man-for-man pass defenses in favor of the zone defense.

Fred's skills and dedicated work habits led him to ten consecutive seasons of 40 or more catches. In 1971 and 1972, after the merger of the AFL into the NFL, he led the NFL with 61 catches for 929 yards and 9 touchdowns, and 58 receptions for 802 yards, respectively. In playoff games he caught 70 passes for 1,167 yards during that same period. Those totals include his performance in Super Bowl XI, in which he caught 4 passes for 79 yards in helping his team to a 32-14 win over the Minnnesota Vikings. He was selected the game's most valuable player.

Fred retired after the 1978 season. During his AFL/NFL career, he caught 589 passes for 8,974 yards and 76 touchdowns, which, at that point,

AFL and NFL Statistics

Season	GP	Rec.	Yds.	Avg.	TD
1965	14	24	331	13.8	0
1966	10	17	272	16.0	3
1967	14	40	876	21.9	5
1968	14	61	1,037	17.0	6
1969	14	54	837	15.5	12
1970	14	45	768	17.1	7
1971	14	61	929	15.2	9
1972	14	58	802	13.8	7
1973	14	48	660	13.8	4
1974	14	42	593	14.1	7
1975	11	43	587	13.7	2
1976	13	43	551	12.8	7
1977	14	33	446	13.5	5
1978	16	20	285	14.3	2
Totals	**190**	**589**	**8,974**	**15.2**	**76**

Notes: GP = games played; Rec. = receptions; Yds. = yards; Avg. = average yards per reception; TD = touchdowns

made him the Raiders' all-time regular-season receiving leader. He played in four Pro Bowls, was elected to the all-AFC squad four times, and he was named to all-NFL teams in 1971 and 1972.

Continuing the Story

After retirement, Fred tried coaching, but he quickly tired of not playing. He came out of retirement in 1980, signing a contract with the Montreal Alouettes of the Canadian Football League. He caught 38 passes for 470 yards and 4 touchdowns, second best on his new team that season, but he found that the old thrill was no longer there. After another retirement, he returned to part-time coaching and public relations work in the San Francisco Bay Area. He also tried acting, securing several roles in television and bit parts in a few movies.

After holding a variety of coaching jobs at the high school, community college, and professional levels, Fred returned to the Raiders in 1989, as an assistant coach. He spent seven seasons working with wide receivers and two seasons in charge of quality control and then became the receivers coach in 1997. After ten years as the Raiders' receivers coach, Fred stepped down in 2007.

In 1994, Fred received an honor of a different kind when the Tallahassee Quarterback Club Foundation inaugurated the Biletnikoff Award for the best receiver of the year in National Collegiate Athletic Association (NCAA) Division 1A football.

Honors, Awards, and Records

1964	Consensus All-American
1965	Chicago College All-Star Team
	Associated Press All-American
	United Press International All-American
1968	Tied NFL record for the most touchdown catches in a postseason game, 3
1968, 1970	AFL All-Star Team
1969	*Sporting News* AFL All-Star Team
1971-72	All-NFL Team
1971-72, 1974-75	NFL Pro Bowl Team
1972-73	*Sporting News* AFC All-Star Team
1977	NFL Super Bowl most valuable player
1980	NFL All-Pro Team of the 1970's
1988	Inducted into Pro Football Hall of Fame
1991	Inducted into College Football Hall of Fame
1994	Biletnikoff Award for college receivers is created

The award's sanctioning by the National College Football Awards Association placed Fred's name alongside those of Dick Butkus, best linebacker award; Jim Thorpe, best defensive back; Bronko Nagurski, best defensive player; and other college football immortals.

Summary

Fred Biletnikoff's success as a professional athlete resulted primarily from his disciplined pass routes, soft hands, work habits, and attention to detail. Those characteristics were instrumental in forcing the development of today's sophisticated pass defenses in the NFL. Fred's career demonstrates that only modest athletic ability is sufficient for a career in professional sports if that ability is augmented by dedication, determination, and hard work.

Paul Madden

Additional Sources

Barber, Phil. "NFL: Football's One Hundred Greatest Players—The Hit Men." *The Sporting News* 223 (November 1, 1999): 12-16.

Flores, Tom, and Matt Fulks. *Tales from the Oakland Raiders.* Champaign, Ill.: Sports, 2003.

"The Greatest Stories Never Told." *Sports Illustrated* 100, no. 4 (February 2, 2004): 60-75.

Lombardo, John. *Raiders Forever: Stars of the NFL's Most Colorful Team Recall Their Glory Days.* Lincolnwood, Ill.: Contemporary Books, 2001.

Doc Blanchard

Born: December 11, 1924
     McColl, South Carolina
Died: April 19, 2009
     Bulverde, Texas
Also known as: Felix Anthony Blanchard, Jr. (full name); Mr. Inside

Early Life

Felix Anthony Blanchard, Jr., was born on December 11, 1924, in McColl, South Carolina, the hometown of his mother, Mary. His father, Felix Anthony Blanchard, Sr., was a physician. A few years after the birth of Felix, Jr., the family moved to Iowa, thinking that life in the Midwest would be easier during the Great Depression. However, the family soon became homesick for South Carolina, and they returned to Bishopville, South Carolina. In Bishopville, Felix, Sr., continued his medical practice and was known as "Doc." To the townspeople Felix, Jr., soon became known as "Little Doc."

Felix, Sr., had been an outstanding football player while he was a student at Tulane University. Therefore, he introduced his son to sports at an early age. Little Doc's football lessons began as soon as he could walk. While growing up in Bishopville, Little Doc was always seen carrying a football. His boyhood was typical: He enjoyed playing sports, especially football and baseball, and had numerous part-time jobs to earn spending money. One thing was unusual about Little Doc though—at the age of fourteen, he weighed 180 pounds.

The Road to Excellence

The first team for which Doc—at 180 pounds he was no longer Little Doc—played was Bishop-ville High School. Because of his size he was assigned to play the line. After a season at Bishopville, he was sent to St. Stanislaus Prep School, a private Catholic school in Bay St. Louis, Mississippi. His father had attended this school and thought it would be good for his son. At St. Stanislaus the coaching staff let Doc carry the ball, and he did so with great success. He was chosen to numerous all-star teams, and a long line of colleges traveled to the prep school to offer Doc college scholarships. He finally chose the University of North Carolina (UNC), where a cousin was the athletic director and football coach.

At UNC, Doc continued to live up to his poten-

Doc Blanchard in 1945. (AP/Wide World Photos)

tial as a first-rate football player. He was a punishing runner who hit would-be tacklers with tremendous force. The United States had recently entered World War II, though, and Doc desired to enter the Naval Reserve unit at the university, but was rejected because of his weight and poor eyesight. At the end of his first year at North Carolina, he left school to enter the Army.

The Emerging Champion

Doc's father always wanted his son to enter the United States Military Academy at West Point (Army) and was able to get him an appointment. In July, 1944, Doc became a West Point cadet. It took very little time for Doc to impress the coaching staff at West Point. Now weighing close to 220 pounds, he continued to run over defenses. He was blessed not only with great size and strength but also with amazing quickness. He was able to change directions quickly, and tacklers were often left trying to grab him from behind. Doc was compared to a charging wild buffalo.

In 1944 and 1945, Doc helped lead the Army team to two undefeated seasons. He did have help, though. Glenn Davis, Doc's running mate in the Army backfield is considered one of the best runners in the history of the game. Davis was capable of outrunning the defense as he ran around the end. Soon, the duo became known as "Mr. Inside," Doc, and "Mr. Outside," Davis.

At the end of his first season, Doc was selected by the Associated Press, United Press International, *Sporting News*, and others as all-American. His second season was even better. He scored 13 touchdowns in nine games and was awarded the Heisman Trophy. His third season was marred by injuries,

NCAA Statistics

Season	Car.	Yds.	Avg.	TD
1944	61	335	5.5	5
1945	101	718	7.1	13
1946	118	630	5.3	8
Totals	**280**	**1,666**	**6.0**	**26**

Notes: Car. = carries; Yds. = yards; Avg. = average yards per carry; TD = touchdowns

but he still led his team to its third consecutive win over archrival United States Naval Academy (Navy) and to its third national championship. Doc was elected to the Associated Press All-American team for the third time.

Continuing the Story

Together, Doc and Davis scored 97 touchdowns and 585 points. The 1944 Army team averaged 56 points per game; the 1945 team averaged 7.64 yards per rushing play. In 1959, in recognition of his accomplishments, Doc was elected to the National Football Foundation's College Football Hall of Fame. After graduation from West Point, Doc turned his football equipment in for the gold bars of a second lieutenant in the U.S. Army. He went on to have a distinguished career in the military. In 1971, he retired as a brigadier general and served as commandant at the New Mexico Military Institute.

Summary

Asked about his keys for success, Doc Blanchard had a simple answer: "I have always enjoyed what I was doing, especially football. That made the hard work easy." There is no doubt that the hard work made Doc into one of the most proficient runners in the history of college football. His name remains legendary along the banks of the Hudson River.

Michael J. Welch

Additional Sources

Bradley, Michael. *Big Games: College Football's Greatest Rivalries.* Washington, D.C.: Potomac Books, 2006.

Fimrite, Ron. "Mr. Inside and Mr. Outside." *Sports Illustrated* 69, no. 23 (November 21, 1988): 76-87.

Wilner, Barry, and Ken Rappoport. *Gridiron Glory: The Story of the Army-Navy Football Rivalry.* Lanham, Md.: Taylor Trade, 2005.

Honors and Awards

1944	United Press International All-American
	Sporting News All-American
1944-46	Associated Press All-American
1945	Heisman Trophy
	Maxwell Award
	Walter Camp Award
	Citizens Savings College Football Player of the Year
	James E. Sullivan Award
1959	Inducted into College Football Hall of Fame

George Blanda

Born: September 17, 1927
   Youngwood, Pennsylvania
Also known as: George Frederick Blanda (full
   name)

Early Life

George Frederick Blanda, the eldest of eleven children, was born in Youngwood, Pennsylvania, on September 17, 1927. His father Michael Blanda, a

George Blanda, who was an NFL quarterback and kicker for twenty-six seasons and set numerous records. (Courtesy of Amateur Athletic Foundation of Los Angeles)

coal miner and devout Catholic of Polish ancestry, was a strict disciplinarian who commanded the respect of his children and encouraged them to participate in sports.

At Youngwood High School, George was the entire track team. He threw the shot, the javelin, and the discus, all without a coach. He caught the eye of college recruiters because of his prowess on the football field, where he was a genuine triple threat, running, passing, and kicking with equal ability. For a time, George considered attending the University of Pennsylvania, but in the end he accepted a scholarship to play football at the University of Kentucky, where he enrolled in 1945.

The Road to Excellence

During his freshman year at Kentucky, George started at quarterback on a team that finished the season with one victory and nine losses. In his memoirs, George revealed that he was disappointed in himself and his choice of teams after the poor record in 1945. However, the fortunes of George and his team turned with the arrival of a new and unknown football coach named Paul W. Bryant.

George's work habits were not on the same level as his physical ability before Bryant's arrival. During the spring and summer of 1945, Bryant brought a number of former servicemen to Kentucky and earned the nickname "Bear" for his legendary practice techniques. George was demoted to the second team during his second and third years at Kentucky, but he learned that hard work and dedication were essential to success on the football field. During his senior year at Kentucky, George impressed Bryant enough to recapture his role as starting quarterback. Bryant's Wildcats started the season slowly with a 3-3 record. With only 44 seconds left in the seventh game, Kentucky trailed Villanova 13-6. George engineered one of the

NFL Kicking Statistics

Season	GP	FGA	FGM	XP	TP
1949	12	15	7	0	21
1950	12	15	6	0	18
1951	11	17	6	26	44
1952	12	25	6	30	48
1953	12	20	7	27	48
1954	8	16	8	23	47
1955	12	16	11	37	70
1956	12	28	12	45	81
1957	12	26	14	23	65
1958	12	23	11	36	69
1960	14	34	15	46	91
1961	14	26	16	64	112
1962	14	26	11	48	81
1963	14	22	9	39	66
1964	14	29	13	37	76
1965	14	21	11	28	61
1966	14	30	16	39	87
1967	14	30	20	56	116
1968	14	34	21	54	117
1969	14	37	20	45	105
1970	14	29	16	36	84
1971	14	22	15	41	86
1972	14	26	17	44	95
1973	14	33	23	31	100
1974	14	17	11	44	77
1975	14	21	13	44	83
Totals	340	638	335	943	1,948

Notes: GP = games played; FGA = field goals attempted; FGM = field goals made; XP = extra points; TP = total points (Blanda also scored nine touchdowns, totaling 54 points, bringing his grand total to 2,002 points.)

of the American Football League (AFL), and, as the starting quarterback, guided the team to the first AFL championship. The Oilers, with George at quarterback, also won the championship in 1961, and finished second in 1962. The Oilers went into decline after 1962, and after four disappointing seasons, George was replaced at quarterback. The next year, in 1967, Houston traded him to the Oakland Raiders. Although George was past forty, he enjoyed his finest and most amazing years in Oakland. His kicking was instrumental in the Raiders' 1967 AFL championship. That year the Raiders had two wins over the Houston team that had traded George; in both games George kicked four field goals. In 1968 and 1969, the Raiders played well but failed to win the AFL championship. In the 1970 season, George, at forty-three, had his finest campaign. In six of the Raiders' games that year, he came off the bench to win games in the last seconds.

Continuing the Story

George engineered more miracles in subsequent years. In 1971, he kicked a last-second field goal to tie Kansas City; this score gave him more points than any player in NFL history. His record of 2,002 career points was not broken until 2000, when placekicker Gary Anderson became the all-time points leader. George went on to play three more seasons as backup quarterback to Ken Stabler and

miracle finishes that became his trademark in later years, and Kentucky won.

The Emerging Champion

After marrying his college sweetheart Betty Harris—with whom he would have eleven children—George was chosen by the Chicago Bears in the twelfth round of the 1949 NFL draft. The Bears already had two outstanding quarterbacks in Sid Luckman and Johnny Lujack, and George was relegated to backup duty, occasionally kicking extra points and field goals. In 1953, George became the Bears' starting quarterback, but because of injuries his team finished with a disappointing 3-8-1 record. George never started another game for the Bears at quarterback, but over the next six seasons he appeared several times late in games to manufacture miraculous victories.

In 1960, George joined the Houston Oilers

NFL Records

Most points, 2,002
Most games played, 340
Most seasons played, 26
Most touchdown passes in a game, 7, in 1961 (record shared)

Honors and Awards

1961, 1967	*Sporting News* AFL All-Star Team
1961, 1968	Newspaper Enterprise Association AFL Player of the Year
1961, 1970	United Press International AFL/AFC Player of the Year
	Sporting News AFL/AFC Player of the Year
1962-64, 1968	AFL All-Star Team
1969	All-Time AFL Team
1970	*Sporting News* AFC Player of the Year
	Bert Bell Award
	Associated Press Male Athlete of the Year
	Citizens Savings Northern California Athlete of the Year
1980	NFL All-Pro Team of the 1970's
1981	Inducted into Pro Football Hall of Fame
1985	AFL-NFL 1960-1984 All-Star Team

as Oakland's regular kicker. He retired at the age of forty-eight. He designated conditioning as the main component of his longevity in a sport in which players are old at thirty. During the off-season he ran 2 miles a day and played golf or handball every day as well. He became a hero to many American males over the age of forty.

After his retirement, George devoted most of his time to his horses and grandchildren. He continued to pursue leisure sports with the same enthusiasm that he devoted to football. He was elected to the Pro Football Hall of Fame in 1981, and later selected to the AFL-NFL 1960-1984 all-star team.

Summary

George Blanda excelled during his football career primarily because of his fierce competitive instinct. The same instinct that pushed him to excel also produced a storm of controversy that followed him throughout his playing days. He often said uncomplimentary things about fellow players, coaches, management, and representatives of the press when he felt he had not received fair treatment. Perhaps the best insight into George came during his spectacular 1970 season. When approached with numerous product endorsement opportunities, George refused to praise any product he did not use regularly, saying it was dishonest. He was fiercely loyal to his friends and never forgot a real or imagined injury perpetrated by his enemies. His overriding will to win and his exhausting work habits made him into a champion.

Paul Madden

NFL Passing Statistics

Season	GP	PA	PC	Pct.	Yds.	Avg.	TD	Int.
1949	12	21	9	.429	197	9.0	0	5
1950	12	1	0	.000	0	0.0	0	0
1951	12	—	—	—	—	—	—	—
1952	12	131	47	.359	664	5.1	8	11
1953	12	362	169	.467	2,164	6.0	14	23
1954	8	281	131	.466	1,929	6.9	15	17
1955	12	97	42	.433	459	4.7	4	7
1956	12	69	37	.536	439	6.4	7	4
1957	12	19	8	.421	65	3.4	0	3
1958	12	7	2	.286	19	2.7	0	0
1960	14	363	169	.466	2,413	6.7	24	22
1961	14	362	187	517	3,330	9.2	36	22
1962	14	418	197	.471	2,810	6.7	27	42
1963	14	423	224	.530	3,003	7.1	24	25
1964	14	505	262	.519	3,287	6.5	17	27
1965	14	442	186	.421	2,542	5.8	20	30
1966	14	271	122	.450	1,764	6.5	17	21
1967	14	38	15	.395	285	7.5	3	3
1968	14	49	30	.612	522	10.7	6	2
1969	14	13	6	.462	73	5.6	2	1
1970	14	55	29	.527	461	8.4	6	5
1971	14	58	32	.552	378	6.5	4	6
1972	14	15	5	.333	77	5.1	1	0
1973	14	—	—	—	—	—	—	—
1974	14	4	1	.250	28	7.0	1	0
1975	14	3	1	.333	11	3.7	0	1
Totals	340	4,007	1,911	.477	26,920	6.7	236	277

Notes: GP = games played; PA = passes attempted; PC = passes completed; Pct. = percent completed; Yds. = yards; Avg. = average yards per attempt; TD = touchdowns; Int. = interceptions

Additional Sources

Blanda, George, and Mickey Herskowitz. *Over Forty: Feeling Great and Looking Good!* New York: Simon and Schuster, 1978.

Lombardo, John. *Raiders Forever: Stars of the NFL's Most Colorful Team Recall Their Glory Days.* Lincolnwood, Ill.: Contemporary Books, 2001.

Masin, Herman L. "A Sweet Streak . . . by George!" *Coach and Athletic Director* 76, no. 10 (May/June, 2007): 6.

Porter, David L., ed. *Biographical Dictionary of American Sports: Football.* Westport, Conn.: Greenwood Press, 1987.

Drew Bledsoe

Born: February 14, 1972
Ellensburg, Washington
Also known as: Drew McQueen Bledsoe (full name)

Early Life

Drew McQueen Bledsoe was born in Ellensburg, Washington, on February 14, 1972, to Mac and Barbara Bledsoe. Drew's father was a football coach and a three-year letter winner at the University of Washington, from 1965 to 1967. His mother, a high school English teacher, also attended the University of Washington, and his younger brother, Adam, played football at Colorado State University. When Drew was one year old, his father began taking him to football camps. By the time Drew was in the sixth grade, his father had moved the family six times, to various coaching jobs throughout eastern Washington. As a child, Drew's favorite athlete was Fred Biletnikoff, a wide receiver for the Oakland Raiders. Drew excelled in all sports in grade school, including baseball, but his favorite was football. In the eighth grade, he began playing quarterback.

The Road to Excellence

At Walla Walla High School in Washington, Drew passed for over 1,600 yards during his junior year to lead the Big Nine Conference. During his senior year at Walla Walla, he became one of the top quarterbacks in the nation. He completed 156 of 272 passes, 57.4 percent, for 25 touchdowns and 2,560 yards. He led his team to a 6-3 record and second place in the conference. He also received numerous awards in recognition of his 509 throwing yards, which set a state record in Washington. He was named to the all-state team and was a Western 100 pick and a "Northwest Nugget." He was also named player of the year in Washington.

In 1990, Drew entered Washington State University (WSU) on a football scholarship.

From 1990 to 1992, he started twenty-eight games and was the first freshman to start for the school in over thirty years. While there, Drew was named all-Pac-10 Conference and was ninth in the nation in total offense, averaging 247 yards per game. During his junior year, he passed for 18 touchdowns and 770 yards and led WSU to a victory over Utah in the Copper Bowl. In 1993, at the end of his junior year, Drew became the number one overall pick and the youngest NFL draft choice, signing with the New England Patriots. In his WSU career,

Buffalo Bills quarterback Drew Bledsoe looks for a receiver in a 2004 game against the Cincinnati Bengals. (Andy Lyons/Getty Images)

Drew had passed for 7,373 yards, 46 touchdowns, and completed 532 attempts.

The Emerging Champion

Drew became the youngest player in NFL history to exceed 7,000 career yards. In 1994, during his second season with the NFL, Drew set an all-time record for 691 passes in a season, 70 attempts in a game, and 45 completions in a game. Drew also set a personal best for passing yards that same season with 4,555. In 1995, he led the American Football Conference (AFC) with more than 3,500 passing yards and 636 pass attempts. On July 20, 1995, Drew signed a seven-year contract extension with the Patriots, which made him one of the highest-paid players in the NFL. That same year he led the Patriots to an AFC division championship.

Drew and his wife, Maura, married in the spring of 1995, in Portland, Oregon, and settled with their son, Stuart, in Brighton, Massachusetts. Drew became involved in numerous community and public service projects. In 1996, he taped a "Rock the Vote" voter registration public service spot for MTV, and he also helped his father and other coaches with a youth summer football camp at the University of Massachusetts at Dartmouth. In 1995, Drew established a $150,000 football scholarship at WSU to honor his grandfather, Albert "Stu" Bledsoe, who graduated with a degree in agriculture in 1947.

Continuing the Story

Two years later, in the 1997 season, Drew produced the highest passing rating of his career, 87.7, and threw a career-best 28 touchdowns in leading the Patriots to a second division title and to the playoffs for the third time in four seasons. At the age of twenty-four, Drew guided his team to Super Bowl XXXI. The Patriots lost 35-21 to the Packers. However, Drew had reached the 3,500-yard passing mark for the fourth year in a row. That same year, he completed 7 passes of 50 yards or more, including 3 to his favorite receiver, Troy Brown. At that time, Drew was ranked third among all NFL quarterbacks for consecutive starts with forty-four. By 1998, he held almost all the Patriots single-season and single-game passing records. He also played in the NFL Pro Bowl in 1996, 1997, and 1998. His most embarrassing moments while playing with the Patriots occurred when he twice lined up behind an offensive guard rather than the center.

Drew played in only two regular season games during the 2001 season, his last with the Patriots, giving way to future Super Bowl most valuable player Tom Brady. However, Drew did play in the AFC title game that year in relief of an ailing Brady, helping lead the Patriots to victory and the Super Bowl. In 2002, Drew was traded to the Bills and played in every game for Buffalo over the next three seasons. Drew's first season with the Bills was productive: He passed for 4,359 yards and 24 touchdowns with a career-best completion percentage of 61.5. His numbers amounted to an impressive 86.0 passer rating for the season, earning him his fourth trip to the Pro Bowl. However, his numbers decreased the following two seasons, and Drew lost his starting job with the Bills to J. P. Losman.

In 2005, Drew signed with the Cowboys, reuniting him with Bill Parcells, his coach in New England, who had made him the number one overall pick. Drew played in all sixteen regular season games that season in Dallas, completing 60.1 percent of his passes for 3,639 yards and 23 touchdowns, tying his third best

NFL Statistics

Season	GP	PA	PC	Pct.	Yds.	Avg.	TD	Int.
1993	13	429	214	.499	2,494	5.81	15	15
1994	16	691	400	.579	4,555	6.59	25	27
1995	15	636	323	.508	3,507	5.51	13	16
1996	16	623	373	.599	4,086	6.56	27	15
1997	16	522	314	.602	3,706	7.10	28	15
1998	14	481	263	.547	3,633	7.55	20	14
1999	16	539	305	.566	3,985	7.39	19	21
2000	16	531	312	.588	3,291	6.20	17	13
2001	2	66	40	60.6	400	6.1	2	2
2002	16	610	375	61.5	4,359	7.1	24	15
2003	16	471	274	58.2	2,860	6.1	11	12
2004	16	450	256	56.9	2,932	6.5	20	16
2005	16	499	300	60.1	3,639	7.3	23	17
2006	6	169	90	53.3	1,164	6.9	7	8
Totals	194	6,717	3,839	57.2	44,611	6.6	251	206

Notes: GP = games played; PA = passes attempted; PC = passes completed; Pct. = percent completed; Yds. = yards; Avg. = average yards per attempt; TD = touchdowns; Int. = interceptions

quarterback rating of 83.7. However, Drew was not as fortunate in the 2006 season, only participating in six games and losing the starting job to emerging star Tony Romo.

At the age of 35, Drew completed his fourteen-year NFL career fifth on the all-time list for pass attempts, with 6,717, and completions, with 3,839. At the time of Drew's retirement, Drew's 44,611 passing yards placed him at number seven on the all-time career list and his 251 touchdown passes were good enough for thirteenth. He started in all sixteen regular season games nine of his fourteen seasons.

Drew and his wife established the Drew Bledsoe Foundation "Parenting with Dignity" program, which aimed to help people improve their parenting skills. In 2005, Drew was enshrined in the World Sports Humanitarian Hall of Fame for his work with the program. He was also involved with the Boys and Girls Clubs and the YMCA. Drew served as International Chairman of the Children's Miracle Network, received the Thurman Munson Humanitarian Award, the NFL Alumni Spirit Award, and in 2004, received the NFL's Walter Payton Man of the Year Award.

Summary

Drew Bledsoe was the youngest quarterback to throw for 7,000 yards in the NFL and the youngest to play in the Pro Bowl. In 1994, his second season, Drew led the New England Patriots to seven straight victories and the team's first playoff ap-

Honors and Awards	
1993	Overall first pick in NFL draft
1994, 1996	NFL All-Pro Team
	Thurman Munson Humanitarian Award
1994, 1996-97, 2002	NFL Pro Bowl Team
2004	Walter Payton Man of the Year Award

pearance in eight years. His leadership enabled the Patriots to move from the twenty-seventh ranked offense to the fourth best. Throughout his career, Drew carried himself and represented his teams with class and dignity. Despite losing his starting job several times to up-and-coming quarterbacks, he continually maintained his focus and prepared for any and all situations, as evidenced by leading the Patriots to victory as a backup quarterback in the 2001 AFC title game.

Lloyd Johnson, updated by Trevor D. Bopp

Additional Sources

Bledsoe, Drew, and Greg Brown. *Make the Right Call.* Somerville, N.J.: Taylor, 1998.

Savage, Jeff. *Drew Bledsoe: Cool Quarterback.* Minneapolis: Lerner, 1999.

Schultz, Randy. *Legends of the Buffalo Bills.* Champaign, Ill.: Sports, 2003.

Shalin, Mike. *Drew Bledsoe: Patriot Rifle.* Champaign, Ill.: Sports, 2000.

Stewart, Mark. *Drew Bledsoe: Stand and Deliver.* New York: Children's Press, 2000.

Tony Boselli

Born: April 17, 1972
     Boulder, Colorado
Also known as: Don Anthony Boselli, Jr. (full
     name)

Early Life
Don Anthony "Tony" Boselli, Jr., was an athletic
young man who played quarterback as a freshman
at Fairview High School in Boulder, Colorado. He
shifted to tight end and linebacker later in his high
school career. He was recruited by many colleges,
including his home state's best-known program,
the University of Colorado, but he chose to play for
the University of Southern California (USC). Tony
had size—at 6 feet 7 inches—strength, and agility
that indicated great promise as a football player.

The Road to Excellence
Tony was awarded a football scholarship by USC,
which traditionally had one of the best college football programs in the United States. During his junior and senior seasons, Tony was a first-team all-
American and all-Pac-10 Conference selection. In
his sophomore season he was a second-team Associated Press All-American. He was awarded the
Morris Trophy during his senior year, which recog-
nizes the outstanding lineman in the conference.
At USC, Tony developed into an effective pass and
run blocker. While in school, he met his wife Angi,
who was a cheerleader for the team and graduated
two years after he did.
     Tony was the first player ever drafted by the ex-
pansion Jacksonville Jaguars and the second overall pick in the 1995 NFL draft. Many scouts considered Tony to be the best collegiate offensive
lineman in a decade.

The Emerging Champion
Tony became an impact player in the NFL immediately. He was selected to the Pro Bowl at the end of
his first season, even though he played in only thirteen games, starting twelve. He earned another
trip to the Pro Bowl for his performance in 1996, a
season in which he started all sixteen games. In
1997, he made the Pro Bowl again, but he missed
four games because of injuries. The next season, he
played in another Pro Bowl, and he started fifteen
games. In 1999, Tony was injury free: He was able to
start and play in all sixteen games and earned his
fifth straight trip to the Pro Bowl. During the next
season, he played in all sixteen games and made
the Pro Bowl as a reserve.
     In 2001, Tony suffered a shoulder injury that re-
quired surgery. He only started and played in three
games that season. However, he was confident that
surgery and rehabilitation would enable him to return to his all-pro status. In his more than six seasons with the Jaguars, he allowed only 15.5 quarterback sacks. He was an integral member of the
Jaguars, helping the team to the playoffs in four
consecutive seasons and to AFC Championship
games in both 1996 and 1999.

Continuing the Story
In 2002, Tony was the first player selected in the ex-
pansion draft by the Houston Texans, which was a
testament to the impact he had made on the
league. Tony was placed on the list of available players because of salary-cap concerns faced by the Jaguars. His shoulder injury, however, prevented him
from playing in any games that season. He spent
the entire season on injured reserve and retired at
the end of the year.
     In 2006, the Jaguars inducted Tony into the Jag-
uars Ring of Honor; he became the first Jacksonville player to be chosen. That year, he signed a
one-day contract that allowed him to retire officially as a member of the Jaguars.
     After retiring from the NFL, Tony engaged in
many endeavors. In addition to working as a football commentator for Fox Sports, he became a

Honors and Awards	
1990's	NFL All-Decade Team
1993-94	All-Pacific Ten Conference
	All-American
1994	Morris Trophy
1996-2000	NFL Pro Bowl
2006	Inducted into Jacksonville Jaguars Ring of Honor

partner in a marketing and advertising firm. Furthermore, became the part owner of several restaurants. He was also a member of Champions for Christ, an outreach ministry based in Jacksonville and established by the organization Every Nation. Also, he established the Boselli Foundation, which assists young people. Despite sustaining serious injuries while playing, he participated in triathlons after his NFL retirement.

Summary

Even with a career shortened because of injuries, Tony Boselli will be remembered as one of the greatest offensive lineman in the history of the NFL. He played the game with great integrity. After the injuries, he made a successful transition to life after football with a business and media career and through significant community service.

Michael Coulter

Additional Sources

Frostino, Nino. *Right on the Numbers: The Debate of the Greatest Players in Sports to Wear the Numbers 0-99.* New Bern, N.C.: Trafford, 2004.

Hawkes, Brian. *The History of the Jacksonville Jaguars.* Mankato, Minn.: Creative Education, 2005.

Terry Bradshaw

Born: September 2, 1948
Shreveport, Louisiana
Also known as: Terry Paxton Bradshaw (full name); the Blond Bomber

Early Life

Terry Paxton Bradshaw was born in Shreveport, Louisiana, about twenty miles from the Texas border, to Bill and Novis Bradshaw, on September 2, 1948. Ranching and farming were what most people in that section of the Bible Belt did, and the Bradshaws were no exception. Terry grew up as the second of three sons in a strong Southern Baptist

Quarterback Terry Bradshaw, who guided the Pittsburgh Steelers to four Super Bowl victories. (Tony Tomsic/NFL/Getty Images)

home, and he learned early the value of hard work and religion in everything he pursued. His father ran a strict household with a curfew and regular Bible readings. Terry, his older brother Gary, and his younger brother Craig were taken to Christian revival meetings by their mother. Terry was "witnessing" from the age of fifteen.

The Road to Excellence

After spending a large portion of his boyhood throwing footballs at tires and buckets, Terry achieved celebrity status early as a star quarterback and record-setting javelin thrower at Shreveport's Woodlawn High School. During his sophomore and junior years at Woodlawn, he spent most of his time on the bench, but after becoming a starting quarterback in his senior season, Terry led his team to an 8-1-1 record and the semifinals of the Louisiana high school championship playoffs. Many colleges, however, sought Terry for track and field after he established a new American high school record with a javelin throw of 244 feet, 11 inches. Not wanting to stray too far from home and deciding to concentrate on football, Terry traveled just eighty miles east to Louisiana Tech University for college. His football success there, where he completed 52 percent of his passes for approximately 7,000 yards and 42 touchdowns, gained Terry national attention. He was named Associated Press first team all-American as a senior. When he was the first college player selected in the 1970 NFL draft, by the Pittsburgh Steelers, he became nationally famous overnight.

The move from Shreveport to Pittsburgh proved drastic for Terry. Having never ventured into the East, Terry was forced to adapt his simple country ways and his strict Baptist beliefs to conform to the sophistication of a large city. He also shouldered a great deal of pressure immediately. The Steelers had not won any sort of championship in the team's thirty-five years in the NFL. In 1969, the season before Terry arrived, the Steelers finished with a 1-13 record. Terry was portrayed as a magician with a strong arm who could turn the team into Super Bowl champions.

The Emerging Champion

Terry did possess a strong arm and a desire to succeed as a professional athlete. In his rookie season, though, he completed only 38.1 percent of his 218 passes. He threw for just 6 touchdowns and was intercepted 24 times—hardly a magical debut. Still, the Steelers finished 5-9, the team's best showing since 1966. Discouraged by his rookie performance, Terry returned to the comfort of Louisiana after the season, and with the support of family and friends he pulled himself together.

Terry returned to Pittsburgh in his second season and completed 203 of 373 passes for 2,259 yards and 13 touchdowns. His performance slipped slightly in 1972, however, and he suffered a shoulder separation in 1973, which caused him to miss four games in the middle of the season. His troubles continued in 1974, when he lost his starting job to third-year man Joe Gilliam. Terry won back his starting job midway through the season, though, and he led Pittsburgh to its first NFL Champion-

---

NFL Records

Super Bowl average in yards per pass, 11.1
Average in yards per pass in a Super Bowl game, 14.7 (1980)

Honors and Awards

1970's	Selected to the NFL's All-Decade Team
1970	Overall first choice in the NFL draft
1976, 1979-80	NFL Pro Bowl Team
1978	Bert Bell Award
1979	Associated Press NFL Player of the Year
	Sport magazine NFL Player of the Year
	Sports Illustrated co-Sportsman of the Year
1979-80	NFL Super Bowl most valuable player
1989	Inducted into Pro Football Hall of Fame
1996	Inducted into College Football Hall of Fame
2007	Named to Pittsburgh Steelers all-time team

---

ship with a 16-6 win over the Minnesota Vikings in Super Bowl IX. The next year, with Terry throwing 18 regular season touchdown passes, the Steelers repeated as champions, defeating the Dallas Cowboys 21-17 in Super Bowl X.

Continuing the Story

Terry led the Pittsburgh Steelers to two more Super Bowl titles, in 1979, with a 35-31 victory over the Dallas Cowboys, and in 1980, with a 31-19 win over the Los Angeles Rams. He was a perfect 4-0 in Super Bowl games; he completed 49 of 84 pass attempts, 9 of them for touchdowns, and threw only 3 interceptions in those four memorable performances. He established Super Bowl passing records for the longest average gain in a career, 11.10 yards, and the longest average gain in a game, 14.71 in Super Bowl XIV, when he completed 21 passes for 309 yards. He was named NFL player of the year by the Associated Press, *Sport* magazine, and the Maxwell Club of Philadelphia following the 1978 season. In 1979, he shared *Sports Illustrated*'s sportsman of the year award with another notable Pittsburgher, the Pirates' Willie Star-

---

NFL Statistics

Season	GP	PA	PC	Pct.	Yds.	Avg.	TD	Int.
1970	12	218	83	.381	1,410	6.7	6	24
1971	14	373	203	.544	2,259	6.1	13	22
1972	14	308	147	.477	1,887	6.1	12	12
1973	10	180	89	.494	1,183	6.6	10	15
1974	8	148	67	.453	785	5.3	7	8
1975	14	286	165	.577	2,055	7.2	18	9
1976	10	192	92	.479	1,177	6.1	10	9
1977	14	314	162	.516	2,523	8.0	17	19
1978	16	368	207	.563	2,915	7.9	28	20
1979	16	472	259	.549	3,724	7.9	26	25
1980	15	424	218	.514	3,339	7.9	24	22
1981	14	370	201	.543	2,887	7.8	22	14
1982	9	240	127	.529	1,768	7.4	17	11
1983	2	8	5	.625	77	9.6	2	0
Totals	168	3,901	2,025	.519	27,989	7.2	212	210

Notes: GP = games played; PA = passes attempted; PC = passes completed; Pct. = percent completed; Yds. = yards; Avg. = average yards per attempt; TD = touchdowns; Int. = interceptions

gell. Terry retired from football just prior to the 1984 NFL season. In 1989, as one of the most productive quarterbacks of all time, he was inducted into the Pro Football Hall of Fame.

Terry's life outside of football was as dramatic as life on the playing field. Married three times, he enjoyed a short career as a country and western singer and even acted in a movie with Burt Reynolds (*Hooper*, 1978). Terry never strayed too far from the things he loved, though. He worked as a television analyst of NFL games for Columbia Broadcast System (CBS) Sports and spent several years in an acclaimed partnership with play-by-play announcer Verne Lundquist. Terry also appeared on *The Super Bowl Today* and *The NFL Today*. In 1993, Terry became a "talking head" on *Fox NFL Sunday*, and continued to hold that position fifteen years later.

In addition to his NFL analysis job for Fox, Terry owned a NASCAR team, *FitzBradshaw Racing*. In 2005, he expressed interest in purchasing the New Orleans Saints after the natural disaster Hurricane Katrina, but the Saints franchise was not for sale.

Terry had many cameos in television shows and commercials, including *Everybody Loves Raymond* and *The Jeff Foxworthy Show*. In addition to his work in television, Terry was in several movies including *Cannonball Run*, *Smokey and the Bandit II*, and *Failure to Launch*. In *Failure to Launch*, Terry appeared naked in a scene. Terry was the first NFL player to have a star on the Hollywood Walk of Fame. In 2007, the Pittsburgh Steelers celebrated the franchise's seventy-fifth season in the NFL, and Terry was named to the Steelers' all-time team.

Summary

Terry Bradshaw was a more complex athlete and person than he was perceived to be early in his career. His strong and accurate arm produced unprecedented results. He was among the first NFL quarterbacks to call his own offensive plays in the huddle and to use the "audible" with effectiveness, proving repeatedly his game sense and competence. He persevered through numerous painful injuries, including dislocated fingers, a fractured nose, a broken collarbone and ribs, a torn hip muscle, and a sprained knee. In fact, Terry played almost the entire 1977 season with a fractured bone in his left wrist. He produced in "clutch" situations and was instrumental in breathing new life into a dismal Pittsburgh Steelers franchise. The Steelers were the first team to win four Super Bowls, and a great deal of credit for those victories belongs to Terry.

Jan Giel, updated by Timothy C. Hemmis

Additional Sources

Aaseng, Nathan. *Football's Winning Quarterbacks.* Minneapolis: Lerner, 1980.

Bradshaw, Terry, and David Fisher. *It's Only a Game.* New York: Pocket Books, 2001.

_____. *Keep It Simple.* New York: Atria Books, 2002.

Bradshaw, Terry, and Buddy Martin. *Looking Deep.* Chicago: Contemporary Books, 1989.

McCullough, Bob. *My Greatest Day in Football: The Legends of Football Recount Their Greatest Moments.* New York: Thomas Dunne Books/St. Martin's Press, 2001.

Tom Brady

Born: August 3, 1977
      San Mateo, California
Also known as: Thomas Edward Patrick Brady, Jr.
    (full name); California Cool; Tom Terrific

Early Life

Thomas Edward Patrick Brady, Jr., was born to Thomas Brady, an insurance consultant, and Galynn Johnson, a former tennis pro. Tom, the youngest of four children and the only boy, grew up

New England Patriots quarterback Tom Brady, who was one of the top players in the first decade of the twenty-first century. (John Capella/ Getty Images)

in a home of religion, academics, competition, and athletics.

When Tom was four, he and his dad attended the 1981 National Football Conference Championship game. Tom witnessed his lifelong hero, San Francisco 49ers quarterback Joe Montana, connect with tight end Dwight Clark for the winning touchdown, a play known in football lore as "the Catch." Tom dreamed of becoming the next Montana.

Tom attended Junipero Serra High in San Mateo, California, lettering in football and baseball. The Montreal Expos chose him in the eighteenth round of the Major League Baseball draft. However, he believed his future was in football. He earned scholarship offers to all the top national programs, eventually choosing the University of Michigan Wolverines. He lettered at Michigan for three years, posting a 20-5 record, but battled for his starting job throughout.

The Road to Excellence

After graduating from college, Tom was picked in the sixth round of the 2000 NFL draft by the New England Patriots. The Patriots had star quarterback Drew Bledsoe and two other quarterbacks on the roster, but Coach Bill Belichick liked Tom's poise and loved his intelligence.

Tom made his first and only pass completion of his rookie year in a lopsided defeat to the Detroit Lions. He went to the 2001 training camp determined to improve and became Bledsoe's backup. During a week-two loss to the New York Jets, Tom was pressed into action after Bledsoe was injured by a vicious hit from Mo Lewis. Bledsoe sheared a blood vessel in his chest and was out indefinitely. Belichick believed Tom could not only substitute for Bledsoe but also be the starting

NFL Statistics

Season	GP	PA	PC	Pct.	Yds.	Avg.	TD	Int.
2000	1	3	1	33.3	6	2.0	0	0
2001	15	413	264	63.9	2,843	6.9	18	12
2002	16	601	373	62.1	3,768	6.3	28	14
2003	16	527	317	60.2	3,620	6.9	23	12
2004	16	474	288	60.8	3,692	7.8	28	14
2005	16	530	334	63.0	4,110	7.8	26	14
2006	16	516	319	61.8	3,529	6.8	24	12
2007	16	578	398	68.9	4,806	8.3	50	8
Totals	112	3,642	2,294	63.0	26,370	7.2	197	86

Notes: GP = games played; PA = passes attempted; PC = passes completed; Pct. = percent completed; Yds. = yards; Avg. = average yards per attempt; TD = touchdowns; Int. = interceptions

quarterback. Tom, buoyed by Belichick's vote of confidence, began to win games and show others what Belichick foretold.

The Emerging Champion

As Bledsoe healed, Tom improved as a player, causing a rift between the two friends. Even when Bledsoe returned, Tom remained the starting quarterback. In the playoffs, Tom and the Patriots were losing to the Oakland Raiders when Tom fumbled attempting a pass. The referees invoked the little known "tuck rule," which designated the fumble as an incomplete pass. The Patriots tied the game on an improbable field goal under blizzard conditions. Tom then completed eight straight passes to allow for the twenty-three-yard game-winning overtime kick. The game, significant in NFL history, became known as "the snow bowl" or "the tuck game." The Patriots advanced to play Pittsburgh. Tom hurt his ankle in the second quarter, allowing Bledsoe to return and win the game.

Matched against the St. Louis Rams in Super Bowl XXXVI, the Patriots had a quarterback dilemma. Many fans wanted Bledsoe to play, but the team wanted Tom, who had led them throughout the season. Belichick chose Tom, who helped the Patriots to the first Super Bowl victory in franchise history. For his efforts, Tom earned most valuable player (MVP) honors for the game. Tom had officially established himself as the Patriots' starting quarterback; Bledsoe was traded to the Buffalo Bills months later.

In 2002, the Patriots finished 9-7 and

missed the playoffs. Tom required postseason shoulder surgery. In the first game of 2003, the team was shut out 31-0 against Bledsoe's Bills. The Patriots rallied and won all fifteen of the remaining regular season games, fighting injuries and the weight of the winning streak. Tom drove his team through the playoffs to defeat the Carolina Panthers in Super Bowl XXXVIII, again earning the game's MVP award. He had become a superstar and his team, a dynasty. Tom developed a knack for comeback wins, and comparisons to his childhood hero, Montana, abounded.

Tom and the Patriots maintained momentum into 2004, as the team cruised through the regular season to a victory over the Philadelphia Eagles in Super Bowl XXXIX. In 2005 and 2006, Tom led the Patriots to the playoffs, but the team did not appear in the Super Bowl.

Continuing the Story

In 2007, Tom was given his strongest complement of offensive players and responded, setting the regular-season touchdown-passing record with 50 and winning the NFL MVP award. His Patriots became the first team in history to finish the regu-

NFL Records

Most completions in Super Bowl, career, 100
Most completions in one Super Bowl, 32 (2004)
Most consecutive wins in the playoffs, 10
Most passing touchdowns in a single season, 50 (2007)

Honors and Awards

1998	All-Big Ten Conference (honorable mention)
2001, 2004-05, 2007	NFL Pro Bowl
2002, 2004	Super Bowl most valuable player
2004	*Sports Illustrated* NFL Player of the Year
2004, 2007	*The Sporting News* Sportsman of the Year
2005	*Sports Illustrated* Sportsman of the Year
2005, 2007	NFL All-Pro
2007	Associated Press NFL Offensive Player of the Year
	Associated Press NFL most valuable player
	Associated Press First-Team All-Pro
	Associated Press Male Athlete of the Year
	Sporting News NFL Player of the Year
	NFL Alumni Quarterback of the Year

lar season 16-0. However, the team was upset by the New York Giants in Super Bowl XXLI. After this remarkable year, however, his 2008 season ended abruptly in the very first game when he sustained a season-ending knee injury.

Tom was named among *People* magazine's fifty most beautiful people and romantically linked with a number of celebrities. He hosted *Saturday Night Live* and became an internationally known celebrity. Tom visited U.S. troops in Iraq and stated an interest in one day becoming a U.S. senator. He also was involved with a number of charitable interests.

Summary

Tom Brady was arguably the most popular and best player in the NFL in the first decade of the 2000's. In his first four Super Bowl appearances, he and the Patriots won three times. His 2007 season was the best for a quarterback in NFL history to that time. Tom's football success was congruent with Joe Montana's, his football idol. A fourth Super Bowl victory would tie Tom with Montana.

Jonathan E. Dinneen

Additional Sources

Holley, Michael. *Patriot Reign: Bill Belichick, the Coaches, and the Players Who Built a Champion.* New York: HarperCollins, 2004.

King, Peter. "Surprise! Surprise." *Sports Illustrated* 15 (September, 2003): 47.

Pierce, Charles P. *Moving the Chains: Tom Brady and the Pursuit of Everything.* New York: Farrar, Straus and Giroux, 2007.

Savage, Jeff. *Tom Brady.* Minneapolis: Lerner, 2006.

Bob Brown

Born: December 8, 1941
    Cleveland, Ohio
Also known as: Robert Stanford Brown (full
    name); Boomer

Early Life

Robert Stanford Brown was born and raised in Cleveland, Ohio, where his father operated a grocery store. Bob started playing football as an overweight eighth grader at Empire Junior High School. He then played football at East Technical High School in Cleveland, a school best known for its basketball and track programs. He had great size, 6 feet 4 inches, and significant strength as a high school player. Based on his high school performance, he was offered a scholarship by the University of Nebraska, where he majored in physical education and graduated in four years.

The Road to Excellence

At Nebraska, Bob was a first-team all-American guard in 1963—the first all-American under hall-of-fame coach Bob Devaney—and lettered in 1961 and 1962. At the time, players were permitted only three years of varsity eligibility. Bob was a key player in the Cornhuskers' turnaround. In 1962, the second year Bob was eligible for varsity football, the team was 9-2, and the next season, the team was 10-1. Bob considers Devaney to be one of the greatest football coaches ever and spoke of the privilege of playing for him.

Bob was chosen by the Philadelphia Eagles as the second pick overall in the 1964 NFL draft. He was also drafted by the Denver Broncos of the American Football League, which was then a rival organization. Bob opted to play for the Eagles in the NFL.

The Emerging Champion

Bob played with the Eagles through the 1968 season. He played in 50 consecutive games before a knee injury in 1967. In 1968, when the Eagles won only two games, Bob had a falling out with the Eagles coach. During this time, Bob embraced year-round training and serious weightlifting when few other players did so. He trained seven days a week and often for five hours each day. In 1966, his third season in the league, he was chosen for the first of his five Pro Bowl appearances. Despite the injury in 1967, he was chosen to the Pro Bowl during that season as well.

Bob was powerful and effective but did not have great technique. He once described himself as "as subtle as a sixteen pound sledgehammer." He also spoke of "taking a toll" on the defensive lineman that he was blocking. He was known for his aggressive style of play. While Bob did not think of himself as subtle, others in the league spoke of him as having great quickness and great strength. Hall-of-fame coach George Allen said that Bob was among the best blockers he ever saw.

Continuing the Story

After the 1968 season, he was traded to the Los Angeles Rams, for whom he played in 1969 and 1970. He was selected to the Pro Bowl in both seasons. After the 1970 season, he was traded to the Oakland Raiders, playing with the team for three seasons. During that time the Raiders were 27-11-4; the team led the American Football Conference in points scored in 1971 and in total offense in 1973. Bob was selected to the Pro Bowl during the 1971 and 1972 seasons. John Madden, the coach of the Raiders at the time, described Bob as the most aggressive offensive lineman who ever played professional football.

Honors and Awards

1960's	NFL All-Decade Team
1963	First-team all-American
1965-66, 1968-70	Associated Press All-Pro first team
1965-66, 1968-71	NFL Pro Bowl
1993	Inducted into College Football Hall of Fame
2004	Inducted into Pro Football Hall of Fame
	Uniform number 64 retired by University of Nebraska

While Bob was not immediately recognized for his on-field greatness, he was honored in retirement. On November 26, 2004, the University of Nebraska retired his number 64. That day was declared Bob Brown Day in Lincoln. At the time, the Nebraska program had only retired fifteen other players' jerseys. Bob was one of only ten players who played at Big Twelve Conference schools to be elected into the National Football Foundation's College Football Hall of Fame and the Pro Football Hall of Fame. He was inducted into the Pro Football Hall of Fame in 2004, twenty-six years after he was first eligible; he had been a finalist five times before he was finally elected. At the Pro Football Hall of fame induction ceremony, teammates and rival players honored Bob's remarkable career.

Summary

Known for his great work ethic and mental toughness, Bob Brown was a dominant offensive lineman during his years in the NFL. He was named to the NFL all-1960's team and was a first-team all-NFL player seven times. Because of his outstanding play, he was also chosen NFL offensive lineman of the year three times.

Michael Coulter

Additional Sources

Didinger, Ray, and Robert S. Lyons. *The Eagles Encyclopedia*. Philadelphia: Temple University Press, 2005.

Forbes, Gordon. *Tales from the Eagles Sideline*. Champaign, Ill.: Sports, 2006.

Jim Brown

Born: February 17, 1936
    St. Simons Island, Georgia
Also known as: James Nathaniel Brown (full name)
Other major sport: Lacrosse

Early Life

James Nathaniel Brown, known as "Jimmy" or "Jim," was born on February 17, 1936, on St. Simons Island, Georgia, part of a string of islands along the state's coastline. The area is rich in black history. The inhabitants of the islands are said to have descended from West African tribes. The Ibo warriors were enslaved and brought to St. Simons Island, and rather than live out their lives as slaves, many marched into the ocean to their deaths.

Jim was raised on St. Simons Island by his great-grandmother, Nora Peterson, until he was seven. His grandmother, Myrtle Johnson, also shared the house in which Jim lived. Jim's father left Jim and his mother when Jim was two weeks old. Jim's mother left when he was two years old to find work near New York City. Jim recalled his life on the island with great fondness. He could grow and play in surroundings of care and love. When Jim was eight, his mother sent for him to live with her in Manhasset, Long Island, New York.

The Road to Excellence

Manhasset was a mostly white city, but Jim's grade school was predominantly black. He was often in trouble in school. Later in high school, he was involved in a gang, but athletics became a dominant factor in his life. At Manhasset High School, Jim excelled in every sport he tried and won thirteen varsity letters. He averaged 18 points per game in basketball and 14.9 yards per carry in football. Forty-five colleges offered him scholarships.

Jim attended Syracuse University, and in 1956, he made all-American teams in both football and lacrosse. In his senior season, Jim set a major college record that stood until 1990, by scoring 43 points—6 touchdowns and 7 extra points—in one game, against Colgate University. The Orangemen played in the 1957 Cotton Bowl, and Jim rushed for 132 yards and scored 21 points, but Syracuse lost to Texas Christian University, 28-27. During his collegiate career, from 1954 to 1956, Jim compiled 2,091 total yards, 25 touchdowns, and 187 points. A high scorer on the basketball team, too, Jim tallied 563 points in forty-three games. He also placed fifth in the national decathlon championship in track. The Cleveland Browns

Jim Brown of the Cleveland Browns scoring his 106th career touchdown in this 1965 game against the Philadelphia Eagles. (AP/Wide World Photos)

selected Jim in the first round of the 1957 NFL draft, after which he played in the college all-star game.

The Emerging Champion

From 1957 to 1965, Jim performed for Cleveland as one of the greatest ball carriers in NFL history. The 6-foot 2-inch, 228-pound fullback, often compared to earlier greats Jim Thorpe and Bronko Nagurski, demonstrated power, speed, and quickness. His running power was most evident to the outside as he moved around and over defenders on a sweep or pitchout. Although he was hit hard by many opponents, Jim never missed an NFL game, and he was seldom stopped. His duels with linebacker Robert "Sam" Huff of the New York Giants and Washington Redskins were unrivaled. Besides his designation as NFL rookie of the year in 1957, Jim led Cleveland

NFL Statistics

Season	GP	Rushing					Receiving			
		Car.	Yds.	Avg.	TD	Rec.	Yds.	Avg.	TD
1957	12	202	942	4.7	9	16	55	3.4	1
1958	12	257	1,527	5.9	17	16	138	8.6	1
1959	12	290	1,329	4.6	14	24	190	7.9	0
1960	12	215	1,257	5.8	9	19	204	10.7	2
1961	14	305	1,408	4.6	8	46	459	10.0	2
1962	14	230	996	4.3	13	47	517	11.0	5
1963	14	291	1,863	6.4	12	24	268	11.2	3
1964	14	280	1,446	5.2	7	36	340	9.4	2
1965	14	289	1,544	5.3	17	34	328	9.6	4
Totals	118	2,359	12,312	5.2	106	262	2,499	9.5	20

Notes: GP = games played; Car. = carries; Yds. = yards; Avg. = average yards per carry *or* average yards per reception; TD = touchdowns; Rec. = receptions

in rushing, in 1957, 1958, 1959, 1962, 1963, and 1965; scoring, in 1958, 1959, 1962, 1963, and 1965; and receiving, in 1963. In seven different seasons, he rushed for more than 1,000 yards. In 1958, Jim led the NFL in scoring with 108 points. On November 1, 1959, Jim scored 5 touchdowns against the Baltimore Colts.

Jim established NFL records for most seasons leading the NFL in rushing, 8; consecutive seasons leading the NFL in rushing, 5; career rushing attempts, 2,359; career rushing yards, 12,312; games with 100 or more yards rushing, 58; career yardage average per gain, 5.2; rushing touchdowns in a season, 17; lifetime rushing touchdowns, 106; and rushing yards in one season; 1,863. Although many of these records have since been broken, Jim set the standard to which other running backs aspire. His 12,312 career rushing yards stood until Walter Payton surpassed the record during the 1984 season. Jim's lifetime statistics for 118 games also included 262 receptions and 756 points scored.

Continuing the Story

In 1958 and 1965, Jim was named the NFL's most valuable player, and he played in three NFL Championship games. Cleveland lost title games to the Detroit Lions in 1957, and the Green Bay Packers in 1965, but captured the 1964 crown with a 27-0 triumph over the Baltimore Colts. An all-NFL selection eight years, Jim was named to the Pro Bowl every

NCAA Division I-A Record

Most points in a game, 43 (1956)

NFL Records

Most career touchdowns, 126 (later broken)
Highest average in yards per carry, 5.2

Honors and Awards

1956	College All-American
1957	Chicago College All-Star Team
	NFL Rookie of the Year
1957, 1965	Associated Press NFL Player of the Year
1958, 1963, 1965	United Press International NFL Player of the Year
	Jim Thorpe Trophy (corecipient 1963)
1958, 1965	Newspaper Enterprise Association NFL Player of the Year
1958-66	NFL Pro Bowl Team
1962-63, 1966	NFL Pro Bowl Player of the Game (corecipient)
1963	Bert Bell Award
1964	Hickok Belt
1970	NFL All-Pro Team of the 1960's
1971	Inducted into Pro Football Hall of Fame
1975	Inducted into Black Athletes Hall of Fame
1982	NCAA Silver Anniversary Award
1985	AFL-NFL 1960-1984 All-Star Team
	Uniform number 32 retired by Cleveland Browns

year of his career and was selected the game's most valuable player twice, in 1962 and 1963. In 1958 and 1965, Jim won the Jim Thorpe Trophy and shared it with Y. A. Title in 1963. With Green Bay's Jim Taylor, he was selected at fullback on the all-pro squad of the 1960's, by the Pro Football Hall of Fame Committee.

In 1971, Jim was elected to the Pro Football Hall of Fame. Jim, who was also elected as a member of the National Lacrosse Hall of Fame, was named to the Pro Football Hall of Fame's American Football League (AFL)/NFL 1960-1984 all-star team. Jim married Sue Jones in 1958, and they had three children: Kim and Kevin, who are twins, and Jim. After his retirement, Jim worked in the motion picture industry, appearing in *The Dirty Dozen* (1967), *Ice Station Zebra* (1968), *I'm Gonna Git You Sucka* (1988), *Any Given Sunday* (1999), and several other films. As a former gang member, Jim volunteered his time with an organization he founded, Amer-I-Can, to help gang members acquire skills to turn their lives around.

Summary

Jim Brown is widely regarded as the toughest and most powerful running back in NFL history. Off the field, too, Jim earned a reputation as a tough, outspoken critic of both football and society at large. He has often spoken out against modern players as pampered and lazy, and he has decried racism in athletics. He has actively promoted black economic causes and has established organizations to assist both athletes and nonathletes in a number of areas.

Kevin R. Lasley

Additional Sources

Barber, Phil. "NFL: Football's One Hundred Greatest Players—The Hit Men." *The Sporting News* 223 (November 1, 1999): 12-16.

Freeman, Michael. *Jim Brown: The Fierce Life of an American Hero.* New York: HarperCollins, 2007.

Jones, Richard Lezin. "Across Years and Yards, Two Old-School Guys." *The New York Times*, September 19, 2004, p. 9.

Tim Brown

Born: July 22, 1966
     Dallas, Texas
Also known as: Timothy Donell Brown (full
    name); Touchdown Timmy

Early Life
Born in Dallas, Texas, on July 22, 1966, Tim Brown displayed his athletic talents in a variety of sports from a young age. At Woodrow Wilson High School, Tim was a prep all-American and selected twice as an all-district running back. In basketball, he starred as a guard and was selected as all-district for his efforts. Tim's skill extended to track and field, where he excelled as a sprinter and established a local record with a 24 foot 3 inch long jump.

The Road to Excellence
Tim's high school accomplishments attracted attention at the next level. He enrolled at the University of Notre Dame and joined the Fighting Irish, playing for sub-par teams under coach Gerry Faust in the 1984 and 1985 seasons. Tim's performance in these years was solid but not spectacular; however, he demonstrated a versatility that became his trademark. Playing the flanker position, Tim caught 28 passes his first season—a Notre Dame freshman record at the time—carried the ball once, and returned one kick. In his second season, he scored touchdowns through receiving, rushing, and kick returning, with a 93-yard return.

In 1986, the fortunes of both Tim and his team improved when Lou Holtz became head coach. Holtz called Tim "the most intelligent player I've ever been around." Tim became a central component of the Irish offensive attack. For the season, he had a Notre Dame record 1,937

all-purpose yards which included punt returns in addition to receiving, rushing, and kickoff returns. His best season was 1987, statistically and from a team perspective. The Irish finished with 8 wins, 4 losses, and the school's first bowl appearance in seven years. Tim again scored touchdowns in three different ways, including his first touchdown via a punt return. In fact, he had consecutive punt returns for touchdowns in a game against Michigan State University.

Tim finished 1987 and his career at Notre Dame as the team's all-time leader in receiving yards. His six return touchdowns—three punt and three kick—tied with Raghib "Rocket" Ismail and Allen Rossum for the most in a career. Tim capped his amateur era by winning the Heisman Trophy, the seventh in Notre Dame history, by 611 votes over the runner-up, quarterback Don McPherson of Syracuse University.

Wide receiver Tim Brown after scoring the winning touchdown to help the Oakland Raiders beat the San Francisco 49ers in 2000. (AP/Wide World Photos)

The Emerging Champion

As had his high school statistics, his college football career and Heisman Trophy drew considerable attention from the next level. On the day of the 1988 NFL draft, Tim awaited the results in his South Bend, Indiana, apartment. He did not have long to wait. The Los Angeles Raiders made him the sixth selection of the first round of the draft.

Tim's professional career began in 1988. Tim quickly displayed the same versatility he had shown in his college football career. Playing in all sixteen regular season games, Tim scored touchdowns rushing, receiving, and returning kicks, and in the process, broke former Chicago Bear Gale Sayers's NFL record for most total yards by a rookie. For his efforts, Tim made the Pro Bowl as a rookie and was named by *The Sporting News* as a kick returner on its NFL all-pro team. Tim's sophomore season, in 1989, was memorable for the wrong reason. In the opening game, and after catching only one pass, he suffered a season-ending knee injury on a kick return. He overcame the injury but believed it left him irredeemably slower than before. After rehabilitation, Tim returned for the 1990 season and until 1992, his numbers lagged behind projections based on his rookie season, in part because of the nature of the Raider offensive game plan.

Honors and Awards

1987	Heisman Trophy
	Walter Camp Award
1988, 1991, 1993-95, 1997	AFC all-conference first team
	Sporting News NFL All-Pro Team
1988, 1991, 1993-97, 1999, 2001	NFL Pro Bowl Team
1990's	NFL All-Decade Team
1993-97	NFL All-Pro Team

Tim became a free agent after the 1991 season, but the Raiders elected to re-sign him. He did not catch as many passes as he had his first year until 1992. While he continued to return punts on a regular basis, he gave up returning kicks. His breakthrough season as a professional came in 1993, when he caught 80 passes, a career high at that point. It also appeared to be his last season as a Raider when, in March, 1994, he signed a lucrative free-agent contract with the Denver Broncos. The Raiders, however, had the option to match the contract and did so five days later. Tim's career then took off.

In each season from 1993 to 1997, Tim was voted an all-pro receiver and earned a ticket to the Pro Bowl. He steadily increased his receptions over those five years, catching 80 in 1993, 89 in 1994 and 1995, 90 in 1996, and a career-best 104 in 1997. In the latter year, Tim had a career-best receiving yards total with 1,408. He was also selected to the Pro Bowl in 1999 and 2001, giving him a total of nine trips to the all-star event.

Tim's strong and consistent performance continued for a team that did not match his level of play. For Tim, this meant experiencing several coaching changes and few playoff games—the Raiders missed the playoffs for six straight seasons going into the 2000 season, when Tim helped lead the team to the conference finals. Tim criticized Raiders owner Al Davis, which led to speculation that the wide receiver might seek another team. Encouraging him to remain were his ties to the Raiders and a new family. He married in 1997 and became a father in 1998.

NFL Statistics

Season	GP	Rec.	Yds.	Avg.	TD
1988	16	43	725	16.9	5
1989	1	1	8	8.0	0
1990	16	18	265	14.7	3
1991	16	36	554	15.4	5
1992	15	49	693	14.1	7
1993	16	80	1,180	14.8	7
1994	16	89	1,309	14.7	9
1995	16	89	1,342	15.1	10
1996	16	90	1,104	12.3	9
1997	16	104	1,408	13.5	5
1998	16	81	1,012	12.5	9
1999	16	90	1,344	14.9	6
2000	16	76	1,128	14.8	11
2001	16	91	1,165	12.8	9
2002	16	81	930	11.5	2
2003	16	52	567	10.9	2
2004	15	24	200	8.3	1
Totals	255	1,094	14,934	13.7	100

Notes: GP = games played; Rec. = receptions; Yds. = yards; Avg. = average yards per reception; TD = touchdowns

Continuing the Story

In 2001, Tim faced a new kind of challenge when the legendary 49ers wide receiver Jerry Rice signed with the Raiders. Football fans everywhere looked forward to seeing how well two of the greatest receivers in NFL history would work together. Tim did well, averaging just under 75 receptions a season from 2001 to 2003. Tim's decision to stay with Raiders through a difficult era was rewarded with an AFC Championship and a trip to the Super Bowl in the 2002 season.

In 2004, after sixteen seasons with the "Silver and Black," Tim opted to sign with Tampa Bay rather than take a reserve role with the Raiders. He was reunited with former Oakland coach Jon Gruden, further souring his relationship with Raiders owner Al Davis. Tim played only a small part in the Bucs season, catching 24 balls for 200 yards and one touchdown. In 2005, Tim, the man dubbed "Mr. Raider," signed a one day contract with Oakland and retired in the silver and black uniform.

At the time of his retirement, Tim was tied with Don Hutson for sixteenth on the NFL's touchdowns list with 105. He was third on the NFL's career receptions list with 1,094. His career receiving yards, 14,934, are second only to former teammate Rice. Tim also had 19,679 all-purpose yards.

Summary

At both the college and professional levels Tim Brown was a consistently strong and multitalented player. Able to catch passes, run back kicks and punts, and run with the ball, Tim displayed versatility. For the Raiders, he was an essential part of the team's offense. His records for most receptions and receiving yards were not lost on Raiders management, as evidenced by the team's decisions to repeatedly re-sign him when he attained free agency and bring him back one last time so that he could retire a Raider.

Steve Hewitt, updated by Trevor D. Bopp

Additional Sources

Barra, Allen. *Big Play: Barra on Football.* Washington, D.C.: Brassey's, 2004.

Carroll, Bob. *Total Football: The Official Encyclopedia of the National Football League.* New York: HarperCollins, 1999.

Marder, Keith, Mark Spellen, and Jim Donovan. *The Notre Dame Football Encyclopedia: The Ultimate Guide to America's Favorite College Team.* New York: Citadel Press/Kensington, 2001.

Tedy Bruschi

Born: June 9, 1973
     San Francisco, California
Also known as: Tedy Lacap Bruschi (full name);
   Bru

Early Life

Tedy Lacap Bruschi was born June 9, 1973, in San Francisco, California, the son of Anthony and Juanita Bruschi. Tedy's parents divorced when he was five; financial struggles plagued his family during his childhood and teen years. When Tedy was in eighth grade, his mother moved the family to Roseville, California, where he played organized football for the first time. In Tedy's freshman year, a couple of his friends tried out for the football team at Roseville High School. Tedy decided to

Tedy Bruschi. (John Pyle/CSM/Landov)

try out with them and made the team. He worked hard and became well known for his competitive spirit and overwhelming desire to win, emerging as a team leader. He was team captain for two years, lettered twice, and earned all-conference, all-Northern California, and all-metro honors as a defensive tackle. Besides football, he wrestled and competed in the track events of shot put, discus, and triple jump, lettering in all three sports.

The Road to Excellence

Tedy enrolled at the University of Arizona and distinguished himself in football as a defensive end. He tied the NCAA Division I-A record for career sacks with 52. He finished his college career ranked sixth in Division I-A history with a total of 74 tackles for losses. He forced 6 fumbles, recovered 5 others, and accrued 185 total tackles during his college career. Tedy was known for his intelligence, competitiveness, and commitment. He graduated from Arizona with a communications degree and was selected in the third round of the 1996 NFL draft by the New England Patriots, as a defensive linebacker. Despite doubts about his ability based on his small stature, his professional football career had begun.

The Emerging Champion

Tedy acquired a reputation as a fierce competitor and team leader. Early in his career, his work ethic distinguished him from other football players. In 1996, his first season with the Patriots, Tedy played in every game as either a pass-rush specialist or special-teams player. He finished his first professional season with 11 tackles and 4 sacks, ranked third on the team with 17 special-teams tackles, and scored his first career touchdown. The Patriots made the Super Bowl. During Super Bowl XXXI, on January 26, 1997, Tedy recorded 2 sacks—just one short of Reggie White's Super Bowl record of 3.

Continuing the Story

Over twelve seasons, Tedy accrued 30½ sacks, 12 interceptions, and nearly 1,000 tackles. He was named American Football Conference defensive player of the week six times. Tedy was also voted a captain of the Patriots defensive unit in 2002, 2003, 2006, and 2007. In total, he played in four Super Bowls, earning three Super Bowl rings.

Tedy appeared in his first Pro Bowl on February 13, 2005. Shortly after returning home, on February 16, Tedy suffered a stroke at the age of thirty-one. His football career seemed to be over. However, Tedy worked hard to overcome his weakened physical condition. After surgery to correct a heart defect and intensive rehabilitation therapy, Tedy, through determination and hard work, returned to mental and physical health. With clearance from his doctors and the support of his family, Tedy returned to the football field just eight months later. In the 2005 season, he accumulated 62 tackles.

Tedy was the first player in the NFL to return from a stroke. In 2005, he shared the NFL's comeback player of the year award with Steve Smith. Tedy continued to play well, averaging 97 tackles from 2004 to 2007 and compiling 461 stops between 2003 and 2006. He was the first player in NFL history to return four consecutive interceptions for touchdowns, and the first Patriots linebacker to score on multiple interceptions in a single season. In 2007, he led the team in tackles, with 92, and solo tackles, with 69. In 2008, he played in only thirteen games but amassed an impressive 75 tackles.

Honors and Awards

1993, 1995	First-Team All-Pacific Ten Conference
1995	All-American
	Morris Trophy
2000, 2005	Ed Block Courage Award
2004	Associated Press Second-Team All-Pro
	Football Digest Second-Team All-Pro
2005	NFL Pro Bowl
	Maxwell Football Club's Spirit Award
	NFL Comeback Player of the Year (award shared with Steve Smith)
2006	Paul E. Tsongas Award
	Inducted into Rhode Island Italian-American Hall of Fame

Summary

Tedy Bruschi embodied hard work, resilience, and determination. Although underestimated as a player, he demonstrated an instinctive ability and passion for football. He proved to be a leader, a record setter, and the captain of the New England Patriots defense. Although he suffered what was thought to be a career-ending stroke, he fought back and proved that, with hard work, obstacles can be overcome. In 2005, he established Tedy's Team, an organization dedicated to raising awareness of stroke victims. He also became a spokesperson for the American Stroke Association and recipient of the Ed Block Courage Award in 2000 and 2005.

Alice C. Richer

NFL Statistics

Season	GP	Tac.	Sacks	FF	FR	Int.
1996	16	11	4.0	1	0	0
1997	16	30	4.0	2	2	0
1998	16	74	2.0	2	0	0
1999	14	107	2.0	1	1	1
2000	16	106	1.0	1	0	0
2001	15	75	2.0	3	1	2
2002	11	66	4.5	1	0	2
2003	16	131	2.0	3	1	3
2004	16	122	3.5	2	0	3
2005	9	62	2.0	1	0	0
2006	15	112	1.5	0	2	1
2007	16	92	2.0	0	0	0
2008	13	75	0.0	0	0	0
Totals	**189**	**1,063**	**30.5**	**17**	**7**	**12**

Notes: GP = games played; Tac. = tackles; FF = forced fumbles; FR = fumble recoveries; Int. = interceptions

Additional Sources

Altobelli, Lisa. "My Sportsman Choice: Tedy Bruschi." *Sports Illustrated* (November 23, 2005).

Boston Globe. Driven: The Patriots Ride to a Third Title. Chicago: Triumph Books, 2005.

Bruschi, Tedy, and Michael Holley. *Never Give Up: My Stroke, My Recovery, and My Return to the NFL.* Hoboken, N.J.: Wiley and Sons, 2007.

Buck Buchanan

Born: September 10, 1940
      Gainesville, Alabama
Died: July 16, 1992
      Kansas City, Missouri
Also known as: Junious Buchanan (full name)

Early Life

Junious "Buck" Buchanan was born on September 10, 1940, in Gainesville, Alabama, to Fannie Mae and Wallace Buchanan. One of the greatest early influences on Buck's life was his older brother, Wallace, whose determination and hard work were an inspiration to Buck. Wallace followed Buck's career closely in college and in professional football. His interest meant a great deal to Buck. Wallace died at an early age, but Buck never forgot the lessons that Wallace taught him: Work hard and never accept anything less than your best.

The Road to Excellence

While a student at Parker High School in Birmingham, Alabama, Buck played basketball and football. In 1960, Buck entered Grambling State University on a basketball scholarship. He earned a letter playing basketball on a team that included future National Basketball Association (NBA) hall of fame member Willis Reed and future Kansas City Chief teammate Ernie Ladd.

At 6 feet 7 inches and 212 pounds, Buck was already a "big man on campus." While at Grambling State University, he grew to almost 275 pounds. Despite his size, Buck was a very fast man. He even ran for the university's track team. In 1962, he ran the 440-yard dash in 49.2 seconds. Some feel that Buck was not only one of the best football players ever to play at a small college but also one of the best all-around athletes. Buck played both offensive and defensive end for the Tigers of Grambling State. He was on the all-conference team in 1960, 1961, and 1962. In 1963, he played in the college all-star game, which pitted the best college football players in the country against the NFL champions. In 1963, the college all-star team beat the Green Bay Packers 20-17. The next time Buck played the Packers was as a professional football player in the

first Super Bowl, in 1967. This time the Packers beat Buck's team, the Kansas City Chiefs, 35-10.

The Emerging Champion

After an outstanding college career in which he helped Grambling State become one of the best small-college football programs in the country, Buck was ready to play professional football. He was the first player selected in the 1963 American Football League (AFL) draft. Buck's selection marked the first time a player from an all-black school was the number-one pick of any professional football league. While the AFL was neither as successful nor as well established as the better known NFL, Buck decided to play for the team that had picked him, the Dallas Texans. The Texans moved to Kansas City soon afterward and changed their name to the Chiefs. Buck was honored to be the first player ever to be a number-one pick from a small black college, and he wanted to prove that good football players could come from small schools as well as big schools.

Success did not come easily at first for Buck, however. He did not play much in his first AFL game and was very upset. He was determined to work even harder in practice, and soon he was one of the best players on the team. As a defensive tackle, Buck was more than just a good player. He had skills and qualities that changed the way people played defensive tackle. He was bigger, stronger, and faster than most other tackles. He was in-

---

Honors and Awards

1960-62	All-Southwest Conference Team
1962	NAIA All-American
1963	Chicago College All-Star Team
	Overall first choice in the AFL Draft
1965-70	AFL All-Star Team
1966-67, 1969	*Sporting News* AFL All-Star Team
1966-68	NFL All-Pro Team
1971-72	NFL Pro Bowl Team
1980	NFL All-Pro Team of the 1970's
1990	Inducted into Pro Football Hall of Fame

telligent and was very quick to learn from his mistakes. He was an honest and fair player, often helping up an opponent he had just knocked down.

Continuing the Story

Buck played for the Kansas City Chiefs for 13 seasons, from 1963 through 1975. He played in a total of six AFL all-star games, two AFC-NFC Pro Bowl games, two AFL Championship games, and two Super Bowls: Kansas City's Super Bowl I loss to the Green Bay Packers in 1967, and the team's 23-7 Super Bowl IV victory over the Minnesota Vikings in 1970. Buck played in a total of 181 professional football games. He missed only one game, in 1974, as the result of a broken hand. His teammates voted him the Chiefs' most valuable player in 1965 and 1967, and he was the team cocaptain in 1968.

Buck was so overwhelming as a player that the Oakland Raiders drafted a college player especially to play against Buck. That player, Gene Upshaw, went on to have an excellent NFL career and was inducted into the Pro Football Hall of Fame in 1987. Upshaw was a bigger, stronger, and faster offensive lineman than others. Upshaw had to be a different type of football player in order to play well against Buck, who not only influenced the way defensive tackles usually played but also made other football teams change the way they played against him.

Buck retired after the 1975 season. He was an assistant coach for the New Orleans Saints in 1976 and 1977, and the Cleveland Browns in 1978. Later, he settled in Kansas City with his wife and three children. He was involved in the Kansas Special Olympics and did charity work. He owned two businesses in the Kansas City area and was a highly respected person in the community. Buck's accomplishments on the football field were honored in August of 1990, when he was inducted into the Pro Football Hall of Fame. He is also a member of the Louisiana, Alabama, National Association of Intercollegiate Athletics (NAIA), and Grambling sports halls of fame. Buck died in 1992.

Summary

Buck Buchanan dramatically changed the way that defensive tackles played football. He was so much bigger and stronger than other defensive tackles that teams tried to find players just like him, or tried to find bigger players to play against him. Size and strength were not his only assets, though. Buck's ability to work hard helped to make him a success on and off the field. In 1995, the National Collegiate Athletic Association (NCAA) established the Buck Buchanan Award, given annually to the top Division I Football Championship Subdivision (FCS) (formerly Division I-AA) player of the year.

Michael Salmon

Additional Sources

Barber, Phil. "NFL: Football's One Hundred Greatest Players—The Hit Men." *The Sporting News* 223 (November 1, 1999): 12-16.

Carroll, Bob. *Total Football: The Official Encyclopedia of the National Football League.* New York: HarperCollins, 1999.

Miller, Jeff. *Going Long: The Wild Ten-Year Saga of the Renegade American Football League in the Words of Those Who Lived It.* New York: McGraw-Hill, 2003.

Zimmerman, Paul. "Gangs of Four." *Sports Illustrated* 83, no. 15 (October 6, 1995): 66-73.

Nick Buoniconti

Born: December 15, 1940
　　　Springfield, Massachusetts
Also known as: Nicholas Anthony Buoniconti, Jr.
　(full name); Skippy

Early Life

Nicholas Anthony Buoniconti, Jr., was born December 15, 1940, in Springfield, Massachusetts. Brought up in a Catholic family, Nick was taught to live by the rules of his parents and his church. Though possessing a fiery disposition, young Nick learned to control his emotions and was looked upon as a respectful boy. As one of the smallest boys in his neighborhood, however, Nick had to learn how to stand his ground. His intensity proved beneficial when he was playing sports with the neighborhood boys, and soon Nick earned the respect of the tallest and strongest among them. As a boy, Nick learned a life of balance. To his elders, he showed respect and admiration. From his peers, he earned respect by his dogged determination on the playing field.

The Road to Excellence

Nick's first real test in organized sports came when he enrolled in Cathedral High School in Springfield. During his first game on the varsity football squad, opposing players had a hard time not laughing when they saw Nick's diminutive figure trot out into the defensive backfield. Those snickers soon turned to groans, however, when Nick leveled ball carriers with ferocious tackles. By his senior season, Nick had evolved into a genuine college prospect.

At the University of Notre Dame, Nick brought a fearsome intensity and quickness to the offensive line, where he played as guard, and to the defensive backfield, where he was a middle linebacker. In 1961, his senior season, Nick was named an all-American, and in the spring of 1962, he graduated with a bachelor of arts degree in economics from Notre Dame. Although Nick was a fine college football player, he was not recommended by his coach, Joe Kuharich, to the NFL scouts who were visiting the Notre Dame campus. Kuharich told them that Nick was too small to play professional football. To Nick, this sounded all too familiar. Once again, he

Miami Dolphins linebacker Nick Buoniconti. (NFL/Getty Images)

was not getting enough respect because of his size. Undaunted by his coach's assessment, Nick decided to try out with the Boston Patriots of the American Football League (AFL). Nick's fiery determination paid off. He was accepted by the team and soon signed a contract to play at the middle-linebacker position.

The Emerging Champion

As a middle linebacker for the Patriots, Nick was an imposing force; he stopped ball carriers cold in their tracks and leaped high in the air to snatch passes away from would-be receivers. Nick played seven seasons for the Patriots, from 1962 to 1968. During that time, he earned a law degree from Suffolk University and was named to the AFL's all-star team six times. Nick became Boston's leading pass interceptor—he grabbed 24 of them—and helped lead the Patriots to the AFL championship game in 1963.

Honors and Awards

1961	College All-American
1964-68	*Sporting News* AFL All-Star Team
1964-68, 1970	AFL All-Star Team
1970	All-Time AFL Team
1973-74	NFL Pro Bowl Team
1980	NFL All-Pro Team of the 1970's

When Nick was traded to the Miami Dolphins in 1969, he provided the experience and leadership the young team needed. In 1970, the Dolphins marched to the first of five consecutive playoff berths, appearing in the Super Bowl in 1971, 1972, and 1973. Nick's statistics as a Dolphin are impressive: He played in eighty-one games, made 475 solo tackles, and assisted in 318 tackles, for a total of 793. He also recovered three fumbles, sacked the quarterback five times, and grabbed 8 interceptions for a total of 89 yards. After losing to the Dolphins in the 1971 American Football Conference (AFC) championship game, Baltimore Colts quarterback Johnny Unitas said of Nick, "If you want to run on the Miami Dolphins, you have to be able to block Buoniconti. Today we couldn't block him."

Nick's winning intensity and quickness rarely failed him as a professional linebacker, in spite of his small size. "When (Dick) Butkus hits you," Nick said, "you fall the way he wants. When I hit you, you fall the way you want. But there's no difference. You still fall." Nick was voted most valuable player by his Dolphin teammates after the 1973 season, and he was selected to play in the Pro Bowl following the 1972 and 1973 seasons. Nick retired as a player in 1976.

Continuing the Story

Because he practiced law in the off-season while with the Dolphins, Nick already had a career in progress when his playing days came to an end. He continued to practice law in Miami to support his wife, Terri, and the couple's three children, Gina, Nick III, and Marc.

Following in his father's footsteps, Marc played as a linebacker for the Citadel, a college in South Carolina. Tragically, however, Marc's career as a football player was cut short in 1985, when he tackled East Tennessee State running back Herman Jacobs. Marc's spinal cord was damaged on the play, leaving him a quadriplegic. From that day on, not only was Marc's life changed, but Nick's life also was transformed.

Inspired by the efforts of Jackson Memorial Hospital in Miami to help Marc and other paralyzed patients, Nick established the Marc Buoniconti Fund. Raising millions of dollars as the fund's director, Nick began to see results. Under the care of specialists, Marc's condition improved, and he was released from the hospital. Although his son was confined to a wheelchair, Nick remained optimistic and determined.

In the 1990's, Nick began working as a sports commentator on HBO Sports' *Inside the NFL*, along with such football notables as Len Dawson and Dan Marino. Nick remained involved with the Marc Buoniconti Fund and the Miami Project to Cure Paralysis, which he helped to create and which is located at the University of Miami School of Medicine. In 2001, Nick was inducted into the Pro Football Hall of Fame.

Summary

Once thought too small to play football, Nick Buoniconti became an all-American for the University of Notre Dame and an all-pro in the NFL. A fiery leader and an inspirational force, Nick became a successful attorney and the director of the Marc Buoniconti Fund, a project to assist paralyzed hospital patients.

Rustin Larson

Additional Sources

Altobelli, Lisa, Mark Bechtel, and Stephen Cannella. "The Beat." *Sports Illustrated* 101, no. 14 (October 11, 2004): 24.

Carroll, Bob. *Total Football: The Official Encyclopedia of the National Football League.* New York: HarperCollins, 1999.

Daniels, Kevin, and Rob Doster. *Game Day: Notre Dame Football—The Greatest Games, Players, Coaches, and Teams in the Glorious Tradition of Fighting Irish Football.* Chicago, Ill.: Triumph Books, 2006.

Mallozzi, Vincent M. "Relentless Pursuit: Buoniconti Keeps Promise, Gives Hope." *The New York Times,* June 19, 2005, pp. 11-12.

_____. "Veteran of 1972 Dolphins Is a Chargers Fan for a Day." *The New York Times,* December 19, 2005, p. D5.

Reggie Bush

Born: March 2, 1985
      San Diego, California
Also known as: Reginald Alfred Bush II (full
   name); Baby Matrix; the President

Early Life

Reginald "Reggie" Alfred Bush II was born in San Diego, California, on March 2, 1985. His biological father abandoned the family soon after Reggie was born. Denise Griffin, his mother, remarried, and Reggie was raised in an urban but unincorporated area of San Diego County by his mother and stepfather, LeMar Griffin. Reggie was an athletic youth who played football and ran track. He attended Helix High School in La Mesa, California, where he

Reggie Bush carrying the ball for the New Orleans Saints against the Chicago Bears in 2008. (Brian Kersey/UPI/Landov)

became a star running back. During his high school career, Reggie rushed for 4,995 yards and scored 450 points. In 2002, he was named a member of *Parade* magazine's all-American football team and a member of *USA Today's* all-USA team.

The Road to Excellence

Reggie was the most sought-after high school football player of his graduating class. He chose to attend the University of Southern California (USC), where he majored in political science. In 2003, as a freshman, he was a reserve tailback and kick returner. Reggie's speed and ability to elude defensive players made him a valuable offensive player. He could run, catch, and return kicks. In one notable game against the University of Washington, Reggie had 270 all-purpose yards. Reggie gained 1,331 total yards during his first year of collegiate play, which set a USC freshman record. He also led the Pac-10 Conference in kickoff returns, averaging 27.3 yards per return, and had one runback for a touchdown. ESPN named Reggie the college football co-newcomer of the year.

Reggie remained a back-up tailback the following year and started only two games. Nevertheless, he accumulated 2,330 total yards, including rushing for 90 yards in a single play. Only Marcus Allen, in 1981, gained more total yards as a USC Trojan, with 2,427. Reggie even threw one touchdown pass. His career-best collegiate performance came in a game against the University of California Los Angeles; he ran for 204 yards and had 335 all-purpose yards. Reggie was the team's most valuable player for 2004. Although a sophomore, he placed fifth in the voting for the Heisman Trophy that year. Mean-

Honors and Awards

2004   University of Southern California team most valuable player

Associate Press Sportsman of the Year

2005   Heisman Trophy

Walter Camp Award

Doak Walker Award

Pacific Ten Conference Offensive Player of the Year

2006   *Pro Football Weekly* All-Rookie Team

NFL Offensive Rookie of the Month (December)

while, USC won the Orange Bowl and the national championship, defeating Oklahoma 55-19.

The Emerging Champion

Reggie's final year of college football was spectacular. He accumulated 2,890 total yards and scored 18 touchdowns. Reggie tied a National Collegiate Athletic Association record with two consecutive seasons of 2,000 or more yards. He led the nation with an average of 222.3 all-purpose yards per game. He also averaged 8.7 yards per carry, 12.9 yards per catch, and 17.6 yards per kickoff return.

Reggie won the Heisman Trophy as well as the Walter Camp and the Doak Walker awards. He was also named as the Associated Press college sportsman of the year. USC ended the 2005-2006 season ranked number one and played Texas in the Rose Bowl to determine the Bowl Championship Series national championship. USC lost the game, 41-38, but Reggie gained 279 all-purpose yards, including 82 rushing yards, 95 receiving yards, and 102 yards in kick returns. He also scored a touchdown. After the game, Reggie announced that he intended to skip his senior year and enter the NFL. His performance in the championship game and the acquisi-

tion of the Heisman Trophy led most to believe Reggie would be the 2006 number-one NFL draft pick. However, the Houston Texans decided to draft Mario Williams, a defensive player. Reggie became the number-two pick of the first round and was signed by the New Orleans Saints for a six-year deal worth $26.3 million. Reggie also received various endorsement deals worth an estimated $50 million. Meanwhile, news reports surfaced that Reggie and his family had received illegal payments from two competing sports agencies that hoped to represent the college player when he entered the NFL.

Continuing the Story

In the aftermath of Hurricane Katrina, in August, 2006, the Saints' selection of Reggie caused considerable excitement in New Orleans. For the first time in team history, the Saints sold out the season. Reggie contributed to a number of local charities and became active in the community. During his first season, Reggie did not achieve the breakaway success that many expected. The Saints often used a two-back offense with Reggie and running back "Deuce" McAllister. Nonetheless, Reggie did turn in several spectacular performances, including a game on December 3, 2006, against the San Francisco 49ers, when Reggie scored four touchdowns. In 2006, Reggie had 88 receptions for 742 yards, setting a record for rookie running backs in the NFL, and 216 yards in punt returns. However, he gained only 565 rushing yards. The Saints won the conference and played for the division championship for the first time in the team's history, losing to the Chicago Bears, 39-14.

In 2007, McAllister was injured, and Reggie became the team's primary running back. He gained 581 running yards, but only 417 receiving yards. During the season, Reggie was criticized for a lack of aggressiveness and unwillingness to run up the middle. He scored only 6 touchdowns during the season and averaged only 3.7 yards per carry. The Saints finished the season with a disappointing record of seven wins and nine losses. Injuries marred Reggie's performance during the 2008 season. The Saints improved their won-

NFL Statistics

Season	GP	Rushing				Receiving			
		Car.	Yds.	Avg.	TD	Rec.	Yds.	Avg.	TD
2006	16	155	565	3.6	6	88	742	8.4	2
2007	12	157	581	3.7	4	73	417	5.7	2
2008	10	106	404	3.8	2	52	440	8.5	4
Totals	38	418	1,550	3.7	12	213	1,599	7.5	8

Notes: GP = games played; Car. = carries; Yds. = yards; Avg. = average yards per carry or average yards per reception; TD = touchdowns; Rec. = receptions

loss record, but Reggie's stats were similar to those of the previous season.

Summary

Reggie Bush was one of the greatest college football players of all time. Although he initially failed to meet the high expectations that accompanied his pedigree as a Heisman Trophy winner, his abilities as running back, receiver, and kick returner allowed him to make an impact on games.

Tom Lansford

Additional Sources

Donnes, Alan, and Chris Myers. *Patron Saints: How the Saints Gave New Orleans a Reason to Believe.* Nashville, Tenn.: Center Street, 2007.

Wharton, David, and Gary Klein. *Conquest: Pete Carroll and the Trojans' Climb to the Top of the College Football Mountain.* Chicago: Triumph, 2005.

Yaeger, Don. *Tarnished Heisman: Did Reggie Bush Turn His Final College Season into a Six-Figure Job?* New York: Pocket, 2008.

Dick Butkus

Born: December 9, 1942
     Chicago, Illinois
Also known as: Richard Marvin Butkus (full
     name)

Early Life

Richard Marvin Butkus was born December 9, 1942, in Chicago, Illinois. He was the youngest of seven children born to his Lithuanian parents. Dick's older brothers introduced him to sports. Although Dick was a good baseball player, he was especially attracted to football. His brothers took him to annual college all-star games played at Soldier Field in Chicago. These games stirred his football interest, and while he was still in grade school, Dick vowed to become a professional football player.

Chicago Bears linebacker Dick Butkus, who was known for his intensity and defensive ferocity. (Courtesy of Amateur Athletic Foundation of Los Angeles)

Dick dedicated his youth to achieving his goal of playing professional football. He even chose to travel several more miles than necessary each day to attend Chicago Vocational High School because of its football program.

The Road to Excellence

In high school, Dick played fullback on offense and linebacker on defense. He was so enthusiastic about football that his coach had to hold him out of scrimmages to keep him from accidentally hurting his own teammates. In his senior year, Dick made the all-state football team as a fullback. In 1961, upon his graduation from high school, Dick received several football scholarship offers. He chose the University of Illinois because of the new football coach Pete Elliot. Although he was dedicated to playing football, Dick realized the importance of balancing academics with athletics. He worked hard at his studies and even harder at football.

Dick played offensive center and defensive linebacker for the University of Illinois football team. He became noted for his fierce defensive play and his ability to strip the football from opposing running backs. While at Illinois, Dick was a two-time all-American. In 1964, he was named American Football Coaches Association player of the year.

In the summer of 1965, Dick was the cocaptain of the college all-star team when it played the Cleveland Browns. He had a great professional debut. He made or assisted on fifteen tackles and blocked a field goal attempt. Dick was runner-up for the game's most valuable player award.

The Emerging Champion

Dick was the Chicago Bears' first choice in the 1965 NFL draft. Drafted ahead of Gale Sayers, who earned fame as a running back, Dick proved to be a valuable addition to the team. The Bears had a tradition of fielding a vicious defense, but the defense had fallen into disarray prior to Dick's arrival. In his rookie year, Dick took over the middle-linebacker position and helped to restore the legendary ferocity of the Bears' defense.

In the season opener against the San Francisco 49ers, Dick made eleven unassisted tackles. In his sixth game with the Bears, he was given the game ball for his outstanding performance. Through his leadership, the Bears defense restored its reputation as "The Monsters of the Midway." In his rookie year, Dick led the Bears in fumble recoveries and pass interceptions. He was runner-up for the NFL rookie of the year award. The winner was his teammate, Sayers, who had made the same kind of impact on offense as Dick had on defense. Dick was named all-pro middle linebacker and was selected to play in the Pro Bowl.

Early in his professional career, Dick became noted for his physical play and reckless style. His quickness and mobility allowed him to cover the football field better than any other player of his day. His punishing hits and tackles distinguished him from other middle linebakers in the league. After turning professional, he married Helen Essenburg, whom he had dated since high school. They had three children, Nikki, born in 1966; Ricky, born in 1967; and Matthew, born in 1971.

Continuing the Story

Many sports professionals distinguish themselves as part of championship teams. Championships, however, eluded Dick. During his nine-year career with the Bears, the team never enjoyed a championship season. In most of those years the Bears did not even have a winning season. However, Dick played every game as though it were his last. Despite the lack of team success, he continued to excel at his position. Sportswriters, fellow players and fans searched for words to describe him accurately. Some called him the meanest, smartest, angriest, strongest, or dirtiest man to ever play the position. Others, such as Green Bay Packers coach Vince Lombardi, called him simply the best.

During his career, Dick did more than dish out bone-jarring hits. He returned 12 kickoffs and

Honors and Awards	
1963-64	Rockne Award
	All-American
1964	American Football Coaches Association Player of the Year
1965	Chicago College All-Star Team
1965, 1967-72	All-NFL Team
1966-73	NFL Pro Bowl Team
1969-70	Halas Trophy
1970	NFL All-Pro Team of the 1960's
1979	Inducted into Pro Football Hall of Fame
1983	Inducted into College Football Hall of Fame
1990	NCAA Silver Anniversary Award
1994	NFL 75th Anniversary All-Time Team
	Uniform number 51 retired by Chicago Bears

once gained 28 yards on a fake punt. On two occasions he caught passes for extra points after fumbled snaps thwarted the kick attempts. One of Dick's favorite plays occurred in 1971, when he caught an extra-point pass that beat the Washington Redskins 16-15.

Dick established a team record for career forced turnovers with 47. His recovery of 25 fumbles was an NFL record when he retired. His 22 pass interceptions became a team record for middle linebackers. Dick was named to the all-NFL team seven of his nine seasons. He played in eight Pro Bowls. A 1970 panel of NFL coaches named him the player they would choose if they were to build a new team from scratch.

Dick's football career was shortened by knee injuries. In 1970, his right knee was injured, but he continued to play. Off-season surgery was not a complete success, and Dick continued to play in pain. During the 1973 season, the pain became too great to bear, and Dick retired in midseason. After his retirement, Dick filed a lawsuit against the Bears for treating his injury improperly. The suit was eventually settled out of court.

In 1995, Dick purchased his own football network, known as the "Dick '51' Butkus Football Network." He later became involved in the startup of a league known as the XFL, which folded shortly after the conclusion of its first season in early 2001. He has also spent time as an actor, appearing in *Necessary Roughness* (1991) and *Any Given Sunday* (1999), among others.

Summary

Dick Butkus was the premier middle linebacker of his era and arguably the best ever. In 1979, Dick's contributions to the game were formally recognized when he was inducted into the Pro Football Hall of Fame. In 1983, he was elected to the College Football Hall of Fame. From his role as a Columbia Broadcasting System (CBS) football commentator to his association with the XFL, Dick continued to make contributions to football and its development.

Duane A. Gill

Additional Sources

Butkus, Dick, and Pat Smith. *Butkus: Flesh and Blood.* New York: Doubleday, 1997.

Reynolds, Neil. *Pain Gang: Pro Football's Fifty Toughest Players.* Washington, D.C.: Potomac, 2006.

Telander, Rick. "Forever Growlin'." *Sports Illustrated* 101, no. 2 (July 12, 2004): 76.

Zimmerman, Paul. "The Greatest Ever." *Sports Illustrated* 95, no. 17 (October 29, 2001): 54-56.

Earl Campbell

Born: March 29, 1955
Tyler, Texas
Also known as: Earl Christian Campbell (full
name)

Early Life
Earl Christian Campbell was born on March 29,
1955, in Tyler, a town in the pine woods of eastern
Texas. Earl's parents were Burk and Ann Collins
Campbell; Earl was the sixth of their eleven children. Earl's childhood was marked by difficulty
and poverty, but was strengthened by firm and loving family values and by a religious upbringing.
The Campbells lived in a weather-beaten farm-
house just outside Tyler. After Earl's father
died in 1966, all the children had to strug-
gle, working in the rose fields around the
house to make ends meet and supplement
their mother's earnings as a housecleaner.
Under the circumstances, Earl was not able
to play organized sports. However, he enjoyed every possible opportunity to throw a
football with friends.

The Road to Excellence
Earl began to develop his football talent in
junior and senior high school. Through
most of his high school career, he played
linebacker. With the help of his coaches,
Earl worked hard to develop the strength
and speed required for this demanding defensive position. By the time he was a senior
at John Tyler High School, Earl was committed to athletic and educational endeavors.
Soon thereafter, his coach moved him to
halfback. The position suited his power, balance, and speed. In his senior year, "the Tyler Rose," as the press called him, rushed for
2,037 yards and led his team to the 1973
Class AAAA state championship.

Earl's achievements earned him honors
on the all-state team and on *Parade* magazine's all-American team. Many colleges recruited Earl. Turning down various offers,
he decided to attend the University of Texas

at Austin to play football under head coach Darrell
Royal.

The Emerging Champion
Earl became an outstanding football player at both
the college and professional levels. From 1974
through 1977, he played for the University of Texas
Longhorns. During his first three years, he was a
fullback in Coach Royal's trademark "wishbone"
formation. With his powerful running style, Earl
gained 928 yards as a freshman and 1,118 yards as a
sophomore. Both years he was selected to the all-
Southwest Conference team. In 1975, he led the
Texas team to victory in the Bluebonnet Bowl and

Earl Campbell, who won the Heisman Trophy in 1977. (Courtesy
of NFL Properties)

was elected to the coaches' all-American team. Earl's junior season was disappointing. A pulled leg muscle kept him out of the lineup for a number of games, and Texas struggled to a mediocre 5-5-1 record.

Earl's senior year, 1977, was the high point of his collegiate career. New head coach Fred Akers changed to a veer offense, in part to take advantage of Earl's blend of speed and power as a running back. Earl turned in an outstanding performance to lead the nation in rushing, with 1,744 yards, and in scoring, with 114 points. The University of Texas went undefeated during the regular season, won the Southwest Conference title, and lost only to Notre Dame in the 1978 Cotton Bowl. In addition, Earl was selected as the winner of the Heisman Trophy, which is awarded annually to the nation's outstanding college football player.

Earl's athletic talents and college record made him an outstanding prospect for professional football. In the 1978 NFL draft, Earl was selected by the

NFL Statistics

| Season | GP | Rushing | | | | Receiving | | | |
		Car.	Yds.	Avg.	TD	Rec.	Yds.	Avg.	TD
1978	15	302	1,450	4.8	13	12	48	4.0	0
1979	16	368	1,697	4.6	19	16	94	5.9	0
1980	15	373	1,934	5.2	13	11	47	4.3	0
1981	16	361	1,376	3.8	10	36	156	4.3	0
1982	9	157	538	3.4	2	18	130	7.2	0
1983	14	322	1,301	4.0	12	19	216	11.4	0
1984	14	146	468	3.2	4	3	27	9.0	0
1985	16	158	643	4.1	1	6	88	14.7	0
Totals	115	2,187	9,407	4.3	74	121	806	6.7	0

Notes: GP = games played; Car. = carries; Yds. = yards; Avg. = average yards per carry *or* average yards per reception; TD = touchdowns; Rec. = receptions

Houston Oilers as the number-one pick in the first round.

Earl's first three years with the Oilers were his most successful. His powerful running style was a major factor in the success the Oilers achieved under Coach O. A. "Bum" Phillips from 1978 through 1980. In his rookie year, 1978, Earl led the NFL in rushing, with 1,450 yards, and was named rookie of the year. In 1979 and 1980, he repeated these performances when he again led the league in rushing; in both seasons he was chosen as the NFL's player of the year. Each of these years the Oilers went to the playoffs, but did not advance to the Super Bowl. In his first four seasons, Earl rushed for 6,457 yards, setting a league record for rushing performance in that span of time.

Earl continued to play professional football through the 1985 season. However, a combination of events limited his performance. In 1981, a coaching change for Houston brought a different formation that gave less scope to Earl's abilities. Finally, in 1984, Earl was traded to the New Orleans Saints, where he was reunited with Bum Phillips. By this time, however, Earl's punishing approach to ball carrying, which drew heavy contact with would-be tacklers, had taken a physical toll. Phillips once said of Earl: "He's got absolutely no regard for his body—or anybody else's body." Earl retired from professional football before the 1986 season. During eight seasons, Earl gained 9,407 yards on 2,187 carries and scored 74 touchdowns. He also caught 121

Honors and Awards

1974-77	All-Southwest Conference Team
1975	Coaches' All-American
1977	Heisman Trophy
	Walter Camp Award
	Sporting News College Player of the Year
	Citizens Savings College Football Player of the Year
	Davey O'Brien Memorial Trophy
	Sporting News College All-American
1978	*Sporting News* AFC Player of the Year
	Associated Press Offensive Rookie of the Year
	United Press International AFC Rookie of the Year
	Sporting News AFC Rookie of the Year
	Bell Trophy
	Overall first choice in the NFL draft
	United Press International AFC Player of the Year
1978-79	*Sporting News* AFC All-Star Team
	Professional Football Writers of America NFL Player of the Year
1978-80	Associated Press Offensive Player of the Year
	Jim Thorpe Trophy
	Seagram's Seven Crowns of Sports Award
1979	Bert Bell Award
1979-82, 1984	NFL Pro Bowl Team
1990	Inducted into College Football Hall of Fame
1991	Inducted into Pro Football Hall of Fame
	Uniform number 34 retired by Houston Oilers

passes for 806 yards. He ranked eighth among the all-time leading rushers in the NFL.

Continuing the Story

After his retirement from professional football, Earl maintained an active career pursuing various business interests. The primary focus of his life continued to be his family and his work with young people. Earl married Reuna Smith, who had been his girlfriend since junior high school. They had two sons, Earl Christian II and Tyler, who were both collegiate athletes. Earl also fulfilled a dream by building his mother a new house on the land in Tyler where Earl was raised.

Earl earned a degree in speech communication from the University of Texas at Austin. He was a special assistant to the vice president of student affairs at the university. For several years, he wrote an advice column for a local paper, the *Austin Weekly*. In print and in his frequent speaking engagements, he emphasizes that students should complete their education and avoid drugs and alcohol abuse. In recognition of his athletic achievements, Earl was inducted into the Pro Football Hall of Fame in Canton, Ohio, in 1991, in his first year of eligibility.

Summary

Earl Campbell's induction into the Pro Football Hall of Fame was a fitting recognition of one of the most powerful and gifted running backs in the history of the sport. As a collegian and as a professional, Earl put all of his 5 feet 11 inches and 225 pounds into every play. His style of play took an exacting toll—he developed trouble with both his back and his knees and needed a wheelchair to help him get around. Regardless of his struggles off the field, he left a lasting impression on all who saw him on it.

Karen Gould

Additional Sources

Campbell, Earl, and John Ruane. *The Earl Campbell Story: A Football Great's Battle with Panic Disorder.* Toronto: ECW Press, 1999.

Carroll, Bob. *Total Football: The Official Encyclopedia of the National Football League.* New York: HarperCollins, 1999.

Menez, Gene, and Richard Deitsch. "The Greatest Longhorns of All Time." *Sports Illustrated Commemorative Edition* 103 (January 7, 2006): 66-71.

Reid, Jan. "Earl Campbell." *Texas Monthly* 29, no. 9 (September, 2001): 106-109.

John Carney

Born: April 20, 1964
Hartford, Connecticut
Also known as: John Michael Carney (full name)

Early Life
John Michael Carney was raised in Florida and played soccer as a boy. He was a strong kicker, a position he filled for the football program at Cardinal Newman High School in West Palm Beach, Florida. He was awarded all-state honors as a kicker. He displayed athletic ability beyond kicking, as he was a hurdler on his school track team.

The Road to Excellence
Based on his high school performance, John was awarded a scholarship to the University of Notre Dame, traditionally one of the best college football programs in the United States. He was the primary kicker for the Fighting Irish during the 1984, 1985, and 1986 seasons and graduated from the university in 1987. For his performance, he was named to *Sports Illustrated*'s all-time Notre Dame team.

Becoming a star professional football player did not happen quickly for John. He was not chosen in the 1987 NFL draft. The Cincinnati Bengals invited him to participate in its training camp, but he was cut before the season began. He did not make a team that year but was a replacement player during the 1987 NFL strike. However, his statistics from that season are not included with his career numbers. In 1988, John did not make an NFL team initially but was signed by the Tampa Bay Buccaneers during the season to replace an injured kicker. In 1989, he was active for only one game, and he failed to score during that opportunity.

The Emerging Champion
In 1990, he earned a roster spot on the San Diego Chargers and went on to have ten successful seasons with the team. In 1990, he set a club record with a .905 field-goal percentage, making 19 of 21 attempts, and led the team with 84 points. In 1991, he repeated as the Chargers' points leader with 88. In 1993, he had 113 points, also a team high.

In 1994, one of five seasons with the Chargers in which John scored more than 100 points, he had a career-high 135 points and was selected to the Pro Bowl. San Diego advanced to the Super Bowl that year, and John scored a field goal in that game. During the 1995 season, he scored a team-leading 95 points and kicked a 54-yard field goal, the longest of his career. In 1996, he was fourth in the AFC with 118 points.

In 1997, John did not play in all sixteen regular-season games for the only time in his Chargers career. That year, he suffered a strained medial collateral ligament in his right knee and played in only four games. He returned with a strong season in 1998, scoring 97 points and making 26 of 30 field-goal attempts. In 1999, he made 31 of 36 attempts.

During his time with the Chargers, John missed only 4 extra point attempts. In seven of his eleven seasons he did not miss a single try. He was also known as one of league's most consistent field-goal kickers during that time.

NFL Statistics

Season	GP	FGA	FGM	XP	TP
1988	4	5	2	6	12
1989	1	0	0	0	0
1990	13	21	19	27	84
1991	16	29	19	31	88
1992	16	32	26	35	113
1993	16	40	31	31	124
1994	16	38	34	33	135
1995	16	26	21	32	95
1996	16	36	29	31	118
1997	4	7	7	5	26
1998	16	30	26	19	97
1999	16	36	31	22	115
2000	16	25	18	27	81
2001	15	31	27	32	113
2002	16	35	31	37	130
2003	16	30	22	36	102
2004	16	27	22	38	104
2005	16	32	25	22	97
2006	16	25	23	20	115
2007	13	14	12	27	63
2008	15	38	35	38	143
Totals	289	557	460	575	1,955

Notes: GP = games played; FGA = field goals attempted; FGM = field goals made; XP = extra points; TP = total points

Continuing the Story

In 2001, John left the Chargers and signed as a free agent with the New Orleans Saints. He spent six successful seasons with the team. In five of those years, he scored more than 100 points; he missed only one regular-season game.

He set several Saints team records, including most points in a season, 130; consecutive games with a field goal, 22; most field goals in a season, 31. Furthermore, he ranked first in Saints history with an 83 percent field-goal average. As of 2008, he was second in Saints history with 661 points and 150 field goals.

New Orleans signed a new kicker for the 2007 season, and John sought employment elsewhere. He was not signed immediately but joined the Jacksonville Jaguars after kicker Josh Scobee was injured in the first game of the season. John played in eight games with Jacksonville but was released when Scobee returned. John played the final five games of 2007 with the Kansas City Chiefs.

As of 2008, John had played in 272 career games and ranked fourth in scoring in NFL history with 1,749 points, trailing only Morten Andersen (2,445), Gary Anderson (2,434), and George Blanda (2,002). John was one of only three players with more than 400 career field goals.

In addition to on-field excellence, John was recognized for his exceptional behavior off the field. In 1999, he was nominated by the Chargers as NFL man of the year because of his service to his community. He led many NFL programs to benefit children in the communities in which he has lived and played. Notre Dame also recognized him with the Moose Krause Award for his outstanding community service.

Milestones

NFL Pro Bowl, 1994
Fourth most points in NFL history, 1,749
Third kicker in NFL history to compile 400 or more field goals (Morten Andersen, Gary Anderson)
Most points in a season, New Orleans Saints, 130
Most field goals in a season, New Orleans Saints, 31
Most games with a field goal, New Orleans Saints, 22
Highest field-goal percentage, New Orleans Saints, .833, 135 (1994)

Summary

Over his lengthy career, John Carney made more than 80 percent of his field-goal attempts and nearly 99 percent of points after touchdowns. John's professional career did not come easily. He had been out of college for three full seasons before he became a starting kicker in the NFL. He trained hard to maintain excellence throughout his lengthy career and is regarded as one of the greatest kickers in the history of the NFL.

Michael Coulter

Additional Sources

Heisler, Karen Croake. *Fighting Irish: Legends, Lists, and Lore.* Champaign, Ill.: Sports, 2006.
Somogyi, Lou. "The All-Time Notre Dame Team." *Sports Illustrated*, September 20, 2006, 50.

Cris Carter

Born: November 25, 1965
     Troy, Ohio
Also known as: Christopher D. Carter (full name)

Early Life

Christopher D. Carter was born in Troy, Ohio, on November 25, 1965. He grew up in a poor family, headed by a single mother who raised six children in the housing projects of Middletown, Ohio. Cris became interested in sports at an early age. He competed in organized sports and, informally, against his three brothers and two sisters. As a teen-ager, Cris's favorite sport was basketball. He played both basketball and football for Middletown High School.

The Road to Excellence

Cris was a good basketball player but excelled at football. His poverty, however, made the process of college recruiting difficult, as his family did not have a telephone. This obstacle was overcome, and he received a scholarship to play football for Ohio State University. He became a great wide receiver for the team. In his three college seasons, he was twice named to the all-Big Ten Conference team. At the end of his Ohio State career, he was the team's all-time leader in catches, with 168, and touchdown receptions, with 27. In 1986, his final season with the team, he set single-season records with 11 touchdown receptions and 1,127 receiving yards.

Cris was not permitted to return for his senior year, as he violated rules for college players established by the National Collegiate Athletic Association. He was talented enough, however, to be drafted into the NFL. The Philadelphia Eagles picked Cris in the fourth round of the 1987 supplemental draft. Cris's first catch as a professional player was for a touchdown. During his three seasons with the Eagles, however, his performance was inconsistent. During that time, he experienced multiple personal problems, as he struggled with drugs and alcohol. After the 1989 season, the Eagles waived him.

The Emerging Champion

In 1990, Cris was acquired by the Minnesota Vikings. During his

Wide receiver Cris Carter gaining yardage after a catch. (Greg Trott/NFL/ Getty Images)

NFL Milestones

Second most career pass receptions, 1,101
Third most pass receptions in a season, 122 (1994)
Third most seasons with at least 1,000 yards receiving, 8 (record shared)
Second most career touchdowns, 130
Third most touchdowns in a season, 17

Honors and Awards

1986	Ohio State University team most valuable player
1990's	NFL All-Decade Team
1993-2000	NFL Pro Bowl
1994, 1995, 1999	NFL All-Pro selection
1999	Walter Payton Award
2000	Member of the Ohio State Football All-Century Team
2003	Uniform number 80 retired by the Minnesota Vikings
	Inducted into the Ohio State Varsity "O" Hall of Fame
	Inducted into Vikings' Ring of Honor

twelve seasons with the Vikings, he developed into one of the best wide receivers in professional football. He was known for stretching out his entire body to catch the ball with his fingertips, while keeping his tiptoes in the playing field. Furthermore, he developed all-around skills at the wide receiver position. He excelled at eluding defenders by running precise routes. In 1993, Cris had the first of eight consecutive seasons with at least 1,000 receiving yards. In 1994, he set the then-NFL record for receptions in a season, with 122, and was named to the all-pro team.

In 1995, Cris duplicated his previous season's number of receptions and again made the all-pro team. His tremendous performance and leadership helped the Vikings become a consistently good team. In Cris's twelve years with the team, the Vikings made the playoffs eight times. In 1998 and 2000, Cris played an important role on teams that went to the National Football Conference Championship game. In 1998, the Vikings had the best regular-season record in the league, going 15-1. When his time with the team ended in 2001, Cris held numerous Vikings' records, with 1,004 receptions, 110 touchdown catches, 12,383 receiving yards, and forty 100-yard receiving games.

Continuing the Story

While Cris improved his football skills with the Vikings, he also successfully addressed his personal problems. In 1996, he was ordained as a minister.

As his personal life improved, he became a leader of the team. He helped mentor teammate Randy Moss. In 1999, Cris was named to the all-pro team for the fourth time. Later, he was named to the NFL's all-decade team for the 1990's.

Cris also became heavily involved in charitable causes. He formed Christian Athletes United for Spiritual Empowerment (CAUSE). He also cofounded the Carter-White Charitable Foundation. Eventually, he was recognized for such efforts; in 1999, he received the NFL's man of the year award, given to a player for his humanitarian actions. In addition to his charitable actions, in the late 1990's Cris established the FAST program—a training facility used by hundreds of athletes, including professionals—in Boca Raton, Florida.

Following the 2001 season, Cris was let go by the Vikings. He ended his career with the Miami Dolphins, playing with the team in the 2002 season. After retiring from playing football, he began a broadcasting career, serving as an analyst on HBO's *Inside the NFL*. He also became a businessman, serving as a co-owner of Carter Brothers L.L.C., a project management company. In 2003, he was inducted into the Vikings' Ring of Honor and had his jersey number, 80, retired. In 2008, he was a finalist for the Pro Football Hall of Fame in Canton,

NFL Statistics

Season	GP	Rec.	Yds.	Avg.	TD
1987	9	5	84	16.8	2
1988	16	39	761	19.5	6
1989	16	45	605	13.4	11
1990	16	27	413	15.3	3
1991	16	72	962	13.4	5
1992	12	53	681	12.8	6
1993	16	86	1,071	12.5	9
1994	16	122	1,256	10.3	7
1995	16	122	1,371	11.2	17
1996	16	96	1,163	12.1	10
1997	16	89	1,069	12.0	13
1998	16	78	1,011	13.0	12
1999	16	90	1,241	13.8	13
2000	16	96	1,274	13.3	9
2001	16	73	871	11.9	6
2002	5	8	66	8.3	1
Totals	**234**	**1,101**	**13,899**	**12.6**	**130**

Notes: GP = games played; Rec. = receptions; Yds. = yards; Avg. = average yards per reception; TD = touchdowns

Ohio. He ranked second on the NFL's list for receptions in a career, with 1,101, and touchdown receptions in a career, with 130. He compiled 13,899 career receiving yards. In 2008, he joined ESPN as an analyst.

Summary

Cris Carter overcame poverty and personal problems to become one of the best wide receivers in the history of football. His commitment to training and conditioning made him a model for other athletes, no matter the sport. He also achieved success off the football field, becoming a broadcaster, businessman, teacher, coach, and philanthropist.

Kevin L. Brennan

Additional Sources

Carter, Butch, and Cris Carter. *Born to Believe*. Halifax, N.S.: Full Wits, 2000.

Dillon, Dennis. "Show of Hands: Football Player Cris Carter." *The Sporting News* (October 30, 2000).

Hooley, Bruce. *OSU's Unforgettables*. Champaign, Ill.: Sports, 2002.

Dutch Clark

Born: October 11, 1906
    Fowler, Colorado
Died: August 5, 1978
    Cañon City, Colorado
Also known as: Earl Harry Clark (full name);
    the Flying Dutchman

Early Life

Earl Harry "Dutch" Clark was born on October 11, 1906, on a farm near Fowler, Colorado. The fourth of five children born to Harry J. and Mary Etta Clark, he was given the nickname "Dutch" at birth. His two older brothers were also called Dutch.

Dutch Clark. (Courtesy of Amateur Athletic Foundation of Los Angeles)

They were referred to as "Big Dutch," brother Carl, "Dutch," brother Fred, and "Little Dutch," Earl. However, Earl made the nickname famous. The Clark family moved to Pueblo, Colorado, when Dutch was very young.

The Road to Excellence

Dutch began his journey to excellence when he entered Central High School in Pueblo, at the age of seventeen. In three years, he earned a total of sixteen letters in four sports. He made the Colorado all-state teams in football and basketball, and was named all-American in basketball. In 1926, Dutch's Central High School basketball team played in the Stagg National Interscholastic Finals in Chicago. Football, though, became Dutch's strength. The 175-pound center was converted to a back by his high school coaches. During his three seasons at Central, he scored a total of 298 points. He helped lead the Central Wildcats to South-Central League titles in 1924 and 1925. Going unbeaten in the 1925 season, Central met and defeated Littleton, Colorado, in the opening playoff game, 58-3, with Dutch scoring five touchdowns. Dutch's accomplishments during his three seasons at Central gave him fame as the greatest high school athlete in the history of Colorado.

Dutch's philosophy helped make him a great athlete. His sister Pearl described him as believing that he could never take anything for granted, that only through hard work and intense training could he excel in sports. Dutch was definitely serious about sports.

The Emerging Champion

Though Dutch was recruited by football powers such as the University of Michigan, he elected to attend Northwestern University. However, he left Northwestern after only one week with a bad case of homesickness. He then enrolled in small Colorado College, where he played freshman football in 1926, and joined the varsity in 1927. As a football player at Colorado College, Dutch became a national figure.

Dutch was switched to quarterback by Coach Hans Van de Graaff and began to become known in college football. In his junior year, he rushed for 1,359 yards in only 135 carries and earned all-American honors from the Associated Press, becoming the first Coloradan so honored. In a game against the University of Wyoming, Dutch carried for 381 yards, completed 8 of 15 passes for 200 more yards, and scored 36 points as Colorado won 48-25.

In his senior year, Dutch scored all the points in a 3-2 victory over the University of Denver. Dutch's squad was unable to make any headway in the first half. In the second half, Dutch, who was also the team's punter, dropped back in the end zone to punt. He was tackled hard, giving Denver a safety and 2 points. Dutch tried in vain to move the ball against Denver's defense, but with only 90 seconds remaining he drop-kicked from the 38-yard line. The ball traveled over the upright, not between, and the referee signaled the kick no good. Dutch called time out and got the referee's attention. Coach Van de Graaff convinced the referee that a field goal is good even if the kick does not split the upright, and persuaded the referee to reverse his decision, giving Colorado the win. In 1930, Dutch ended his collegiate football career by participating in the East-West Shrine Game and graduated from Colorado with a bachelor's degree in biology.

Honors and Awards

1926-30	All-Rocky Mountain Conference Team (football)
	All-Rocky Mountain Conference Team (basketball)
1928	Associated Press All-American
1930	East-West Shrine Game team captain
	All-Rocky Mountain Conference Team (baseball)
	All-Rocky Mountain Conference Team (track)
1931-32, 1934-37	NFL All-Pro Team
1951	Inducted into College Football Hall of Fame
1963	NFL All-Pro Team of the 1930's
	Inducted into Pro Football Hall of Fame
1973	Inducted into Greater Pueblo Sports Association Hall of Fame
1989	Inducted into Colorado High School Activity Association Hall of Fame
	Uniform number 7 retired by Detroit Lions

Dutch began his professional football career with the Portsmouth, Ohio, Spartans of the NFL. Times were hard in Portsmouth during the Depression. More fans showed up for practice than for the games, and from time to time the players got paychecks only to find there was no money in the bank to cover them.

Dutch led the NFL in scoring in 1932, 1935, and 1936. During the 1933 season he bowed out of professional football briefly to become the athletic director and football and basketball coach at the University of Colorado, but he soon returned to the NFL. In 1934, the Portsmouth franchise moved to Detroit and became the Lions. That year, Dutch was named all-pro quarterback for the third time. In 1935, Dutch helped lead the Lions to an NFL title.

Dutch ended his playing career with the Lions in 1938 while serving as one of the last player-coaches in the NFL. Known as the "Flying Dutchman" during his professional playing days, he was often considered to be the greatest triple-threat back of his era. He was not only a running back but also the team's passer and field-goal kicker. In addition, he was a safety on defense.

Continuing the Story

Dutch stayed in professional football through the next thirteen years. He coached the Cleveland Rams for four years before joining the coaching staff of the Pacific Coast Professional Foot-

NFL Statistics

Season	GP	Rushing				Receiving			
		Car.	Yds.	Avg.	TD	Rec.	Yds.	Avg.	TD
1932	—	111	461	4.2	2	10	107	10.7	2
1934	—	123	763	6.2	6	7	72	10.3	2
1935	—	120	412	3.4	4	9	124	13.8	2
1936	—	123	628	5.1	6	1	5	5.0	1
1937	—	96	468	4.9	5	2	33	16.5	1
1938	—	7	25	3.6	0	0	0	0.0	0
Totals		580	2,757	4.8	23	29	341	11.8	8

Notes: GP = games played; Car. = carries; Yds. = yards; Avg. = average yards per carry *or* average yards per reception; TD = touchdowns; Rec. = receptions

ball League's (PCPFL's) Seattle Bombers. Dutch ended his professional coaching career with the All-America Football Conference's (AAFC's) Los Angeles Dons.

In 1951, he was appointed head football coach and athletic director at the University of Detroit. He stayed there until 1955, when he resigned to be a representative of a Detroit tool-and-die firm. He retired in 1963 and lived in Royal Oaks, Michigan, until 1976, when he decided to return to his native state. The Clarks built a home in Cañon City, Colorado, where Dutch lived until his death on August 5, 1978.

Summary

Dutch Clark was a quiet, soft-spoken man off the field. He stayed out of the spotlight and avoided admiring fans. On the playing field, though, he was aggressive and confident, a bold leader who made decisions rapidly and with precision. He was a master strategist, constantly probing for a weakness in the opposition. When the Pro Football Hall of Fame opened in 1963, Dutch was made one of the original members in recognition of his many accomplishments.

Jessie F. Banks

Additional Sources

Carroll, Bob. *Total Football: The Official Encyclopedia of the National Football League.* New York: Harper-Collins, 1999.

"Clark, Dutch." *American National Biography* 4 (1999).

Peterson, Robert. *Pigskin: The Early Years of Pro Football.* New York: Oxford University Press, 1997.

Porter, David L., ed. *Biographical Dictionary of American Sports: Football.* Westport, Conn.: Greenwood Press, 1987.

Willis, Chris. *Old Leather: An Oral History of Early Pro Football in Ohio, 1920-1935.* Lanham, Md.: Scarecrow Press, 2005.

Larry Csonka

Born: December 25, 1946
     Stow, Ohio
Also known as: Lawrence Richard Csonka (full
    name); the Lawnmower; Zonk

Early Life

Lawrence Richard Csonka was born on Christmas Day in 1946, in the working-class town of Stow, Ohio. He was raised on a farm near Stow along with his older brother, Joe, by his mother, Mildred, and his father, Joseph.

Larry was known for his hard work around the farm. His nose was first broken by a steer that was frightened while Larry was tending to it. His nose was broken eight more times in football.

When Larry was nine years old, his father took him to watch his brother, Joe, play in a high school game. His brother played end, and when he caught a pass, Larry was instructed by his dad to take a dollar to his brother on the sideline as a reward. The excitement of the sideline and the players under the lights caught Larry's attention. He wanted to be a football player.

The Road to Excellence

Larry was large for his age, so when it came time for football, the coaches put him on the line. Larry wanted to carry the football, though. He had to fight his way, literally, into the backfield of his high school team. One of Larry's teammates told him to play as a lineman when he came over to the running backs to practice. An argument and a fight followed, and Larry remained mostly on the line until he ran back a kickoff in a varsity game as a sophomore. Larry ran over everyone in his path. From then on, he was the varsity fullback.

After high school, Larry attended Syracuse University. There, too, the coaches wanted Larry to be a lineman on defense.

One Syracuse coach later said putting Larry on the line was the worst mistake he ever made. He also said that the smartest move he ever made was to put Larry back on offense.

Larry was not a great student in college. He overcame obstacles with hard work. He married during his sophomore year in college and supported his family by working nights, even during football season.

Larry broke all the rushing records at Syracuse, including those set by Jim Brown, Ernie Davis, and

Larry Csonka, whose bruising running style was a primary reason for the Miami Dolphins' undefeated season in 1972. (Focus on Sport/Getty Images)

Floyd Little. He was all-American as a junior and senior, and he was the first player named the outstanding player in both the 1968 college all-star game and the coaches' all-American game.

The Emerging Champion

Larry was the first running back chosen in the 1968 American Football League (AFL) draft. The Miami Dolphins signed him as a fullback. After the 1969 season, Don Shula became head coach of the Dolphins and began to build a football dynasty. Larry was the cornerstone. His powerful running forced opponents to play tight defenses, which allowed Larry's talented Dolphin teammates Bob Griese, Paul Warfield, Mercury Morris, and Jim Kiick more room to operate.

Shula worked the team very hard, especially Larry. They developed a mutual respect. Larry said that the games were fun, but it was the practices for which he was paid.

Larry became known as the one of the finest fullbacks ever, on one of the best teams ever. He reminded people of Bronko Nagurski with his power, quickness, and aggressiveness. Larry often carried would-be tacklers with him as he ran. At times he seemed to look for an opponent to run over as he carried the ball. His battering style resulted in several injuries to his head, elbow, and back. Even when Larry was hobbled, his teammates could still

count on him to help them win. He claimed the pain did not bother him much, because it proved he had contributed in the game.

Continuing the Story

In 1972, the Dolphins went undefeated and won the Super Bowl. The next year they lost only two games and again won the Super Bowl, and "Zonk" was named the game's most valuable player. With all of his success, Larry remained humble. After the 1974 Super Bowl, Larry said "What I do around here is no big deal. We have a great offensive line." He and Jim Kiick became known for a time as "Butch Cassidy and the Sundance Kid." They were close friends and exciting athletes. Even so, when Kiick was replaced by Mercury Morris, Larry remained a team player and helped Morris to succeed just as he had helped Kiick.

In 1974, Larry and two of his teammates were signed away from the Dolphins by a team in the newly formed World Football League (WFL). Larry played one season for the Memphis Southmen of the WFL, but the new league had immediate financial troubles. When the league folded, Larry returned to the NFL and signed with the New York Giants. He played little with the Giants as a result of a severe

AFL, NFL, and WFL Statistics

Season	GP	Rushing Car.	Yds.	Avg.	TD	Receiving Rec.	Yds.	Avg.	TD
1968	11	138	540	3.9	6	11	118	10.7	1
1969	11	131	566	4.3	2	21	183	8.7	1
1970	14	193	874	4.5	6	11	94	8.5	0
1971	14	195	1,051	5.4	7	13	113	8.7	1
1972	14	213	1,117	5.2	6	5	48	9.6	0
1973	14	219	1,003	4.6	5	7	22	3.1	0
1974	12	197	749	3.8	9	7	35	5.0	0
1975	7	99	421	4.3	1	5	54	10.8	1
1976	12	160	569	3.6	4	6	39	6.5	0
1977	14	134	464	3.5	1	2	20	10.0	0
1978	16	91	311	3.4	6	7	73	10.4	0
1979	16	220	837	3.8	12	16	75	4.7	1
NFL-AFL Totals	148	1,891	8,081	4.3	64	106	820	7.7	4
WFL Totals	7	99	421	4.3	1	5	54	10.8	1

Notes: GP = games played; Car. = carries; Yds. = yards; Avg. = average yards per carry *or* average yards per reception; TD = touchdowns; Rec. = receptions

Honors, Awards, and Records

1967-68	College All-American
1968	Chicago College All-Star Game Outstanding Player
	Coaches' All-American Game Outstanding Player
	Overall first choice in the AFL draft
1971-73	*Sporting News* AFC All-Star Team
1971-75	NFL Pro Bowl Team
1973	NFL record for the most touchdowns in a postseason game, 3 (record shared)
1974	NFL Super Bowl most valuable player
1980	NFL All-Pro Team of the 1970's
1987	Inducted into Pro Football Hall of Fame
1989	Inducted into College Football Hall of Fame

knee injury. Larry finished his career by playing one final season with the Dolphins in 1979. He made a great comeback by rushing for 837 yards and 12 touchdowns, and he helped lead Miami to a division title. He finished his career with 8,081 yards rushing in twelve pro seasons. Larry was voted into the Pro Football Hall of Fame in 1987.

Summary

Larry Csonka was arguably the best fullback ever to play football. He was a powerful and bruising ball carrier, a team player, and a champion. After his retirement Larry became involved in professional football's labor disputes, and in that arena, too, his forcefulness helped make him one of the game's most respected figures.

Kevin R. Lasley

Additional Sources

Carroll, Bob. *Total Football: The Official Encyclopedia of the National Football League.* New York: Harper-Collins, 1999.

Deitsch, Richard, Mark Bechtel, and Stephen Cannella. "Q and A: Larry Csonka." *Sports Illustrated* 103, no. 21 (November 28, 2005): 28-29.

Hyde, Dave, and Don Shula. *Still Perfect! The Untold Story of the 1972 Miami Dolphins.* Miami Springs, Fla.: Dolphin Curtis, 2002.

Randall Cunningham

Born: March 27, 1963
        Santa Barbara, California
Also known as: Rocket Man; Rockin' Randall
    Cunningham; Starship 12; the Ultimate
    Weapon

Early Life

Randall Cunningham was born on March 27, 1963, in Santa Barbara, California, to Samuel Cunningham, a porter on the Southern Pacific Railroad, and Mabel Cunningham, a nurse. Randall spent his childhood in Santa Barbara, a coastal city about one hundred miles north of Los Angeles.

The Cunninghams were an athletic family. Randall's brother Sam played at the University of Southern California (USC) as a running back and later had a long professional career. At Santa Barbara High School, Randall became a star quickly. He played quarterback and defensive back and also punted for the team, which won a league championship in Randall's junior year.

The Road to Excellence

Randall developed his wide-open, scrambling style of quarterbacking in high school. Many college recruiters were wary of his flashy style, however, fearing he was too undisciplined to run a college-level offense. USC offered him a scholarship as a defensive back, but Randall wanted to play quarterback, so he chose to attend the University of Nevada at Las Vegas (UNLV), the only school that guaranteed him a chance to compete for the starting job at that position.

The college years were difficult at first for Randall. His mother died of cancer in November of 1981, and his father passed away a year later after a heart attack.

On the football field, Randall adjusted to the rigors of the college game. He continued to be a versatile player, handling the quarterbacking duties and the punting for the Rebels during his varsity career. Randall became only the third player to pass for more than 2,500

yards for three straight seasons in college; the other two were former Heisman Trophy winner Doug Flutie of Boston College and Stanford's John Elway.

The Emerging Champion

A professional career awaited Randall. Following his standout career at UNLV, Randall was selected by the Philadelphia Eagles in the second round of the 1985 NFL draft.

The mid-1980's were a period of transition for the Eagles. The team had been to the Super Bowl in 1980, but many of the players were getting old,

Randall Cunningham passing for the Minnesota Vikings during the 1998 season. (AP/Wide World Photos)

NFL Statistics

Season	GP	PA	PC	Pct.	Yds.	Avg.	TD	Int.
1985	6	81	34	42.0	548	6.77	1	8
1986	15	209	111	53.1	1,391	6.66	8	7
1987	12	406	223	54.9	2,786	6.86	23	12
1988	16	560	301	53.8	3,808	6.80	24	16
1989	16	532	290	54.5	3,400	6.39	21	15
1990	16	465	271	58.3	3,466	7.45	30	13
1991	1	4	1	25.0	19	4.75	0	0
1992	15	384	233	60.7	2,775	7.23	19	11
1993	4	110	76	69.1	850	7.73	5	5
1994	14	490	265	54.1	3,229	6.59	16	13
1995	7	121	69	57.0	605	5.00	3	5
1997	6	88	44	50.0	501	5.69	6	4
1998	16	425	259	60.9	3,704	8.72	34	10
1999	7	200	124	62.0	1,475	7.38	8	9
2000	6	125	74	59.2	849	6.79	6	4
2001	6	89	54	60.7	573	6.4	3	2
Totals	163	4,289	2,429	56.6	29,979	7.0	207	134

Notes: GP = games played; PA = passes attempted; PC = passes completed; Pct. = percent completed; Yds. = yards; Avg. = average yards per attempt; TD = touchdowns; Int. = interceptions

and younger players such as Randall were coming in to replace them. Randall played only occasionally in his first two seasons, backing up aging veteran Ron Jaworski. Eagles coach Buddy Ryan often used Randall as the quarterback on third-and-long plays, on which Randall was able to use his scrambling ability and strong arm to pick up the necessary yardage for a first down.

In 1987, Randall first began to learn about the excitement—and the pain—inherent in his role as a starting quarterback in the NFL. He was named the starter at the beginning of the season and played in twelve of the sixteen games. He completed almost 55 percent of his passes, threw for 23 touchdowns, and rushed for 505 yards and 3 more touchdowns. However, the news was not all good. The Eagles' young offensive line did not provide much protection, and Randall was sacked 72 times, an NFL record at the time. Still, his 23 touchdown passes were the third-best mark in the conference, and his 505 rushing yards led the team.

Continuing the Story

The 1988 season was Randall's breakthrough year. He played in all sixteen games as the Eagles' starter, tossed 24 touchdown passes, and threw for more than 3,800 yards. He also rushed for more than 600 yards and added another half-dozen touchdowns on the ground. For his efforts, he was selected to the NFC Pro Bowl team, and he was voted the most valuable player in the annual postseason contest in Hawaii.

Randall was rapidly becoming known throughout the league as a dangerous runner and passer. Opponents simply could not get to him the way they had in years past. When he had time to pass, Randall was deadly; if the pass rush forced him out of the pocket, Randall hurt teams with his running. "He may be the best athlete ever to play the (quarterback) position," said Buddy Ryan, the Eagles' head coach at the time. To let everyone know how much he valued his prize quarterback, Ryan jokingly referred to Randall as "The Boss" and then designed his whole offensive scheme to take advantage of his star quarterback's abilities.

Randall also was voted to the Pro Bowl after the 1989-1990 and 1990-1991 seasons. He continued to improve; in 1990-1991, he completed 58 percent of his passes, tossed a career-best 30 touchdowns, and rushed for an amazing 942 yards. The 1,000-yard milestone is considered the mark of an excellent running back, and Randall nearly reached that level while playing at quarterback.

Randall lost the 1991-1992 season to a knee injury, but he rebounded in 1992-1993 to throw 19 touchdown passes and run for 5 more touchdowns.

Honors and Awards

1984	College All-American
1988	Professional Football Writers Association's NFL Player of the Year
1988, 1990, 1998	Bert Bell Award
1988-90, 1998	NFC Pro Bowl Team
1988	NFL Pro Bowl most valuable player
1990	United Press International Player of the Year
	Professional Football Writers Association NFL most valuable player
1992	NFL Comeback Player of the Year
1998	Pro Bowl Team

In 1993-1994, the talented Eagles were expected to contend for the Super Bowl title and got off to a fast start, but in the fourth game, Randall was injured again. He missed the remainder of the season, and the Eagles stumbled to an 8-8 record, leaving fans to hope for better things when he returned.

Randall sat out the 1996 season in retirement but came back in 1997, playing for the Minnesota Vikings. He led the Vikings to new heights, especially in 1998, when he passed for more than 3,000 yards. That same year, Randall led the league with a 106.0 quarterback rating. He won the Bert Bell Award. He was only the second quarterback, after Johnny Unitas, to receive the trophy three times. On June 2, 2000, Randall was released by the Vikings, but he was signed a few days later by the Dallas Cowboys to a three-year deal that included a $500,000 signing bonus and a $500,000 salary for the 2000 season.

Randall played sparingly for one year for Dallas, starting in three games and appearing in three others. He completed 74 passes for 849 yards and 6 touchdowns and 4 interceptions. His completion percentage was over 60 percent, above his career average. In addition, he rushed for 89 yards on 23 attempts, scoring one touchdown. In 2001, he signed with the Baltimore Ravens but made only two starts and four other appearances. He passed for 573 yards in 54 attempts, throwing 3 touchdowns and 2 interceptions; he rushed for 40 yards and 1 touchdown in 14 attempts.

After the season, Randall retired for the second, and final, time. He played 163 games, starting 135, in sixteen NFL seasons—eleven with Philadelphia. A four-time all-pro, he completed 2,429 passes for 29,979 yards, with 207 touchdowns and 134 interceptions. His completion percentage was 56.6 and his quarterback rating 81.5. He also had rushed for 4,928 yards in 775 attempts, scoring 35 touchdowns.

After retirement, Randall returned to the University of Nevada, Las Vegas to finish his degree. He opened a music production business called Studio 7. In 2004, he reconfirmed his religious faith by becoming a born-again Christian. He was ordained as a minister, becoming a senior pastor at Remnant Ministries nondenominational church in Las Vegas. The church also served as a recording studio for Christian music and hosted live concerts. Randall also coached high and broad jump for a Las Vegas high school.

Summary

Randall Cunningham brought to professional football a combination of passing and running ability not often seen in a quarterback. Those abilities helped him become one of the most exciting offensive weapons in the NFL and a stylistic predecessor of quarterbacks such as Michael Vick and Donovan McNabb.

John McNamara, updated by Frederick B. Chary

Additional Sources

Cunningham, Randall, and Steve Wartenberg. *I'm Still Scrambling*. New York: Doubleday, 1993.

Lawrence, Andrew. "Catching up with Randall Cunningham, Quarterback." *Sports Illustrated* 103, no. 19 (November 14, 2005): 16.

Murphy, Austin. "Pro Football: Second Coming Rejuvenated After a Year in Retirement, Randall Cunningham Is Setting the League on Its Ear and Leading the Vikings to New Heights." *Sports Illustrated* 86, no. 23 (December 7, 1998): 36-41.

"Randall Cunningham." In *Who's Who Among African Americans*. 21st ed. Farmington Hills, Mich.: Gale, 2008.

Ernie Davis

Born: December 14, 1939
New Salem, Pennsylvania
Died: May 18, 1963
Cleveland, Ohio
Also known as: Ernest R. Davis (full name);
Elmira Express

Early Life
Ernie Davis was born on December 14, 1939, in New Salem, a small town in the coal-rich southwest corner of Pennsylvania. Ernie's father was killed in

an accident before Ernie was born, and so, when Ernie was fourteen months old, his mother left him to live with his grandparents in nearby Uniontown, Pennsylvania, while she searched for a job to support her only child.

Although Ernie's grandfather worked as a coal miner, it was difficult for him to support the family. He had twelve children of his own, and the family lived in poverty.

Ernie dreamed, as a child, of becoming a professional athlete. His heroes were baseball star Stan Musial and Chicago Bears quarterback Johnny Lujack, men whose athletic skills had helped them escape the coal mines and steel mills of western Pennsylvania, where Ernie grew up.

The Road to Excellence
When Ernie was twelve years old, his mother settled in Elmira, New York, a community that became his adopted home. Even as early as grade school, Ernie displayed the talents that eventually led to greatness. He could run faster, throw harder, and kick farther than anyone else in the school.

Ernie attended Elmira Free Academy High School, where he won eleven varsity letters. Many believed that he was a better basketball player than a football player, and his basketball statistics were certainly impressive. He set the all-Southern Tier Conference career scoring record with 1,605 points, averaging 18.4 points per game. In addition, his team won fifty-two consecutive games during his last two years at the school.

Ernie was a great player who could control a game. However,

Running back Ernie Davis, who flourished at Syracuse University, leading the team to an undefeated season and a national championship in 1959. (National Football Foundation Hall of Fame)

NCAA Statistics

Season	GP	Rushing Car.	Yds.	Avg.	TD
1959	—	98	686	7.0	—
1960	—	114	877	7.7	—
1961	—	150	823	5.5	—
Totals	—	362	2,386	6.6	35

Notes: GP = games played; Car. = carries; Yds. = yards; Avg. = average yards per carry *or* average yards per reception; TD = touchdowns

if his team had a sizable lead, he did not shoot or rebound or, sometimes, play defense. He let other players—even his opponents—have the opportunity to score points and to perform well in the game.

Ernie's ambition, in spite of his basketball successes, had always been to be the best professional football player anywhere. Ernie therefore chose to concentrate on football instead of basketball.

The Emerging Champion

Although he had always dreamed of playing halfback for Notre Dame, Ernie chose to attend Syracuse University from among the thirty colleges that offered him a football scholarship, because he felt that Syracuse provided him with the best opportunity to run with the football. Once at Syracuse, he quickly became known as the "Elmira Express" because of his running ability.

Ernie wore number 44, the same number worn by a previous Syracuse great, Jim Brown. During the three years that Ernie played, he broke most of Brown's records, including marks for total rushing yards, 2,386; yards per carry, 6.6; total touchdowns, 35; and total points, 220.

In his sophomore year, Ernie gained 686 yards and scored 64 points. Those numbers represented totals greater than the combined totals of all ten of Syracuse's opponents that year. Playing both offense and defense, Ernie led the Orangemen to a 23-14 victory over Texas in the Cotton Bowl that year. In that game, he scored 16 of Syracuse's points on 2 touchdowns and 2 two-point conversions, and set up the other touchdown with a pass interception. The win completed an undefeated season and enabled Syracuse to gain the number-one ranking in the country.

In his senior year, Ernie was awarded the Heis-

man Trophy as the best college football player in the United States. He was the first black player ever to receive the award. Perhaps his biggest thrill, though, occurred when President John F. Kennedy shook his hand following the Heisman ceremonies.

Ernie set an example of excellence for others both on and off the field. His grandfather, who had raised him until he was twelve years old, had been a strict disciplinarian, and Ernie's character reflected this upbringing. Ernie was thoughtful and polite. He did not smoke, swear, or drink, and he willingly helped others when they needed assistance. He was a hero to many children, but especially to those in Elmira. At his college graduation, he was selected marshall by his fellow senior students and led his classmates into graduation ceremonies.

Continuing the Story

Playing in the NFL had always been Ernie's dream. When he was drafted by the Cleveland Browns and was going to join Jim Brown in the same backfield, his dream seemed to be realized.

However, Ernie never got to play in the NFL. In July of 1962, Ernie was diagnosed as having leukemia, and he died from this disease in Cleveland, Ohio, on May 18, 1963, at the age of twenty-three.

People still remember his funeral. He was so well respected and liked that thousands of people attended, including almost the entire Cleveland Browns football team. There were lines of mourners two blocks long waiting to pay their respects.

The people of Elmira never forgot Ernie or the courage, sportsmanship, and other good qualities that he displayed. Elmira Free Academy was renamed Ernie Davis Junior High School, and in 1988, to commemorate the twenty-fifth anniversary of Ernie's death, a life-size bronze statue of him was dedicated in front of the school. A city park, located across the street from the school, also

Honors and Awards

1961	Heisman Trophy
	Walter Camp Award
1962	Overall first choice in the NFL draft
1979	Inducted into College Football Hall of Fame
1987	Inducted into Pro Football Hall of Fame
	Uniform number 45 retired by Cleveland Browns

bears his name. Football has not forgotten Ernie either. In 1987, in spite of never having played a down in professional football, Ernie was voted into the Pro Hall of Fame. However, his fame has lived on. In 2008, Rob Brown portrayed Ernie in *The Express*, a feature film celebrating his career.

Summary

Ernie Davis was one of the greatest players in college football history. He set many records at Syracuse University and became the first black player ever to win the Heisman Trophy. His courage and outstanding character made him a hero and an inspiration to many people, but especially to children. His death at a very young age prevented him from playing in the NFL and took away the oppor-

tunity for him to reach even greater heights of achievement.

Stephen Schwartz

Additional Sources

Gallagher, Robert C. *Ernie Davis, the Elmira Express: The Story of a Heisman Trophy Winner.* Silver Spring, Md.: Bartleby, 1999.

Pitoniak, Scott. *Syracuse University Football.* Charleston, S.C.: Arcadia, 2003.

Savage, Jeff. *Top Ten Heisman Trophy Winners.* Springfield, N.J.: Enslow, 1999.

Youmans, Gary, and Maury Youmans. *'59: The Story of the 1959 Syracuse University National Championship Football Team.* Oklahoma City, Okla.: Campbell Road Press, 2003.

Glenn Davis

Born: December 26, 1924
     Claremont, California
Died: March 9, 2005
     La Quinta, California
Also known as: Glenn Woodward Davis (full
    name); Mr. Outside

Early Life

Irma and Ralph Davis received a double surprise on the day after Christmas in 1924. Irma gave birth to twin boys, Ralph, Jr., and Glenn, in Claremont, California. Glenn, who was born nine minutes after his brother, was later nicknamed "Junior." As a teenager growing up in Southern California,

Glenn Davis, who won the Heisman Trophy in 1946 and, along with backfield partner Doc Blanchard, guided Army to undefeated seasons in 1944, 1945, and 1946. (Courtesy of Amateur Athletic Foundation of Los Angeles)

Glenn developed into a fine all-around athlete. He was a fast sprinter in track, a strong-armed center fielder in baseball, and a swift runner in football. At Bonita High School, he played four varsity sports, baseball, football, basketball, and track, and earned sixteen varsity letters. Glenn was not only chosen to a high school all-star team in baseball, but he also won the Knute Rockne Trophy as Southern California's best high school track performer in 1943. Football was Glenn's ticket to greatness, however. In his senior year, he scored a remarkable 236 points and was chosen football player of the year in his conference.

The Road to Excellence

After graduating from high school, Glenn and twin brother Ralph were appointed to the United States Military Academy at West Point in 1943. Glenn quickly established himself as one of the greatest athletes to enter West Point. He scored a record 962.5 points out of a possible 1,000 in the Army Master of the Sword physical fitness test. In his first year, Glenn failed a mathematics course and was forced to drop out. He was disappointed, but he worked hard in mathematics at another college to catch up. His work paid off, and Glenn was permitted to reenter West Point in 1944.

By 1944, Army football coach Earl "Red" Blaik had assembled a powerful football team, including gifted quarterbacks Doug Kenna and Arnold Tucker, as well as strong tackle DeWitt "Tex" Coulter and talented end Barney Poole. A powerful fullback from South Carolina, Felix "Doc" Blanchard, also joined the team. Glenn and Blanchard formed a running duo that became legendary in college football. Glenn, an all-around player, was known for excelling at receiving, passing, blocking, and defending. With his exceptional speed and powerful leg drive, he was superb at shedding tacklers, leaving them floundering in his wake.

The Emerging Champion

Glenn and Blanchard complemented each other perfectly. Glenn, smaller than Blanchard at 5 feet 9 inches and 170 pounds, was a fast and elusive open-field runner. At 6 feet and 205 pounds, Blanchard was a classic power fullback and blocker who shredded opposing defensive lines for yardage. Later known as "Mr. Inside," Blanchard, and "Mr. Outside," Davis, this remarkable pair's glory days had just begun.

In their sophomore year, Glenn and Blanchard led Army to an undefeated season. They destroyed opposing teams by scores of 83-0, 76-0, 69-7, and 59-0. Glenn and Blanchard became known as the "Touchdown Twins." Glenn scored 20 touchdowns that year and averaged an incredible 11 yards each time he carried the ball. In other words, he averaged a first down each time he ran. Glenn's spectacular year earned him the Maxwell Award and Walter Camp Award as player of the year. He also made the Helms Athletic Foundation All-Time All-American team.

The next two seasons were more of the same. Army was the national champion in 1945 and tied for the title in 1946. Glenn starred in every game. In fact, he never once played in a losing game during his three years with the team. As a result, he was repeatedly chosen as an all-American and won the coveted Heisman Trophy. Glenn scored 59 touchdowns, an average of nearly 2 per game. Blaik hailed Glenn as the best player he had ever seen. In addition, many football authorities have rated the

NCAA Statistics

Season	GP	Rushing Car.	Yds.	Avg.	TD	Receiving Rec.	Yds.	Avg.	TD
1943	95	634	6.7	7	—	—	—	—	1
1944	58	667	11.5	14	—	—	—	—	4
1945	82	944	11.5	15	—	—	—	—	3
1946	123	712	5.8	7	—	—	—	—	6
Totals	358	2,957	8.3	43	—	—	—	—	14

Notes: GP = games played; Car. = carries; Yds. = yards; Avg. = average yards per carry *or* average yards per reception; TD = touchdowns; Rec. = receptions

1945 Army team as the best college team ever. After finishing second in Heisman Trophy balloting two years in a row, Glenn finally won the trophy in 1946. That same year he was also named college player of the year by *The Sporting News* and was voted male athlete of the year by the Associated Press.

Continuing the Story

Glenn was a dedicated athlete who trained hard. He was the epitome of the clean-cut, all-American athlete. Because of his tremendous running speed, Glenn was offered a contract to play baseball with the Brooklyn Dodgers in 1947, but he turned it down.

After graduating from West Point, Glenn was required to serve in the U.S. Army until 1950. Consequently, his professional football career was postponed. After serving in Korea, Glenn resigned his Army commission in 1950 to give pro football a try.

As the best running back in college football history, Glenn joined the Los Angeles Rams and became an important part of a great team. He led the team in rushing and receiving and was a runner-up for the rookie of the year award. An old knee injury began to hamper him, and he retired from football in 1952.

A year later, Glenn married Harriet Lancaster. He had one son, Ralph, and a stepson, John Slack. After retiring from pro football, Glenn accepted a position as promotions director for the *Los Angeles Times* newspaper. He directed special events for the paper and administered the paper's charitable fund-raising activities. In 1961, he was chosen for the National Football Foundation's College Football Hall of Fame.

A contented man, Glenn considered himself lucky to have accomplished all that he did.

Honors and Awards

1944	Associated Press Outstanding College Football Player
	Maxwell Award
	Walter Camp Award
	Consensus All-American
	Helms Athletic Foundation All-Time All-American Team
1944, 1946	Citizens Savings College Football Player of the Year
1945	World Trophy
	Citizens Savings Southern California Athlete of the Year
1945-46	Unanimous All-American
1946	Heisman Trophy
	Sporting News College Player of the Year
	Associated Press Male Athlete of the Year
1951	NFL Pro Bowl Team
1961	Inducted into College Football Hall of Fame

Eventually, Glenn gave his Heisman Trophy to his alma mater, Bonita High School in La Verne, California. In turn, the high school's football stadium was renamed Glenn Davis Stadium in honor of the distinguished alumnus.

Summary

One of the fastest running backs in college football history, Glenn Davis was also one of the best. He and Doc Blanchard combined to form one of the most potent running combinations of all time. The two backs led Army to three straight undefeated football seasons. Glenn's great talent, combined with his dedication, made him a terrific athlete and an inspiration to all players of the game.

Nan White

Additional Sources

Bradley, Michael. *Big Games: College Football's Greatest Rivalries.* Washington, D.C.: Potomac Books, 2006.

Pennington, Bill. *The Heisman: Great American Stories of the Men Who Won.* New York: ReganBooks, 2004.

Sugar, Bert R. *The One Hundred Greatest Athletes of All Time.* New York: Citadel Press, 1995.

Terrell Davis

Born: October 28, 1972
   San Diego, California
Also known as: Terrell Lamar Davis (full name);
   TD; Boss Hog

Early Life

Denver Broncos running back Terrell Davis achieved football stardom despite taking a perilous road to the NFL. Born on October 28, 1972, Terrell was the youngest of six boys. Growing up in east San Diego, California, Terrell played Little League at first. Then he discovered the joys of Pop Warner League football, earning the nickname "Boss Hog" for his tenacious playing style. In 1986, when Terrell was fourteen, his father, John, died of lupus, leaving his mother, Kateree, to raise the rambunctious boys.

Money, according to Terrell's recollections, was hard to come by, but he always believed that sports were his ticket to bigger and better things. His first chance to prove that came when he transferred from Morse High School to Lincoln Prep in San Diego. He played six different positions at Lincoln, including nose guard, before he graduated in 1990. Although he was destined to become a running back in college, Terrell scored only three touchdowns during his whole high school career.

The Road to Excellence

Encouraged by his older brother Reggie, Terrell earned a scholarship to California State University, Long Beach, where, as a redshirt freshman, he played for legendary coach George Allen. Terrell's running ability and tenacity was apparent to Allen, who began to groom Terrell. Adversity struck when Allen died of a heart attack after the 1990 season, and the Long Beach football program was dismantled. Terrell reluctantly transferred to the University of Georgia, which used a passing offense that did not showcase Terrell's speed. Playing for three seasons, Terrell, at 5 feet 11 inches and 210 pounds, still finished his career at Georgia with 1,657 yards on 317 carries, for a 5.2 average, and 15 touchdowns. He also caught 46 passes

for 529 yards and 4 touchdowns. As a senior, he led the team with 445 yards and 7 touchdowns on 97 carries, for a 4.6 average, in addition to 31 receptions for 330 yards.

Nevertheless, Terrell did not leave Georgia as a top NFL prospect. In fact, he was selected by the Broncos as the 196th player in the sixth round of the 1995 draft, a placement that usually relegates one to practice-player status, not superstardom.

The Emerging Champion

Undaunted, Terrell took his rookie season by storm, starting fourteen games in the season and rushing for 1,117 yards on 237 carries and 7 touchdowns. He also caught 49 passes for 367 yards and 1 touchdown. For his efforts, his teammates voted him the club's offensive most valuable player (MVP). Furthermore, he finished second for NFL offensive rookie of the year. Terrell's output landed him in the record books as well. He became the lowest drafted player in NFL history to rush for over 1,000 yards in his rookie season.

Terrell's numbers continued to improve. In his second season, he led the American Football Conference (AFC) and was second in the NFL in both rushing yards, 1,538 on 345 carries, and total yards from scrimmage, 1,848. He led the NFL in first downs earned, with 108, and was second in the AFC and third in the league in both rushing touchdowns, 13, and total touchdowns, 15. He also set franchise single-season records in rushing attempts, rushing yards, and total yards.

Honors and Awards

1995	UPI All-AFC second team
1996-98	NFL All-Pro Team
	NFL Pro Bowl Team
1996, 1998	Associated Press NFL Offensive Player of the Year
1997	Super Bowl most valuable player
1998	Associated Press NFL most valuable player
	Professional Football Writers Association NFL most valuable player
2007	Elected to Denver Broncos Ring of Fame

By 1997, Terrell began to show the brilliance that led him to the upper echelons of the game. Starting the first fifteen games, Terrell finished his third season with 1,750 yards on 369 carries, a 4.7 average, and 15 rushing touchdowns. All his rushing numbers were career and franchise highs. He won the NFL rushing title that year.

Continuing the Story

Terrell's greatest triumph came on January 23, 1998, in his hometown, when he rushed for 157 yards and set a Super Bowl record, scoring 3 touchdowns, to lead the Broncos to a Super Bowl victory, all while suffering from a severe migraine headache. Terrell started at halfback in all sixteen games that season and won the rushing title with a career and Broncos' best 2,008 yards, along with 21 touchdowns on 392 carries. In doing so, Terrell became only the fourth player in league history to top the 2,000-yard mark in a single season. His total ranked third-best behind Eric Dickerson's 2,105 in 1984 and Barry Sanders's 2,053 in 1997; both players were inducted in the Pro Football Hall of Fame. The season also helped Terrell become the Broncos' all-time career rushing leader with 6,413 yards, surpassing Floyd Little's mark of 6,323, set between 1967 and 1975.

In 1998, Terrell continued his triumphant play by helping Denver win a second, consecutive Super Bowl title. Terrell rushed for 102 yards against the Atlanta Falcons in Super Bowl XXXIII. After five seasons, Terrell had earned two Super Bowl rings,

had appeared in three Pro Bowls, and had been voted MVP of Super Bowl XXXII. He also became the first 2,000-yard rusher to win a Super Bowl.

Terrell's numbers in the playoffs placed him in any discussion concerning all-time great postseason performers. In eight career playoff appearances, he averaged 142.5 rushing yards per game, with 1,140 total yards, on 5.6 yards per carry, and scored 12 touchdowns. Terrell tallied 581 yards rushing over three games during the 1997 playoffs and 468 over three playoff games in 1998, both concluding with Super Bowl victories. His seven straight postseason games rushing at least 100 yards was a playoff record.

Knee injuries—medial collateral ligament (MCL) and anterior cruciate ligament (ACL) tears—spoiled Terrell's 1999 and 2000 seasons, in which he played four and five games, respectively. He totaled only 493 rushing yards in those nine games. In 2001, Terrell showed signs of healing, playing in eight games and rushing for 701 yards; however, he did not score a single touchdown on 167 carries. His injuries continued to worsen, and Terrell was placed on the injured reserve list for the 2002 season. He officially retired in 2004. He played his entire seven year careeer with the Broncos.

Despite a premature end to his career, consisting of only two full seasons and seven overall, Terrell rushed for 7,607 yards, caught 169 balls for 1,280 receiving yards, and scored a total 65 touchdowns. His dominance during his healthy playing time was evident in his four straight all-pro selections, from 1995 to 1998, and three straight Pro Bowl appearances, from 1996 to 1998. His career average of 97.5 rushing yards per game was in the upper ranks on the NFL's all-time career list. In 2007, Terrell was voted into the Denver Broncos Ring of Fame. In retirement, Terrell worked as an analyst on the NFL Network and cohost of *NFL Total Access.*

Summary

Never considered a gifted football player growing up, Terrell Davis surpassed many expectations by displaying grit and drive. His determined attitude

NFL Statistics

Season	GP	Rushing Car.	Yds.	Avg.	TD	Receiving Rec.	Yds.	Avg.	TD
1995	14	237	1,117	4.7	7	49	367	7.5	1
1996	16	345	1,538	4.5	13	36	310	8.6	2
1997	15	369	1,750	4.7	15	42	287	6.8	0
1998	16	392	2,008	5.1	21	25	217	8.7	2
1999	4	67	211	3.1	2	3	26	8.7	0
2000	5	78	282	3.6	2	2	4	2.0	0
2001	8	167	701	4.2	0	12	69	5.8	0
Totals	78	1,655	7,607	4.6	60	169	1,280	7.6	5

Notes: GP = games played; Car. = carries; Yds. = yards; Avg. = average yards per carry *or* average yards per reception; TD = touchdowns; Rec. = receptions

was a staple of his playing style. Terrell did not forget his roots and continued to be a part of his San Diego community. In 2000, Terrell returned to Lincoln Prep to a hero's welcome, complete with marching band and a ceremony in which his number 7 jersey was retired. In kind, Terrell donated a check for $10,000 to the school.

A. K. Ruffin, updated by Trevor D. Bopp

Additional Sources

Davis, Terrell, and Adam Schefter. *TD: Dreams in Motion.* New York: HarperPaperbacks, 1999.

Griffith, Howard. *Laying It on the Line: Notes of a Team Player.* Champaign, Ill.: Sports, 2000.

Saunders, Patrick. "Davis Carries Himself as Well as He Does the Football." *The Denver Post,* September 12, 1999.

Len Dawson

Born: June 20, 1935
    Alliance, Ohio
Also known as: Leonard Ray Dawson (full name);
    Lenny the Cool

Early Life
The son of English immigrants James and Annie Dawson, Leonard Ray Dawson was born on June 20, 1935, in Alliance, Ohio. Len's father worked as a machinist in a pottery factory in order to feed his eleven children. Len's childhood was like that of many youngsters who grew up during the Depression, and who came from a small town and a large family. Such children developed remarkable survival skills in order to get their share at the dinner table.

Since Len was the youngest of the Dawson children, he learned to live by his wits. As a fourteen-year-old, he calculated that at his weight of only 125 pounds, he had better play baseball rather than football. Len hit .400 in American Legion baseball.

Len was also a talented basketball player. His football-playing brothers did not leave him alone until he played their sport as well, so he did, but he did not enjoy it. Playing football meant facing mammoth linemen whom he feared. Furthermore, he hated the violence; he hated getting hit. Len came up with his own way of coping. He developed a quick release that enabled him to pass the ball before defenders could get close to him, and, in his high school years, he managed to complete 100 out of 200 passes for 1,615 yards and 19 touchdowns. His senior year, he was the first athlete at Alliance High to earn all-state honors in both football and basketball. Players nicknamed him "Lenny the Cool" for his calm, calculating ability to survive and triumph.

The Road to Excellence
After graduating from high school in 1953, Len attended Purdue University, where he lettered in basketball and starred in football

as a quarterback. He worked with assistant coach Hank Stram, who later played an important role in Len's professional career. For three years, Len led the Big Ten Conference in passing and total offense. In 1956, he graduated with a degree in physical education and was an academic all-American, having finished his college career with a B average and with 3,325 yards passing.

Then began the most difficult phase of Len's career. Although the Pittsburgh Steelers selected him in the first round of the NFL draft, the team already boasted Bobby Layne as its quarterback. So Len spent most of his time on the bench as reserve quarterback. From Layne, the quiet Len learned to

Quarterback Len Dawson, who led his final team, the Kansas City Chiefs, to victory in Super Bowl IV. (Courtesy of Amateur Athletic Foundation of Los Angeles)

Honors and Awards

1956   Academic All-American
1962   *Sporting News* AFL Player of the Year
        Newspaper Enterprise Association AFL Player of the Year
1962, 1966   *Sporting News* AFL All-Star Team
        All-League Team
1963, 1965, 1967-70   AFL All-Star Team
1969   AFL All-Star Game Co-Outstanding Offensive Player
1970   NFL Super Bowl most valuable player
1972   NFL Pro Bowl Team
1973   NFL Man of the Year
1987   Inducted into Pro Football Hall of Fame
        Uniform number 16 retired by Kansas City Chiefs

be more aggressive with his teammates, to chew them out when they erred. However, this was not his personality, and his new toughness eventually backfired.

In 1960, Pittsburgh's coach, Buddy Parker, traded Len to the Cleveland Browns. Sadly, Len's jinx continued, for he was benched most of the time. Coaches seemed to feel he lacked the competitive spark—that he was there to serve time, not to win. Consequently, in Len's first year with Cleveland he played so rarely that he threw only 13 passes; in his second, only 15. After five frustrating years as a pro, Len had thrown a total of only 45 passes. He felt that he had wasted all those years.

The Emerging Champion

Luckily, Len's former coach from college, Stram, invited him to join the Dallas Texans of the American Football League (AFL), where Stram was coaching. When Len arrived, he had been inactive for so long that his footwork was clumsy and his passing arm weak. Stram did not recognize him as the player he had coached at Purdue and had second thoughts about keeping him. He did, however, figuring time would sharpen Dawson's skills. Meanwhile, the team's promoters had a difficult time attracting fans to watch a quarterback who had never been

more than a substitute. Consequently, only a few thousand spectators came to Len's first game.

Given the chance at last to perform, Len became an immediate star. He showed what a daring play-caller he was and how deadly accurate his passing arm could be. He was also great at scrambling. Soon, he set a league record by completing 61 percent of his passes. Throughout the season, "Lenny the Cool" either made every big play or enabled his teammates to do so. By year's end, Len had led the Texans to the championship and was chosen AFL player of the year. After all it had taken to get there, Len felt like he had been reborn.

Nevertheless, the Dallas Texans were not receiving enough support from local fans. The franchise soon moved to Kansas City and was renamed the Chiefs. The team got off to a slow start in their new home, losing as many games as they won. They improved rapidly, though, winning AFL championships in 1966 and 1969 and compiling the highest winning percentage in pro football.

Len's greatest triumph came in 1970. First, though, Len, the AFL's top-rated quarterback had

NFL and AFL Statistics

Season	GP	PA	PC	Pct.	Yds.	Avg.	TD	Int.
1957	3	4	2	.500	25	6.3	0	0
1958	4	6	1	.167	11	1.8	0	2
1959	12	7	3	.429	60	8.6	1	0
1960	2	13	8	.615	23	1.8	0	0
1961	6	15	7	.467	85	5.7	1	3
1962	14	310	189	.610	2,759	8.9	29	17
1963	14	352	190	.540	2,389	6.8	26	19
1964	14	354	199	.562	2,879	8.1	30	18
1965	14	305	163	.534	2,262	7.4	21	14
1966	14	284	159	.560	2,527	8.9	26	10
1967	14	357	206	.577	2,651	7.4	24	17
1968	14	224	131	.585	2,109	9.4	17	9
1969	8	166	98	.590	1,323	8.0	9	13
1970	13	262	141	.538	1,876	7.1	13	14
1971	14	301	167	.555	2,504	8.3	15	13
1972	14	305	175	.574	1,835	6.0	13	12
1973	9	101	66	.653	725	7.2	2	5
1974	14	235	138	.587	1,573	6.7	7	13
1975	12	140	93	.664	1,095	7.8	5	4
Totals	209	3,741	2,136	.571	28,711	7.7	239	183

Notes: GP = games played; PA = passes attempted; PC = passes completed; Pct. = percent completed; Yds. = yards; Avg. = average yards per attempt; TD = touchdowns; Int. = interceptions

to go through a difficult test. On the eve of Super Bowl IV, when the Chiefs were to face the Minnesota Vikings, television newscasters reported that Len and other quarterbacks were friendly with a professional sports gambler who bet on football games illegally. Although Len's teammates called him "the Puritan," he was distressed. He knew his fans considered him a marked man. If he gave anything but a flawless performance during the following day's Super Bowl—if he fumbled or was intercepted—he would appear guilty of the unwarranted charges.

Len gave that game his highest effort. He pitched to one teammate for a 46-yard touchdown, completed 12 of 17 passes for 142 yards, and led the Chiefs to three field goals. Kansas City won the championship, 23-7, and Len won the most valuable player award.

Continuing the Story

Some credit for Len's success should be given to Stram. Since Len's arm was not strong enough to throw long passes, Len compensated by becoming the most accurate passer football had known. Stram's innovative offense of "play-action" passes and a movable pass pocket enabled Len to shine as a quarterback, highlighting his strengths without exposing his weaknesses. Len was noted not only for his passing accuracy but also for his quick release in throwing the ball. He always remained "Lenny the Cool" when under pressure. He was never the kind to raise his voice—if a fellow player did anything wrong, Len simply gave him a look that meant he should shape up. Usually the player did.

By the time he retired in 1975, Len held impressive professional career statistics. He ranked eighth in completions and passing yardage, seventh in games played, fourth in passing efficiency and touchdown passes, and third in seasons as an active player. Named to the AFL all-star team six times, he also held AFL career records for passing efficiency, touchdown passes, total passing yardage, yards gained per pass, and lowest interception percentage.

Len's achievements did not end with his NFL career, though. After his retirement he worked briefly as a commentator on televised NFL games; later, he worked for a time as a football analyst on radio. At the same time, Len worked for many charities and civic organizations, in recognition of which he was honored as the NFL's man of the year for 1973. In 1987, he was elected to the Pro Football Hall of Fame. Len had married Jacqueline Puzder in 1953; they had two children, Len, Jr., and Lisa. In the 1990's, Len worked as a commentator for HBO Sports' weekly *Inside the NFL* and later broadcast in the Chiefs' hometown of Kansas City.

Summary
Len Dawson went from a benchwarmer to one of the great passers in professional football history. Although many doubted his ability for the first five years of his professional career, when finally given an opportunity, Len became a hall-of-fame quarterback and a Kansas City Chiefs icon.

Nicholas White

Additional Sources
Carroll, Bob. *Total Football: The Official Encyclopedia of the National Football League.* New York: HarperCollins, 1999.

Dawson, Len. *Len Dawson: Pressure Quarterback.* New York: Cowles, 1970.

Stallard, Mark. *Kansas City Chiefs Encyclopedia.* Champaign, Ill.: Sports, 2004.

Stram, Hank, and Lou Sahadi. *They're Playing My Game.* Chicago: Triumph Books, 2006.

Eric Dickerson

Born: September 2, 1960
     Sealy, Texas
Also known as: Eric Demetric Johnson (birth
    name); Eric Demetric Dickerson (full name);
    Mr. Fourth Quarter

Early Life

On September 2, 1960, in the small town of Sealy, Texas, a son was born to Robert Johnson and his sixteen-year-old wife. The boy was named Eric Demetric. Because his mother was so young at the time, Eric was legally adopted by his great-aunt and great-uncle, Viola and Kary Dickerson, and became known as Eric Demetric Dickerson. The

Pro Football Hall of Fame running back Eric Dickerson, who began his career with the Los Angeles Rams. (NFL/Getty Images)

Dickerson family also lived in Sealy, a town located 50 miles from Houston.

Eric had a simple childhood. His family did not have much money, thus Eric developed a habit of living frugally. He learned to be happy with what he had. This inner contentment came from family and spilled over into the rest of his life; he came to be known for his friendliness, charm, and a balanced sense of self-esteem.

As a boy, Eric was an athlete with high standards. He used to feel disappointed whenever he watched O. J. Simpson run and yet fail to gain 100 yards in a game. Eric was a fine runner himself. Even as a boy, his legs barely seemed to move when he ran, and he looked as though he were gliding. His running talent served him well in the future.

The Road to Excellence

At Sealy High School, Eric participated in track, basketball, and football. In track, he won the state 100-yard dash championship in the excellent time of 9.4 seconds. Eric's track success came as no surprise to those who had watched him run as a child. In football, he became a running back. Eric found he liked football more than other sports.

By the time Eric was a high school senior, he had become a superb running back, and he rushed for 2,653 yards that year. In the state high school championship game, he scored four touchdowns and led Sealy to the title. For his achievements, Eric was *Parade* magazine's choice as all-American and the best high school running back of 1978.

The next fall, Eric enrolled in Southern Methodist University (SMU). There, he had many injuries playing football as a freshman. As a sophomore, though, he played five games in which he rushed for more than 100 yards. After two years at SMU, Eric wanted to drop out, but his adoptive mother convinced him to stay in school.

In Eric's junior year, he was selected as Southwest Conference (SWC) player of the year after he had rushed for the second-best yardage total in SWC history. He also set scoring records at SMU with 114 points and 19 touchdowns.

More records came Eric's way as a senior. His 48 career touchdowns set a record at SMU. That year, he made consensus all-American and ranked third nationally with 147 rushing yards per game. As a result of his success in college football, Eric was the second choice in the NFL's 1983 draft. Eric was drafted by the Los Angeles Rams, and he joined the team before the 1983 NFL season.

The Emerging Champion

In several respects Eric was fortunate that the Rams had chosen him. The team had a good offensive line, and its coach, John Robinson, was a strong proponent of the running game. Still, Eric did not become a hero overnight. During his first three games, he fumbled six times—and one of the fumbles set up a field goal that caused the Rams to lose the game.

Eric's fourth game was another matter, though. He made an 85-yard touchdown that was the longest NFL run of the year at that time. He continued breaking records that season, setting the rookie rushing record while leading the Rams into the playoffs. Other 1983 honors earned by Eric included unanimous Pro Bowl selection and the United Press International National Football Conference (NFC) player of the year award.

The following season, Eric learned to be more patient on the field and to choose the holes through which he rushed more carefully. He began to recognize his limits, realizing he could not possibly gain 100 yards every week, as many people expected. In 1984, the more selective approach helped Eric break Simpson's 1973 NFL record for single-season rushing. That season, Eric gained at least 100 yards in a game eleven times. For his performance, he was chosen as NFC offensive player of the year, named to the all-NFL team, and selected to play in the Pro Bowl.

Continuing the Story

Eric became best known for his remarkable speed and durability. Size helped him, too. He stood 6 feet 3 inches and weighed

NFL Statistics

Season	GP	Rushing				Receiving			
		Car.	Yds.	Avg.	TD	Rec.	Yds.	Avg.	TD
1983	16	390	1,808	4.6	18	51	404	7.9	2
1984	16	379	2,105	5.6	14	21	139	6.6	0
1985	14	292	1,234	4.2	12	20	126	6.3	0
1986	16	404	1,821	4.5	11	26	205	7.9	0
1987	12	283	1,288	4.6	6	18	171	9.5	0
1988	16	388	1,659	4.3	14	36	377	10.5	1
1989	15	314	1,311	4.2	7	30	211	7.0	1
1990	11	166	677	4.1	4	18	92	5.1	0
1991	10	167	536	3.2	2	41	269	6.6	1
1992	16	187	729	3.9	2	14	85	6.1	1
1993	4	26	91	3.5	0	6	58	9.7	0
Totals	146	2,996	13,259	4.4	98	281	2,137	7.6	6

Notes: GP = games played; Car. = carries; Yds. = yards; Avg. = average yards per carry *or* average yards per reception; TD = touchdowns; Rec. = receptions

NFL Records

Most rushing touchdowns in a rookie season, 18 (1983)
Most rushing yards in a season, 2,105 (1984)
Most rushing yards in a rookie season, 1,808 (1983)
Most rushing yards in a postseason game, 248 (1985)

Honors and Awards

1980	All-Southwest Conference Team
1981	Southwest Conference Player of the Year
	College All-American
1982	Hula Bowl All-Star Team
	Japan Bowl All-Star Team
	Consensus All-American
1983	*Sporting News* NFL Player of the Year
	Associated Press Offensive Rookie of the Year
	United Press International NFC Rookie of the Year
	Seagram's Seven Crowns of Sports Award
	Sports Illustrated NFL Player of the Year
1983-84, 1986	United Press International NFC Offensive Player of the Year
1983-84, 1986-88	*Sporting News* NFL All-Star Team
1983-85, 1987-90	NFL Pro Bowl Team
1984, 1986	All-NFL Team
1999	Inducted into Pro Football Hall of Fame

218 pounds. Together, these qualities made Eric one of the finest running backs ever. Whenever he ran, he started out slowly, but somehow he always seemed to be six yards or so downfield before any opponent could reach him. Then he switched to overdrive and glided by the defense, his legs barely seeming to move. People enjoyed just watching Eric run, because he did it so beautifully.

Off the field, Eric was popular with fans. Articulate and charming, he made frequent appearances on television and acted in several commercials. In 1987, though, a long-simmering salary dispute between Eric and the Rams' management boiled over, and Eric was traded to the Indianapolis Colts in one of the biggest deals in NFL history. The Rams received eight players from the Colts in return for Eric.

Eric had an immediate effect on the hapless Colts. In 1986, Indianapolis had gone 3-13 and finished last in the American Football Conference's (AFC's) Eastern Division. With Eric in the backfield the next season, the Colts improved to 9-6 and won the Eastern Division title. Eric finished his playing career with the Los Angeles Raiders in 1992 and the Atlanta Falcons in 1993. He retired having gained 13,259 career rushing yards. In 1999, Eric was inducted into the Pro Football Hall of Fame. The following year, he joined the broadcasting team of *Monday Night Football* as a field commentator. Later, he returned to Los Angeles and became a sports commentator for the local Columbia Broadcasting System (CBS) affiliate.

Summary

Eric Dickerson combined speed, power, and grace in a way few other running backs ever have. Eric was often described as the "prettiest" runner in the game, and even the great O. J. Simpson, whose single-season rushing record was broken by Eric, conceded that Eric may have been the best running back ever.

Nan White

Additional Sources

Carroll, Bob. *Total Football: The Official Encyclopedia of the National Football League.* New York: HarperCollins, 1999.

Dickerson, Eric, and Richard Graham Walsh. *Eric Dickerson's Secrets of Pro Power.* New York: Warner Books, 1989.

Dingus, Anne. "Eric Dickerson." *Texas Monthly* 27, no. 9 (September, 1999): 216.

Dan Dierdorf

Born: June 29, 1949
Canton, Ohio
Also known as: Daniel Lee Dierdorf (full name)

Early Life
Daniel Lee Dierdorf was born and raised in Canton, Ohio, and played football at Glenwood (now GlenOak) High School. He was recruited by home-state rival University of Michigan, where he had three successful seasons. The Wolverines had success during Dan's tenure. In 1968, Michigan was 8-2; in 1969, the team was the Big Ten Conference champion; and in 1970, the Wolverines finished 9-1. The team averaged nearly 30 points per game during those seasons.

Dan Dierdorf watching from the sideline during a 1976 St. Louis Cardinals game. (NFL/Getty Images)

Dan was all-conference in both 1969 and 1970. The latter year, he was named a consensus all-American and was recognized as one of the premier linemen in college football. He was selected to play in several postseason all-star games, including the East-West Shrine Game and the Hula Bowl, after his senior year.

The Road to Excellence
In the 1971 NFL draft, Dan was selected in the second round, as the forty-third overall pick, by the St. Louis Cardinals (now Arizona Cardinals). His first year with the Cardinals, he played twelve games as a right guard. During the 1972 and 1973 seasons, Dan played backup left tackle, entering all the regular-season games but starting none. These three seasons were particularly unsuccessful for the Cardinals, which compiled 4-9-1 each season.

In 1974, Dan became a starter at right tackle, a position he played for the next eight seasons. Furthermore, that year signified the first of five straight seasons in which Dan was selected as an all-pro and played in the Pro Bowl game. From 1974 to 1978, he missed only two regular-season games because of injuries.

Coinciding with Dan's role as a starter, the Cardinals had some successful seasons. In 1974 and 1975, the team finished 10-4 and 11-3, respectively, and made the playoffs both seasons. In 1976, the Cardinals had a 10-4 record. Dan was a key member of the successful offensive team.

The Emerging Champion
Beginning in 1976, Dan was voted National Football Conference lineman of the year for three consecutive seasons. He did not give up a sack during the entire 1976 and 1977 seasons. He was the first agile, nearly 300-pound linemen in the NFL, setting the standard for all of the league's linemen to follow. His quickness and athleticism allowed him to stay healthy, a fact exhibited by his performance over seven seasons, until a broken jaw forced him to sit out two games in 1977. In 1979, Dan suffered another injury: A dislocated knee forced him to miss fourteen of the sixteen games in the season. In

Honors and Awards

1970's	NFL All-Decade Team
1970	Consensus All-American
1974-78, 1980	NFL Pro Bowl
1976-78	NFC Offensive Lineman of the Year
1987-89	Emmy Award for Outstanding Sports Analyst
1996	Inducted into University of Michigan Athletic Hall of Honor
	Inducted into Pro Football Hall of Fame
1999	Inducted into Missouri Sports Hall of Fame
2000	Inducted into College Football Hall of Fame
2002	Inducted into St. Louis Walk of Fame
2008	Pete Rozelle Radio-Television Award

1980, he returned with another Pro Bowl season.

In 1982, Dan played center during a desperate time for the team. He contributed in all nine games of the strike-shortened season, and his team made the playoffs. In 1983, at the age of thirty-four, he played in only seven games, starting four.

Continuing the Story

After retiring from playing football, Dan began a successful career in business and in sports broadcasting. He was part of the radio broadcast team for the Cardinals in 1984 and joined CBS in 1985. In 1987, he was added to the Monday Night Football team, one of the highest-profile broadcast positions in sports at the time. He stayed with ABC for twelve seasons. After a shake-up at ABC following the 1998 season, he was immediately rehired by CBS and became part of the networks' top broadcast team. In 1987, 1988, and 1989, for his work on television, he was awarded an Emmy Award for Outstanding Sports Analyst.

Dan was so appreciated in St. Louis, where he remained after his playing career, that he was awarded a star on the St. Louis Walk of Fame. He served more than fifteen years on the board of trustees at the Cardinal Glennon Children's Hospital and the Trauma Center. He also served as a board member of the Cystic Fibrosis Foundation in St. Louis.

Dan was inducted into the Pro Football Hall of Fame, the National Football Foundation's College Football Hall of Fame, and the University of Michigan Athletic Hall of Honor. He was also selected to the Missouri Sports Hall of Fame in 1999.

Summary

Dan Dierdorf was a gifted athlete who, with hard work and intelligence, became one of the best offensive linemen in the NFL during the 1970's. In fact, Dan was named to the NFL team of the decade for the 1970's. He was a remarkably durable player who battled in the trenches of a tough game. Dan also had a successful postplaying career as a sports announcer.

Michael Coulter

Additional Sources

Brandstatter, Jim. *Tales from Michigan Stadium, Volume II.* Champaign, Ill.: Sports, 2005.

Madej, Bruce, Rob Toonkel, Mike Pearson, and Greg Kinney. *Michigan: Champions of the West.* Champaign, Ill.: Sagamore, 1997.

Smith, Ron, and Dan Dierdorf. *Pro Football's Heroes of the Hall.* St. Louis: Sporting News, 2003.

Mike Ditka

Born: October 18, 1939
　　Carnegie, Pennsylvania
Also known as: Michael Keller Ditka, Jr. (full
　name); Iron Mike

Early Life
Michael Keller Ditka, Jr., was born October 18, 1939, in Carnegie, Pennsylvania. He and his younger brothers and sisters grew up in a government housing project in Aliquippa, Pennsylvania, where the only future that lay ahead for most children was a life in the steel mills. Mike's father, the son of a Ukrainian immigrant, worked in the Jones and Laughlin steel mill and on the railroad. He instilled in his children a belief in the value of hard work.

As a boy, Mike excelled in sports, primarily because of his hatred of losing. He started out playing Little League baseball because he was too small for most sports. By the time he was in fifth grade, he joined the football team because he enjoyed the head-to-head contact. He was so determined to become a good football player that he lifted weights and did push-ups through junior high and high school. As a result of his grueling workouts, Mike was able to play offensive end on the Aliquippa High School team that won the state championship in his junior year.

In high school, Mike's fierce desire to win a college athletic scholarship was fueled by his refusal to work in the mills as his father and grandfather had. Although he wanted to attend Notre Dame, Mike went to the University of Pittsburgh, because he wanted to enter its dental school. While playing defense for the Pitt Panthers, he earned a reputation as an aggressive player who expected every player to give 100 percent to the game.

The Road to Excellence
After his senior year in college, Mike signed a $12,000 contract with the Chicago Bears of the NFL. Soon afterward, the Houston Oilers of the rival American Football League (AFL) offered him a $50,000 contract. Still, Mike had no regrets about joining the Bears, because he wanted to be part of a hard-hitting team.

Mike had no sooner joined the Bears than he began gaining recognition as an exceptional offensive tight end. In 1961, he was voted NFL rookie of the year. In 1963, he helped the Bears to win the NFL title.

However, Mike's determination and commitment to greatness did not become fully apparent

Mike Ditka, who reinvented the tight-end position, adding the skills of a receiver to the toughness of an offensive lineman. (Courtesy of Amateur Athletic Foundation of Los Angeles)

until he became injured. In 1965, he played every game and caught 36 passes, even though he had severely injured his right foot just prior to the season's opening day. The following year, he caught 32 passes, despite the fact that his injury was slowing him down.

Mike believed that God arranged for him to be traded to the Philadelphia Eagles at the end of the 1966 season so that he could "learn a little humility." Mike spent most of the 1967 and 1968 seasons on the bench because of his pulled muscles and torn ligaments. He was also forced to sit out as punishment for his public criticism of his team, and he began drinking to escape his depression.

In 1969, the Eagles traded Mike to the Dallas Cowboys. Under the influence of Dallas coach Tom Landry, Mike worked hard to get himself back into shape. Mike's renewed enthusiasm helped propel the Cowboys to the Super Bowl in the 1970 and 1971 seasons. However, when back pain robbed Mike of his former strength and speed, he decided to retire as a player in 1972.

The Emerging Champion

Mike loved football so much that he took a position as a Dallas assistant coach under Landry in 1973, even though his salary was cut in half. Still, he accepted his pay cut because of the invaluable lessons that he was learning from Landry about analyzing game films and dealing with individualistic players. He served eight years as an offensive coordinator for the Cowboys.

In 1981, Mike's patience was rewarded with his appointment as head coach of the Chicago Bears, a

NFL Statistics

Season	GP	Rec.	Yds.	Avg.	TD
1961	14	56	1,076	19.2	12
1962	14	58	904	15.6	5
1963	14	59	794	13.5	8
1964	14	75	897	12.0	5
1965	14	36	454	12.6	2
1966	14	32	378	11.8	2
1967	9	26	274	10.5	2
1968	11	13	111	8.5	2
1969	12	17	268	15.8	3
1970	14	8	98	12.3	0
1971	14	30	360	12.0	1
Totals	144	410	5,614	13.7	45

Notes: GP = games played; Rec. = receptions; Yds. = yards; Avg. = average yards per reception; TD = touchdowns

team that had had only two winning seasons in the previous thirteen. Mike tried so hard to justify the team owners' faith in him that he often flew into fits of rage. He even broke his hand punching a steel trunk in the Bears' locker room.

By 1984, Mike had completely revamped the team by firing lazy players and hiring new ones. The new Bears were a team of strong-willed individualists. Mike had the ability to mold a group of such distinct personalities as quarterback Jim McMahon and defensive coordinator Buddy Ryan into a formidable team. Fans across the nation turned Mike and his players into celebrities.

Mike piloted the Bears to a 15-1 season in 1984, and the Bears crushed the New England Patriots in the Super Bowl 46-10. Mike, who had become the best-known football coach in the United States since Vince Lombardi, was named coach of the year by the Associated Press, United Press International, and *The Sporting News.*

Continuing the Story

After the Super Bowl, Mike became Chicago's most famous citizen. He appeared on more billboards and made more television commercials than any public figure in Chicago's history. He became so well known throughout the entire nation that sportswriter Peter Gent dubbed him "the John Wayne of the NFL."

Mike retained his determination to keep winning after the Super Bowl. He did perhaps his best coaching job in 1988, when he coached a 12-4 season out of an aging team. By the end

Honors and Awards

1960	*Sporting News* College All-American
1961	United Press International NFL Rookie of the Year
	Bert Bell Award
	Sporting News NFL Rookie of the Year
1961-65	*Sporting News* NFL Western Conference All-Star Team
1962-66	NFL Pro Bowl Team
1985	Associated Press Coach of the Year
	Sporting News Coach of the Year
1985, 1988	United Press International NFC Coach of the Year
1986	Inducted into College Football Hall of Fame
1988	Inducted into Pro Football Hall of Fame

of the decade, his team had won five National Football Conference Central Division titles.

In 1988, though, Mike found that he could no longer maintain his volatile coaching style. At the end of a disappointing season in 1988, Mike suffered a minor heart attack just before he was supposed to introduce former vice president George Bush at a campaign rally in Lake Forest, Illinois. Only eleven days later, Mike was back on the sidelines of a Bears game with the Washington Redskins. He later explained that he "coach[ed] by crisis," and that he was not happy unless he had something to fight and overcome.

Still, Mike seemed to have learned that he was not invulnerable. He started a cholesterol-free diet and curtailed his drinking. He also has an artificial hip, the result of his football injuries. He still smoked his trademark cigars, though.

At the end of the 1989 season, Mike was so embittered by the fact that his team had lost ten of its last twelve games that he almost quit. Mike's frustration surfaced in front of television cameras in 1990, when he yanked the clipboard out of the Bears' defensive coordinator's hand and began calling the plays himself. Once again, he had made the point that only winning satisfied him. In 1992, Mike was fired as head coach of the Chicago Bears. In 1997, he was hired as head coach of the New Orleans Saints. Mike continued his hard-driven coaching style, but the Saints did not do well. During Mike's three seasons as the Saints' head coach,

the team's record was 15-33. He was fired from that club in January, 2000.

The tenacity that Mike displayed on the field as a player and on the sidelines as a coach was later showcased in his vocal campaign in support of an adequate pension plan for former NFL players. Mike felt that the NFL, a highly successful and lucrative business, had not taken care of the players who sacrificed their bodies to help form the league. In all of life's ventures, Mike remained a fighter.

Summary

Mike Ditka became a folk hero, the champion of the all-American work ethic. As a player, he was one of the toughest men in the history of the sport. As a coach, he pushed his players as hard as he had pushed himself when he played. He emerged as a hard-driven man fueled by the courage of his convictions.

Alan Brown

Additional Sources

Ditka, Mike, and Rick Telander. *Mike Ditka Reflections on the 1985 Bears and Wisdom from Da Coach.* Champaign, Ill.: Sports, 2007.

Whittingham, Richard. *Sunday's Heroes: NFL Legends Talk About the Times of Their Lives.* Chicago: Triumph Books, 2004.

Wolfe, Rich. *Da Coach.* Chicago: Triumph Books, 2001.

Clint Dolezel

Born: March 25, 1970
　　　Lorena, Texas

Early Life

Clint Dolezel grew up in tiny Lorena, Texas. After high school he attended Cisco Junior College in Cisco, Texas, where he lettered in football. He transferred to East Texas State University (now Texas A&M-Commerce) in Commerce, Texas. The school competed in National Collegiate Athletic Association Division II athletics. At East Texas State, Clint was a two-time all-Lone Star Conference second-team selection. He played for the Lions in 1992 and 1993, the only two seasons in which he was eligible, and passed for 3,152 yards and 33 touchdowns. He also lettered in golf when attending East Texas State. At 6 foot 5 inches, Dolozel had the size to be a great quarterback.

The Road to Excellence

In 1994, Clint was not drafted into the NFL and did not make a team as a free agent. He did not give up on his dream of playing professional football: He tried out for and made a team in the Arena Football League (AFL) in 1995. The AFL was founded in 1987 and received little attention during its early years. Later it became better known because of national-television exposure. The AFL began with only four teams but, by 1995, had expanded to thirteen teams; the league had as many as nineteen teams. Arena football has rules that enable high amounts of scoring. The field is only 50 yards long and 85 feet wide, approximately half of the size of a regulation football field. Eight players, instead of eleven, are on the field for each team. There are limitations on blitzing by the defense and punting is not permitted. The league has even had rules requiring players to play both offense and defense.

Clint joined the league in 1995 as a member of the Milwaukee Mustangs. He was a backup quarterback that year, attempting only 12 passes and completing 10. In 1996, he was again a member of the Mustangs and spent that season as a backup, attempting only 16 passes and completing 9. In both of those seasons, he threw 2 touchdown passes and 1 interception.

The Emerging Champion

In 1997, Clint became the starting quarterback for the Texas Terror, which finished 6-8. He completed 259 of 388 passes, threw 69 touchdowns, and had only 15 interceptions. In 1998 and 1999, he was the starting quarterback for the Houston Thunderbears. During those seasons, he threw more than 1,100 passes, completing more than 700. In 1998 and 1999, he threw 81 and 80 touchdown passes,

Clint Dolezel. (L. Scott Wambsganss/WireImage/Getty Images)

Arena Football League Statistics

Season	PA	PC	Pct.	Yds.	TD	Int.
1995	12	10	83.3	121	2	1
1996	16	9	56.3	103	2	1
1997	388	259	66.8	3,377	69	15
1998	558	343	61.5	4,228	81	17
1999	556	374	67.3	4,336	80	19
2001	574	364	63.4	3,952	80	10
2002	505	339	67.1	3,878	79	19
2003	545	361	66.2	4,431	89	15
2004	585	381	65.1	4,428	93	12
2005	465	302	64.9	3,505	78	16
2006	573	375	65.4	4,685	105	11
2007	533	375	70.4	4,474	107	9
2008	388	257	66.2	3,046	66	10
Totals	5,698	3,749	65.8	44,564	931	155

Notes: PA = passes attempted; PC = passes completed; Pct. = percent completed; Yds. = yards; TD = touchdowns; Int. = interceptions

respectively. In those two seasons combined he threw only 36 interceptions. In 1998, Houston was 8-6 and won the central division. Clint missed the 2000 AFL season because he was invited to try out with the Chicago Bears. He did not make the team.

In 2001, Clint started the first of three seasons with the Grand Rapids Rampage, which went 11-3. He passed 574 times and completed 364 passes, including 80 for touchdowns. He threw only 10 interceptions that season. He was second-team AFL. In 2002, he threw more than 500 passes and completed 339, including 79 for touchdowns. In 2003, he completed 361 passes in 545 attempts, throwing 89 touchdown passes. Clint had mastered the art of quarterbacking in the high-scoring AFL.

In 2004, he signed with the Las Vegas Gladiators and played two great seasons. In the first year of his contract, he set career-high totals in pass attempts, 585, and completions, 381. He threw for 93 touchdowns that season and only 12 interceptions. In 2005, he had 465 attempts, 302 completions, and 78 touchdowns. Both seasons, the Gladiators went 8-8.

Continuing the Story

In 2006, he signed with the Dallas Desperados and had two tremendous seasons in terms of personal statistics and team success. He threw 573 passes in 2006 and 533 passes in 2007. Both seasons he completed 375 passes. In 2006, threw 105 touchdowns;

in 2007, he threw 107. In those two seasons, he threw for a combined 9,000 yards. He completed 65 and 70 percent of his passes in those seasons, respectively. Amazingly, he had a total of only 20 interceptions in the two-year period. His quarterback ratings were among the highest in AFL history. In 2006, he was named first-team AFL. The following year he made second-team AFL.

The Desperados were impressive as a team during those seasons. In 2006, the team finished 13 and 3. The following year, the Desperados went 15 and 1, one of the best seasons for a team in the history of the AFL. After the 2007 season, Clint had 865 career touchdown passes, the most in AFL history. He hoped to throw for more than 1,000 by the end of his career.

After the 2007 season, Clint was third all-time in the AFL in passing yards. He had the second-highest career completion percentage and the third-most passing attempts. He had the sixth-highest lifetime quarterback rating.

Summary

Even after not getting a scholarship to play in a major college football program and missing out on an NFL career, Clint Dolezel pursued a dream of becoming a professional football player. He adapted his skills to arena football and mastered this fast-moving and high-scoring game.

Michael Coulter

Additional Sources

Archer, Todd. "Desperados' Dolezel Rings Up No. 800." *Dallas Morning News,* April 17, 2007.

Schmaedeke, Chris. "Air Dolezel Cleared for Take-off." *Rocky Mountain News,* March 3, 2007, p. 9.

Taylor, Jean-Jacques. "Desperados' Dolezel Sets TD Mark in 82-38 Win." *Knight Ridder Tribune Business News,* May 13, 2006, p. 1.

Honors and Awards

2001	Arena Bowl XV Championship
2006	All-Arena Football League first team
2007	All-Arena Football League second team

Tony Dorsett

Born: April 7, 1954
     Rochester, Pennsylvania
Also known as: Anthony Drew Dorsett (full
    name); Hawk

Early Life

Anthony "Tony" Drew Dorsett was born on April 7, 1954, in Rochester, Pennsylvania. The sixth of seven children, Tony grew up in a conservative churchgoing family. Tony's mother, Myrtle, instilled in her son the values of respecting other people and getting a first-rate education. His father, Westley, supported the family by working in a steel mill. His fa-

Running back Tony Dorsett, who won the 1976 Heisman Trophy before helping the Dallas Cowboys to a Super Bowl victory the following year. (Courtesy of Amateur Athletic Foundation of Los Angeles)

ther gave Tony the nickname "Hawkeye," often abbreviated to "Hawk," and the name stuck with fans and sportswriters.

Tony worked at developing muscle strength and aggressiveness during his childhood years. Many believe that this determination was spurred by his rejection from a midget-league football team when he was twelve.

The Road to Excellence

Tony's determination to build himself into an athlete paid off. As an outside linebacker for Hopewell High School, Dorsett was known as "monster man" who streaked out of nowhere to make crushing tackles. As a junior, Tony was made a running back by Coach Butch Ross.

Dorsett led Hopewell to the Midwestern Athletic Conference Championship. As a senior, he rushed for 1,238 yards and 23 touchdowns and was named first-team all-state and scholastic all-American by *Parade, Scholastic,* and *Coach and Athlete* magazines.

A top college prospect, Tony was finally convinced by Coach Johnny Majors to attend the University of Pittsburgh. Tony was certain that the Panthers, who had gone through nine losing seasons, could only improve with his help as a running back. His assumption proved to be true.

Coach Majors observed that Dorsett was "like a man possessed in his dedication." Tony added power to his 5-foot 10-inch frame by working with weights, and grew from 157 to 190 pounds. The increased power was evident in his freshman season, as he rushed for 1,586 yards and led the Pittsburgh Panthers to a 6-4-1 record in 1973. For that, Tony became the first freshman all-American since 1944, when Doc Blanchard won the same honor.

The next season, Pittsburgh improved its record to 8 wins and 4 losses, and Tony increased his total yards accumulated in college to 2,590. Tony's proudest achievement that year was a 303 yard rushing performance against the University of Notre Dame.

The Emerging Champion

Tony's greatest season in a University of Pittsburgh uniform came in 1976, his senior year. The Panthers finished that season undefeated and went to the Sugar Bowl, where the team defeated the University of Georgia.

Including his performance in the Sugar Bowl, Tony rushed for 2,050 yards in his senior year. The Panthers were named national champions in both the Associated Press and United Press International polls, and Tony was awarded the Heisman Trophy, the Maxwell Award, and numerous player of the year citations.

After he was selected in the first round of the NFL draft by the Dallas Cowboys, Tony signed a five-year $1.1 million contract. Immediately, Tony exceeded expectations, as he surprised the Dallas Cowboy coaches with his excellent catching and blocking abilities.

A position on the first team of the Cowboys had

NFL Statistics

Season	GP	Rushing					Receiving			
		Car.	Yds.	Avg.	TD		Rec.	Yds.	Avg.	TD
1977	14	208	1,007	4.8	12		29	273	9.4	1
1978	16	290	1,325	4.6	7		37	378	10.2	2
1979	14	250	1,107	4.4	6		45	375	8.3	1
1980	15	278	1,185	4.3	11		34	263	7.7	0
1981	16	342	1,646	4.8	4		32	325	10.2	2
1982	9	177	745	4.2	5		24	179	7.5	0
1983	16	289	1,321	4.6	8		40	287	7.2	1
1984	16	302	1,189	3.9	6		51	459	9.0	1
1985	16	305	1,307	4.3	7		46	449	9.8	3
1986	13	184	748	4.1	5		25	267	10.7	1
1987	12	130	456	3.5	1		19	177	9.3	1
1988	16	181	703	3.9	5		16	122	7.6	0
Totals	**173**	**2,936**	**12,739**	**4.3**	**77**		**398**	**3,554**	**8.9**	**13**

Notes: GP = games played; Car. = carries; Yds. = yards; Avg. = average yards per carry *or* average yards per reception; TD = touchdowns; Rec. = receptions

to wait, however. At first, Tony was used sparingly, warming the bench while veteran Preston Pearson played at the running back position. Though Tony was on the second team, playing half of each game, he still led the team in touchdowns and rushing at midseason. By the tenth game of the season, Tony was put on the first team. He won the rookie of the year award easily, and in the 1978 Super Bowl he was the leading rusher, contributing one touchdown in the win over the Denver Broncos.

Among the Dallas club records Tony held were longest scoring catch of the 1978 season, 91 yards; most yards gained in a season, 1,325 yards; 484 yards rushing and 5 touchdowns in the playoffs; and 101 yards rushing in the NFC Championship game.

When the Cowboys' passing game slumped, the offense turned to Tony's running to pick up the slack. In a 1979 game against the New York Giants, Tony carried the ball twenty-nine times for 108 yards, a career high. The Cowboys won that game 28-7 and later that season, won their fifth straight divisional championship.

Continuing the Story

Whenever Tony got the ball he left a wake of dazed defensive backs. About his incredible running ability, he has said, "I see a guy, and if I can spin on him, I spin. If you do it wrong, you get hit dead center in the back." His college coach said Tony could "Stop on a dime . . . take three little bitty steps and be off again." The

NCAA Division 1-A Records

Most rushing yards, 6,082

Honors and Awards

1973-76	College All-American
1976	Heisman Trophy
	Maxwell Award
	Walter Camp Award
	Sporting News College Player of the Year
	Citizens Savings College Football Player of the Year
	Sporting News College All-American
1977	Associated Press Offensive Rookie of the Year
	United Press International NFC Rookie of the Year
	Sporting News NFC Rookie of the Year
	Bert Bell Award
1979, 1982-84	NFL Pro Bowl Team
1981	United Press International NFC Player of the Year
	Sporting News NFL All-Star Team
1994	Inducted into Pro Football Hall of Fame

fastest tacklers who pursued him were often left grasping air.

After eleven stellar seasons in Dallas, Tony was traded by the Cowboys to the Denver Broncos shortly before the start of the 1988 season. Tony played one season with the Broncos and appeared in all sixteen of the team's games before retiring at the season's end. In 1994 Tony was inducted into the Pro Football Hall of Fame.

Tony was described as affable and articulate, walking with a fluid bounce. His son, Anthony Drew Dorsett, Jr., also played football at the University of Pittsburgh and in the NFL.

Summary

Not since O. J. Simpson had there been a greater breakaway running back in professional football than Tony Dorsett. Tony was a four-time all-American at the University of Pittsburgh, where he led the team to a national championship and won the Heisman Trophy. As a Dallas Cowboy he used his great offensive ground speed to break rushing records, and he helped the team to a world's championship in the Super Bowl.

Rustin Larson

Additional Sources

Dorsett, Tony, and Harvey Frommer. *Running Tough: Memoirs of a Football Maverick.* New York: Doubleday, 1989.

Monk, Cody. *Legends of the Dallas Cowboys.* Champaign, Ill.: Sports, 2004.

Spong, John. "Bar Stool Arguments." *Texas Monthly* 34, no. 9 (September, 2006): 151-154.

Waxman, Matthew. "Tony Dorsett." *Sports Illustrated* 105, no. 1 (July 3, 2006): 124-125.

Warrick Dunn

Born: January 5, 1975
     Baton Rouge, Louisiana
Also known as: Warrick De'Mon Dunn (full name)

Early Life

Warrick De'Mon Dunn was born on January 5, 1975, the oldest of six children. He was reared by his mother, Betty Smothers, a Baton Rouge, Louisiana, police corporal. By the time Warrick was eighteen years old, he was a standout option quarterback for Baton Rouge Catholic High School, which won the 1991 Class 4A state championship in Warrick's junior season. Warrick earned a football scholarship to play running back for Florida State University. What should have been a time of personal triumph became a tragic turning point in Warrick's life. In January, 1993, Warrick's mother was killed during a late-night bank robbery while she worked her second job as a security officer. Warrick became a surrogate parent for his younger brothers and sisters, and he purchased a home in Baton Rouge. There, Warrick's grandmother, Willie Wheeler, watched over the rest of the family as Warrick pursued his college career with the Seminoles.

The Road to Excellence

As a freshman, Warrick had the good fortune to become the roommate of senior Florida State quarterback Charlie Ward. The two soft-spoken football players quickly formed a friendship, and their chemistry on the field transformed the Seminoles into a national championship contender. The signature play of Warrick's freshman year came late in a victory against the rival University of Florida Gators. Ward threw a 79-yard touchdown pass to Warrick to clinch the win that secured a berth in the national championship game against Nebraska, at the 1994 Orange Bowl in Miami. Warrick carried only once for three yards in that game, but the Seminoles defeated the Cornhuskers, 18-16, to give Florida State its first national championship.

In 1994, Warrick lost his roommate and mentor when Ward, the 1993 Heisman Trophy winner, went to the National Basketball Association. However, even with Ward gone, Warrick cemented his place among Florida State's all-time greats by finishing his college career as the school's career leader in rushing yards, with 3,959, and touchdowns, with 47. He was the first Florida State running back to rush for more than 1,000 yards in three consecutive seasons and was named all-Atlantic Coast Conference three times. His jersey number,

Tampa Bay Buccaneers running back Warrick Dunn rushing with the ball against the Green Bay Packers in 2008. (Ronald C. Modra/Getty Images)

NFL Statistics

Season	GP	Rushing Car.	Yds.	Avg.	TD	Receiving Rec.	Yds.	Avg.	TD
1997	16	224	978	4.4	4	39	462	11.8	3
1998	16	245	1,026	4.2	2	44	344	7.8	0
1999	15	195	616	3.2	0	64	589	9.2	2
2000	16	248	1,133	4.6	8	44	422	9.6	1
2001	13	159	447	2.8	3	68	557	8.2	3
2002	15	230	927	4.0	7	50	377	7.5	2
2003	11	125	672	5.4	3	37	336	9.1	2
2004	16	265	1,106	4.2	9	29	294	10.1	0
2005	16	280	1,416	5.1	3	29	220	7.6	1
2006	16	286	1,140	4.0	4	22	170	7.7	1
2007	16	227	720	3.2	4	37	238	6.4	0
2008	15	186	786	4.2	2	47	330	7.0	0
Totals	181	2,669	10,967	4.1	49	510	4,339	8.5	15

Notes: GP = games played; Car. = carries; Yds. = yards; Avg. = average yards per carry or average yards per reception; TD = touchdowns; Rec. = receptions

28, was one of seven to be retired by the Florida State program.

The Emerging Champion

At 5 feet 9 inches, 178 pounds, Warrick's potential inability to withstand the physical punishment absorbed by running backs in the NFL was the only weakness scouts noted as Warrick prepared for the 1997 NFL draft. He was quick, elusive, sure-handed as a receiver, and surprisingly effective as a blocker, despite his lack of size. The Tampa Bay Buccaneers selected Warrick in the first round, the twelfth pick overall, and envisioned a two-running-back system featuring the speed of Warrick and the power of fullback Mike Alstott.

The Warrick-Alstott combination, known as "Thunder and Lightning," quickly emerged as the offensive centerpiece for a team that had not made the playoffs since 1982. The Buccaneers began Warrick's rookie season with five consecutive victories and secured the National Football Conference (NFC) Central Division championship. Warrick earned the NFC rookie of the year award and a berth in the Pro Bowl. He gained 978 yards on 224 carries and caught 39 passes for 462 yards, dispelling the notion that he might not be durable enough for the NFL.

As he met with success on the football field, Warrick turned his attention to philanthropy, first in the Tampa Bay community, then beyond. To honor his mother's memory, Warrick focused on helping single moms buy houses for their families. In 1997, he began the Homes For the Holidays program, through which he personally selected a single mother to receive the down payment on a furnished home on or around Thanksgiving Day. The next year, Warrick expanded the program to include his hometown of Baton Rouge, and later he added Tallahassee, Florida—the site of Florida State University—and Atlanta, Georgia. Through 2007, Warrick's program had placed more than seventy-five single parents and nearly two hundred children in homes of their own.

Continuing the Story

Warrick continued to thrive with the Buccaneers. In 1998 and 2000, he rushed for more than 1,000 yards. An ankle injury slowed him in 1999, but the Buccaneers reached the NFC Championship game before losing to the eventual Super Bowl champion St. Louis Rams. Warrick's fifth and final season with Tampa Bay came in 2001, which also happened to be the final season for Buccaneers' head coach Tony Dungy, who had an immediate affinity for Warrick when they were united in 1997. Dungy moved on to coach the Indianapolis Colts, while

Florida State University Records

Most career rushing yards, 3,959
Most rushing yards in a season, 1,418
First player to have three consecutive 1,000-yards rushing seasons

Honors and Awards

1997	Associated Press NFL Offensive Rookie of the Year
1997, 2000, 2005	NFL Pro Bowl
2004	Walter Payton Award
	Jessie Tuggle Humanitarian Award
2007	Home Depot NFL neighborhood most valuable player
	Inducted into Florida State University's Alumni Association's Circle of Gold

Warrick signed a free agent contract with the Atlanta Falcons.

In Atlanta, Warrick revived the thunder-and-lightning backfield concept with teammate T. J. Duckett, a running back in the mold of Alstott. From 2004 to 2006, Warrick compiled three consecutive 1,000-yard rushing seasons with the Falcons and earned his third trip to the Pro Bowl by rushing for a career-best 1,416 yards in 2005. That same season, Warrick again experienced the heartbreak of losing in the NFC Championship game when the Falcons fell to the Philadelphia Eagles.

The 2007 season was tumultuous for the Falcons. Quarterback Michael Vick was sent to prison for running an illegal dog-fighting ring in Virginia. The season was emotionally trying for Warrick, who visited both Vick and one of his mother's killers on death row. By the time the season ended, Warrick had become the twenty-third player in NFL history to rush for more than 10,000 yards in a career. In March, 2008, after eleven seasons in the NFL, Warrick was released by the Falcons and became a free agent. Even at the age of thirty-three, he insisted he still could play. He signed a two-year contract to play for his former team, the Buccaneers. During the 2008 season, he played in fifteen games and rushed for 786 yards.

Summary

Warrick Dunn proved that a running back did not have to be a big man to succeed in the NFL. Off the field, he was honored as the 2004 NFL's Walter Payton Man of the Year, an award reserved for those in the game whose charitable contributions transcended sports. The commitment to others outside the game, in memory of his mother, became his ultimate legacy.

Carter Gaddis

Additional Sources

Dunn, Warrick, and Don Yaeger. *Running for My Life: My Journey in the Game of Football and Beyond.* New York: HarperEntertainment, 2008.

Harry, Chris, and Joey Johnston. *Tales from the Bucs Sideline.* Champaign, Ill.: Sports, 2004.

Ross, Alan. *Away from the Ball: Off-the-Field Heroes from the NFL.* Nashville, Tenn.: Cumberland House, 2008.

Kenny Easley

Born: January 15, 1959
      Chesapeake, Virginia
Also known as: Kenny Mason Easley, Jr. (full
   name)

Early Life

Kenny Mason Easley, Jr., was born in Chesapeake, Virginia, on January 15, 1959, and grew up with several sisters under the care of their mother, Juanita. A passionate competitor from an early age, he participated in a variety of athletic activities. By the time he reached Oscar F. Smith High School, he had grown tall and strong and starred in multiple sports. His specialty was football, and as a defensive back from 1973 to 1977, he was named to all-Southeastern District, all-Tidewater, all-State, all-South, and all-American teams.

The Road to Excellence

After graduation from high school, Kenny was recruited to attend the University of California at Los Angeles (UCLA). As he had in high school, he starred as a free safety, demonstrating superior skills both in the science of hitting opponents and in the art of picking off passes. During his four-year collegiate career, he set school records for interceptions, with 19, and tackles, with 324. At UCLA, Kenny was a three-time all-American and was named to the all-Pac-10 Conference team four consecutive years. In 1980, he was considered for the Heisman Trophy and finished ninth in the voting.

NFL Statistics

Season	GP	Sacks	FR	Int.
1981	14	0	4	3
1982	8	2.0	1	4
1983	16	3.0	3	7
1984	16	0	1	10
1985	13	2.0	1	2
1986	10	1.0	0	2
1987	12	0	0	4
Totals	89	8.0	10	32

Notes: GP = games played; FR = fumble recoveries; Int. = interceptions

Once Kenny's college career ended, professional teams came calling. In 1981, the Chicago Bulls of the National Basketball Association drafted the all-around athlete in the tenth round. However, Kenny wanted to play football and was happy when the Seattle Seahawks of the NFL chose him as the fourth overall pick of the 1981 draft. He was less happy at training camp when he learned the team wanted him to play strong safety, the position opposite the opponent's tight end, rather than his accustomed role as free safety, a position that allows the player to make quick decisions after the ball is snapped.

Despite the new position, Kenny learned his tasks quickly and, as always, excelled. As a hint of things to come, he logged 3 interceptions for 155 yards and 1 touchdown in his first year as a professional. Kenny's performance earned him honors as American Football Conference (AFC) defensive rookie of the year.

The Emerging Champion

In the next several seasons, Kenny continued to improve, playing in four consecutive Pro Bowls from 1982 to 1985 and making the all-pro first team in three consecutive years from 1983 to 1985. In 1983, he had 7 interceptions and was named AFC defensive player of the year. In 1984, he stole ten passes, leading the NFL in interceptions, and twice scored touchdowns after the pickoffs. At the end of the season, he was named NFL defensive player of the year and signed a five-year contract with the Seahawks that boosted him toward the top of the salary list for defensive players.

In 1986, Kenny's season was interrupted by an ankle injury and subsequent surgery. Upon the recommendation of team doctors, he took over-the-counter medication to dampen the pain during his recovery but was limited to just ten games that year.

Entering the 1987 season, Kenny had gained weight and did not look like or perform to his all-pro status. Concerned that he had lost speed because of additional pounds, Kenny undertook an extreme diet, consuming just an apple and water at lunch, but his weight did not drop. Though Kenny played well enough to record 4 interceptions in twelve games and was named to the 1987 Pro Bowl, the Seahawks decided to trade him to the Phoenix (now Arizona) Cardinals in April, 1988, for quarterback Kelly Stouffer. During a physical examination prior to the completion of the trade—which was eventually canceled—doctors discovered that Kenny had irreversible kidney disease: the organ was failing. He needed dialysis and, inevitably, a transplant. His life in jeopardy should he continue to play professional football, Kenny announced his retirement. In his abbreviated seven-year career, he compiled 32 interceptions for 538 return yards and scored 3 defensive touchdowns. He had also returned 27 punts for an aggregate 302 yards.

Continuing the Story

With his career prematurely cut short, Kenny regularly underwent dialysis while awaiting an organ donor. He filed a lawsuit against the Seattle Seahawks, the team trainer, and the team physicians for bad medical advice: Evidence indicated that the pain medication he had been prescribed had caused his kidney to deteriorate. The lawsuit was settled out of court, but it did not reduce hard feelings between the Seahawks and Kenny.

In 1990, Kenny received a new kidney during a 4-hour operation at the University of Washington Medical Center. Later, Kenny returned to Virginia, settling in Norfolk with his wife Gail and their three children: Kendrick, Gabrielle, and Giordanna. A successful businessman and entrepreneur, he was part owner of a semiprofessional football team, the Norfolk Nighthawks, until the franchise folded in 2003.

After his retirement from pro football, Kenny garnered numerous honors. He was inducted into the Oscar Smith High School Hall of Fame and was chosen to the all-Tidewater Golden Jubilee Team (1932-1982). In 1991, he was inducted into the UCLA Athletic Hall of Fame and the National Football Foundation's College Football Hall of Fame;

Honors and Awards

1977-80	All-Pacific Ten Conference
1978-80	All-American
1981	AFC Defensive Rookie of the Year
1982-85, 1987	NFL Pro Bowl
1983	AFC Defensive Player of the Year
1984	NFL Defensive Player of the Year
1990	NFL All-Decade Team (1980's)
1991	Inducted into UCLA Athletic Hall of Fame
	Uniform number 5 retired by UCLA
	Inducted into College Football Hall of Fame
1998	Inducted into Virginia Sports Hall of Fame
2002	Inducted into Seattle Seahawks Ring of Honor

UCLA also retired his jersey number 5. He was selected for the NFL's all-decade team during the 1980's. In 2002, he was elected to the Seattle Seahawks Ring of Honor, which finally amended the relationship between Kenny and the Seahawks.

Summary

One of the finest all-around athletes of his era, Kenny Easley performed as an outstanding defensive football player on both amateur and professional levels. His pro career was shortened by a kidney ailment exacerbated by ingredients in the pain medication he ingested during recovery from an injury. Coaches, teammates, and opponents alike considered him one of the best safeties in NFL history.

Jack Ewing

Additional Sources

Cluff, Chris. *The Good, the Bad, and the Ugly Seahawks: Heart-Pounding, Jaw-Dropping, and Gut-Wrenching Moments from Seattle Seahawk History.* Chicago: Triumph Books, 2007.

Gilbert, Sara. *The History of the Seattle Seahawks.* Hadley, Mass.: Creative Education, 2005.

Raible, Steve. *Steve Raible's Tales from the Seahawks Sideline.* Champaign, Ill.: Sports, 2004.

Carl Eller

Born: January 15, 1942
　　　Winston-Salem, North Carolina
Also known as: Carl Lee Eller (full name); Moose

Early Life
Carl Lee Eller was born on January 15, 1942, in Winston-Salem, North Carolina, the son of Clarence McGee and Ernestine Eller. When Carl was in high school, his father died. Therefore, Carl worked construction jobs in the summer to help support the family. He went to Atkins High School, where he made all-state in football, lettered in track, served as class president, and acted the lead role in Sophocles' *Antigone*. Needless to say, Carl was a dedicated and well-rounded person.

The Road to Excellence
Carl did not get into organized football until his sophomore year in high school. Even then, most people in town knew about the 185-pound ninth-grader playing sandlot football. By the conclusion of his senior season, Carl was considered a prime collegiate prospect. In 1960, Carl graduated from high school and accepted a football scholarship to the University of Minnesota. Carl joined fellow North Carolinian Bobby Bell to give Minnesota one of the finest pairs of defensive tackles ever to play college football together. In 1962, Carl and Bobby anchored the best college defense against the run in the nation. They held opponents to only 52.2 yards rushing per game. They also set a Big Ten Conference record by allowing opponents a total of only 58.2 yards per game. While Carl was a star on defense, he was also a fine blocker on offense. After his senior year, Carl was selected as an

all-American tackle, and he played for the East in the East-West Shrine All-Star Game in 1963.

Carl was in the shadow of the more outgoing Bell. Both players started as sophomores and compiled similar statistics and awards, but Carl was not the colorful and witty team clown that Bobby was. Carl was described as quiet, reflective, and dignified—a "gentlemanly giant." Carl enjoyed reading, theater, and jazz. On the field for the Gophers, Carl was known for his quick, overwhelming pass-rush

Defensive end Carl Eller, who was the NFL defensive player of the year in 1971 and an integral member of the stalwart Minnesota Vikings' defense known as the "Purple People Eaters." (Courtesy of Amateur Athletic Foundation of Los Angeles)

Honors and Awards

1963	East-West Shrine All-Star Team
	College All-American
1968-71	NFL All-Pro Team
1969-72, 1974-75	NFL Pro Bowl Team
1971	Halas Trophy (corecipient)
1980	NFL All-Pro Team of the 1970's
2004	Inducted into Pro Football Hall of Fame
2006	Inducted into College Football Hall of Fame

and jarring tackles. His coaches noticed that he was even better as an offensive blocker, however. Carl was willing to do whatever it took to help the team, even if it was not always noticeable to the fans.

At 6 feet 6 inches and 245 pounds, Carl had impressive speed. He could run the 40-yard dash in 4.5 seconds, a mark faster than many NFL running backs could achieve. The NFL's Minnesota Vikings selected Carl in the first round of the 1963 NFL draft. During training camp, he was switched to defensive end. Carl liked the change, because he had more freedom to use his speed to rush the passer, and he could use his size to knock down passes.

The Emerging Champion

With all of his apparent success as an athlete, Carl had not quite found himself as a person. He was considered shy during his early days with the Vikings. He felt awkward with newspaper reporters and had trouble answering their questions. Also, the Vikings were having difficulties between some of the black and white players on the team.

Along with Vikings teammate Jim Marshall, Carl helped ease and eventually eliminate these racial tensions. Carl's apartment in Minneapolis became a meeting place for players to discuss their problems. The responsibility helped Carl open up, and he became a leader on and off the field for the entire Vikings organization. He became a source of inspiration to his teammates, and was known for his effective halftime speeches. Sometimes he shouted, and sometimes he whispered, but the effect was always dramatic. His teammates knew that Carl tried hard to win every time he played.

Carl became one of football's most respected defensive ends during his career, which lasted from 1964 to 1979. He was named all-pro four times and

played in six Pro Bowl games. He even occasionally joined the offensive line on short-yardage situations. He was once awarded a game ball for a block he threw that enabled a Vikings back to score and win the game. He was a part of the "Purple People Eaters," a fearsome defensive line that included Alan Page, Jim Marshall, and Gary Larsen. Some of the modern rules governing pass-rushers, such as outlawing the head slap technique, were designed to control the dominance of the "Purple People Eaters." Marshall said that he and the other three players reached a point that they knew what the others were doing and where they were throughout the entire game. The four won numerous team and league awards. In 1971, Carl received the George Halas trophy as the NFL's best defensive player.

Off the field, Carl was known for his taste in clothes and his business ventures. He formed a business partnership with Marshall and a high school friend called Eller, Marshall and Blue, Inc. He was even featured once in a *Life* magazine story about his stylish home and clothes. Marshall and Carl were roommates on road games. They both were known to get tense before games. Sometimes they had water fights or pillow fights or even played chess to ease the tension. Even though Carl was fearsome on the field, he was always gracious to fans, often coming out of the locker room to chat with them after a tough game. Carl played fifteen years with the Vikings before playing one final year with the Seattle Seahawks.

Continuing the Story

After his retirement from professional football in 1979, Carl encountered more adjustment problems. He confronted his problems and sought help. As a result, Carl started a counseling program for NFL drug rehabilitation. He also started his own career counseling company, called Triumph Life Center. Furthermore, Carl was involved in the development of some of the principles of sport psychology. Before entering the counseling profession, Carl's imposing features landed him some acting roles and some television commercials. Performing remained a side interest in light of Carl's business interests.

Carl later became a consultant to corporations and government programs. Trained as a specialist on behavioral and mental health provider networks, his client list included Fortune 500 companies, sports organizations, colleges and universities, and professional and community groups from across the United States and abroad. At the state of Minnesota's department of human services, Carl developed and expanded health services for children and families, with an emphasis on children of color.

Summary

Carl Eller was an imposing, intense, and dedicated lineman in the NFL. Before that, he was considered one of the best defensive tackles ever to have played in the Big Ten Conference. Carl overcame obstacles and always strove to improve himself. A quiet man, Carl let responsibility make him a leader as an athlete, businessman, and person. In 2004, he was elected to the Pro Football Hall of Fame; two years later he was inducted into the National Football Foundation's College Football Hall of Fame.

Kevin R. Lasley

Additional Sources

Carroll, Bob. *Total Football: The Official Encyclopedia of the National Football League.* New York: Harper-Collins, 1999.

Eller, Carl. "A Sure Super Bowl Winner: Civil Rights." *USA Today,* February 2, 2007.

McDonell, Chris. *The Football Game I'll Never Forget: One Hundred NFL Stars' Stories as Told to the Editors of Football Digest.* Richmond Hill, Ont.: Firefly Books, 2004.

Zimmerman, Paul. "Gangs of Four." *Sports Illustrated* 83, no. 14 (October 6, 1995): 66-73.

John Elway

Born: June 28, 1960
　　Port Angeles, Washington
Also known as: John Albert Elway, Jr. (full name);
　　Duke of Denver; Wood

Early Life

John Albert Elway, Jr., one of the most gifted athletes to play quarterback in the NFL, was born on June 28, 1960, in Port Angeles, Washington. The son of Jack and Janet Elway, John grew up in a close, affectionate family. He had an especially warm relationship with his twin sister, Jana. Since John's father was a college football coach, the Elway family left Washington's rugged Olympic peninsula and moved frequently while the children were growing up. John's father always found time to play various sports with him.

Although John's father never pressured him to excel at sports, he instructed him in football, basketball, and baseball. When John was three years old, he swung his first plastic baseball bat, holding it in a perfect right-hander's stance. His father taught him how to swing from the left side as well, so he learned to bat from both sides of the plate. When the family moved to Los Angeles, John's father searched for a school for John with a football team known for its passing attack. Having chosen the best school district for his boy, he then began the search for a home to buy in that district.

The Road to Excellence

At Granada Hills High School, John made straight A's and played varsity football, throwing as many as 40 passes in a game. After John had passed for 3,000 yards in twelve games, his coach began to realize he was professional quarterback material. John's father had long known this. Even when John was young, he had exceptional vision. He was able to see everything happening on the basketball court or the football field. In football, he could see the whole field without distraction from his focus on the primary receiver.

After high school, John decided to play football at Stanford University. He played starting quarterback in his sophomore year; after that season, his coach predicted that John would eventually win the Heisman Trophy. In fact, he was the first sophomore in eighteen years to be a first-team all-American, and was chosen as West Coast and Pac-10 Conference player of the year.

Meanwhile, Elway studied economics, maintaining a B average. He was awarded the National Collegiate Athletic Association (NCAA) Today's Top Five award not only for his athletic success and leadership qualities, but also for his academic prowess. He also participated in the Fiesta Bowl-NCAA drug education program. In the summers,

Denver Bronco John Elway looks for an open receiver down field during this mid-1980's game. (Chris Smith/Hulton Archive/ Getty Images)

John played baseball. As a senior, he was contracted to play baseball for the New York Yankees farm team for $140,000.

In 1982, John returned to Stanford for his last football season, and he led the NCAA Division I with 24 touchdown passes. He set NCAA Division I career records for completions, interception avoidance, passing attempts, and most games with 200 or more passing yards. He was a consensus all-American, but he came in second in the Heisman Trophy voting.

The Emerging Champion

Not surprisingly, John was chosen first in the 1983 NFL draft, but he refused to play for the Baltimore Colts, the team that had selected him. He threatened to become a baseball player rather than play for the Colts' coach, who was known to be a brutal disciplinarian. A week later, the Colts traded the rights to John to the Denver Broncos, who soon signed him to a long-term contract.

Even before starting his professional football career, John was the best-known rookie quarterback since Joe Namath. His arrival in Denver caused tremendous commotion, with fans and media around

NFL Statistics

Season	GP	PA	PC	Pct.	Yds.	Avg.	TD	Int.
1983	11	259	123	47.5	1,663	6.4	7	14
1984	15	380	214	56.3	2,598	6.8	18	15
1985	16	605	327	54.0	3,891	6.4	22	23
1986	16	504	280	55.6	3,485	6.9	19	13
1987	12	410	224	54.6	3,198	7.8	19	12
1988	15	496	274	55.2	3,309	6.7	17	19
1989	15	416	223	53.6	3,051	7.3	18	18
1990	16	502	294	58.6	3,526	7.0	15	14
1991	16	451	242	53.7	3,253	7.2	13	12
1992	12	316	174	55.1	2,242	7.1	10	17
1993	16	551	348	63.2	4,030	7.3	25	10
1994	14	494	307	62.1	3,490	7.1	16	10
1995	16	542	316	58.3	3,970	7.3	26	14
1996	15	466	287	61.6	3,328	7.1	26	14
1997	16	502	280	55.8	3,635	7.2	27	11
1998	13	356	210	59.0	2,806	7.9	22	10
Totals	234	7,250	4,123	56.9	51,475	7.1	300	226

Notes: GP = games played; PA = passes attempted; PC = passes completed; Pct. = percent completed; Yds. = yards; Avg. = average yards per attempt; TD = touchdowns; Int. = interceptions

him at all times. He became known as the "Duke of Denver." John, whose twin sister described him as happiest behind a mask at a Halloween party, was never comfortable with too much attention. He had to get used to it, however, as he gained increasing national prominence.

John began his first season under the weight of high expectations and had a tough season. He was not prepared for the speed at which professionals play the game, and he could not figure out the complex NFL defenses. As a result, John completed only 47.5 percent of his 259 passes, for 1,663 yards. He thought about quitting football.

Because of John's competitiveness, he persevered. He studied films during the off-season and worked out with weights, building himself up. By his third NFL season it all paid off: He led the NFL in total offense and completed 54 percent of his 605 passes, throwing 22 touchdowns.

While John had matured as a player, he still threw too many interceptions. He believed stubbornly that he could do anything with his all-powerful arm and fast feet. At times, he tried to make great plays all the time—as his fans expected—relying on improvisation

Honors and Awards

1980, 1982	*Sporting News* College All-American
1982	Walter Camp Award
1983	NCAA Today's Top Five Award
	Overall first choice in the NFL draft
1986-87, 1993-94, 1996	NFL Pro Bowl Team
1987	Associated Press NFL Player of the Year
	United Press International AFC Offensive Player of the Year
	Sporting News NFL All-Star Team
1993	AFC most valuable player
	United Press International AFC Offensive Player of the Year
1999	Super Bowl most valuable player
	Inducted into Denver Broncos Ring of Fame
	Uniform number 7 retired by Broncos
2000	Inducted into College Football Hall of Fame
2003	Inducted into Bay Area Sports Hall of Fame
2004	Inducted into Pro Football Hall of Fame

and instinct. He soon learned he was trying to do too much, and that he needed to play smart, read defenses better, and accept what the defenses gave him.

By the 1986 season, he posted numbers that showed he had achieved the greatness long predicted for him: 280 of 504 passes for 3,485 yards and 19 touchdowns. That year, he threw only 13 interceptions. In 1986, 1987, and 1989, he led the Broncos to victories in the American Football Conference (AFC) championship games and on to the Super Bowl. Some said John was a one-man team.

Continuing the Story

In 1990, in Super Bowl XXIV, Denver lost badly to the San Francisco 49ers, 55-10. Joe Montana, of the 49ers, earned most valuable player honors. John and his father stayed up all that night playing ping-pong, both of them grudging losers unable to call it quits.

In 1993, John was named AFC most valuable player by the NFL Placekickers Association and AFC offensive player of the year by United Press International. He was the starting quarterback in the 1994 Pro Bowl after a regular season in which he lead the AFC in all six major quarterback statistical categories. John's 1993 statistics and rankings included a 92.8 rating, first in the AFC, third in the NFL; 551 attempts, first in the NFL; 348 completions, first in the NFL; a 63.2 completion percentage, first in the AFC, third in the NFL; 25 touchdown passes, first in the AFC, second in the NFL; and 4,030 yards, first in the AFC.

In 1996, John earned his fifth Pro Bowl selection and was again a statistical leader. That year he moved into third place in all-time career passing yards and became the third NFL player to throw for 45,000 yards in a career. John also surpassed hall-of-famer Fran Tarkenton as the winningest starting quarterback in NFL history.

In 1997 and 1998, John continued to be a statistical leader, cementing his place in NFL history as one of the top quarterbacks of all time. He capped his career in Super Bowl XXXII on January 25, 1998, by leading the Broncos to a 31-24 victory over the Green Bay Packers, and in Super Bowl XXXIII on January 31, 1999, by contributing to a 34-19 win against the Atlanta Falcons. With two Super Bowl victories to his credit, John announced his retirement from professional football in April, 1999.

When his playing days ended, John entered the business world. He owned several auto dealerships and was the proprietor of two steak houses in the Denver area. He also became co-owner of the Colorado Crush, an Arena Football League team. In 2004, John was elected to the Pro Football Hall of Fame in his first year of eligibility.

Summary

John Elway is considered by some to be the most gifted athlete ever to play quarterback in the NFL. After he joined the Denver Broncos in 1984, the team became the AFC's premier franchise. After a number of attempts, John and the Denver Broncos finally triumphed in the Super Bowl in 1998 and 1999.

Nan White

Additional Sources

"John Elway: On the Road to Relief." *Saturday Evening Post* 277, no. 4 (July/August, 2005): 24.

Latimer, Clay. *John Elway, Armed and Dangerous.* Rev. ed. Lenexa, Kans.: Addax, 2002.

Sabino, David, Kostya Kennedy, and Mark Bechtel. "John Denver." *Sports Illustrated* 100, no. 7 (February 16, 2004): 24-26.

Boomer Esiason

Born: April 17, 1961
      West Islip, New York
Also known as: Norman Julius Esiason (full
    name)

Early Life

Norman Julius "Boomer" Esiason was born in West Islip, New York, on April 17, 1961. He acquired the nickname "Boomer" before he was born. While Boomer's mother was pregnant, a friend from his father's college football team came to visit the family. The friend, upon seeing Boomer's mother react to her baby kicking, said that she had quite a boomer. The nickname stuck. During his childhood, Boomer had such an aversion to his given name, Norman, that he routinely fought anyone who called him that. This toughness helped him as he began playing sports.

Boomer Esiason, who led the Cincinnati Bengals to Super Bowl XXIII. (Ron Vesely/Getty Images)

When Boomer was seven years old, his mother passed away. Sports filled part of the void he felt from the death of his mother. Boomer's father traveled two hours to Manhattan each day, which left Boomer alone much of the day. Sports not only kept Boomer occupied but also gave him structure. During high school, Boomer did not limit his focus to football. He played basketball and baseball also. In fact, he was so good at baseball that, in his senior year, he was named the Yastrzemski Award winner as the best baseball player on Long Island.

Boomer's football career might never have begun if he had not played basketball. A University of Maryland football coach was in New York to scout a player on a team opposing Boomer's. When Boomer outplayed the other player, he was offered a visit to Maryland—the school for which he eventually played collegiate football.

The Road to Excellence

At the University of Maryland, Boomer blossomed into an excellent quarterback. Under the tutelage of Coach Bobby Ross, who later became an NFL head coach, and Ralph Friedgen, an innovative offense coordinator, Boomer was challenged and developed the skills that helped him in the NFL.

Even though Maryland recruited a bigger name to play quarterback while Boomer was there, Boomer's drive to succeed pushed him to remain the starter. By graduation, Boomer had set seventeen school records and was named an all-American honorable mention for both 1982 and 1983.

With a cache of gaudy statistics and a body built for the NFL, Boomer was excited to take the next step. His enthusiasm was thwarted when he was selected in the second round, at thirty-seventh overall, by the Cincinnati Bengals. He was perceived as a first-round talent and was amazed that he had not been selected earlier. However, he was the first quarterback taken in the draft.

The Emerging Champion

In Boomer's first start, on October 7, 1984, he led the Bengals to a victory over the Houston Oilers (now Tennessee Titans), 13-3. The win was not

NFL Statistics

Season	GP	PA	PC	Pct.	Yds.	Avg.	TD	Int.
1984	10	102	51	50.0	530	5.2	3	3
1985	15	431	251	58.2	3,443	8.0	27	12
1986	16	469	273	58.2	3,959	8.4	24	17
1987	12	440	240	54.5	3,321	7.5	16	19
1988	16	388	223	57.5	3,572	9.2	28	14
1989	16	455	258	56.7	3,525	7.7	28	11
1990	16	402	224	55.7	3,031	7.5	24	22
1991	14	413	233	56.4	2,883	7.0	13	16
1992	12	478	144	51.8	1,407	5.1	11	15
1993	16	476	288	60.9	3,421	7.2	16	11
1994	15	440	255	58.0	2,782	6.3	17	13
1995	12	389	221	56.8	2,275	5.8	16	15
1996	10	339	190	56.0	2,293	6.8	11	14
1997	7	186	118	63.4	1,478	7.9	13	2
Totals	187	5,205	2,969	57.0	37,920	7.3	247	184

Notes: GP = games played; PA = passes attempted; PC = passes completed; Pct. = percent completed; Yds. = yards; Avg. = average yards per attempt; TD = touchdowns; Int. = interceptions

enough to make Boomer the full-time starter. The Bengals still had Ken Anderson, the quarterback who had taken the Bengals to the Super Bowl two years earlier. However, the following year, 1985, Boomer took over the starting position.

From that point forward, Boomer excelled at his position. He was named to three Pro Bowls with the Bengals—1986, 1988, 1989—and won a league most valuable player award in 1988. That year, Boomer led his team to the Super Bowl. With the help of a tough defense and excellent special teams, Boomer guided his team to a 16-13 lead with slightly more than two minutes remaining in the Super Bowl. However, Joe Montana led the San Francisco 49ers down the field to score a touchdown with thirty-four seconds remaining, which gave the 49ers a 20-16 win.

Continuing the Story

Boomer played for the Bengals for another four years but was unable to duplicate his success. In 1993, he signed with the New York Jets. That year, he earned another Pro Bowl invitation. He stayed in New York through the 1995 season before switching to the Arizona Cardinals, where

he played for one year. When his contract expired, Boomer contemplated retiring but, instead, was persuaded to play one more year, for the Cincinnati Bengals. Though a thirteen-year veteran, he still displayed the skills that had made him special.

In 1993, Boomer experienced a life-changing event. His son, Gunnar, was diagnosed with cystic fibrosis. Boomer became a noted speaker and fund-raiser to help cure the disease. The Boomer Esiason Foundation raised more than $60 million for this cause.

Summary

When Boomer Esiason retired, he was considered one of the top fifteen quarterbacks ever to have played football. He is considered one of the best left-handed quarterbacks in NFL history. After his football career, he turned to broadcasting. He was an analyst on CBS's *NFL Today* and host of a radio show in New York.

P. Huston Ladner

Additional Sources

Cannizzaro, Mark. *Tales from the New York Jets Sideline.* Champaign, Ill.: Sports, 2007.

Esiason, Boomer, and Jacqueline Rogers. *A Boy Named Boomer.* New York: Scholastic, 1995.

Wertheim, L. Jon. "Where Are They Now?" *Sports Illustrated* 107, no. 1 (July 2, 2007): 80-83.

Zaslow, Jeffrey. "Straight Talk." *USA Weekend*, October 9, 1998.

Honors and Awards

1986, 1988-89, 1993	NFL Pro Bowl
1988	NFL most valuable player
	United Press International AFC Player of the Year
	Pro Football Writers of America NFL most valuable player
1995	Walter Payton Award
2006	Joe DiMaggio Award

Marshall Faulk

Born: February 26, 1973
New Orleans, Louisiana
Also known as: Marshall William Faulk (full
name)

Early Life

Marshall William Faulk was born in New Orleans, Louisiana, in 1973. He grew up, with his mother and five brothers, in the Desire housing project in the rough ninth ward of New Orleans. Later, he attended George Washington Carver High School. He excelled at football and started as running back, quarterback, wide receiver, and cornerback. He also lettered in track and worked summers at a law firm in New Orleans.

Many college football coaches recruited Marshall to play defense. He eventually chose to attend San Diego State University (SDSU) because it was the only school that allowed him the chance to play running back. While there, he majored in public administration.

The Road to Excellence

As a freshman at SDSU in 1991, Marshall set several National Collegiate Athletic Association (NCAA) Division I-A records. He was the first freshman to lead the nation in scoring, at 15.6 points per game, and rushing, with 158 yards per game. He also rushed for 386 yards and scored 7 touchdowns in his second game of the season. He finished ninth in the Heisman Trophy balloting as a freshman, won Associated Press (AP) all-American first team honors, and was named United Press International freshman of the year.

As a sophomore and the full-time starting running back, Marshall became only the fifth player to win back-to-back NCAA rushing titles. He also became the second running back in the NCAA to rush for more than 3,000 yards in the first two years of a college career. Marshall became a double threat to defenders by developing into an accomplished receiver coming out of the backfield; he caught 18 passes for 128 yards. In 1992, he finished sec-

ond in the Heisman Trophy balloting and was named to the AP all-American team again.

Though rumors spread after the season that Marshall would leave college to enter the NFL draft, he remained at SDSU. In his junior year, he ranked fifth in NCAA rushing, finished fourth in the Heisman race, and earned his third consecutive all-American selection. Finally, he decided to turn professional and was selected second overall in the 1994 NFL draft by the Indianapolis Colts.

The Emerging Champion

As a rookie, Marshall rushed 314 times for 1,282 yards and caught 52 passes for 522 yards. Based on these performances, he earned NFL offensive rookie of the year honors and was named as a starter for the Pro Bowl. In 1995, he led the Colts in rush-

Marshall Faulk. (Ezra Shaw/Getty Images)

ing attempts, rushing yards, and receptions. He ranked twelfth in the NFL for rushing and earned his second consecutive Pro Bowl berth. At the Pro Bowl, he was named the game's most valuable player (MVP).

In the 1996 season, Marshall was injured for three games but still managed to lead the Colts in rushing for his third consecutive season. He also accumulated more than 1,000 yards of offense from scrimmage, both rushing and receiving, for the third time in his career. In 1997, he returned to top form and rushed for his third 1,000-yard season and had a career-best four 100-yards-rushing games. He ranked thirteenth in the NFL for rushing that year. Marshall set the Colts' single-season record and led the NFL with 2,227 total yards in 1998. He was the only player with 100-yard-rushing and receiving games and earned his third trip to the Pro Bowl.

Continuing the Story

The Colts traded Marshall to the St. Louis Rams on April 14, 1999, in exchange for the Rams' second- and fifth-round draft picks. Marshall responded

with his best season ever. He became only the second player in the history of the NFL—Roger Craig was the first, in 1985—to have more than 1,000 yards of rushing and receiving in a single season. He rushed for 1,381 yards and had 1,048 receiving yards, which helped lead the Rams to success in regular-season and postseason play. The Rams won Super Bowl XXXIV, beating the Tennessee Titans 23-16, and Marshall was named the NFL offensive player of the year. He was selected for his fourth Pro Bowl in six seasons.

In 2000, Marshall became the first running back in the NFL to lead his team in receptions in five separate seasons. He also set an NFL record with 26 touchdowns, had 2,189 total yards, was the NFL MVP and the offensive player of the year, and was selected to his fifth Pro Bowl. During the 2001 season, Marshall had a career-high 1,382 rushing yards. Furthermore, he led the NFL in yards per rushing attempt, with 5.3; rushing yards per game, with 98.7; touchdowns, with 21; and points scored, with 128. The Rams advanced to the Super Bowl but

---

Honors, Awards, and Milestones

1994	Consensus NFL Offensive Rookie of the Year
	Only rookie to appear in this year's Pro Bowl
	Set Pro Bowl records for rushing yardage, highest average gain per attempt, yards from scrimmage, and longest run from scrimmage
1994-95, 1998-99, 2000-01	Pro Bowl
1995	Led team in rushing attempts, rushing yardage, and receptions
	Pro Bowl most valuable player
1998	Set Colts single-season record and led the NFL with 2,227 total yards from scrimmage
	Only player in NFL with at least 900 yards rushing and receiving
	Led Colts and all NFL running backs in receptions with team record: 86 catches for 908 receiving yards
1999-2000	Associated Press NFL Offensive Player of the Year
2000	NFL most valuable player
	Sporting News Sportsman of the Year (shared with Kurt Warner)
2007	Uniform number 28 retired by St. Louis Rams

NFL Statistics

| Season | GP | Rushing | | | | Receiving | | | |
		Car.	Yds.	Avg.	TD	Rec.	Yds.	Avg.	TD
1994	16	314	1,282	4.1	11	52	522	10.0	1
1995	16	289	1,078	3.7	11	56	475	8.5	3
1996	13	198	587	3.0	7	56	428	7.6	0
1997	16	264	1,054	4.0	7	47	471	10.0	1
1998	16	324	1,319	4.1	6	86	908	10.6	4
1999	16	253	1,381	5.5	7	87	1,048	12.0	5
2000	14	253	1,359	5.4	18	81	830	10.2	8
2001	14	260	1,382	5.3	12	83	765	9.2	9
2002	14	212	953	4.5	8	80	537	6.7	2
2003	11	209	818	3.9	10	45	290	6.4	1
2004	14	195	774	4.0	3	50	310	6.2	1
2005	16	65	292	4.5	0	44	291	6.6	1
Totals	176	2,836	12,279	4.3	100	767	6,875	9.0	36

Notes: GP = games played; Car. = carries; Yds. = yards; Avg. = average yards per carry *or* average yards per reception; TD = touchdowns; Rec. = receptions

lost to the New England Patriots, 20-17. However, for the third year in a row, Marshall was named the NFL offensive player of the year and to his sixth Pro Bowl.

Over the next four seasons, Marshall was unable to equal his previous seasons. He never again rushed for more than 1,000 yards, and he suffered numerous injuries. Prior to the 2006 season, Marshall underwent reconstructive knee surgery and sat out the entire year. During that time, he served as an analyst for the NFL Network's *NFL Total Access.* Finally, after much speculation, on March 26, 2007, Marshall announced his retirement from football. He then easily transitioned into a full-time football analyst on *NFL Total Access.*

Marshall also made significant contributions off the football field. When he was drafted into the NFL in 1994, he established the Marshall Faulk Foundation to benefit children's charities and organizations. This foundation donated more than $150,000 to underprivileged children in New Orleans, Indianapolis, and St. Louis.

Summary

For a decade, beginning in 1994, Marshall Faulk became one of the most exciting players in the NFL. He combined his speed, power, and elusiveness to outmaneuver defenders. He amassed more than 10,000 rushing and 5,000 receiving yards and was the first player to have 100 rushing and more than 30 receiving touchdowns. In his thirteen-year professional career, Marshall became one of the most prolific running backs in the sport.

Tinker D. Murray,
updated by Lamia Nuseibeh Scherzinger

Additional Sources

Bell, Lonnie. *The History of the St. Louis Rams.* Mankato, Minn.: Creative Education, 2004.

Dillon, Dennis. "Grand Marshall." *The Sporting News,* December 27, 1999, 42-43.

Pierce, Charles P. "The Magnificent Seven." *Esquire,* September, 2000, 208-217.

Rains, Rob. *Marshall Faulk: Rushing to Glory.* Champaign, Ill.: Sports, 2000.

Brett Favre

Born: October 10, 1969
Gulfport, Mississippi
Also known as: Brett Lorenzo Favre (full name);
Country

Early Life
Brett Lorenzo Favre was born on October 10, 1969, in Gulfport, Mississippi. His father, Irvin, was a football and baseball coach as well as a driver's education teacher at Hancock North Central High School, while his mother, Bonita, was a special education teacher. He also had two brothers, Scott and Jeff, and a sister, Brandi.

Brett Favre moving out of the pocket, looking for a receiver in a 2007 game against the Minnesota Vikings. (Jonathan Daniel/Getty Images)

In high school, Brett played quarterback and safety, but because of the team's weak offense, he was not recruited to play quarterback for any Division I-A college football programs. However, the University of Southern Mississippi offered him a scholarship to play defensive back, an offer that he accepted. Working his way up the depth chart, he eventually became the starting quarterback and led Southern Mississippi to two bowl appearances and twenty-nine victories over four years. Despite a major injury between his junior and senior seasons, Brett was drafted thirty-third overall in the 1991 NFL draft by the Atlanta Falcons. On draft day, he was so little known that he was announced as "quarterback, Brett Fay-verer."

The Road to Excellence
In 1992, the Falcons traded Brett to the Green Bay Packers for a first-round draft pick. That same year, Brett brought the Packers within one game of the playoffs and made the Pro Bowl for the first time in his career. At twenty-three years old, he became the youngest quarterback at that time to receive that honor. During the season he threw 471 passes and connected on 302, while passing for 3,227 yards and 18 touchdowns. In 1993, the Packers' acquired Pro Bowl defensive end Reggie White. He and Brett represented the resurgence of the Packers dynasty.

The Emerging Champion
Brett continued to play well. In 1995, he became only the third 4,000-yard passer in team history. He finished the season with an NFL best of 4,413 passing yards and became the first player in team history to post four 3,000-yard seasons. He led the National Football Conference (NFC) with a 99.5 passer rating and threw 3 or more touchdown passes in a game on seven occasions. He started in the Pro Bowl and was named the NFL's most valuable player (MVP). Brett led the

NFL Statistics

Season	GP	PA	PC	Pct.	Yds.	Avg.	TD	Int.
1991	2	5	0	.000	0	0.00	0	2
1992	15	471	302	.641	3,227	6.85	18	13
1993	16	522	318	.609	3,303	6.33	19	24
1994	16	582	363	.624	3,882	6.67	33	14
1995	16	570	359	.630	4,413	7.74	38	13
1996	16	543	325	.599	3,899	7.18	39	13
1997	16	513	304	.593	3,867	7.54	35	16
1998	16	551	347	.630	4,212	7.64	31	23
1999	16	595	341	.573	4,091	6.88	22	23
2000	16	580	338	.583	3,812	6.57	20	16
2001	16	510	314	61.6	3,921	7.7	32	15
2002	16	551	341	61.9	3,658	6.6	27	16
2003	16	471	308	65.4	3,361	7.1	32	21
2004	16	540	346	64.1	4,088	7.6	30	17
2005	16	607	372	61.3	3,881	6.4	20	29
2006	16	613	343	56.0	3,885	6.3	18	18
2007	16	535	356	66.5	4,155	7.8	28	15
2008	16	522	343	65.7	3,472	6.7	22	22
Totals	273	9,280	5,720	61.6	65,127	7.0	464	310

Notes: GP = games played; PA = passes attempted; PC = passes completed; Pct. = percent completed; Yds. = yards; Avg. = average yards per attempt; TD = touchdowns; Int. = interceptions

Packers to the NFC Central Division championship with a record of 11-5.

After three straight losses in the NFC Championship game, Brett finally led the Packers to the Super Bowl. A 30-13 victory over the Carolina Panthers in the NFC Championship game brought Brett and the Packers to Super Bowl XXXI. At the Louisiana Superdome, Brett led the Packers to a 35-21 victory over the New England Patriots, giving him his first Super Bowl championship.

In 1996, when he threw 39 touchdown passes, Brett set NFC and Green Bay records for most touchdown passes in a season for the second straight year; his total was the third highest in a single NFL season at that time. He also threw for an NFC-best 3,899 yards and ranked highest in fourth-quarter passing, 96.2, and third-down passing, 93.6. Brett also rushed for 136 yards and 2 touchdowns. He was voted into the Pro Bowl as starting quarterback and was voted the NFL's most valuable player for the second time.

Prior to the 1996 season, Brett revealed that he had become addicted to painkillers, which he had been using for his many injuries. He spent forty-six days in the Menninger Clinic in Topeka, Kansas, for drug and alcohol treatment. Through sheer will and determination, Brett was able to overcome this problem.

Continuing the Story

After that, Brett signed a $47.25 million, seven-year contract with the Packers. His 108 touchdowns from 1997 to 2000 led all NFL quarterbacks during that time span. Brett threw for 3,000 or more yards in sixteen consecutive seasons. He has started 253 consecutive regular-season games, the longest streak of any active quarterback in the league history.

In 1997, Brett led the NFL with 35 touchdown passes and finished third in the NFL's quarterback ratings with a mark of 92.6. He was named co-MVP of the NFL with running back Barry Sanders of the Detroit Lions. Once again, the Packers won the NFC Championship game, defeating the San Francisco 49ers 23-10. This led to a second straight Super Bowl appearance, but Brett could not lead the Packers to victory, and the team was defeated by the Denver Broncos, 31-24, in Super Bowl XXXII.

The Packers did not win another Super Bowl with Brett as quarterback. Some of his supporting cast retired or moved on and his coach soon left for the Seattle Seahawks. It seemed as if everything was changing in Green Bay except for Brett. Although the Packers did not win another Super Bowl under Brett's guidance, Green Bay fans lived on the edge of their seats on Sundays. However, "America's quarterback" was far from done when it came to winning football games.

In December, 2003, Brett lost his father, who suffered a heart attack at the age of fifty-eight. The day after "Big Irv" died, Favre defeated the Oakland Raiders on Monday Night Football in a game that NFL fans will never forget.

Brett married his high school sweetheart, Deanna Tynes, and had two daughters, Brittany and Breleigh. In March, 2008, Brett officially retired. He and his family adjourned to their 465 acre ranch in Hattiesburg, Mississippi. However, he was not ready to quit and returned to the NFL in the

2008 season, playing for the New York Jets. He led the Jets to a 9-7 record, but their failure to reach the playoffs was a disappointment. In February, 2009, Brett again announced his retirement.

Summary

Brett Favre stands among the great quarterbacks of all time. His accurate passing and powerful arm not only led him to personal greatness, with three MVP awards, but also led the Green Bay Packers to team greatness in two Super Bowl appearances and one championship. He was an eight-time Pro Bowler and set the NFL records for most touchdown passes, most career completions, most career attempts, most regular season wins by a quarterback, and most consecutive 3,000-yard passing seasons.

Richard Slapsys,
updated by Shane L. Hudson

Honors and Awards

1990's	NFL All-Decade Team
1992-93, 1995-97, 2001-03, 2007-08	NFL Pro Bowl Team
1995-96	Newspaper Enterprise Association NFL most valuable player
	Bert Bell Award
	Associated Press NFL Offensive Player of the Year
1995-97	NFL All-Pro first team
	Associated Press NFL most valuable player
1996	NFL Pro Bowl Team
	Pro Bowl most valuable player
1996-97	Professional Football Writers Association NFL most valuable player
	Super Bowl most valuable player
1999	Number 82 on *Sporting News* list of greatest football players
2003	Named Toughest Person in America by *Men's Health Magazine*
2004	Wisconsin declares November 29 Brett Favre Day
2005	Number 5 on *Sporting News* list of greatest quarterbacks
2007	*Sports Illustrated* Sportsman of the Year
	Chris Greicius Celebrity Award
	U.S. Sports Academy Male Athlete of the Year Award

Additional Sources

Cameron, Steve. *Brett Favre: Huck Finn Grows Up.* Kalamazoo, Mich.: Masters Press, 1997.

Carlson, Chuck, and Vernon J. Biever. *Brett Favre, QB.* Kalamazoo, Mich.: Masters Press, 1996.

_____. *Celebrating the Legend of Brett Favre: America's Quarterback.* Chicago: Triumph Books, 2007.

Favre, Brett, and Chris Havel. *Favre: For the Record.* New York: Doubleday, 1997.

Kertscher, Tom. *Brett Favre: A Packer Fan's Tribute.* Rev. ed. Nashville, Tenn.: Cumberland House, 2007.

McHale, Mark. *Ten to Four: Brett Favre's Journey from Rotten Bayou to the Top of the NFL.* Macon, Ga.: Indigo, 2007.

Doug Flutie

Born: October 23, 1962
      Baltimore, Maryland
Also known as: Douglas Richard Flutie

Early Life

Douglas Richard Flutie grew up in Melbourne Beach, Florida, where he played quarterback in the Pop Warner league. His father, a computer engineer, moved the family to Natick, Massachusetts, when Doug was thirteen, which was not entirely to Doug's liking. The move meant he had to leave behind his friends and life on the beach.

Doug attended Natick High School, where he eventually earned eight varsity letters and all-league honors in football, basketball, and baseball. He was also a model student, earning straight A's in the classroom. Doug's dream was to play major college football, but because of his small size, the 5-foot, 10-inch, 173-pounder received few scholarship offers from major college programs. Eventually, however, the Boston College Eagles offered Doug a scholarship, and he eagerly accepted it.

The Road to Excellence

Doug began far down the Eagles' depth chart as a quarterback. In fact, at one time he contemplated switching to wide receiver. Doug's big break came in the fourth game of his freshman season in 1981, when he was inserted into the lineup against Penn State University with the Eagles trailing 38-0. Doug proceeded to complete 8 of 18 pass attempts for 135 yards, and threw 1 touchdown and 1 interception. This effort earned him the starting quarterback job, and he played in more than half of the Eagles' remaining games. In his sophomore season, Doug played in all eleven regular-season games and led his team to an 8-2-1 record. He completed 162 of 348 pass attempts, for 2,749 yards and a 46.6% completion percentage. Against Penn State that year, he passed for 520 yards, which was a career best and a Boston College record. Boston College, in its first bowl appearance in forty years, faced the Auburn Tigers in the Tangerine Bowl, but lost the game 33-26. Nevertheless, Doug completed 22 of 38 passes for 299 yards and 2 touchdowns and was named the game's most valuable player.

San Diego Chargers quarterback Doug Flutie passing his team to a victory over the Minnesota Vikings in 2003. (Mike Blake/Reuters/Landov)

In his junior year, Doug completed 177 of 345 pass attempts for 2,724 yards, 18 touchdowns, and 15 interceptions. Doug guided Boston College to a 9-2 record and into the Liberty Bowl, where the Eagles lost to Notre Dame, 19-18. In his senior season, Doug completed 233 of 386 passes for 3,454 yards, 27 touchdowns, and 11 interceptions. During his senior year, Doug enjoyed one of his most memorable games, engineering a 47-45 victory over the defending national champion Miami Hurricanes. Doug's game-ending, 48-yard "Hail Mary" touchdown pass to Gerard Phelan capped an improbable come-from-behind victory. He went on to lead the Eagles to another 9-2 regular-season record and a win over the University of Houston in the Cotton Bowl, 45-28. In this game, Doug connected on 13 of 37 passes for 180 yards and 2 touchdowns. For his achievements during this season, Doug was awarded the Heisman Trophy and was named the *Sporting News* college football player of the year. By the time Doug finished his collegiate career, he had passed for what was then a record 10,579 yards.

The Emerging Champion

Upon graduation from college, NFL scouts, like the college recruiters before them, were troubled by Doug's diminutive stature and indicated they were not interested in his services. Therefore, Doug signed a pro contract in the United States Football League (USFL) with the New Jersey Generals. During his rookie year for the Generals, Doug completed 134 of 281 passes for 2,109 yards and 13 touchdowns. However, Doug's season ended early when he fractured his collarbone in a game against the Memphis Showboats. In 1986, the USFL suspended operations, and Doug moved to the NFL, where he played with the Chicago Bears and New England Patriots. As one of the most popular collegiate athletes in Boston history, Doug became an immediate favorite with the Patriots' fans. While he managed to register several exciting victories, he was never able to meet the high expectations held by fans who wanted Doug to do for the Patriots what he had done for Boston College. In 1989, after his release from New England, Doug headed for the Canadian Football League (CFL) where a bigger field and a wide-open style ideally suited his scrambling tendencies.

Continuing the Story

During his CFL career, Doug played for the British Columbia Lions, Calgary Stampeders, and Toronto Argonauts. He led the league in passing yardage five times, won the CFL's most outstanding player award an unprecedented six times, and led his teams to three Grey Cup Championships—the equivalent of a Super Bowl victory. During a title game against Saskatchewan in 1997, Doug, playing for Toronto,

NFL Statistics

Season	GP	PA	PC	Pct.	Yds.	Avg.	TD	Int.
1986	—	46	23	.500	361	7.85	3	2
1987	—	25	15	.600	199	7.96	1	0
1988	—	179	92	.514	1,150	6.42	8	10
1989	—	91	36	.396	493	5.42	2	4
1998	13	354	202	.571	2,711	7.66	20	11
1999	15	478	264	.552	3,171	6.63	19	16
2000	11	231	132	.571	1,700	7.36	8	3
2001	16	521	294	56.4	3,464	6.6	15	18
2002	1	11	3	27.3	65	5.8	0	0
2003	7	167	91	54.5	1,097	6.6	9	4
2004	2	38	20	52.6	276	7.3	1	0
2005	5	10	5	50.0	29	2.9	0	0
Totals	103	2,151	1,777	54.7	14,715	6.8	86	68

Notes: GP = games played; PA = passes attempted; PC = passes completed; Pct. = percent completed; Yds. = yards; Avg. = average yards per attempt; TD = touchdowns; Int. = interceptions

Honors and Awards

1983	Liberty Bowl most valuable player
1984	Heisman Trophy
	Sporting News College Football Player of the Year
	Walter Camp Award
	Davy O'Brien National Quarterback Award
	Maxwell Award
1991-94, 1996-97	Canadian Football League most outstanding player
1992, 1996-97	Grey Cup most valuable player
1998	NFL Pro Bowl Team
	NFL Comeback Player of the Year
2003	San Diego Chargers most inspirational player award
2007	Elected to College Football Hall of Fame
2008	Inducted into Canadian Football Hall of Fame

completed 30 of 38 pass attempts and threw 3 touchdowns. He also rushed 5 times for 35 yards and 1 touchdown, leading the Argonauts to a 47-23 victory.

After eight seasons in the CFL, Doug returned to the NFL in 1998, signing with the Buffalo Bills as a free agent. He returned triumphantly, leading the Bills to a playoff berth and earning a Pro Bowl selection. He also won NFL comeback player of the year honors. Doug took over the starting quarterback position five games into the season and guided the Bills to a 7-3 record in his ten regular-season starts. Despite building a winning record with the Bills, Doug was eventually released by the team.

In 2001, Doug signed with the San Diego Chargers as a free agent. He started all sixteen games with the Chargers and set a career high with 3,464 yards passing. This yardage total was the seventh-highest in Chargers' team history. Following the 2001 season, Doug was relegated to backup quarterback behind Drew Brees. In 2003, at the age of forty-one, Doug gained more time, replacing an ineffective Brees, and performed well. During this season, Doug was the corecipient of the Chargers' Emil Karas Award for most inspirational player, after starting five of seven games. This performance prompted San Diego to sign him to a 3-year contract in 2004; however, Doug was released by the Chargers the following year.

In April, 2005, Doug signed with the Patriots as a backup to Tom Brady. On the final play of his career, Doug infamously drilled a drop-kick extra point through the uprights in a meaningless January game against the Miami Dolphins. After the 2005 season, Doug officially retired from pro football. In 2007, Doug was elected to the National Football Foundation's College Football Hall of Fame. The following year, he was inducted into the Canadian Football Hall of Fame.

Summary

The sight of Doug Flutie, as a diminutive quarterback, outmaneuvering and outfoxing players twice his size is an enduring image. Throughout his distinguished career, Doug utilized perseverance and flexibility to overcome enormous odds as a smaller athlete engaged in a big man's sport. Few professional quarterbacks of Doug's physical stature have been able to attain similar success. Doug's determination also served him well in his personal life, helping him cope with his son's autism, a condition that led him to establish the Doug Flutie, Jr. Foundation for Autism, which focused on raising awareness of the disorder and support for the afflicted. In 1998, this cause also spurred the creation of Flutie Flakes, the frosted-corn-flakes breakfast cereal named in honor of Doug. A large portion of the profits garnered from sales of Flutie Flakes were donated to the Doug Flutie, Jr. Foundation for Autism. After his retirement, Doug worked as a college football analyst for both ESPN and ABC Sports.

William H. Hoffman, updated by Michael Stellefson

Additional Sources

Flutie, Doug. *Flutie.* Toronto: Warwick, 1998.

————. *Never Say Never.* Dallas: Taylor, 1999.

Kirkpatrick, R. *Doug Flutie: International Football Star.* New York: PowerKids Press, 2000.

Looney, Douglas. "A Little Man on Campus." *Sports Illustrated* 59 (September 26, 1983): 38-45.

Wulf, Steve. "Mr. Touchdown Scores Again." *Sports Illustrated* 62 (February 4, 1985): 20-27.

Dan Fouts

Born: June 10, 1951
      San Francisco, California
Also known as: Daniel Francis Fouts (full name)

Early Life

Daniel Francis Fouts was born into football. His father, Bob Fouts, was the play-by-play announcer for the San Francisco 49ers, and as a child, Dan was the team's ball boy. At St. Ignatius High School in San Francisco, Dan tried out for all the major sports teams. He could not run, jump, or hit the curve ball, but he could throw a football. As quarterback he led the team to the city championship. His lack of athleticism meant that only one major college, the University of Oregon, recruited him. At Oregon, he started at quarterback in his sophomore through senior years, recording 5,995 passing yards and 57 touchdowns. Those numbers garnered him a selection in the third round of the 1973 NFL draft, by the San Diego Chargers.

The Road to Excellence

In his first year with the Chargers, Dan began as the backup to Johnny Unitas, one of the greatest quarterbacks ever. Unitas, however, had been worn down by years of play and injuries, and he was not the quarterback he once had been. After Unitas started the first four games, Dan took over.

The Chargers were not very good at that point. In Dan's first three years the team's record was 9-32-1, but Dan was improving. One person who noticed his improvement was Bill Walsh, who came to the Chargers as offensive coordinator in 1976, on his way to glory with the San Francisco 49ers. That season Dan threw for 2,535 yards; Walsh called him the greatest leader he had ever coached.

In 1977, Walsh took the head coaching position at Stanford University, and the Chargers planned to replace Dan with newly acquired James Harris. Dan announced his retirement, moved to a log cabin in Oregon,

and joined seventeen other players in a lawsuit to overturn the league's collective bargaining agreement, which impeded free agency.

Dan lost the suit but was offered a lucrative contract to re-sign with the Chargers. Dan returned in the middle of the 1977 season. Dan's fortunes radically changed when Don Coryell took over as the Chargers' head coach in the fifth game of the 1978 season.

The Emerging Champion

Coryell had an offensive approach, known as "Air Coryell," that emphasized the pass. Dan had the strong arm on which to carry the team. Only one

Dan Fouts, who passed for more than 43,000 yards in his career. (Rogers Photo Archive/Getty Images)

NFL Statistics

Season	GP	PA	PC	Pct.	Yds.	Avg.	TD	Int.
1973	10	194	87	44.8	1,126	5.8	6	13
1974	11	237	115	48.5	1,732	7.3	8	13
1975	10	195	106	54.4	1,396	7.2	2	10
1976	14	359	208	57.9	2,535	7.1	14	15
1977	4	109	69	63.3	869	8.0	4	6
1978	15	381	224	58.8	2,999	7.9	24	20
1979	16	530	332	62.6	4,082	7.7	24	24
1980	16	589	348	59.1	4,715	8.0	30	24
1981	16	609	360	59.1	4,802	7.9	33	17
1982	9	330	204	61.8	2,883	8.7	17	11
1983	10	340	215	63.2	2,975	8.8	20	15
1984	13	507	317	62.5	3,740	7.4	19	17
1985	14	430	254	59.1	3,638	8.5	27	20
1986	12	430	252	58.6	3,031	7.0	16	22
1987	11	364	206	56.6	2,517	6.9	10	15
Totals	181	5,604	3,297	58.8	43,040	7.7	254	242

Notes: GP = games played; PA = passes attempted; PC = passes completed; Pct. = percent completed; Yds. = yards; Avg. = average yards per attempt; TD = touchdowns; Int. = interceptions

quarterback—Joe Namath, in 1967—had ever passed for 4,000 yards in a single season, but Dan attained that feat three consecutive years, beginning in 1979. Throwing to hall-of-famers Kellen Winslow and Charlie Joiner, as well as Wes Chandler and John Jefferson, and handing off to Chuck Muncie, Dan operated one of the most dominant offenses in NFL history. In 1979, he was chosen as the Pro Football Writers of America (PFWA) most valuable player (MVP) and the United Press International (UPI) American Football Conference (AFC) player of the year, and he began a five-year run in the Pro Bowl.

The defense, however, did not quite measure up, and though the Chargers went to the playoffs from 1979 to 1982, the team never managed to reach the Super Bowl. The Chargers came closest in 1981, when Dan's 4,802 passing yards were the most in league history at the time. San Diego's first playoff game that year, against the Miami Dolphins, was of epic status. The Chargers had a 24-0 lead, allowed Miami to catch up, then finally won it 41-38 in overtime. Dan completed 33 of the 53 passes for 433 yards and 3 touchdowns. The next week, the Chargers had to play one of the coldest games in NFL history and lost to the Cincinnati Bengals.

In the strike-shortened 1982 season, Dan,

playing only nine games, threw for 2,883 yards. He repeated as PFWA MVP and UPI AFC player of the year and was chosen as the NFL offensive player of the year. Still, he could not take the team to the Super Bowl. His 333 yards and 3 touchdowns led the team to victory in the first week of the playoffs, but the Chargers lost to the Dolphins the following week.

Continuing the Story

Dan had never been a particularly mobile quarterback, so he took many hits. After Dan's stellar 1982 season, the team regressed. Dan made the Pro Bowl in 1983 and 1985, and averaged a respectable 3,200 yards per season over his last six years. In 1988, he retired with totals of 3,297 completions for 43,040 yards and 254 touchdowns. The Chargers retired his uniform number, 14. In 1993, his first year of eligibility, he was elected to the Pro Football Hall of Fame.

After retiring as a player, Dan followed in his fa-

Chargers Records

Most career touchdowns, 254

Most touchdowns in a game, 6 (1981)

Most career passing yards, 43,040

Most passing yards in a season, 4,802 (1981)

Most career pass attempts, 5,604

Most career pass completions, 3,297

Most consecutive completions in a game, 15 (September 7, 1981)

Honors and Awards

1979	Pro Bowl most valuable player
1979-83, 1985	NFL Pro Bowl
1979, 1982	Pro Football Writers of America NFL most valuable player
	United Press International AFC Player of the Year
1980's	NFL All-Decade Team
1982	NFL most valuable player
	NFL Offensive Player of the Year
1988	Uniform number 14 retired by San Diego Chargers
1993	Inducted into Pro Football Hall of Fame
1997	Inducted into Bay Area Sports Hall of Fame

ther's footsteps, serving as a sports anchor for KPIX-TV in San Francisco from 1994 to 1997. He also broadcast college football games for CBS. In 2001, Monday Night Football hired him as a counterbalance to Dennis Miller. After that failed, he returned to announcing college football, broadcasting Pac-10 Conference games with Keith Jackson.

Summary

Dan Fouts was a traditional quarterback with a skinny body and slow legs but a powerful and accurate arm. He was one of the greatest pure passers ever, and when he was surrounded with suitable talent and given a system that maximized his abilities, he led a powerful offense.

Arthur D. Hlavaty

Additional Sources

DuFresne, Jim. *Quarterbacks: McMahon, Eason, Elway, Fouts.* Worthington, Ohio: Willowisp, 1986.

King, Peter. *Greatest Quarterbacks.* Des Moines, Iowa: Sports Illustrated Books, 1999.

Moseley, Rob, and Dan Fouts. *Game Day: Oregon Football—The Greatest Games, Placekickers, Coaches, and Teams in the Glorious Tradition of Duck Football.* Chicago: Triumph Books, 2007.

Benny Friedman

Born: March 18, 1905
      Cleveland, Ohio
Died: November 23, 1982
      New York, New York
Also known as: Benjamin Friedman (full name);
    the Boy Scout of Ann Arbor

Early Life

Benjamin "Benny" Friedman was born on March 18, 1905, in Cleveland, Ohio, the son of Russian immigrants. He grew up in an Orthodox Jewish household, supported by a father who worked as a tailor.

Tall for his era, at 5 feet 10 inches, but slight of build, Benny was a natural athlete. He played basketball and baseball at Cleveland's East Technical High School. However, he was deemed too fragile to play football, a sport in which, with the founding of the NFL in 1920, possibilities for a professional career existed. Denied the opportunity to play at East Technical High School, Benny transferred to Glenville High School. There, as quarterback, he played well enough not only to guide the team to citywide and national championships but also to earn a football scholarship to the University of Michigan.

The Road to Excellence

Not allowed to play varsity football in his freshman year, 1923, at Michigan, Benny used the time to increase his strength and stamina. Since the football of the era was fatter and blunter than the modern streamlined version, Benny worked hard to develop his fingers, hands, wrists, and forearms to grip the ball more firmly. He carried a squeezable handball or tennis ball everywhere and stretched his fingers to improve their span.

The hard work paid dividends. In the 1924-1925 season, after the Michigan Wolverines lost badly to the University of Illinois, Benny was selected to start as quarterback against the University of Wisconsin. He made an immediate impact, throwing for a touchdown and running for another to help win the game. Under Benny's leadership Michigan had four consecutive victories. Benny was named an all-Midwest honorable mention.

In 1925, as full-time starting quarterback—in addition to playing defensive back, halfback, kicker, and kick returner—Benny led the Wolverines to the Big Ten Conference title. In the process, the team outscored its opponents 227-3, as Benny ran, passed, and kicked his way to all-American first-team honors. Named team captain his senior year, Benny again led the Wolverines to the Big Ten Conference Championship, while earning conference most valuable player and first team all-American awards. Benny's prowess on the field, and his clean-cut popularity off it, helped spur construction of 100,000-seat Michigan Stadium, one of the nation's largest sports venues, which opened in 1927.

The Emerging Champion

Though legal since 1906, passing did not become a major part of football until Benny came along.

Benny Friedman in 1926. (AP/Wide World Photos)

Throwing to all-American end Bennie Oosterbaan, Benny changed the game of college football from a plodding, rugby-like tussle dominated by the run, into a considerably more exciting spectator sport.

Benny continued his pioneering ways in the fledgling NFL. Though Benny originally intended to enter law, his father grew sick and could not work. He seized the opportunity to help support the family by playing pro football and signed with the NFL's Cleveland Bulldogs in 1927. Benny excelled despite a plump, clumsy football and rules that hampered the quarterback: passers had to stand at least 5 yards behind the scrimmage line, there was no quarterback-roughing penalty, and two incomplete passes in a row earned a penalty.

Between 1927 and 1931, playing for the Bulldogs, the Detroit Wolverines, and the New York Giants, Benny led the NFL in passing yards and passing touchdowns. He won all-pro honors all four years and became the first professional football player to earn a $10,000 salary. In 1928, he led the NFL in passing, scoring, extra points, and rushing yards, and was the first player in league history to lead in passing and rushing in the same season. In 1929, the first year in which the Giants showed a profit, Benny completed 20 touchdown passes while leading his team to a 13-1-1 record.

Continuing the Story

Following a knee injury, in 1932, Benny signed as quarterback and coach with the NFL's Brooklyn Dodgers. At the same time, he served as backfield coach at Yale University. After leading the NFL in completion percentage in 1931 and making the all-pro team in 1933, he retired after the 1934 season, In his career he completed more than 50 percent of his passes for more than 7,000 yards and 68 passing touchdowns. He also rushed for more than 2,000 yards, scoring 18 touchdowns, and occasionally caught passes, kicked extra points and field goals, punted, and returned punts.

Benny's greatest contribution, however, was in helping make pro football a pastime worth watching. Largely because of Benny's passing abilities, the shape of the football was changed in 1933. Moreover, because of his presence, pro football became established in New York, helping solidify the NFL.

Following his professional career, Benny coached football at City College of New York until 1941. During World War II, he served in the U.S. Navy.

Honors and Awards	
1926	First-team all-American
	Big Ten Conference most valuable player
1933	All-Pro Team
1951	Inducted into College Football Hall of Fame
1979	Inducted into International Jewish Sports Hall of Fame
1980	Inducted into University of Michigan Athletic Hall of Honor
2005	Inducted into Pro Football Hall of Fame

After the war, he became head football coach—until 1959, when the sport was dropped—and athletic director at Brandeis University, remaining until 1963. After 1964, he ran a football school in Maine. In 1970, he unsuccessfully tried to obtain NFL pension benefits for early professional players. In 1978, Benny, a diabetic, had to have a leg amputated. Four years later, suffering from depression and ill health, he shot himself. In 2005, Benny, a member of the National Football Foundation's College Football Hall of Fame, the University of Michigan Athletic Hall of Honor, and the International Jewish Sports Hall of Fame, was finally enshrined in the Pro Football Hall of Fame.

Summary

College and professional football's first outstanding passer, multitalented Benny Friedman was instrumental in changing the nature of the sport. Originally dominated by the run, football, thanks to Benny, was transformed from a defense-oriented battle to an offensive game. The only player to lead the league in both passing and rushing touchdowns in the same season in the NFL's more than eighty years of existence, he set the stage for professional football's subsequent popularity.

Jack Ewing

Additional Sources

Goldman, David J. *Jewish Sports Stars: Athletic Heroes Past and Present*. Minneapolis: Kar-Ben, 2006.

Greenberg, Murray. *Passing Game: Benny Friedman and the Transformation of Football*. New York: PublicAffairs, 2008.

Siegman, Joseph M. *Jewish Sports Legends: The International Jewish Sports Hall of Fame*. Dulles, Va.: Potomac Books, 2005.

Slater, Robert. *Great Jews in Sports*. New York: Jonathan David, 2005.

Rich Gannon

Born: December 20, 1965
      Philadelphia, Pennsylvania
Also known as: Richard Joseph Gannon (full
   name)

Early Life

Born in Philadelphia in 1965, Richard Joseph
Gannon went to high school at Saint Joseph's Pre-
paratory, a Jesuit school for boys in the same city.
There he was a three-sport athlete who earned
three varsity letters in both football and crew and
two in basketball. However, football was his best

sport. He played quarterback and also punted.
During his senior year, he passed for 1,567 yards
and earned all-city honors as both a quarterback
and a punter.

The Road to Excellence

After high school Rich attended the University of
Delaware, a Division 1-AA school that is only about
thirty-five miles southwest of Philadelphia. There
he became the starting quarterback in Coach Tubby
Raymond's wing-t offense during his sophomore
year. By the time he graduated, he had set twenty-
one school records. In 1986, he earned
all-American honors and was voted the
Yankee Conference's player of the year.

The Emerging Champion

In 1987, after Rich graduated from Delaware, the New England Patriots selected
him in the fourth round of the NFL draft,
making him the ninety-eighth pick overall. The Patriots wanted to convert him to
a defensive back, but when he was reluctant to make the change, they traded him
to the Minnesota Vikings. During Rich's
first two seasons in the NFL, he served as a
backup quarterback. In 1990, he replaced
Wade Wilson as the Vikings' starter. However, he was replaced by Sean Salisbury
toward the end of the 1992 season. After
the season ended, he had rotator cuff
surgery.

In 1993, Rich joined the Washington
Redskins, but after starting only three
games as their quarterback, he was released. He then sat out the 1994 season
before signing with the Kansas City Chiefs
in 1995. After backing up quarterbacks
Steve Bono and Elvis Grbac, Rich finally
got his chance to start when Grbac was
injured during the 1997 season. Rich
then led the Chiefs to the playoffs, only
to watch his team lose its first playoff
game after Coach Marty Schottenheimer
started Grbac instead of him.

Rich Gannon, who won the 2002 NFL most valuable player award.
(Terry Schmitt/UPI/Landov)

Over the next two seasons, Rich shared quarterbacking chores with Grbac until he was released in 1999. Fearing that he might not make another NFL roster, he tried out with the Winnipeg Blue Bombers of the Canadian Football League. That team offered him a contract, but he decided to turn it down because playing in Canada might hurt his chances of getting back into the NFL.

By that time, Rich had gone through eleven undistinguished seasons with three different NFL teams and might easily have given up on his football career. However, he still had faith in himself. Professional stardom finally came to him after he signed with the Oakland Raiders as a free agent in 1999. Raider coach John Gruden used the so-called West Coast offense, which was built on short passes and ball control. This system proved ideal for Rich.

After leading the Raiders through a rebuilding season in 1999, Rich led his new team to three consecutive division championships from 2000 to 2002. Along the way, he was selected for the Pro Bowl three straight years. In the 2001 and 2002 Pro Bowl games, he became the first person voted most valuable player (MVP) in two consecutive years.

In 2000, Rich won the NFL's most prestigious honor, the Bert Bell player of the year award, which was also awarded to him in 2002. During the 2002 season, he passed for 4,689 yards and 26 touchdowns and set an NFL record for the number of 300-yard passing games. However, his otherwise great season was spoiled when the Raiders were crushed by the Tampa Bay Buccaneers in the 2002 Super Bowl. In that game, Rich threw 5 interceptions, several of which were run back for touchdowns.

Part of the reason for Rich's disastrous performance in the Super Bowl was the fact that Tampa Bay was coached by Gruden. As the former coach of the Raiders, Gruden was not only intimately familiar with the Raiders' playbook—which he had helped write—but he also knew Rich's mannerisms and the audibles he used to change plays at the line of scrimmage.

Consequently, Gruden's Buccaneers knew exactly what Rich was going to do on almost every play. It was an unprecedented situation, and few quarterbacks could have succeeded in similar circumstances. Nevertheless, despite the crushing disappointment of his Super Bowl loss, Rich bounced back only one week later with another strong performance in the NFL Pro Bowl. Only the outstanding play of Miami running back Ricky Williams prevented him from winning his third consecutive MVP award in that game.

Continuing the Story

Over the next two seasons, Rich suffered serious injuries. In week seven of the 2003 season, a shoulder injury sidelined him for the rest of the year. Early the following year, he suffered a season-ending neck injury during a helmet-to-helmet collision with an opposing player. That injury also effectively ended his playing career. The Raiders went 4-12 and 5-12 during his final two seasons.

Rich officially retired in August, 2005, after an eighteen-year playing career. During that same year, he was inducted into the University of Delaware Athletic's Hall of Fame and was hired as an NFL analyst for CBS-TV. He and his wife, Shelley, the daughter of Minnesota Vikings running back Bill

NFL Statistics

Season	GP	PA	PC	Pct.	Yds.	Avg.	TD	Int.
1987	4	6	2	33.3	18	3.0	0	1
1988	3	15	7	46.7	90	6.0	0	0
1989	0	0	0	0	0	0	0	0
1990	14	349	182	52.1	2.278	6.5	16	16
1991	15	354	211	59.6	2,166	6.1	12	6
1992	12	279	159	57.0	1,905	6.8	12	13
1993	8	125	74	59.2	704	5.6	3	7
1995	2	11	7	63.6	57	5.2	0	0
1996	4	90	54	60.0	491	5.5	6	1
1997	9	175	98	56.0	1,144	6.5	7	4
1998	12	354	206	58.2	2,305	6.5	10	6
1999	16	515	304	59.0	3.840	7.5	24	14
2000	16	473	284	60.0	3,430	7.3	28	11
2001	16	549	361	65.8	3,828	7.0	27	9
2002	16	618	418	67.6	4,689	7.6	26	10
2003	7	225	125	55.6	1.274	5.7	6	4
2004	3	68	41	60.3	524	7.7	3	2
Totals	157	4,206	2,533	60.2	28,743	6.8	180	104

Notes: GP = games played; PA = passes attempted; PC = passes completed; Pct. = percent completed; Yds. = yards; Avg. = average yards per attempt; TD = touchdowns; Int. = interceptions

Brown, had two daughters. Rich became a staunch supporter of the Brave Kids Organization, which combats Celiac disease, from which one of his daughters suffered.

Summary

Rich Gannon's story is one of persistence, determination, courage, and preparation. After spending years as a journeyman backup quarterback, he finally found his niche in a system, the so-called West Coast offense, that allowed him to both pass and run his way to success and recognition. With Rich, the Oakland Raiders were of championship caliber; when he was injured and unable to play, the team was mediocre or worse. His size and speed enabled him to run over secondary defenders. However, his running was also responsible for the injuries that brought his career to an end.

Thomas L. Erskine

Additional Sources

Baldinger, Brian. "Magic Man." *Sporting News* 226, no. 42 (October 21, 2002): 29.

Barber, Phil. "The Greatness of This Raider." *Sporting News* 226, no. 52 (December 30, 2002): 16.

Dillon, Dennis. "NFL Awards 2002: Player of the Year, Rich Gannon." *Sporting News*, 227, no. 5 (February 3, 2003): 10.

"Key to Gannon's Success: Painstaking Preparation." *USA Today*, December 13, 2002, p. 8C.

"Raider of the Lost Art." *Sports Illustrated* 95, no. 15 (October 19, 2001): 66.

Raiders Records

Most games with at least 300 passing yards, 24
Most career completions, 1,533
Best completion percentage, 62.6

Honors and Awards

1999-2002	NFL Pro Bowl
2000-01	Pro Bowl most valuable player
2000-02	NFL All-Pro
2000, 2002	Bert Bell Award
2002	NFL most valuable player
	Pro Football Writers of America NFL most valuable player
2005	Elected to the University of Delaware Athletics Hall of Fame

Antonio Gates

Born: June 18, 1980
Detroit, Michigan
Also known as: Antonio D. Gates (full name)
Other major sport: Basketball

Early Life

Antonio Gates was born in Detroit, Michigan, in 1980. In high school, he was a heavily recruited basketball and football player. As a two-sport star, he earned first-team all-state honors in both sports, while leading the Detroit Central High School football team to the Michigan state class A championship in 1997. He played both tight end and linebacker. He was not a blocking tight end, but his pass-catching ability was superb. However, Antonio's poor blocking did not stop Nick Saban, the head coach of the Michigan State University football team at the time, from offering Antonio a football scholarship.

The Road to Excellence

A stipulation to Antonio accepting the scholarship to Michigan State was that he could also try out for the school's basketball team. However, he was a Proposition 48 qualifier and had to sit out the 1998 football season. He did not meet academic requirements in his first semester of college. Coach Saban decided that if Antonio wanted to play for the football team, he could not join the basketball team. Antonio was angered by the decision and transferred to Eastern Michigan University to play basketball. Antonio played for the Eastern Michigan

NFL Statistics					
Season	GP	Rec.	Yds.	Avg.	TD
2003	15	24	389	16.2	2
2004	15	81	964	11.9	13
2005	15	89	1,101	12.4	10
2006	16	71	924	13.0	9
2007	16	75	984	13.1	9
2008	16	60	704	11.7	8
Totals	93	400	5,066	12.7	51

Notes: GP = games played; Rec. = receptions; Yds. = yards; Avg. = average yards per reception; TD = touchdowns

basketball team during the 1999-2000 season but was dismissed from the team because of his chronic academic problems.

Antonio then attended the College of the Sequoias in Visalia, California, and Henry Ford Community College in Dearborn, Michigan, before playing basketball for Kent State University in 2001. Antonio flourished as a power forward for Kent State and became a two-time all-Mid America Conference (MAC) selection. He also led Kent State to consecutive MAC championships and to the Elite Eight of the National Collegiate Athletic Association Basketball Tournament. By the end of his senior year at Kent State, Antonio was sixth on Kent State's all-time scoring list. Even with this impressive resume, National Basketball Association's scouts labeled Antonio a "tweener," meaning he was not big enough to be a professional power forward and not slim enough to be a professional small forward. However, San Diego Chargers tight ends coach Tim Brewster saw Antonio as a Charles Barkley in shoulder pads.

The Emerging Champion

Antonio tried to impress the NBA scouts at the 2003 Portsmouth Invitational Tournament but sprained his ankle, which essentially ruined his chances for an NBA career. However, the next week, at the Kent State Field House, Antonio worked out in front of NFL scouts and coaches from the San Francisco 49ers, the Pittsburgh Steelers, the Indianapolis Colts, the Cleveland Browns, and the San Diego Chargers. Only one scout, Brewster, knew about Antonio's sprained ankle. Antonio had a miserable workout: He ran a 4.8-second 40-yard dash and had poor agility and route-running drills. Brewster recommended ending the workout early, and the other NFL team representatives agreed to do so. Knowing about the sprained ankle and that Antonio had not played football since high school, Brewster emphasized that Antonio's potential was too great to pass up. The Chargers signed Antonio to a contract with only a $7,000 signing bonus.

In the summer of 2003, Chargers coach Marty Schottenheimer saw the same potential in Antonio

Honors and Awards

2004	Single-season record for touchdown reception by a tight end, 13
2004-06	NFL All-Pro
2004-07	NFL Pro Bowl
2005	Second tight end to compile at least 10 touchdowns and 1,100 receiving yards in one season (record shared with Todd Christensen)
2005-06	Associated Press NFL all-pro tight end

that Brewster had. Schottenheimer was so impressed with Antonio's vision, hands, speed, and body control that he stated: "It became clear real fast that [Antonio] was going to make the team . . . you just can't find that type of athleticism in men his size." On November 2, 2003, Antonio played tight end for the Chargers against the Chicago Bears. The next week, against the Minnesota Vikings, he caught his first NFL touchdown pass. On December 10, he was the first Chargers rookie to record 100 yards receiving in a game since Wayne Walker in 1989. By the end of the 2003 season, Antonio ranked third among all Chargers' receivers for catches, with 24.

Continuing the Story

Antonio had a breakout year in 2004. On November 28, against the Kansas City Chiefs, he broke the Chargers record for touchdowns by a tight end with his eleventh. On December 26, against the Colts, he broke the NFL record for touchdowns by a tight end with his thirteenth of the year. Because of his 2004 season, Antonio became a starter at the American Football Conference's (AFC's) Pro Bowl. In addition to his Pro Bowl selection, Antonio earned multiple first-team all-pro selections. In 2005, he had another stellar season. He was chosen for another trip to the Pro Bowl, and he earned multiple first-team all-pro selections, despite missing the first game of the season because of a "roster exemption." In 2006, he was once again a first-team all-pro selection.

Antonio started the 2007 NFL season strongly, scoring the Chargers' first touchdown of the year on a 17-yard halfback-option pass from LaDainian Tomlinson. During the 2007 regular season, Antonio caught 75 passes for 984 yards and had 9 touchdowns before tearing the plantar plate in his left foot, which resulted in a dislocated toe during the AFC wild card playoff game against the Tennessee Titans. Antonio played in the next round of the playoffs against the Colts and caught a touchdown. The toe injury forced him to miss the 2008 Pro Bowl. In February, 2008, Antonio decided to have the toe surgically repaired and was not sure if he would be ready for the 2008 NFL season. However, he played in the first game of the 2008 NFL season against the Carolina Panthers and recorded a touchdown. He went on to play in every game and finished the season with 60 receptions, 704 receiving yards, and 8 touchdowns.

Summary

In 2005, Tim Brewster admitted that "If I had been truthful to the [Chargers] about what I saw that day we probably wouldn't have signed Antonio," referring to that dismal workout at Kent State. Brewster did stretch the truth, allowing Antonio Gates to eventually flourish as a professional. Antonio wanted to be known as one of the greatest tight ends to play in the NFL, and, after his initial seasons, he was on the path to his goal.

Paul C. Alexander II

Additional Sources

Chadiha, Jeffri. "The Tight End: Version 2.0." *Sports Illustrated* 105, no. 12 (September 25, 2008).

Jenkins, Lee. "San Diego Chargers." *Sports Illustrated* 109, no. 8 (September 1, 2008).

Kimmich, Ian. *Antonio Gates.* Broomall, Pa.: Mason Crest, 2008.

Eddie George

Born: September 24, 1973
  Philadelphia, Pennsylvania
Also known as: Edward Nathan George, Jr. (full
  name)

Early Life

Edward Nathan "Eddie" George, Jr., was born on September 24, 1973, in Philadelphia, Pennsylvania, to Donna and Eddie George, Sr. In 1980, Eddie's parents separated. While his mother worked two or three jobs to provide for the family, Eddie began to hone his football skills. Though Eddie began at Abington High School, his lack of discipline made his mother transfer him to Fork Union Military Academy in Virginia after his sophomore year. Known for instilling a work ethic and self-esteem

Eddie George rushes for the Tennessee Titans in a 2001 play-off game. (Jonathan Daniel/Allsport/Getty Images)

into its cadets, Fork Union was also an institution where Eddie could improve both his grades and his skills as a running back. However, when he did not draw much attention from recruiters, he stayed at the academy for a postgraduate year and ended the season with an average of 275 yards per game and 1,372 yards for the season. This allowed Eddie to garner the attention he needed, and he was awarded a scholarship to Ohio State University.

The Road to Excellence

Though Eddie struggled at first at Ohio State, including fumbling twice his freshman year in a game against the University of Illinois, he continued working hard and improving. After his sophomore year as a third-string running back, Eddie entered his junior year as the starter and ran for more than 1,400 yards, scoring 12 touchdowns. However, Eddie really showcased his talent in his senior year. He rushed for 1,927 yards, a school record, and 24 touchdowns; had an average of more than 152 yards a game; and had twelve consecutive games in which he ran for more than 100 yards a game. Furthermore, during his senior year, he was able to redeem himself against Illinois: This time, Eddie ran for a school-record 314 yards and scored 3 touchdowns. Eddie's dedication to improvement and his athletic ability led to the Doak Walker Award, given to the top running back in the nation each year; the Maxwell and the Walter Camp player of the year awards, both given to the top collegiate football player in the nation; and the Big Ten Conference most valuable player award. In addition, he won the coveted Heisman Trophy, drawing national attention.

Eddie ended his college football career with 3,668 rushing yards, second in Ohio State history, and 44 rushing touchdowns, third in the school's history. Furthermore, he rushed for more than 200 yards five times, a school record, and rushed for more than 100 yards twelve times. He entered the 1996 NFL draft and was

NFL Statistics

Season	GP	Rushing					Receiving			
		Car.	Yds.	Avg.	TD		Rec.	Yds.	Avg.	TD
1996	16	335	1,368	4.1	8		23	182	7.9	0
1997	16	357	1,399	3.9	6		7	44	6.3	1
1998	16	348	1,294	3.7	5		37	310	8.4	1
1999	16	320	1,304	4.1	9		47	458	9.7	4
2000	16	403	1,509	3.7	14		50	453	9.1	2
2001	16	315	939	3.0	5		37	279	7.5	0
2002	16	343	1,165	3.4	12		36	255	7.1	2
2003	16	312	1,031	3.3	5		22	163	7.4	0
2004	14	132	432	3.3	4		9	83	9.2	0
Totals	**142**	**2,865**	**10,441**	**3.6**	**68**		**268**	**2,227**	**8.3**	**10**

Notes: GP = games played; Car. = carries; Yds. = yards; Avg. = average yards per carry *or* average yards per reception; TD = touchdowns; Rec. = receptions

picked fourteenth in the first round by the Houston Oilers (now Tennessee Titans).

The Emerging Champion

During his rookie season, Eddie started each game and by the end of the season, had rushed for 1,368 yards, which was one of the reasons he won the NFL rookie of the year award. His first four seasons were monumental: He started all sixty-four games and led the Titans in rushing yards in fifty-seven of those games. With 5,365 yards, he ranked second in franchise history and fifth in league history for rushing yards in a player's first four seasons. He was also named to the Pro Bowl four times, from 1997 to 2000.

In 2000, Eddie assisted the Titans to Super Bowl XXXIV against the St. Louis Rams. In the game, he rushed for 95 yards and 2 touchdowns. In the final, dramatic play of the game, the Titans, losing 23-16, finished 1 yard short of scoring the winning touchdown. However, Eddie had one of his best years as a professional, with 1,509 rushing yards, 50 receptions, and 16 total touchdowns.

Continuing the Story

Eddie never had another season like he did in 2000. In 2004, he signed a one-year contract with the Dallas Cowboys after he was released by the Titans. When the season ended, Eddie retired from football. He transferred to television work as a host of pregame football shows. He also became the co-owner of two sports-themed restaurants, one in Nashville, Tennes-

see, and one in Columbus, Ohio. In 2006, he was appointed spokesperson for Tennessee's GetFitTN, an initiative aimed at promoting a healthier, more active lifestyle. He also started a nonprofit organization, Visions with Infinite Possibilities, with his wife, Tamara, to support women and children of domestic abuse.

Summary

Over almost a decade of football, Eddie George amassed 10,441 rushing yards, 268 receptions, 2,227 receiving yards, and 78 touchdowns and averaged more than 300 carries per season. He was only the second running back to rush for 10,000 yards while never missing a start and was second behind Walter Payton for consecutive regular-season games started by a running back, with 128 games.

Lamia Nuseibeh Scherzinger

Additional Sources

Baptist, Bob. "The Eddie George Story." *The Columbus Dispatch*, December, 1995.

Mayer, Larry. "The Amazing Journey: Tennessee Titans' Eddie George." *Football Digest*, August, 2000.

Thornley, Stew. *Super Sports Star Eddie George.* Berkeley Heights, N.J.: Enslow, 2003.

Ohio State University Records

Most rushing yards in one game, 314 (1995)
Most rushing yards in one season, 1,927 (1995)
Most rushing yards per game in one season, 148.2 (1995)
Most games in a season with at least 100 rushing yards, 20 (1995)
Most games in a career with at least 200 rushing yards, 5
Most catches in one season by a running back, 47 (1995)

Honors and Awards

1995	Heisman Trophy
	All-American (first-team)
	Walter Camp Award
	Maxwell Award
	Doak Walker Award
1996	NFL Offensive Rookie of the Year
1996, 1999-2000	NFL All-Pro
1997-2000	NFL Pro Bowl
2001	Uniform number 27 retired by Ohio State University

Frank Gifford

Born: August 16, 1930
      Santa Monica, California
Also known as: Francis Newton Gifford (full
    name)

Early Life

Frank Gifford was born on August 16, 1930, in
Santa Monica, California, to Weldon Wayne and
Lola Mae (Hawkins) Gifford. One of three children—he had a brother, Weldon Wayne, Jr., and a
sister, Winona—Frank enjoyed an unsettled but
comfortable childhood even during the rugged
years of the Great Depression. His father was a
driller in the California oil industry, who moved
the family to such oil field communities as Taft,
Stockton, and Long Beach. When Frank was fourteen, his family settled in Bakersfield, California,
and young Frank, always a gifted athlete, enrolled
at Bakersfield High School, where his long and successful career got its start.

The Road to Excellence

At Bakersfield High School, Frank demonstrated
his versatility by playing several positions on the
football team. He played quarterback, halfback,
and end for Coach Homer Beatty. At tailback in the
single-wing offense, however, he really excelled. At
this position he could utilize his superior skills as a
passer, runner, and blocker. In 1948, his senior
year, Frank led Bakersfield to the conference
championship. He spent one semester at Bakersfield Junior College, where he starred as a triple-
threat halfback. His running, passing, and receiving led the team to the Junior Rose Bowl.

    Frank's athletic skills won him a full scholarship
to the University of Southern California (USC). He
began his career as a defensive back, but eventually
played both offense and defense, which was not unusual for a player during the 1940's and 1950's.
What was unusual was Frank's mastery of both the
offensive tailback position and the defensive back
position. He directed Coach Jess Hill's offense tire-
lessly, then stayed in the game to tackle and defend
passes when his opponents had the ball. In addition, Frank kicked extra points and field goals, and

New York Giant Frank Gifford, who in 1956 won the NFL
most valuable player award and guided his team to the
NFL Championship game. (Courtesy of Amateur Athletic Foundation of Los Angeles)

was the team's punter. In recognition of his ability,
he was named his senior year to the all-American
team on both offense and defense, and he was chosen to play in the North-South and East-West all-
star games.

The Emerging Champion

Although Frank wanted to be drafted by the NFL's
Los Angeles Rams, he was the top draft choice of
the New York Giants, with whom he played his entire professional career. His rookie season at halfback was a disappointment for the college star; he
rushed for just more than one hundred yards,
caught only five passes, and failed to score a point
the entire year. At first, his teammates doubted
Frank's toughness and dubbed him "Tippy Toes"

because of his elusive style of running. He was almost cut from the team. Neither Frank nor his head coach, Steve Owen, gave up on him, though. The faith was rewarded when, in his second season, Frank scored forty-seven points on offense while also playing defensive back well enough to make the all-NFL Defensive team.

In 1954, the Giants' new head coach, Jim Lee Howell, recognized his young halfback as one of the chief building blocks of a championship team. New offensive assistant coach Vince Lombardi designed an offensive scheme built around the power sweep, with Frank running the ball. Frank credits the studious Lombardi with changing his football life by giving him a definite role in the offense and motivating him to excel. Lombardi claimed that Frank was able to spot a defense's weaknesses better than any player he had ever coached. In 1956, the rebuilt Giants won the Eastern Conference crown and went on to defeat the Chicago Bears 47-7 for the NFL title, the team's first championship in eighteen years. That year Frank ranked in the league's top five in rushing, with 819 yards, and pass receptions, with 51 for 603 yards. He was the first NFL player to finish that high in both categories in the same year. For his accomplishments, Frank was named NFL

player of the year. George Halas, the legendary owner of the Chicago Bears, called him the best all-around back in the league in twenty years. Frank's versatility and superb conditioning helped him lead the Giants to NFL Eastern Conference titles in both 1958 and 1959.

Continuing the Story

In 1960, an event occurred that almost ended Frank's career. In a game with the Philadelphia Eagles, Frank was blindsided by Eagles linebacker Chuck Bednarik while catching a pass. The tackle resulted in an acute brain concussion. Many writers and fans criticized Bednarik for the vicious hit, but Frank refused to place blame, saying the tackle was part of the game.

After a brief retirement, Frank returned to football. In 1962, he moved to flanker for Coach Allie Sherman. Slowed by a training camp injury, he wondered if his return had been a mistake; however, he kept working hard. The year turned out a great success, with Frank catching 39 passes for 796 yards and 8 touchdowns. As a

Honors and Awards

1952	North-South All-Star Team
	East-West All-Star Team
	College All-American
1953	All-NFL Defensive Team
1954-57, 1959-60, 1964	NFL Pro Bowl Team
1955	*Sporting News* NFL All-Star Team
1955-57, 1959	NFL All-Pro Team
1956	United Press International NFL Player of the Year
	Newspaper Enterprise Association NFL Player of the Year
	Jim Thorpe Trophy
	Sporting News NFL Player of the Year
1956-59	*Sporting News* Eastern Division All-Star Team
1959, 1963	NFL Pro Bowl most valuable player
1962	United Press International Comeback Player of the Year
1963	NFL All-Pro Team of the 1950's
1964	Catholic Youth Organization Sportsman of the Year
1972	NCAA Prominent National Media Salute
1975	Inducted into College Football Hall of Fame
1977	Inducted into Pro Football Hall of Fame
	Emmy Award for Outstanding Sports Personality

NFL Statistics

Season	GP	Rushing Car.	Yds.	Avg.	TD	Receiving Rec.	Yds.	Avg.	TD
1952	10	38	116	3.1	0	5	36	7.2	0
1953	12	50	157	3.1	2	18	292	16.2	4
1954	9	66	368	5.6	2	14	154	11.0	1
1955	11	86	351	4.1	3	33	437	13.2	4
1956	12	159	819	5.2	5	51	603	11.8	4
1957	12	136	528	3.9	5	41	588	14.3	4
1958	10	115	468	4.1	8	29	330	11.4	2
1959	11	106	540	5.1	3	42	768	18.3	4
1960	8	77	232	3.0	4	24	344	14.3	3
1962	14	2	18	9.0	1	39	796	20.4	7
1963	14	4	10	2.5	0	42	657	15.6	7
1964	13	1	2	2.0	1	29	429	14.8	3
Totals	136	840	3,609	4.3	34	367	5,434	14.8	43

Notes: GP = games played; Car. = carries; Yds. = yards; Avg. = average yards per carry *or* average yards per reception; TD = touchdowns; Rec. = receptions

reward for his bravery and talent, he received the United Press International's NFL comeback player of the year award.

Frank's career with the Giants continued through the 1964 season. During his years in the NFL, he scored 484 points, 77 touchdowns, and gained more than 9,000 yards rushing and receiving. He appeared in seven Pro Bowls and was twice the game's most valuable player (1959 and 1963). In 1964, he was named sportsman of the year. He was inducted into the Pro Football Hall of Fame in 1977. After retiring from football, Frank continued his distinguished career as a sportscaster, author, motion picture actor, fashion model, and spokesperson for various charities.

Summary

Few athletes have demonstrated the versatility and sheer courage of Frank Gifford. From his disap-

pointing rookie season and his career-threatening injury to his willingness to put his reputation on the line each week as an announcer on live television, Frank has consistently stood for those values most admired in athletes.

Harold R. Blythe, Jr.

Additional Sources

Carroll, Bob. *Total Football: The Official Encyclopedia of the National Football League.* New York: Harper-Collins, 1999.

Conerly, Perian. *Backseat Quarterback.* Jackson: University Press of Mississippi, 2003.

Gifford, Frank, and Harry Waters. *The Whole Ten Yards.* Thorndike, Maine: Thorndike Press, 1994.

McCullough, Bob. *My Greatest Day in Football: The Legends of Football Recount Their Greatest Moments.* New York: Thomas Dunne Books/St. Martin's Press, 2001.

George Gipp

Born: February 18, 1895
       Laurium, Michigan
Died: December 14, 1920
       South Bend, Indiana
Also known as: The Gipper

Early Life

George Gipp was born in the small town of Laurium, Michigan. The young man, who would become one of the best-known college football

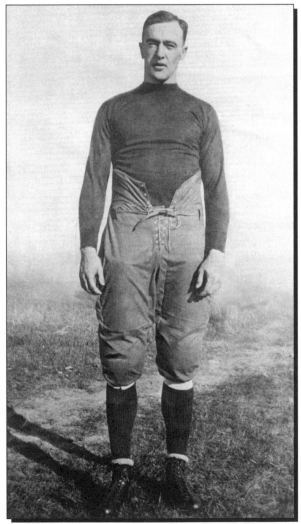

George Gipp, who was named the most outstanding college football player of 1920. (AP/Wide World Photos)

players of all time, was a natural athlete. Football was not his primary sport, however; he did not play on an organized football team in high school. Always an avid sports enthusiast, he actively participated in track, hockey, sandlot football, and organized baseball. He loved baseball, and throughout high school he was an outstanding player on the Calumet High School team. George aspired to be a professional baseball player and worked toward that dream while attending the University of Notre Dame. In addition to playing football, he was the center field for the Irish; he planned to play professional baseball with the Chicago Cubs following his graduation from Notre Dame.

The Road to Excellence

George's career as a football player was almost accidental. One early autumn afternoon in September, 1916, he was kicking a football on a practice field with another student when football coach Knute Rockne spotted him. Rockne was impressed by George's natural athletic style and grace—he repeatedly kicked the football 50 yards or more with both precision and accuracy without the benefit of football boots. Rockne asked George to join the freshmen on the football field the following day. George, wanting to make the most of every opportunity available to him at Notre Dame, did so, thereby beginning his college football career.

The Emerging Champion

George played football at Notre Dame from 1916 to 1920. His playing has been unparalleled in the history of the university. George stood 6 feet 2 inches and weighed 185 pounds. He was fast on his feet, running 100 yards in 10.2 seconds. He was also an intelligent player on the field. He could kick remarkably well, and he was one of the most accomplished passers of his day. Even as a freshman George was well regarded and recognized as the best player on the Fighting Irish team.

In 1918, George joined the Student Army Training Corp. He was not drafted during World War I and was able to continue playing football. During his years at Notre Dame, not a single pass was completed in his protective zone when he played defense. During his career, Notre Dame's football team compiled an astonishing 27-2-3 record. For the last twenty games in which George participated, Notre Dame's record was 19-0-1. With George on the team, the Irish outscored their competition 506-97. George led the team in rushing and passing yards each of his last three seasons. His career mark of 2,341 yards rushing was a school record that stood until Jerome Havens broke it in 1978. In 1920, George was named the outstanding college player in the United States by coach Walter Camp.

George's final statistics might have been better but for some strict officiating. In a 1919 game against Kalamazoo, George had three touchdown plays recalled when penalties were assessed against the Notre Dame players. Following the nullification of the third score, a frustrated George reportedly asked the official to signal one whistle to stop and two to keep going the next time he carried the ball.

Continuing the Story

On November 20, 1920, during his final season, George injured his shoulder in a game against Illinois, just a week before an important game against Northwestern. He also contracted a serious throat infection and was not slated to play in the Northwestern game. Rockne kept him off the field until the crowd demanded George make an appearance. George took the field with a few minutes left to play and threw a fifty-five-yard touchdown pass to his teammate. That was his final football game: The streptococcic infection he had contracted worsened after the game against Northwestern.

George was subsequently hospitalized. On his deathbed, he supposedly requested that Rockne ask the team to "win one for the Gipper." In Ameri-

can sports, this phrase became the rally cry for downtrodden teams. Rockne invoked that memory for his team during Notre Dame's game against Army in November, 1928; the Fighting Irish won 12-6.

George died on December 14, 1920, of complications from his throat infection and pneumonia. Just two weeks after he was named Notre Dame's first all-American, George was dead at the age of twenty-five. His legend lived on in the film *Knute Rockne, All American* (1940), starring Ronald Reagan as George Gipp. He was later named to the Michigan Hall of Fame, the College Football Hall of Fame, and the Upper Peninsula Hall of Fame. The George Gipp Award, established in 1934, is awarded to an outstanding senior athlete at Calumet High School. His legacy has become part of college football lore, at Notre Dame

NCAA Statistics

RUSHING

Season	GP	Car.	Yds.	TD	Avg.
1917	5	63	244	0	3.87
1918	6	98	541	6	5.52
1919	9	106	729	7	6.88
1920	8	102	827	8	8.11
Totals	28	369	2,341	21	6.34

PASSING

Season	GP	PA	PC	Yds.	TD	Pct.
1917	5	8	3	40	1	.375
1918	6	45	19	293	1	.442
1919	9	72	41	727	3	.569
1920	8	62	30	709	3	.484
Totals	28	187	93	1,769	8	.497

RETURN YARDAGE

Season	GP	Punt returns No.	Punt returns Yards	Kickoff returns No.	Kickoff returns Yards
1917	5	8	99	0	0
1918	6	0	0	3	80
1919	9	1	12	8	166
1920	8	7	106	11	208
Totals	28	16	217	22	454

Notes: GP = games played; Car. = carries; Yds. = yards; TD = touchdowns; Avg. = average; PA = passes attempted; PC = passes completed; Pct. = percent

Honors and Awards

1920	Consensus All-American
1940	Portrayed by future U.S. president Ronald Reagan in *Knute Rockne, All American*
1943	U.S. Liberty Ship *George Gipp* named in his honor
1951	Inducted into College Football Hall of Fame
1957	Inducted into Michigan Sports Hall of Fame
2008	Number 22 on ABC Sports Top 25 College Football Players

and beyond. His legacy remained topical nearly ninety years after his death. In 2007, George's body was exhumed for a DNA sample in response to a claim that he fathered a child. The accusation proved to be false.

Summary

George Gipp's name has become synonymous with football worldwide. Frank Coughlin, captain of the 1920 Notre Dame team, said of his friend: "George Gipp was the greatest athlete I have ever known. He will forever be remembered as a friend, a student, an athlete, and a gentleman, for to know him was to love him."

Kathleen Schongar

Additional Sources

Chellan, Patrick. *One for the Gipper.* Lumas, Calif.: Arrowhead, 1996.

"Gipp, George." *American National Biography* 9 (1999).

Klosinski, Emil. *Gipp at Notre Dame: The Untold Story—Finally, the Truth About "The Gipper."* Baltimore: PublishAmerica, 2003.

Tony Gonzalez

Born: February 27, 1976
       Torrance, California
Also known as: Anthony David Gonzalez (full
   name); Tony G
Other major sport: Basketball

Early Life

Anthony "Tony" David Gonzalez was born and raised in Torrance, California. In high school, Tony was a three-season athlete who competed in football, basketball, and baseball, lettering in each. While a senior at Huntington Beach High School, he caught 62 passes for a total of 945 yards and 13 touchdowns. Tony excelled at football and was selected for an all-American team as both a linebacker and a tight end. He also was an extremely good basketball player. Averaging 26 points per

Tight end Tony Gonzalez scoring a touchdown catch against the Denver Broncos in 2008. (Dave Kaup/Reuters/Landov)

game, Tony was awarded the Sunset League most valuable player award. In his senior year he was also named the Orange County High School athlete of the year, sharing the honor with famous golfer Tiger Woods.

The Road to Excellence

After high school, Tony attended the University of California, at Berkeley. He majored in communications and continued to play both football and basketball. His basketball career was highlighted with the advancement of his team to the "Sweet Sixteen" in the NCAA Basketball Tournament. Tony credited many of his moves and his quick athleticism on the football field to his background in basketball. While at Berkeley, Tony also played for Steve Mariucci, who later became the head coach of the San Francisco 49ers and the Detroit Lions. In Tony's most successful season, in his junior year, he caught 46 passes for 699 yards and 5 touchdowns. At Berkeley, Tony was an all-Pac-10 Conference and all-American selection. He forfeited his final year of athletic eligibility to declare for the NFL draft. Tony was rated as the number-one tight end in the 1997 draft, and the Kansas City Chiefs decided to choose him. To draft Tony, the Chiefs made a trade with the Houston Oilers and managed to attain the number thirteen selection.

In his rookie season with the Kansas City Chiefs, Tony caught 33 passes for 368 yards and 2 touchdowns. In 1998, he started in all sixteen games and caught 59 passes for a total of 621 yards and 2 touchdowns.

The Emerging Champion

By 1999, Tony's record with the Chiefs improved drastically: He caught 76 passes, scored 11 touchdowns, and gained a total of 849 yards. Tony was selected to his first of eight consecutive Pro Bowls. In 2000, he continued to improve his statistics. He caught 93 passes for a total of 1,203 yards and 9 touchdowns. In just three years of playing for the Kansas City Chiefs, Tony was ranked sixth in the American Football Conference and tenth in the NFL for total receptions. In 2001, Tony was selected to start in his third consecutive Pro Bowl but was unable to play because of a knee injury. In 2003, Tony had 916 receiving yards and 71 receptions, which ranked him first among all tight ends in the NFL.

Statistically, Tony's best season was 2004. He set a new NFL record for a tight end when he caught 102 passes for 7 receiving touchdowns and a total of 1,258 yards. The record also made Tony the first tight end since 1986 to lead the NFL in receptions.

Tony continued to break records. In 2005, Tony made his one hundredth consecutive start. In 2006, he broke the Chiefs' franchise records for receiving yards, previously held by Otis Taylor, and yards-from-scrimmage, surpassing Priest Holmes. During that season, he recorded 73 receptions for a team-high 900 yards. On October 14, 2007, in a game against Cincinnati, Tony caught a three-yard pass from Damon Huard to break the record of career touchdown receptions for a tight end, previously held by Shannon Sharpe. Only a few weeks later, on December 23, 2007, Tony set a new record for the most receptions of all time by a tight end.

Continuing the Story

Tony published an autobiographical children's book to inspire children to achieve all they can in spite of their situations. Tony also worked with the Boys & Girls Club and the Shadow Buddies Organi-

NFL Statistics

Season	GP	Rec.	Yds.	Avg.	TD
1997	16	33	368	11.2	2
1998	16	59	621	10.5	2
1999	15	76	849	11.2	11
2000	16	93	1,203	12.9	9
2001	16	73	917	12.6	6
2002	16	63	773	12.3	7
2003	16	71	916	12.9	10
2004	16	102	1,258	12.3	7
2005	16	78	905	11.6	2
2006	15	73	900	12.3	5
2007	16	99	1,172	11.8	5
2008	16	96	1,058	11.0	10
Totals	190	916	10,940	11.9	76

Notes: GP = games played; Rec. = receptions; Yds. = yards; Avg. = average yards per reception; TD = touchdowns

zation. In 1998, he founded the Tony Gonzalez Foundation. Tony's ethnicity was a blend of Hispanic, African American, and Cape Verdean. He embraced his Hispanic culture and made it a priority in his life: He remained active in the Hispanic Chamber of Commerce in Kansas City and California. His volunteer work and outstanding attitude garnered him the Kansas City Chiefs man of the year award. In 2007, he signed a contract assuring Kansas City that he would remain with the Chiefs for another five years. In 2008, he rewarded the Chiefs with 96 receptions for 1,058 yards and 10 touchdowns.

Summary

Tony Gonzalez was not just an athlete. He served as a role model to his communities in Kansas City and in California. His professional achievements included nine consecutive Pro Bowls, and he shattered numerous records for the Kansas City Chiefs and the NFL. Personally, he served others by mentoring young people, volunteering his free time, and aiding the Hispanic community.

Kathryn A. Cochran

NFL Records

Most seasons with at least 1,000 receiving yards as a tight end, 3
Most receptions as a tight end in a career, 816
Most receiving touchdowns as a tight end in a career, 66
Most receptions as a tight end in one season, 102 (2004)

Honors and Awards

1994	Orange County high school athlete of the year
1997	All-Pacific Ten Conference
	All-American
1999-2007	NFL Pro Bowl
	NFL All-Pro

Additional Sources

Althaus, Bill. *The Good, the Bad, and the Ugly: Kansas City Chiefs—Heart-Pounding, Jaw-Dropping, and Gut-Wrenching Moments from Kansas City Chiefs History.* Chicago: Triumph Books, 2007.
Gonzalez, Tony, and Greg Brown. *Catch and Connect.* Kirkland, Wash.: Positively for Kids, 2004.

Otto Graham

Born: December 6, 1921
    Waukegan, Illinois
Died: December 17, 2003
    Sarasota, Florida
Also known as: Otto Everett Graham, Jr. (full
    name); Automatic Otto
Other major sport: Basketball

Early Life
Otto Everett Graham, Jr., was born in Waukegan, Illinois, on December 6, 1921. The son of two music instructors, he grew up loving music. Early on, he proved to be a musically talented child, learning to play the piano, the cornet, the violin, and the French horn. During his teenage years, Otto developed other talents. He was an exceptional, all-around athlete. At Waukegan High School, he won varsity letters in baseball, football, track, and tennis. Long before he graduated, he made his parents proud by becoming not only his school's best basketball player but also the best high school player in the state. Otto was offered many college scholarships for his basketball skills, and soon earned the title of all-American basketball player at Northwestern University.

The Road to Excellence
Otto played intermural football but did not take the sport seriously until the day he attracted the attention of Lynn "Pappy" Waldorf, a football coach. Pappy persuaded Otto to join Northwestern's football team. By 1941, Otto was playing tailback on the team's single-wing offense. No one was surprised that Otto excelled as a quarterback. Before long, he had completed a record 156 passes in 321 attempts, for 2,162 yards. In 1943, Otto won all-American honors for helping Northwestern finish second in its conference. He was chosen the conference's most valuable player. Before that season, Otto played for the college all-stars against the Washington Redskins, and he intercepted a pass and made a remarkable 97-yard touchdown. The qualities that helped make Otto shine as a collegiate athlete were his daring, his excellent sense of timing, and his ability to throw long, accurate passes.

When it came time for Otto to leave Northwestern University, World War II was still raging. Otto wanted to become a professional football player but, instead, he left school in mid-year to join the United States Naval Flight Training Program. In 1944, he finally earned his bachelor's degree from Northwestern. Just before the war ended, Otto received an excellent offer from Paul Brown, a renowned collegiate football coach. Brown had recently founded a new professional team called

Otto Graham posing at a Cleveland Browns practice in 1949. He later wore number 14. (AP/Wide World Photos)

AAFC and NFL Statistics

Season	GP	PA	PC	Pct.	Yds.	Avg.	TD	Int.
1946	14	174	95	.546	1,834	10.5	17	5
1947	14	269	163	.606	2,753	10.2	25	11
1948	14	333	173	.520	2,713	8.2	25	15
1949	13	285	161	.565	2,785	9.8	19	10
1950	12	253	137	.542	1,943	7.7	14	20
1951	12	265	147	.555	2,205	8.3	17	16
1952	12	364	181	.497	2,816	7.7	20	24
1953	12	258	167	.647	2,722	10.6	11	9
1954	12	240	142	.592	2,092	8.7	11	17
1955	12	185	98	.530	1,721	9.3	15	8
Totals	127	2,626	1,464	.558	23,584	9.0	174	135

Notes: GP = games played; PA = passes attempted; PC = passes completed; Pct. = percent completed; Yds. = yards; Avg. = average yards per attempt; TD = touchdowns; Int. = interceptions

the Cleveland Browns. As soon as the war ended, the team began to play in the new All-America Football Conference (AAFC). Otto, a three-letter athlete and an all-American in both football and basketball, joined the Browns.

The Emerging Champion

Otto began his professional football career as the Browns' first quarterback. With his astonishing ability to throw long forward passes, Otto completed 95 of 174 passes, 17 of which were touchdowns. He led the team to the league championship, winning thirteen out of fifteen games. For this, he earned the nickname "Automatic Otto." As the seasons continued, Otto's ability to inspire and control his team made him the heart of the Cleveland Browns. For four successive seasons, his efficient forward passes brought the Browns four league championships. Shortly after the Browns' fourth championship, though, the AAFC collapsed.

The Browns were considered a team of minor status, but, nevertheless, they were invited to join the proud and tough NFL. Critics said "Automatic Otto" would be fortunate to gain any victories for his team in the face of major competition. Otto proved his critics wrong in his first season in the NFL. His passes took his competition by surprise, and the Browns became the professional football champions of the world. Year after year, Otto pitched his team into the championship title game, where he always played his best. In seven out of ten

years, Otto's teams claimed the league championship, while Otto set records for most yards gained, most passes completed, and most touchdown passes in the NFL's history to that point.

Continuing the Story

In 1954, Otto chose to quit football when he was thirty-two years old. He wanted to leave the game while he was still a champion. However, Paul Brown, his coach, inspired him to play one last season as pro football's greatest quarterback. Otto won another world championship. Afterward, Otto nearly retired from his brief but fabulous football career. Again, Paul Brown somehow persuaded him to give one more year to his team, and to football history, and "Automatic Otto" played his final year. In his last game, before a crowd of 100,000, he played magnificently. He threw two long touchdown passes, and the Browns beat the Los Angeles Rams 38-14 for another NFL title.

That game marked the end of Otto's career. His place in football history was secure, though. His 88 touchdown passes were only two short of the record held by Frankie Albert of San Francisco. While playing in the AAFC, Otto won passing honors for four years, and was voted the AAFC most valuable player in 1947, 1948, and 1949. In the

Honors and Awards

1943	Chicago College All-Star Team
	College All-American (football)
	College All-American (basketball)
1947-49	AAFC most valuable player (1948 co-recipient)
1951	NFL Pro Bowl Player of the Game
1951-55	NFL Pro Bowl Team
	NFL All-Pro Team
1953, 1955	United Press International NFL Player of the Year
	Newspaper Enterprise Association NFL Player of the Year
1955	Hickok Belt
1956	Inducted into College Football Hall of Fame
1963	NFL All-Pro Team of the 1950's
1965	Inducted into Pro Football Hall of Fame
	Uniform number 14 retired by Cleveland Browns

NFL, he led the league in passing in 1953 and 1955. From 1951-1955 he was the all-NFL selection at quarterback. He also was selected as NFL player of the year in 1953 and 1955.

Otto was elected to the College Football Hall of Fame in 1956 and to the Pro Football Hall of Fame in 1965. Some football historians feel he was the finest professional quarterback ever. In his ten-year professional career, he completed 1,464 of 2,626 forward passes for 23,584 yards and 174 touchdowns. His winning streak was unparalleled, and seems unlikely to be equaled.

Summary

"Automatic Otto" Graham was one of the greatest quarterbacks ever to play pro football. He was renowned for his highly efficient passing ability. He led the Cleveland Browns to championship games for ten successive years, and won championships seven of those ten times.

Nan White

Additional Sources

Aikman, Troy. "Ranking the Greatest Quarterbacks Is a Winning Proposition." *Sporting News* 228, no. 41 (October 11, 2004): 44.

Attner, Paul. "The Best There Ever Was." *Sporting News* 227, no. 52 (December 29, 2003): 5.

Graham, Duey. *Ottomatic: The Remarkable Story of Otto Graham.* Wayne, Mich.: Immortal Investments, 2004.

Sugar, Bert R. *The One Hundred Greatest Athletes of All Time.* New York: Citadel Press, 1995.

Zimmerman, Paul, Kostya Kennedy, and Mark Bechtel. "Pass Perfect." *Sports Illustrated* 99, no. 25 (December 29, 2003): 36.

Red Grange

Born: June 13, 1903
      Forksville, Pennsylvania
Died: January 28, 1991
      Lake Wales, Florida
Also known as: Harold Edward Grange (full
    name); the Galloping Ghost

Early Life

Harold Edward "Red" Grange was born June 13, 1903, in Forksville, Pennsylvania, where his father worked as a foreman in a lumber camp. When he was five years old, his mother died. Needing help to raise his sons, Red's father moved the family to Wheaton, Illinois—where he had relatives—and became a policeman and, eventually, chief of police.

In high school and college, Red earned his spending money delivering ice. In those prerefrigerator days, families kept food cold in a box that required a new 100-pound block of ice every few days. Carrying those heavy slabs on his back helped build strength in the husky redhead's legs. Sportswriters later referred to him as "The Wheaton Ice Man." Red became a star athlete at Wheaton High School, winning sixteen letters in football, basketball, baseball, and track. Of the four sports, football was his least favorite. In track, he won all nineteen events he entered as a senior, and he often said he "could play basketball or baseball all day, but football was work."

The Road to Excellence

Impressed by the 75 touchdowns Red scored as a Wheaton halfback, Robert Zuppke encouraged Red to attend the University of Illinois, where Zuppke was head coach. In the fall of 1922, Red enrolled at the university and became a member of the varsity team the next year. In his first game for the Illini, Red rushed for 208 yards and scored 3 touchdowns. That fall, he led the nation in rushing, and was named to Walter Camp's All-American team.

Red had unusual speed and plenty of power. But his greatest attribute was a mystifying change of pace that left tacklers grasping empty air. The famous sportswriter Grantland Rice dubbed Red "The Galloping Ghost." Red's greatest game came against archrival Michigan when Illinois dedicated its new Memorial Stadium in 1924. Red ran the opening kickoff back 95 yards for a touchdown, then scored 3 more touchdowns in the next 12 minutes on runs of 67, 56, and 44 yards. After sitting out the second quarter, he ran 15 yards for a fifth touchdown in the third quarter. In the final period,

Halfback Red Grange, who played with the Chicago Bears and New York Giants and was a star in the early days of the NFL. (Courtesy of Amateur Athletic Foundation of Los Angeles)

he threw a touchdown pass to account for all of his team's points in a 39-14 win. In 1924, he was a unanimous all-American. In 1925, Red gained 363 yards on a muddy field to lead Illinois over Pennsylvania; he again was named all-American.

The Emerging Champion

Red was the biggest star in football. Huge crowds came to see him. His quiet modesty and dedication to hard work added to his popularity. Many football fans across the country wrote to Red urging him against playing professional football, which was a minor sport at the time and considered unsavory compared to the "pure" college game. However, Red felt it was more honest for him to make money as a football player than to use his name as a front for some enterprise he knew nothing about. Midway through his final season at Illinois, he made a handshake agreement to let Charles C. Pyle, an Illinois theater owner, manage his career. Pyle thus became, in effect, the first player agent.

After Red's final college game, he went to Chicago with Pyle and signed a contract with George Halas of the NFL's Chicago Bears. The following Thursday, Thanksgiving Day, he took the field for the Bears against the crosstown Chicago Cardinals before the first pro football sellout in Wrigley Field history. After drawing another packed house on Sunday, Red and the Bears launched a barnstorming tour in which the team played as many as four games a week against league and nonleague teams. The crowds were enormous. In New York, where the Giants were struggling through their first season, the magic of Red's appeal brought out an estimated 70,000 fans. When the tour ended in California, in January, Red, who received 30 percent of the gate, was a wealthy man.

Continuing the Story

In 1926, when Red and Pyle could not reach a contract agreement with the Bears, they tried to start their own NFL franchise, proposing to play in New York's Yankee Stadium. The Giants, who played at the Polo Grounds, had exclusive rights to the city as far as the league was concerned. Rebuffed, Red and Pyle launched their own American Football League, with Red as the featured star of the New York Yankees. Although the "Grange League" was a financial failure, the NFL was forced to take the Yankees in as a new franchise in 1927.

Midway through the 1927 season, Red's knee was badly damaged in a pileup. He limped through the rest of the schedule, but announced his retirement for 1928. Without him, the Yankees collapsed and handed the franchise back to the league. During 1928, Red starred in several forgettable movies, made radio appearances, and endorsed various products. Though he was making money, he yearned to get back into football. In 1929, he rejoined the Chicago Bears. Red always maintained that the 1928 knee injury took away his maneuverability and left him "just an ordinary halfback," but he earned all-NFL honors in 1930 and 1931 and played for league championship teams in 1932 and 1933. In addition to his running, he became known as the league's best defensive back.

NFL Statistics

Season	GP	Rushing Car.	Yds.	Avg.	TD	Receiving Rec.	Yds.	Avg.	TD
1925	17	204	1,024	5.0	—	—	—	—	—
1926	16	191	961	5.0	—	—	—	—	—
1927	14	154	762	4.9	—	—	—	—	—
1929	14	130	552	4.3	—	—	—	—	—
1930	14	88	382	4.3	—	—	—	—	—
1931	12	72	288	4.0	—	—	—	—	—
1932	9	57	132	2.3	3	11	168	15.3	3
1933	13	81	277	3.4	1	3	74	24.7	0
1934	12	32	136	4.3	1	2	46	23.0	2
Totals	121	1,009	4,514	4.5	5	16	288	18.0	5

Notes: GP = games played; Car. = carries; Yds. = yards; Avg. = average yards per carry or average yards per reception; TD = touchdowns; Rec. = receptions

Honors and Awards

1923	Walter Camp All-American
1924	Citizens Savings College Football Player of the Year World Trophy
1924-25	Consensus All-American
1930-31	All-NFL Team
1951	Inducted into College Football Hall of Fame
1963	NFL All-Pro Team of the 1920's
	Inducted into Pro Football Hall of Fame
	Uniform number 77 retired by Chicago Bears

After his football career, Red served as a Bear's assistant coach through 1937. He then worked at a successful insurance business in Chicago, where he also became a popular play-by-play announcer for college and professional games on radio and television. After a 1951 heart attack, Red and his wife retired to a pleasant life of golf, fishing, and boating in Florida. He died in 1991.

Summary

Red Grange's career at Illinois was remarkable, and many still consider him the greatest runner in college football history. His unprecedented popularity was the result of his unassuming personality, sensational running, and the fact that sports became front page news in the 1920's. Red's professional career, though excellent, was not as spectacular. Nevertheless, by bringing sell-out crowds to professional games for the first time, he popularized the sport and raised its stature tremendously.

Bob Carroll

Additional Sources

Carroll, John M. *Red Grange and the Rise of Modern Football.* Urbana: University of Illinois Press, 2004.

Grange, Red, and Ira Morton. *The Red Grange Story: An Autobiography.* Urbana: University of Illinois Press, 1993.

Platt, Jim, and James Buckley. *Sports Immortals: Stories of Inspiration and Achievement.* Chicago: Triumph Books, 2002.

Whittingham, Richard. *What a Game They Played: An Inside Look at the Golden Era of Pro Football.* Lincoln: University of Nebraska Press, 2002.

Hugh Green

Born: July 27, 1959
    Natchez, Mississippi
Also known as: Hugh Donell Green (full name)

Early Life

Hugh Donell Green was born in Natchez, Mississippi, on July 27, 1959. He grew up in poverty without a father. When Hugh's mother died not long after his sixth birthday, his aunt, Lucy Berry, and uncle, Eltee Berry, a mason, took him in. The Berrys taught Hugh self-sufficiency and such practical skills as cooking and sewing: Hugh learned to make his own clothes. He began playing football in junior high school and gained recognition at North Natchez High School, where he was credited with 116 solo tackles and 58 assists in his senior year. After graduating in 1976, Hugh signed a letter of intent to attend Mississippi State University but later accepted an athletic scholarship at the University of Pittsburgh.

The Road to Excellence

At the University of Pittsburgh, Hugh wore number 99 while playing defensive end for the Panthers. An intense and dominating presence on the field, the 6-foot 2-inch, 220-pound Hugh had an outstanding college career. In 1978, 1979, and 1980, he was a consensus all-American and led the team to a cumulative 39-8-1 record; the Panthers won three of four bowl games in this time span. In his senior year, when Pitt went 11-1 to finish second in the national polls, Hugh was credited with 123 tackles and 17 quarterback sacks, completing a stellar collegiate career in which he totaled 441 tackles and 53 sacks: more sacks than anyone in National Collegiate Athletic Association (NCAA) history. That year, he finished second in balloting for the Heisman Trophy with the highest number of votes ever for a strictly defensive player. Though University of South Carolina running back George Rogers won the Heisman, Hugh was otherwise honored. He garnered the Walter Camp Award, a coaches' and sports information directors' recognition of the player of the year; the Maxwell Award, given by sportscasters, sportswriters, and NCAA coaches to

the nation's best college football player; and the Lombardi Award, annually bestowed on the best college football lineman or linebacker.

The Emerging Champion

After Hugh graduated in 1981, the Tampa Bay Buccaneers selected him as the seventh overall pick in the first round of the NFL draft. Though he played respectably, Hugh did not have as much an impact as a professional as he had in college. Part of the problem was that he was playing a new position. The Buccaneers, instead of using the natural aggressiveness and speed that had made Hugh a hostile and agile defensive end at Pittsburgh, pressed him into service as a linebacker, a role that limited his tackles and sacks totals. Another part of the problem was a series of injuries and personal problems that cut into his playing time.

Hugh made all-pro as a linebacker after the 1982 and 1983 seasons; in the latter year he returned 2 interceptions for touchdowns. During the middle of the 1984 season, he was hurt in an automobile accident, suffering a fracture near his eye that required surgery. Halfway through the 1985 season, he was traded to the Miami Dolphins. Injuries continued to plague him, and Hugh played only a total of twelve games during the 1986 and 1987 seasons. In 1989, during a party celebrating

NFL Statistics

Season	GP	Sacks	FR	Int.
1981	16	0	1	2
1982	9	2.3	0	1
1983	16	3.5	2	2
1984	8	4.0	0	0
1985	16	7.5	1	1
1986	3	4.0	0	0
1987	9	0.0	0	0
1988	16	2.5	1	0
1989	16	7.5	2	0
1990	16	2.0	0	0
1991	11	1.0	0	0
Totals	**136**	**34.3**	**7**	**6**

Notes: GP = games played; FR = fumble recoveries; Int. = interceptions

Honors and Awards

1978-80	Consensus All-American
1980	Walter Camp Award
	Maxwell Award
	Lombardi Award
1983, 1984	NFL Pro Bowl
1996	Inducted into College Football Hall of Fame
2009	Inducted into Mississippi Sports Hall of Fame

his thirtieth birthday, he was arrested on a charge of battery for striking his twenty-two-year-old wife, Monique Stallings-Green. In 1991, after again missing significant playing time, he retired. In 136 professional games spread over eleven seasons, he recorded a total of 34.3 sacks and 6 interceptions.

Continuing the Story

After leaving the professional ranks, Hugh returned to Mississippi. He remarried, and he and his wife, Guy, and their four children lived quietly on a farm in Fayette, near his birthplace. In 1996, Hugh was enshrined in the National Football Foundation's College Football Hall of Fame; afterward, he was named to a number of national polls as one of the best collegiate players of all-time.

In 2000, hoping to return to football in a coaching capacity, Hugh attended the NFL's coaching internship program. He later became defensive coordinator of the Miami Tropics in the short-lived Spring Football League and afterward served briefly as an assistant coach for the Barcelona Dragons of NFL Europe and in the Canadian Football League as a coach with the Montreal Alouettes.

Among many enterprises, Hugh headed a training camp for the NFL Minority Coaching Fellowship program. In association with other investors, his company marketed "Legends of the Decades," hosted Super Bowl parties, staged fantasy camps, applied for federal grants to build sports facilities for youth, and raised money for charities such as the Ronald McDonald House. Hugh and his investment group attempted to gather funds for a multimillion-dollar athletic complex—incorporating baseball and softball fields, a water park, and a golf course—in Vicksburg, Mississippi. In 2007, ESPN listed Hugh as the fourteenth best player on its list of the top twenty-five college players in football history. Hugh was inducted into the Mississippi Sports Hall of Fame in 2009.

Summary

Voted in numerous polls as one of the best collegiate players of all time, Hugh Green starred as a defensive end at the University of Pittsburgh, setting a national record for quarterback sacks in the process. Though he did not fully live up to his college reputation as a professional, he played through injuries during an eleven-year career as a linebacker with the Tampa Bay Buccaneers and the Miami Dolphins.

Jack Ewing

Additional Sources

Gruden, Jon, and Vic Carucci. *Do You Love Football? Winning with Heart, Passion, and Not Much Sleep.* New York: HarperCollins, 2003.

Quirk, James P. *The Ultimate Guide to College Football: Rankings, Records, and Scores of the Major Teams and Conferences.* Urbana: University of Illinois Press, 2004.

Sciullo, Sam, Jr. *Tales from the Pitt Panthers.* Champaign, Ill.: Sports, 2004.

Joe Greene

Born: September 24, 1946
     Temple, Texas
Also known as: Charles Edward Greene (full
    name); Mean Joe Greene

Early Life

Charles Edward "Joe" Greene was born on September 24, 1946, in Temple, Texas. He grew up in a poor family. When Joe was a young boy, his parents divorced; Joe was brought up by his mother. Although she had to work hard as a domestic worker, Joe's mother did an excellent job bringing up her son, for even as a child he was unselfish and considerate of people's feelings. However, Joe was also shy

Defensive lineman Joe Greene helping the Pittsburgh Steelers to victory in Super Bowl IX. (Manny Rubio/NFL/ Getty Images)

and uncomfortable at meeting people. Perhaps it was this lack of sociability that helped him earn his future football nickname, "Mean Joe." Or perhaps it was his strength and intensity. Even at the age of fourteen, when he first started playing football, he was the scourge of enemy quarterbacks and of anyone else who crossed his path. When he played middle linebacker at Dunbar High School in Temple, he intimidated opposing teams.

The Road to Excellence

At North Texas State University, Joe majored in physical education and played for the university's football team. He was part of the defense squad nicknamed the Mean Green, because of the team's green jerseys. Naturally, the nickname stuck to Joe, the team's toughest member. As Joe was fast approaching his eventual playing size of 6 feet 4 inches and 270 pounds, his coach described him as "a fort on foot." In addition to his exceptional quickness, Joe was also an excellent leader. By the time he was a senior, Joe had been named consensus all-American, as well as Missouri Valley Conference athlete of the year. He was also chosen as the nation's top college defensive lineman by a nearly unanimous vote.

In 1969, although there were some doubts about his competitive spirit, he was drafted by the Pittsburgh Steelers of the NFL in the first round of the NFL draft. The selection did not please many of the Steelers' fans, who considered Joe an insignificant defensive tackle from an unknown university, not a big name who was worthy of a first-round choice. Joe made things worse by showing up twenty-three days late for training camp, since he was holding out in a contract dispute.

When Joe arrived, two veteran Steelers decided to teach the rookie a lesson. When Joe lined up against them in a two-way drill, the two planned to get him with a high-and-low double-team block. Mean Joe grabbed one by the shoulder pads, the other by the neck, tossed them like rag dolls, and was onto the quarterback in a half-second. Suddenly, the Steelers realized they had a rookie who was head and shoulders above them all.

The Emerging Champion

Not surprisingly, Joe was honored as the NFL's defensive rookie of the year, and played in his first of ten Pro Bowls. The following year, he made the all-NFL team for the first of five consecutive seasons. In 1974, Joe developed a new tactic of lining up at a sharp angle between the guard and center; this disrupted the opposition's blocking assignments. As a result, the "unknown kid from Texas" soon turned into the cornerstone of his franchise. He was the heart of the Steelers' intimidating defensive unit, the "Steel Curtain," which helped the team to four Super Bowls.

For years, Joe clobbered opposition players. He was known for a kind of inspired savagery and enthusiasm that resulted in superb plays and also led to the revival of his "Mean Joe" image. That did not please Joe, since the name marked him as a dirty player. By the time he reached the climax of his career, Joe was so good that he was able to dominate a game nearly single-handedly. He came to symbolize the invincible Steelers during the team's heyday. The Steelers—who dominated the NFL during the 1970's—boasted many superstars, but Joe was the one who kept the team together through good and bad times. Too strong to be overpowered and too smart to be fooled, Joe was possibly the greatest player on one of the greatest teams ever. He was instrumental in turning the team around at a time when it was rebuilding. As leader of the "Steel Curtain" defensive unit, he was a dominant force that led the team to six consecutive playoff appearances and four Super Bowl victories. Joe was unanimously selected to the NFL's 1970's Team of the Decade.

Continuing the Story

For the first ninety-one season games of his career, Joe was lucky: He remained free of injuries. In 1975, though, he was suddenly sidelined with groin, back, and neck injuries. After his injuries, he played more conservatively, funneling the play to someone else if he could not make it. Joe never fully regained his sense of health and invincibility, and in 1981, he retired.

Before retiring, Joe appeared in minor films and television commercials. One commercial, for which he won a Clio Award, did much to revamp

Honors and Awards

1969	Missouri Valley Conference Athlete of the Year
	All-Missouri Valley Conference Team
	Senior Bowl Outstanding South Lineman
	East-West Shrine All-Star Team
	Chicago College All-Star Team
	Consensus All-American
1970	*Sporting News* Eastern Conference All-Star Team
	Associated Press NFL Defensive Rookie of the Year
1970-74, 1979	*Sporting News* AFC All-Star Team
1970-75, 1977-79	United Press International All-AFC Team
1970-77, 1979-80	NFL Pro Bowl Team
1971-76	Associated Press All-AFC Team
1972	United Press International AFC Lineman of the Year
1972, 1974	Associated Press NFL Defensive Player of the Year
	Halas Trophy
	Newspaper Enterprise Association All-Pro Team
1972-74, 1979	Professional Football Writers of America All-Pro Team
1974	Seagram's Seven Crowns of Sports Award
1977	Associated Press All-Pro Team
1980	NFL All-Pro Team of the 1970's
1984	Inducted into College Football Hall of Fame
1985	AFL-NFL 1960-1984 All-Star Team
1987	Inducted into Pro Football Hall of Fame

his Mean Joe image. In it, Joe gives his jersey to a small boy in return for a soft drink, thereby showing television viewers the real, kind-hearted Joe. Later, Joe served as assistant coach with the Steelers. In 1985, Joe was elected to the Pro Football Hall of Fame and named to its AFL-NFL 1960-1984 all-star second team.

Summary

Joe Greene went from the "unknown kid from Texas" to one of the greatest defensive tackles ever. He was the heart of the Pittsburgh Steelers' intimidating defensive unit. He is remembered as one of the NFL's toughest and most skillful defenders.

Nicholas White

Additional Sources

Barber, Phil. "NFL: Football's One Hundred Greatest Players—The Hit Men." *The Sporting News* 223 (November 1, 1999): 12-16.

Carroll, Bob. *Total Football: The Official Encyclopedia of the National Football League.* New York: HarperCollins, 1999.

Mendelson, Abby. *The Pittsburgh Steelers: The Official Team History.* Lanham, Md.: Taylor Trade, 2006.

Wexell, Jim. *Tales from Behind the Steel Curtain.* Champaign, Ill.: Sports, 2004.

Forrest Gregg

Born: October 18, 1933
        Birthright, Texas
Also known as: Alvis Forrest Gregg (full name)

Early Life

Alvis Forrest Gregg was born on October 18, 1933, in the small town of Birthright, Texas. He was one of eleven children and did not have an easy childhood. There were endless chores to do since his family lived on a large farm. When Forrest was fifteen years old, he left home to attend Sulfur Springs High School to play football. Forrest also participated in basketball, baseball, and track and field. Sulfur Springs football coach C. L. Davis arranged for Forrest to live in a garage apartment. Although meager, this arrangement seemed like a king's life to Forrest; he had his own room and as much to eat as he needed.

The Road to Excellence

The next stop for Forrest was Southern Methodist University (SMU), coached by Chalmer Woodard. When Forrest reported to his first football practice as a freshman, he weighed 195 pounds and was not a standout player. He played tackle and by his junior year he was a solid 225 pounds of muscle and could hit hard. In 1953, 1954, and 1955, he earned varsity letters. In 1954 and 1955, he was first-team all-Southwest Conference; in the latter year, he played in the East-West Shrine Game and the Hula Bowl. Forrest gave 100 percent effort both on and off the field, and eventually earned a bachelor's degree in physical education. His admiration for his coaches gave him the desire to become a coach someday. The idea of playing professionally did not occur to Forrest until his junior year, when some former SMU players began returning to campus with new suits and new cars. During his senior year Forrest was drafted by the NFL's Green Bay Packers.

The Emerging Champion

Green Bay seemed liked a foreign country to Forrest. He had never been to Wisconsin, and he thought everyone talked funny because they did not have a Texas accent. His $7,500 annual salary made him more willing to withstand the cold of Wisconsin. Coach Vince Lombardi was a demanding coach, expecting nothing less than the best. That was no problem for an athlete like Forrest. Lombardi said that Forrest was one of the finest players he had ever coached.

Many of Forrest's teammates thought he was one of the best offensive tackles they had ever seen. He never got excited and always exuded a calmness that rubbed off on other players in a positive way. In 1965, Forrest did something unusual for the good of the team. He switched back and forth between tackle and guard because so many other

Forrest Gregg played in 188 consecutive games and anchored the offensive line for a Green Bay Packers team that won multiple NFL Championships and Super Bowls in the 1960's. (Courtesy of Amateur Athletic Foundation of Los Angeles)

Honors and Awards

1954-55	All-Southwest Conference Team
1955	East-West All-Star Team
	Hula Bowl All-Star Team
1960-65, 1967-69	NFL Pro Bowl Team
1960-67	NFL All-Pro Team
1970	NFL All-Pro Team of the 1960's
1976	Associated Press Coach of the Year
1977	Inducted into Pro Football Hall of Fame
1981	United Press International AFC Coach of the Year
1986	Inducted into Texas Sports Hall of Fame
1994	NFL 75th Anniversary All-Time Team

players were injured. Few other athletes would have been able to make such a difficult move, but Forrest made it look easy because he was so talented and focused.

Continuing the Story

Forrest was a consensus all-pro performer from 1960 to 1967 and was a member of the West Pro-Bowl team from 1960 through 1965, and from 1967 through 1969. Even though Forrest had to switch positions, he still continued to perform on a level higher than many players in the NFL. Forrest's attitude separated him from the rest of the league. He took pride in his job.

Forrest began to explore coaching. In 1965, he quit the team to become an assistant coach at the University of Tennessee. He returned to the Packers the next year only to quit again to become an assistant coach for the Packers in 1969. Finally, he returned for one last season with the Dallas Cowboys, helped the team win a Super Bowl in 1971, and then finally quit for good at the age of thirty-nine. Through sixteen seasons, many division titles, three Super Bowl victories, and one hundred eighty-seven consecutive games, Forrest proved to be one of the finest defensive linemen of

all time. His fellow players and his coaches always considered him a special and outstanding champion.

After retiring as a player, Forrest entered into a new football career as a coach. He first coached the Cleveland Browns (1975-1977), then the Cincinnati Bengals (1980-1983), and finally his former team, the Green Bay Packers (1984-1987). In 1979, he coached in the Canadian Football League (CFL) with the Toronto Argonauts. He was the head football coach at his alma mater SMU in 1989 and 1990. In 1994, he returned to CFL to coach the Shreveport Pirates. The same year, Forrest was selected to the NFL's seventy-fifth anniversary all-time team. In 2005, he became the vice president of football operations for the CFL's Ottawa Renegades.

Summary

In the 1960's, Forrest Gregg helped the Packers win five NFL championships in seven years. Six years after he retired in 1971, Forrest was inducted into the Pro Football Hall of Fame. He reached the Super Bowl as a player and a coach, guiding the Bengals to an AFC championship during the 1981 season.

Brooke K. Zibel

Additional Sources

Barber, Phil. "NFL: Football's One Hundred Greatest Players—The Hit Men." *The Sporting News* 223 (November 1, 1999): 12-16.

Carroll, Bob. *Total Football: The Official Encyclopedia of the National Football League.* New York: HarperCollins, 1999.

MacCambridge, Michael. *America's Game: The Epic Story of How Pro Football Captured a Nation.* New York: Random House, 2004.

Smith, Ron, and Dan Dierdorf. *Heroes of the Hall.* St. Louis: Sporting News, 2003.

Bob Griese

Born: February 3, 1945
      Evansville, Indiana
Also known as: Robert Allen Griese (full name);
  Rag

Early Life

Robert Allen Griese, one of the greatest NFL quarterbacks, came from a humble background. He was born on February 3, 1945, in Evansville, Indiana. He was one of three children raised by Sylverious and Ida Griese. His father owned a plumbing business in Evansville.

In 1955, when Bob was ten, his father died. His mother had to sell her husband's plumbing business and take a job as a secretary in order to pay the family's bills. Saddened by his father's death, young Bob became a loner. However, he enjoyed sports. While attending Rex Mundi High School in Evansville, he participated in football, baseball, track and field, and basketball. These sports gave him a sense of purpose and a goal: to become a great athlete.

The Road to Excellence

In high school, Bob captained the football, basketball, and baseball teams. He was named Indiana's best high school quarterback during his junior and senior years. As a baseball pitcher, he compiled a 17-0 record and led his team to the American Legion World Series. In 1963, when Bob graduated from Rex Mundi High School, he was swamped with offers from forty colleges. He selected Purdue, in his home state. At Purdue, Bob continued on the road to greatness. He was a great all-around athlete, playing both basketball and football. As a quarterback, Bob really excelled, though. Previously, he had been a sidearm passer, but at Purdue, he changed to throwing the ball overhand, and became even better.

As a junior, Bob led his Purdue team to an upset 25-21 victory over the top-ranked Notre Dame team. In that game, Bob completed an incredible 19 of 22 passes, including 13 in a row. As a result of his outstanding year, he was selected to the all-American team, and finished second in the voting for the prestigious Heisman Trophy. In his senior year, Bob led Purdue to the Rose Bowl and a 14-13 victory over the University of Southern California (USC). He was again selected to the all-American team. In 1967, Bob graduated from Purdue with a B.S. in industrial management. He is remembered as one Purdue's all-time greatest quarterbacks.

Quarterback Bob Griese of the Miami Dolphins. (Al Messerschmidt Archive/Getty Images)

The Emerging Champion

Bob Griese's great collegiate career did not go unnoticed. He was selected in the first round of the 1967 American Football League (AFL) college draft by the Miami Dolphins. He became the team's starting quarterback in the first game of the season, when the regular quarterback was injured. Bob established himself as a professional in his rookie year. On October 29, 1967, he set an AFL record for the highest pass completion percentage in one game by completing 17 of 21 passes for an 81 percent completion rate.

Despite Bob's promise as a professional quarterback, the Dolphins were not good. In Bob's first three seasons with the team, the Dolphins won only eleven games. Then in 1970, Don Shula took over as head coach, and the team became far more successful. By 1971, Bob had become the leading quarterback in the American Football Conference (AFC). His passing accuracy was uncanny, and his play calling excellent. That year he led the Dolphins to the AFC championship and to the Super Bowl. Although the Dolphins lost the Super Bowl to the Dallas Cowboys, the team was established as a championship contender. For the next two years, Bob helped the Dolphins become one of the greatest teams in football history. In 1972, they finished the season undefeated at 17-0, the first time that had been done. They won the Super Bowl both that year and the next. Bob's sharp passing skills and intelligent leadership were key ingredients to the team's success.

Continuing the Story

Bob continued playing pro football through the 1980 season. He remained one of the top quarterbacks in football until he retired. In 1977, he passed for 22 touchdowns and won the Bert Bell Award as the NFL player of the year. In 1978, he completed 63 percent of his passes, a career high. Though the Dolphins did not win another Super Bowl, Bob led them to the playoffs almost every year.

On the day Bob became the fourteenth quarterback to pass for more than 25,000 yards, he suffered a shoulder injury that ended his career. Miami Dolphins owner Joe Robbie described Bob as the "cornerstone of the franchise" and retired his number 12 jersey. He was later inducted into the Florida Sports Hall of Fame, the National Football Foundation's College Football Hall of Fame, and the Pro Football Hall of Fame.

According to Bob, the keys to his success were competitiveness, intelligence, determination, and desire. He was also a cool leader

---

Honors and Awards

1966-67	College All-American
1968-69	AFL All-Star Team
1970-71, 1973	*Sporting News* AFC All-Star Team
1971	Jim Thorpe Trophy
	Sporting News AFC Player of the Year
	Newspaper Enterprise Association AFC Co-Player of the Year
1971-72, 1974-75, 1978-79	NFL Pro Bowl Team
1971, 1977	NFL All-Pro Team
1977	Bert Bell Award
	NFL Player of the Year
1979	Inducted into Florida Sports Hall of Fame
1985	Inducted into College Football Hall of Fame
1990	Inducted into Pro Football Hall of Fame
	Uniform number 12 retired by Miami Dolphins

AFL and NFL Statistics

Season	GP	PA	PC	Pct.	Yds.	Avg.	TD	Int.
1967	12	331	166	.502	2,005	6.0	15	18
1968	13	335	186	.524	2,473	6.9	21	16
1969	9	252	121	.480	1,695	6.7	10	16
1970	14	245	142	.580	2,019	8.2	12	17
1971	14	263	145	.551	2,089	7.9	19	9
1972	6	97	53	.546	638	6.5	4	4
1973	13	218	116	.532	1,422	6.5	17	8
1974	13	253	152	.601	1,968	7.7	16	15
1975	10	191	118	.618	1,693	8.8	14	13
1976	13	272	162	.596	2,097	7.7	11	12
1977	14	307	180	.586	2,252	7.3	22	13
1978	11	235	148	.630	1,791	7.6	11	11
1979	14	310	176	.568	2,160	6.9	14	16
1980	5	100	61	.610	790	7.9	6	4
Totals	**161**	**3,409**	**1,926**	**.562**	**25,092**	**7.3**	**192**	**172**

Notes: GP = games played; PA = passes attempted; PC = passes completed; Pct. = percent completed; Yds. = yards; Avg. = average yards per attempt; TD = touchdowns; Int. = interceptions

who was excellent at reading defenses and calling the right play. As a team player, Bob also believed that the quarterback received too much credit if the team won, as well as too much blame if the team lost.

In the 1980's Bob became one of network television's most respected football analysts, first for NBC's NFL coverage and then for ABC's college game of the week and bowl game coverage. His frank commentary, insider's analysis, and genial chemistry with longtime broadcast partner Keith Jackson made him one of the most respected names in sport coverage.

Bob became involved in investments and property management before becoming director of visual education for American Optical. Bob has also been active in children's charities. He has three sons: Scott, Jeff, and Brian—who succeeded John Elway as quarterback of the Denver Broncos in the late 1990's. Bob and Brian wrote together a book entitled *Undefeated*. The book helped Bob cope with his wife's death.

Summary

Bob Griese will be remembered as one of the most intelligent and efficient quarterbacks of all time. He was a true champion, and knew what it took to win in both college and professional football. He was one of the most accurate passers who ever played the game. He was a quiet leader; not flashy or spectacular, but calmly efficient on the field.

Nan White

Additional Sources

Carroll, Bob. *Total Football: The Official Encyclopedia of the National Football League.* New York: Harper-Collins, 1999.

Griese, Bob, Brian Griese, and Jim Denney. *Undefeated: How Father and Son Triumphed over Unbelievable Odds Both on and off the Field.* Nashville, Tenn.: T. Nelson, 2000.

McCullough, Bob. *My Greatest Day in Football: The Legends of Football Recount Their Greatest Moments.* New York: Thomas Dunne Books/St. Martin's Press, 2002.

Archie Griffin

Born: August 21, 1954
Columbus, Ohio
Also known as: Archie Mason Griffin (full name)

Early Life

Archie Mason Griffin was born on August 21, 1954, in Columbus, Ohio, to James and Margaret Griffin. Archie was the fourth of seven Griffin boys, each of whom went on to play major college football, and three of whom played in the NFL. Archie's sister was also a good athlete. This athletic family of eight children was held together by Archie's kind and patient mother and hard-working father. At one point Archie's father worked three different jobs to support his family: He was a sanitation truck driver by day and a school custodian and steel foundry worker by night.

Archie Griffin, who is the only player to win two Heisman Trophies, doing so in 1974 and 1975. (Courtesy of Amateur Athletic Foundation of Los Angeles)

As Archie was growing up, many of his friends teased him with nicknames such as "Butterball" and "Tank" because he was relatively short and somewhat overweight. However, he excelled at football, playing as an offense and defense lineman. One day when the regular fullback failed to show up for a game, Archie filled in and never played another game at lineman. His hard work and disciplined attitude had paid off; he worked out to strengthen his torso and upper body to withstand the wear and tear of life as a running back.

The Road to Excellence

By the time Archie finished junior high school, he was already becoming known as one of the best football players in his area. He was also renowned for his scholastic achievement. One of his teachers spoke of him as a highly motivated, model student whose pursuit of excellence on the field was matched by his in-class performance.

Standing 5 feet 8 inches and weighing a rather slim 167 pounds, Archie quickly became the regular halfback at Columbus Eastmor High School, where he starred for three years. What Archie lacked in size or build, he made up for in determination and desire. He earned all-district honors as a junior, and, in 1972, was honored as a member of the all-state team in Ohio after leading his team to the city championship his senior year. Archie also wrestled for his high school and competed in sprints and relays on the track team. His destiny was football, though, and Archie planned to go to Northwestern University in Evanston, Illinois, a private Big Ten school with a reputation for academic excellence and mediocre football teams.

The Emerging Champion

Archie had leaned toward attending Northwestern because of the school's academic reputation, and also because the campus and student body were smaller than those at other Big Ten schools—like his hometown Ohio State University. Northwestern's atmosphere seemed to be the proper balance between academics and athletics. The legendary Woody Hayes, coach of the Ohio State Buckeyes, nevertheless worked hard to recruit Archie to stay home and play for him at Ohio State. By his own admission, Archie says that Coach Hayes charmed him and his parents into accepting the challenge of playing at a university with a rich football reputation.

Archie had gained 15 pounds, but he was still undersized for a halfback in the Big Ten. As a freshman in 1972, he did not expect to play much, but he did. After he had played less than two minutes in the season's opening game against Iowa, Archie was inserted into the Ohio State starting lineup against the University of North Carolina (UNC) in the season's second game. In that game, Archie broke the all-time Ohio State rushing record by gaining 239 yards, and he also scored a touchdown to give twelfth-ranked UNC its only loss of the season. In his sophomore year—a year filled with amazing exploits—Archie began his remarkable record of consecutive 100-yard performances. After breaking his own Buckeye record with 246 yards against Iowa in a late-season contest, he led his team to a lopsided victory over the eighth-ranked University of Southern California (USC), completing the season 10-0-1 and earning a second-place ranking in the final national polls.

In the 1974 and 1975 seasons, Archie gained 1,620 and 1,357 yards, respectively, and became the

NFL Statistics

| Season | GP | Rushing | | | | Receiving | | | |
		Car.	Yds.	Avg.	TD	Rec.	Yds.	Avg.	TD
1976	14	138	625	4.5	3	16	138	8.6	0
1977	12	137	549	4.0	0	28	240	8.6	0
1978	16	132	484	3.7	0	35	284	8.1	3
1979	16	140	688	4.9	0	43	417	9.7	2
1980	15	85	260	3.1	0	28	196	7.0	0
1981	16	47	163	3.5	3	20	160	8.0	1
1982	9	12	39	3.3	1	22	172	7.8	0
Totals	**98**	**691**	**2,808**	**4.1**	**7**	**192**	**1,607**	**8.4**	**6**

Notes: GP = games played; Car. = carries; Yds. = yards; Avg. = average yards per carry *or* average yards per reception; TD = touchdowns; Rec. = receptions

first college football player to earn two Heisman Trophy awards as the country's outstanding college football player. At the end of the 1975 season, with a berth in the Rose Bowl on the line, the Buckeyes completed an undefeated season by defeating Michigan 21-14. However, the Wolverines ended Archie's 100-yard rushing streak at thirty-one games by holding him to 46 yards.

Continuing the Story

Archie was the second pick of the Cincinnati Bengals in the first round of the 1976 NFL draft. He played for the Bengals for eight seasons, gradually shifting his offensive responsibilities from ball carrier to pass receiver. Soon after he left college and began his NFL career, Archie wrote a well-received and inspirational autobiography that detailed the source of his character and personal discipline:

his faith in Christ. A long-time participant in the Fellowship of Christian Athletes and the Campus Crusade for Christ, Archie became a much sought-after evangelistic and motivational speaker.

In 1983, Archie retired from the Cincinnati Bengals as the team's fourth-leading all-time rusher—2,808 yards, with an average of 4.0 yards per carry—and fifth-leading all-time receiver—192 receptions. After an ill-fated business enterprise with two brothers, James, Jr., and Ray, Archie joined the Ohio State staff to work in public relations and fund-raising. In 1985, Archie revived his career briefly when he joined the United States Football League (USFL) franchise in Jacksonville as a running back, but he returned to Ohio State in midsea-

Honors and Awards

1973	College All-American
1973-74	Silver Football Trophy
1974-75	Heisman Trophy
	United Press International College Football Player of the Year
	Walter Camp Award
	Sporting News College Player of the Year
	Citizens Savings College Football Player of the Year
	Consensus All-American
1975	Maxwell Award
	Sporting News Man of the Year
1976	NCAA Today's Top Five Award
1986	Inducted into College Football Hall of Fame

son after seeing limited action on the field. He settled in Columbus with his wife, Loretta, and their children. He later became the President of the Ohio State University Alumni Association.

Summary

Archie Griffin had a respectable professional football career, but his name will forever be associated with collegiate football excellence. The short and stocky Archie frequently played hurt and was physically unimpressive—until the game began. There have been bigger, faster, and stronger men who have played football—but few have ever had a bigger heart than Archie.

Bruce L. Edwards

Additional Sources

Dienhart, Tom. "Winners for Life." *Sporting News* 231, no. 29 (July 16, 2007): 7.

Hooley, Bruce. *Greatest Moments in Ohio State Football History.* Chicago: Triumph Books, 2006.

Pennington, Bill. *The Heisman: Great American Stories of the Men Who Won.* New York: ReganBooks, 2004.

Lou Groza

Born: January 25, 1924
      Martins Ferry, Ohio
Died: November 29, 2000
      Middleburg Heights, Ohio
Also known as: Louis Roy Groza (full name); the
      Toe

Early Life

Louis Roy Groza, the man who would become known as "The Toe" for his remarkable kicking ability, was born on January 25, 1924, in Martins Ferry, Ohio. Most young men of Martins Ferry, a small, working-class town, either worked in coal mines and steel mills, or they played football. Lou and all of his brothers chose football. Lou especially enjoyed kicking, and he used to practice by booting a ball over a telephone line at one end of a vacant field. Lou was big for a boy—he grew to 6 feet 3 inches and 210 pounds at maturity—and his size was an advantage in sports. At Martins Ferry High School, he played baseball, football, and basketball. Eventually, he captained teams in all three sports, and helped lead Martins Ferry to the state high school basketball championship.

The Road to Excellence

Many Midwest colleges sought Lou because of his athletic talent, but he chose to attend Ohio State University. The school was known for its strong football and basketball teams. In 1942, his freshman year, Lou played in the first three football games, but because of the outbreak of World War II, he left school and joined the U.S. Army. From 1943 to 1945, he served with the 96th Infantry Division in Asia. During his time in the U.S. Army, Lou still managed to practice kicking footballs during breaks in the fighting. His college coach at Ohio State, the legendary Paul Brown, kept in touch with Lou and even sent football equipment to him overseas.

Paul Brown had a significant effect on Lou's football career. He recognized Lou's talent, and asked him to play for his new professional football team, the Cleveland Browns of the All-America Football Conference. He also persuaded Lou to finish his college education in the off-season. In 1949, Lou graduated from Ohio State with a bachelor's degree in busi-

Lou Groza, who played both kicker and offensive lineman for the Cleveland Browns. (Courtesy of Amateur Athletic Foundation of Los Angeles)

NFL Statistics

Season	GP	FGA	FGM	XP	TP
1946	14	29	13	45	84
1947	12	21	7	39	60
1948	14	19	8	51	75
1949	12	7	2	34	40
1950	10	19	13	29	68
1951	12	23	10	43	73
1952	12	33	19	32	89
1953	12	26	23	39	108
1954	12	24	16	37	85
1955	12	22	11	44	77
1956	12	20	11	18	51
1957	12	22	15	32	77
1958	12	19	8	36	60
1959	12	16	5	33	48
1961	14	23	16	37	85
1962	14	31	14	33	75
1963	14	23	15	40	85
1964	14	33	23	49	115
1965	14	25	16	45	93
1966	14	23	9	51	78
1967	14	23	11	43	76
Totals	268	481	265	810	1,602

Notes: GP = games played; FGA = field goals attempted; FGM = field goals made; XP = extra points; TP = total points

ness administration. While still in the U.S Army, Lou had signed a contract to play for the Browns, which he was finally able to do in 1946. Lou played offensive tackle and also became the team's place-kicker.

The Emerging Champion

Lou excelled at both positions. As a 250-pound tackle, he was bruising and effective. As a placekicker, he emerged as a star. Until that time, football had been a game dominated by passing and running. Lou's great kicking ability added another dimension to the game. He was able to kick long field goals with amazing accuracy.

The Browns dominated the All-America Football Conference during that league's four seasons of existence; they won the league championship each year. Then in 1950, the Browns joined the NFL and soon became champions in that league as well. The Browns won the 1950 league championship over the Los Angeles Rams 30-28 when Lou kicked a field goal with 20 seconds left in the game. During the same season, Lou kicked a then

league record of 13 field goals. That was only the beginning of Lou's great kicking feats. He was nicknamed "The Toe" because of his remarkable skill.

Led by Lou and the brilliant quarterback Otto Graham, the Browns finished first in the Eastern Division of the NFL seven out of eight years. Lou led the league in field goals in five of those years. In 1953, he set a record for accuracy by making an incredible 23 field goals in 26 attempts for an 88.5 percent success rate. Then in 1957, he won the league scoring title with 77 points. He was chosen to the NFL all-star team nine times and was selected to the all-pro team as a tackle six times.

Continuing the Story

In 1960, a back injury ended Lou's career as a tackle. However, in 1961, he returned and concentrated on kicking for the next seven seasons. In 1964 and 1965, Lou made football history: He became the first player to score 1,000 career points, and he kicked his 200th career field goal.

Lou achieved great success as a professional football player, although he played almost no college football. When he retired from the sport at the age of forty-three, he had played pro football for twenty-one years—longer than anyone before him. By then he had become a football legend. He finished with 1,602 points, a record that would stand for several years. Lou was an important part of the great Cleveland Brown teams of the 1950's and 1960's that won four league championships. In

NFL Record

Most extra points kicked in a postseason game, 8 (1954)

Honors and Awards

1951-55, 1957	NFL All-Pro Team
1951-56, 1958-60	NFL Pro Bowl Team
1963	NFL All-Pro Team of the 1950's
1974	Inducted into Pro Football Hall of Fame
1992	Palm Beach County Sports Commission established Lou Groza Collegiate Place-Kicker Award
1999	Cleveland Browns rename the street in front of their training facility, making the address Lou Groza Boulevard
2000	Cleveland Browns players wore number 76 on helmets following Groza's death through season's end
	Uniform number 76 retired by Cleveland Browns

1974, he was elected to the Pro Football Hall of Fame. He and his wife, Jackie, had four children, Jeff, Jill, John, and Jud. Lou died of a heart attack on November 29, 2000.

Summary

Lou Groza changed football forever. Before he arrived, football had been a game of passing and running. Lou's powerful leg added another dimension to the game. With Lou on the field, his team became a scoring threat as soon as they passed midfield. Lou kicked many field goals from 40 to 50 yards, which was unheard of in the 1950's. His great scoring ability convinced players and coaches that kicking field goals was a good way to score points.

His reliable toe changed the strategy of football; the era of the kicking specialist had begun.

Nan White

Additional Sources

Boyer, Mary Schmitt. *Browns Essential: Everything You Need to Know to Be a Real Fan!* Chicago: Triumph Books, 2006.

Groza, Lou, and Mark Hodermarsky. *The Toe: The Lou Groza Story.* Dubuque, Iowa: Kendall/Hunt, 1996.

Henkel, Frank M. *Cleveland Browns History.* Chicago: Arcadia, 2005.

Smith, Ron, and Dan Dierdorf. *Heroes of the Hall.* St. Louis: Sporting News, 2003.

Ray Guy

Born: December 22, 1949
        Swainsboro, Georgia
Other major sport: Baseball

Early Life

Ray Guy was born on December 22, 1949, in Swainsboro, Georgia, a small town about 150 miles southeast of Atlanta. At an early age, Ray's profound athletic ability was already evident. One of his favorite activities was trying to punt a football over the telephone lines near his house. With focus and determination he was soon able to punt the football high enough to clear the lines. He could always master athletic skills quickly and believed that he was born with the ability to do well in sports.

The Road to Excellence

Ray displayed his natural athletic talent for four years at Thomson High School in Swainsboro. He won a total of 14 varsity letters in baseball, basketball, football, and track. His athletic talent and determination were recognized with numerous honors and offers. He was selected to the Georgia all-state basketball team. As a pitcher, he was drafted by the Cincinnati Reds, who offered him a six-figure contract to play baseball.

Ray was also named to the Georgia all-state football team and was selected with honorable mention to the all-American high school football team. By the time of his graduation, he had been named Thomson High School's most valuable player in football, baseball, and basketball.

The Emerging Champion

After high school, Ray chose to attend the University of Southern Mississippi (USM), where a family friend was on the football coaching staff. When he arrived in Hattiesburg, Mississippi, for his official visit, he knew that USM was where he belonged. He decided to major in health and physical education and play baseball and football. Ray enjoyed a brilliant baseball career and set many USM baseball rec-

ords. During his senior year in 1972, he struck out 17 batters in a victory over Mississippi College. Later that season, he threw a no-hit shutout against crosstown rival William Carey College.

In addition to his stellar baseball career, Ray excelled on the football field. P. W. Underwood, head football coach at USM, said that Ray had more pure athletic ability than anyone he had ever seen. He was so athletic that he was capable of playing any position on the field. Ray could have played quarterback, but Underwood decided to play Ray at defensive safety because he was the best tackler on the team. Besides intercepting passes and making tackles as a safety, he also did the kicking. He once kicked a 61-yard field goal in a snowstorm against Utah State.

Punter Ray Guy, who appeared in seven Pro Bowls in his career with the Raiders. (NFL/Getty Images)

In punting, however, Ray made his mark on college football. Many people went to the USM football games just to see him punt. In fact, it was not unusual for USM fans to arrive early to watch the pregame warm-up and see Ray kick. In 1972, he was voted all-American and led the nation in punting with a 46.2-yard average. During that season, against the University of Mississippi, he punted a ball from the end zone that soared over the punt returner's head and finally stopped 120 yards later, when it hit a retaining wall at the back of the other end zone. During his senior year many of the professional football teams were keeping close tabs on him.

Continuing the Story

In 1973, the Oakland Raiders shocked the football world by drafting Ray in the first round, even though he had broken his ankle in the last game of his senior year. He became the first punter ever taken in the first round and played with the Raiders for the next fourteen years. He led the NFL in punting in 1974, 1975, and 1977. Besides having a top punting average, Ray was also known for his accuracy and dependability. He was a master at punting the ball high and forcing opponents to make fair catches. He was also an expert in punting the ball out of bounds inside the opponents' 20-yard line and denying good field position. Moreover, he was often the first Raider to reach the punt returner and make the tackle.

Ray's athletic ability allowed him to punt the ball quickly, and as a result the Raiders went six seasons without having a punt blocked. In fact, Ray had only three punts blocked during his entire fourteen-year career. He appeared in 207 straight games without missing a single game. His punting was a reason why the Raiders often made the playoffs and won the Super Bowl in 1977, 1981, and 1984.

NFL Statistics

Season	Punts	Yds.	Avg.	Long
1973	69	3,127	45.3	72
1974	74	3,124	42.3	66
1975	68	2,979	43.8	64
1976	67	2,785	41.6	66
1977	59	2,552	43.3	74
1978	81	3,462	42.7	69
1979	69	2,939	42.6	71
1980	71	3,099	43.6	66
1981	96	4,195	43.7	69
1982	47	1,839	39.1	57
1983	79	3,384	42.8	67
1984	91	3,809	41.9	63
1985	89	3,627	40.8	68
1986	90	3,620	40.2	64
Totals	1,050	44,541	42.4	74*

Notes: Yds. = yards; Avg. = average; Long = longest punt of year; * = longest of career

Ray was selected to the Pro Bowl seven times. At the 1977 Pro Bowl held in the New Orleans Superdome he accomplished a feat thought impossible. For years, punters had been trying to hit one of the television screens hanging from the Superdome ceiling. No one had ever done it, and people said Ray could not do it. He accepted the challenge, and during the first half of the game he aimed for the screen and hit it just for fun.

Punting was not Ray's only task with the Raiders. He was the team's emergency quarterback, and in that capacity he could use his strong and accurate arm. He could kneel down on the 50-yard line and throw the ball out of the end zone, a distance of more than 60 yards. As the quarterback for the Raiders, he completed two of three passes and rushed nine times. He even kicked an extra point.

In 1987, at the age of thirty-seven, Ray retired from the Oakland Raiders because of a chronic back problem. He was proud of the team's success and the contribution he made to that success. Raiders' owner Al Davis called Ray "the best to ever play his position in the history of the sport." Ray believed that his football career inspired young kickers around the United States. In fact, he began operating a kicking camp that teaches youngsters correct punting techniques. Shane Lechler, a placekicker from Texas A&M and one of the punting counselors at the camp, was selected by the Oakland

Honors and Awards

1970's	NFL All-Decade Team
1973-78	NFL All-Pro first team
1973-78, 1980	NFL Pro Bowl Team
1979-80	NFL All-Pro second team
1984	Named to NFL all-time team
1989	Named to Sports Illustrated college team of the twentieth century
1994	Inducted into Mississippi Sports Hall of Fame
1997	Inducted into Georgia Sports Hall of Fame
2005	Inducted into College Football Hall of Fame

Raiders in the fifth round in the 2000 draft, twenty-seven years after Ray was drafted. In 2000, the Ray Guy Award was instituted and given annually to the best collegiate punter in the United States.

Summary

Ray Guy redefined the role of a punter and highlighted the importance of punting as an offensive weapon for a football team. Some said that Ray's punting gave the Raiders a net 50 yards a game extra. Many of the Raiders' victories and defeats rested on his right foot. In 1989, *Sports Illustrated* created its college team of the twentieth century and selected Ray as its punter on the eighty-five-man squad. Five years earlier, a fifteen-person NFL panel selected Ray as the punter on its all-time NFL team. In later years, Ray's name came up regularly in the list of finalists considered for induction into the Pro Football Hall of Fame. However, as late as 2009, he still had not been inducted, and the only full-time kicker in the Hall of Fame was placekicker Jan Stenerud. By then, even Ray himself was publicly questioning why no pure punter was represented in the Hall of Fame.

William G. Durick

Additional Sources

Carroll, Bob. *Total Football: The Official Encyclopedia of the National Football League.* New York: Harper-Collins, 1999.

Flores, Tom, and Matt Fulks. *Tom Flores' Tales from the Oakland Raiders.* Champaign, Ill.: Sports, 2007.

Guy, Ray, and Rick Sang. "Punting the Ray Guy Way." *Scholastic Coach and Athletic Director* 64, no. 9 (April, 1995): 16-19.

Jack Ham

Born: December 23, 1948
Johnstown, Pennsylvania
Also known as: Jack Raphael Ham, Jr. (full name)

Early Life

The son of mining mechanic John Ham and Caroline Ham, Jack Raphael Ham, Jr., was born on December 23, 1948, in Johnstown, Pennsylvania. Johnstown was a coal mining town when Jack was growing up, and Jack learned to love the tough breed of people who work in the mines. From their example, he learned to become a tough, hardworking, determined, and dedicated young man. All of these qualities served him well in his football career. Jack was small for a football player, so he did

Pittsburgh Steeler Jack Ham (59), often considered the best outside linebacker in NFL history, rushing Cincinnati Bengals' quarterback Ken Anderson (14). (Courtesy of Pittsburgh Steelers)

not shine at Bishop McCort High School. As a sophomore, he was only a third-string offensive tackle. He did not play linebacker until his senior year. As a result, he had little confidence in himself, and thought that he had no future in football.

The Road to Excellence

Despite his lack of confidence, Jack was recruited by Virginia Military Institute. At the institute he gained valuable experience playing with fine teammates. He disliked military life, though, and transferred to Penn State. Joe Paterno, Penn State's head coach, was impressed with Jack, who had plenty of speed and excellent jumping ability. More important, Jack was a poised, mature player, not easily flustered on the field. He was extremely competitive as well.

While majoring in real estate and insurance, Jack played linebacker and gradually gained confidence in his playing ability. Some critics suggested he was too small—he then weighed 220 pounds. He simply used his intelligence, speed, and toughness to make up for his size and to prove his detractors wrong. In spite of his slow start as a football player, Jack made all-American as a senior and was made team captain. In 1968 and 1969, the Penn State Nittany Lions were undefeated and played in postseason Orange Bowls both years.

The Emerging Champion

When he graduated, Jack was still considered small, so he did not impress NFL scouts enough to be drafted in the first round. Luckily, however, the Pittsburgh Steelers, who were in the process of rebuilding, drafted Jack in the second round. Another situation in Jack's favor was that professional football was changing. By the 1970's, zone defenses and quick defensive linemen had made it difficult for quarterbacks to throw long passes. As a result, quarterbacks had to make frequent passes to their running backs, and teams needed agile linebackers to stick with the running backs. For the first time ever, linebackers who were lighter in weight than the norm were considered an asset—they were agile and fast enough to cover running backs coming out of the backfield. Jack had found his niche in football at last. In fact, his special combination of speed, strength, and agility set new standards for his position.

Jack's opponents soon learned how quick he could be. They had to get a jump on him, to get him out of position, or else they would get hurt. They also discovered Jack's other great asset, his intuition. Players call it the ability to "ball-react." Jack simply followed the quarterback's eyes and knew intuitively where he would throw the ball. In 1971, his first season, Jack was named to the NFL's all-rookie team. The next year, he was an all-NFL selection. In fact, for the remainder of the 1970's, he was chosen annually to the all-NFL first team. In 1974, he made it to the Pro Bowl for the first of eight times. He also had thirty-two interceptions during his career. Jack was a crucial part of the famous "Steel Curtain" defense that enabled the Steelers to win four Super Bowls in the 1970's.

Continuing the Story

The quietest man on his team, Jack never talked much about himself, but he certainly gave others reason to talk about him. One sportswriter once described Ham as the ultimate professional athlete, citing his perseverance and constant effort to improve. At Steelers games, Pittsburgh fans used to hold up signs that read "dobre shonka," Polish for "good ham."

In late 1979, Jack broke his ankle while playing against Houston, and was never able to properly heal. The next year he broke his arm. In 1982, Jack

---

Honors and Awards

1970	College All-American
1971	NFL All-Rookie Team
1972-80	All-NFL Team
1974-79, 1980-81	NFL Pro Bowl Team
1975	*Pro Football Weekly* NFL Defensive Player of the Year
1988	Inducted into Pro Football Hall of Fame
1990	Inducted into College Football Hall of Fame
1994	NFL 75th Anniversary All-Time Team

---

decided to retire. Jack and his wife, Joanne, remained in Pittsburgh after Jack's retirement. Already one of the finest racquetball players in Western Pennsylvania, Jack began to spend even more time on racquetball courts. He also worked as a broker for Neville Coal Sales in Pittsburgh, where he learned the business from the ground up. On the side, he helped with fund-raising efforts for the American Cancer Society.

Summary

Jack Ham and his linebacking corps were a crucial part of the Pittsburgh Steelers' famous "Steel Curtain" defense. A relatively small player, Jack relied on quickness and the ability to anticipate plays—both skills vital to his team's success. In the course of his career, his special combination of speed, strength, and agility set new standards for linebacking.

Nicholas White

Additional Sources

McCullough, Bob. *My Greatest Day in Football: The Legends of Football Recount Their Greatest Moments.* New York: Thomas Dunne Books/St. Martin's Griffin, 2002.

Prato, Lou, and Scott Brown. *What It Means to Be a Nittany Lion: Joe Paterno and Penn State's Greatest Players.* Chicago: Triumph Books, 2006.

Rappoport, Ken. *Penn State Nittany Lions: Where Have You Gone?* Champaign, Ill.: Sports, 2005.

John Hannah

Born: April 4, 1951
     Canton, Georgia
Also known as: John Allen Hannah (full name);
  Hog

Early Life

John Allen Hannah was born on April 4, 1951, in Canton, Georgia, to Herbert and Geneva Hannah. He grew up in Albertsville, Alabama, along with his two brothers. His father owned a small farming supply business. As both an industrious farmer and a small-businessman, Herbert Hannah instilled his farmers' work ethic in each of his sons.

John attended Baylor School for Boys in Chattanooga, Tennessee, where he won the National Prep Wrestling Championship. Later he attended Albertsville High School and starred in football, wrestling, and track. Football was a big part of the Hannah boys' lives. John's father, Herbert, played tackle for the New York Giants of the NFL during the 1950's. His two brothers starred at the University of Alabama. One of them, Charley, played for the Los Angeles Raiders. John, though, was destined for even greater achievements.

The Road to Excellence

In 1969, John entered the University of Alabama and continued to excel as an all-around athlete. He was undefeated as a freshman wrestler, and he won the Southeastern Conference (SEC) shotput and discus championships in track. However, football was his primary sport. John's father had a major impact on his son's success as a football player. He never pushed John, but taught him all he knew, and encouraged him to do his best. As an outstanding offensive lineman himself, Herbert Hannah knew what it took to excel, and he passed it on to his son. He also taught John how to hustle and to enjoy the game. At Alabama, John played under the legendary Bear Bryant, who taught John how to win and reinforced the work ethic that John had been taught.

John was selected to the all-SEC team three times as an offensive guard. He was chosen to all-American teams in 1971 and 1972. In his senior

year, he won the Rockne Award as college lineman of the year and was one of four finalists for the prestigious Lombardi Award. He led his Alabama teams to postseason bowl games for three straight years.

The Emerging Champion

John followed in his father's footsteps all the way to the professional football ranks. He was selected in the first round of the 1973 NFL draft by the New England Patriots. As John entered professional football, one skill he had to learn was pass blocking. His high school and college teams had rarely passed, but the professionals often did, and this required protecting the quarterback. John studied films of pass blocking and worked hard practicing techniques to protect the quarterback. He soon mastered the techniques and developed into a great pass blocker. As a result, he had an immediate impact in his first year, and was selected to the NFL's all-rookie team in 1973.

As the years went on, John continued to refine and master his skills as an offensive guard, and he soon became one of the best in the game. He was selected for the Pro Bowl team an incredible nine times. In 1977, he received the Mack Truck Award, given to the best offensive lineman by fellow NFL players. John received every award that an offensive lineman could earn and became known

Honors and Awards	
1971-72	College All-American
1971-73	All-Southeastern Conference Team
1972	Rockne Award
1973	College All-Star Team
	NFL All-Rookie Team
1974, 1976, 1978-79	*Sporting News* AFC All-Star Team
1977	Mack Truck Award
1977, 1979-85	NFL All-Pro Team
1977, 1979-86	NFL Pro Bowl Team
1978, 1980	Seagram's Seven Crowns of Sports Award
1980-81, 1984-85	*Sporting News* NFL All-Star Team
1985	AFL-NFL 1960-1984 All-Star Team
1991	Inducted into Pro Football Hall of Fame
1994	NFL 75th Anniversary All-Time Team
1999	Inducted into College Football Hall of Fame

throughout the NFL as the best offensive lineman in the game—possibly the best of all time. As skilled as John was in his career, a team championship always eluded him. He helped lead the Patriots to the playoffs in 1976, 1978, and 1985. In 1985, the Patriots won the American Football Conference (AFC) championship, but they were crushed in the Super Bowl by the Chicago Bears 46-10.

Continuing the Story

One of the keys to John Hannah's success was his strength. Blocking straight ahead, John could drive a defensive lineman back five yards. He could push small defenders even farther. Most of his strength came from his huge, 33-inch thighs. At Alabama, he was known as "Hamhocks." With the Patriots, he was called "Hog." John was also known for his quickness and agility, rare abilities for a man his size. Those skills were especially helpful to John when he was protecting the quarterback from opposing linemen.

A former coach with the Patriots said that John did things on the football field that were unbelievable. For a man his size, he had great speed. He could run the 40-yard dash in 4.8 seconds, which was exceptional for a lineman. He also had great balance, which helped him to stay on his feet and continue blocking downfield to help his team advance the ball. In addition to his great physical qualities, John possessed the inner abilities needed to become the best at his profession. He had great determination and worked hard. He possessed a strong will to win and took pride in doing his best on the field.

In 1985, John retired from football after leading his team to the Super Bowl. He went to work as a stockbroker for the international firm of L. F. Rothschild in Boston and worked as hard at his new profession as he had at football. He and his wife, Page, a former Alabama cheerleader, have one son, named Seth, and a daughter named Mary Beth. John eventually received the ultimate accolades. In 1991, he was inducted into the Pro Football Hall of Fame. In 1994, John was named to the NFL's seventy-fifth anniversary all-time team. In 1999, he was inducted into the College Football Hall of Fame. In 2005, he coached his former high school team at Baylor School, but left his position following the season.

Summary

John Hannah's combination of strength, speed, quickness, and agility set him apart from other linemen. He was a great football player and a great athlete. Those attributes, combined with his fierce desire to win, led him to be selected as an all-pro eight times in his career, an honor that many players dream of receiving even once. John is regarded by many as the greatest offensive lineman in NFL history.

Nan White

Additional Sources

Anderson, Lars. "John Hannah, Hall of Fame Guard." *Sports Illustrated* 92, no. 6 (February 14, 2000): 22.

Attner, Paul, Sean Stewart, Phil Simms, and Dave Sloan. "Football's One Hundred Greatest Players: Better than All the Rest." *Sporting News* 223, no. 45 (November 8, 1999): 58-64.

Barber, Phil. "NFL: Football's One Hundred Greatest Players—The Hit Men." *The Sporting News* 223 (November 1, 1999): 12-16.

Barnhart, Tony. *Southern Fried Football: The History, Passion, and Glory of the Great Southern Game*. Chicago: Triumph Books, 2000.

Wade, Don. *Always Alabama: A History of Crimson Tide Football*. New York: Simon & Schuster, 2006.

Tom Harmon

Born: September 28, 1919
     Rensselaer, Indiana
Died: March 15, 1990
     Los Angeles, California
Also known as: Thomas Dudley Harmon (full
    name); Old 98

Early Life
Thomas Dudley Harmon was born in Rensselaer, Indiana, on September 28, 1919. As a boy, Tom developed a fascination with radio, which in the 1920's was becoming a national craze. He began thinking even then about a career in that rapidly expanding industry.

The Road to Excellence
Tom was a talented, versatile athlete. He earned fourteen letters in four high school sports: football, baseball, basketball, and track. He had powerful legs and was a fast runner. In fact, he was the state high school champion in the 100-yard dash and the 200-yard low hurdles. In football, Tom revealed the great range of his athletic prowess. He could do everything: run, pass, block, tackle, punt, and kick. However, he never set out to develop his talents as a professional player. In 1937, he entered the University of Michigan to major in speech and radio technique, determined to pursue a career in radio broadcasting. Luckily for Wolverine fans, Tom was also determined to play college football.

The Emerging Champion
At Michigan, Tom gained national recognition, primarily as a tailback in the old single-wing formation. In his college career, he rushed for a total of 2,134 yards in just twenty-four games. He averaged 5.4 yards per carry and almost 90 yards per game. He also scored 33 touchdowns, two more than the legendary Red Grange had scored for the University of Illinois more than a decade earlier.

Tom, who was often compared with Grange, was a more versatile player, as his last college game showed. In that 1940 contest with Ohio State, he led the Wolverines to a 40-0 rout by running for 3 touchdowns, passing for 2 others, kicking 4 extra points, and punting three times for a 50-yard average. Not surprisingly, Michigan fans were calling their school "Thomas Harmon University." On his best days, Tom, dubbed "Old 98," put on a spectacular one-man show. One opposing coach reportedly said he would trade his whole team for Tom.

Despite the recognition and glory that came his way as a football player, Tom remained fixed in his career plans to become a broadcaster. Although he played college baseball, basketball, and football, he still had no intention of becoming a professional athlete, as he affirmed in his 1940 speech accepting college football's most prestigious award, the Heisman Trophy. Before finishing his degree, Tom even sacrificed his college eligibility by accepting a fee for performing on radio with comedian Eddie Cantor, thereby forfeiting his last seasons of basketball and baseball.

Tom Harmon, who won the Heisman Trophy in 1940 and later entered a career in sports broadcasting. (Courtesy of Amateur Athletic Foundation of Los Angeles)

NFL Statistics

Season	GP	Rushing Car.	Yds.	Avg.	TD	Receiving Rec.	Yds.	Avg.	TD
1946	10	47	236	5.0	2	10	199	19.9	2
1947	12	60	306	5.1	1	5	89	17.8	1
Totals	22	107	542	5.1	3	15	288	19.2	3

Notes: GP = games played; Car. = carries; Yds. = yards; Avg. = average yards per carry *or* average yards per reception; TD = touchdowns; Rec. = receptions

To Tom, career opportunities were very important. In fact, after graduating, Tom starred in a movie, *Harmon of Michigan* (1941), which was based on his life. Later, when picked first by the powerful Chicago Bears in the 1941 NFL draft, Tom declined to join the team, and signed instead to play for the New York Americans. Tom's professional debut was short-lived. In his single game, he ran for only thirty-seven yards in ten attempts, and he left the team before playing another game not because of his lackluster performance but because he wanted to concentrate on broadcasting. Tom soon had to put even that dream on hold, however.

Continuing the Story

In December of 1941, after the Japanese attack on Pearl Harbor, Tom was called to active duty in the Army Air Corps. He served as a fighter pilot, winning both the Silver Star and the Purple Heart. Twice he was listed as missing in action. In 1943, he bailed out of his P-38 fighter plane when it was shot down over a lake in China. Badly hurt, he survived only with the help of Chinese guerrilla bands, who led him back to the American base through territory under Japanese control.

After the war, Tom returned to professional football, in part to pay a federal tax debt incurred

Honors and Awards

1939	Citizens Savings College Football Player of the Year
1939-40	College All-American
1940	Heisman Trophy
	Maxwell Award
	Walter Camp Award
	Associated Press Male Athlete of the Year
1941	Overall first choice in the NFL draft
1954	Inducted into College Football Hall of Fame

by his movie earnings. He signed with the Los Angeles Rams, but Tom soon found out that his war injuries had taken their toll. Although he averaged five yards per carry and scored nine touchdowns in two years with the Rams, he had lost some of his speed and power. He decided to retire after the 1947 season. Tom never looked back with regret. His playing days over, he turned to sports announcing in radio and television, as he had always planned. He settled in Los Angeles with his wife, actress Elyse Knox, and raised his family of three, including son Mark, a well-known film and television actor.

Tom broadcast all sorts of sporting events, including professional baseball, college football, Winter Olympics, and golf, with both NBC and CBS affiliates. In 1961, he became the host of a nightly ABC-TV sports program, serving, too, as its producer and writer. In 1974, he took the post of sports director with the Hughes Television Network, where he ended his career as one of the deans of sports announcing. On March 15, 1990, Tom died of a heart attack shortly after winning a golf tournament at the Bel Air Country Club in Los Angeles.

Summary

Tom Harmon carried, kicked, and threw a football to collegiate glory in an era when the best players were on the field most of the game, playing both offense and defense. His great versatility made him a genuine triple threat, and he prided himself as much on his hard blocking and tackling as he did on his spectacular running and solid passing, punting, and kicking. Although there has always been speculation about the professional football player Tom might have been, his wartime injuries and career aims make all such conjecture moot.

John W. Fiero

Additional Sources

Gauruder, Dana, and Rob Doster. *Game Day: Michigan Football—The Greatest Games, Players, Coaches, and Teams in the Glorious Tradition of Wolverine Football.* Chicago: Triumph Books, 2006.

Pennington, Bill. *The Heisman: Great American Stories of the Men Who Won.* New York: ReganBooks, 2004.

Franco Harris

Born: March 7, 1950
　　　　Fort Dix, New Jersey

Early Life

Franco Harris was born on March 7, 1950, in Fort Dix, New Jersey. His father, Cadillac, was an African American World War II veteran. His mother, Gina, is Italian. Franco's father was a strict disciplinarian, which helped motivate Franco to do well in school. Franco was very athletic as a boy, and played baseball, basketball, and football. Because Franco was the third in a family of nine children, he learned leadership and teamwork as he grew up. Those qualities helped him to become one of the greatest running backs of all time. He was a high school football all-American at Rancocas Valley High, where he scored twenty touchdowns as a junior. He also had part-time jobs at a gas station and a grocery store, so Franco was no stranger to hard work.

The Road to Excellence

Franco worked hard enough in high school to win an athletic scholarship to Penn State University, where he played under coach Joe Paterno. Franco had mixed success in his college career, making the honorable mention all-American team as a sopho-

more, but failing to do so his last two years. He joined Lydell Mitchell in the Penn State backfield, but Mitchell became the primary ball carrier and center of attention. Still, Franco rushed for 2,002 yards and 24 touchdowns, and played in the Senior Bowl and the college all-star game as a senior. Although he was a good player, few would have picked Franco to become one of the premier running backs in professional football.

The Pittsburgh Steelers, a struggling, mediocre team at the time, saw something special in Franco, and picked him in the first round of the 1972 NFL draft. During the early 1970's, the Steelers acquired players they hoped would make a competitive team. What the Steelers needed most was a big-play running back. They found one in Franco, a 6-foot 2-inch 225-pound speedster. Franco's training camp performance was not impressive, though, and some of the coaching staff wondered if he would even make the team. But after a 70-yard touchdown run in an exhibition game, Franco's doubters turned into believers.

The Emerging Champion

Franco's big break came in a game against the Houston Oilers. Losing 7-0, the Steelers sent Franco into the game. In an exciting turn-around, Franco carried nineteen times for 115 yards, leading his team to a 24-7 victory. Two weeks later, Franco started a streak of six straight 100-yard games, the longest such streak of his career. The rookie had arrived, and just in time. The Steelers won five in a row for the first time since 1958, and nine of the next ten games. Franco finished his first year with 1,055 yards rushing and another 180 yards receiving. Franco won the American Football Conference (AFC) rookie of the year honors, and led his team to the playoffs and the AFC Central Division championship, the

NFL Statistics

Season	GP	Rushing Car.	Yds.	Avg.	TD	Receiving Rec.	Yds.	Avg.	TD
1972	14	188	1,055	5.6	10	21	180	8.6	1
1973	12	188	698	3.7	3	10	69	6.9	0
1974	12	208	1,006	4.8	5	23	200	8.7	1
1975	14	262	1,246	4.8	10	28	214	7.6	1
1976	14	289	1,128	3.9	14	23	151	6.6	0
1977	14	300	1,162	3.9	11	11	62	5.6	0
1978	16	310	1,082	3.5	8	22	144	6.5	0
1979	15	267	1,186	4.4	11	36	291	8.1	1
1980	13	208	789	3.8	4	30	196	6.5	2
1981	16	242	987	4.1	8	37	250	6.8	1
1982	9	140	604	4.3	2	31	249	8.0	0
1983	16	279	1,007	3.6	5	34	278	8.2	2
1984	8	68	170	2.5	0	1	3	3.0	0
Totals	173	2,949	12,120	4.1	91	307	2,287	7.4	9

Notes: GP = games played; Car. = carries; Yds. = yards; Avg. = average yards per carry *or* average yards per reception; TD = touchdowns; Rec. = receptions

Steelers first title of any kind in forty years of NFL play.

Franco grabbed the attention of the sports world in the Steelers' first-round playoff game against the Oakland Raiders. With only five seconds remaining in the game, the Steelers were trailing the Raiders, 7-6. Steelers quarterback Terry Bradshaw rifled a pass downfield to Frenchy Fuqua, but the play was broken up by Jack Tatum, a Raiders defender. As Tatum collided with Fuqua, the football bounced back into the ready hands of Franco, and he raced sixty yards into the end zone for the winning touchdown. This remarkable play, called "The Immaculate Reception," provided a storybook finish to Franco's fantasy-like rookie season.

Franco's success became Pittsburgh's success. The Steelers had never made the playoffs before Franco's arrival, but the team made the playoffs each of the next eight years, and ten years out of the twelve Franco was on the team. The Harris-led Steelers did more than just make the playoffs, though. With Franco leading the ground attack, the Steelers won four Super Bowls and became the NFL's dynasty of the 1970's. In Pittsburgh's first Super Bowl victory, Franco rushed for a then-record 158 yards to win the most valuable player honors. Franco was valuable to his team in many ways throughout his illustrious career. Praising Franco's overall contribution to the Steelers, quarterback Terry Bradshaw said, "Franco is simply the finest team-man I have ever seen in my life." Franco was a key part of one of the finest teams ever.

Continuing the Story

By the end of his phenomenal career, Franco had made extraordinary accomplishments. He held or shared twenty-four NFL records at his retirement. He rushed 2,949 times for 12,120 yards. He rushed for more than 100 yards in forty-seven games, and scored 100 touchdowns. He also had 14,640 combined net yards. He had eight 1,000-yard seasons.

Honors, Awards, and Records

1972	Senior Bowl All-Star Team
	College All-Star Team
	United Press International AFC Rookie of the Year
	Sporting News AFC Rookie of the Year
1972, 1975, 1977	*Sporting News* AFC All-Star Team
1973-81	NFL Pro Bowl Team
1974	NFL record for the most rushing touchdowns in a postseason game (3), record shared
1975	NFL Super Bowl most valuable player
1976	NFL Man of the Year
1977	Pittsburgh Man of the Year
1980	*College and Pro Football Newsweekly* NFL Player of the 1970's
	NFL All-Pro Team of the 1970's
	New York Association of the Blind, Humanitarian Award
	NFL record for the most rushing touchdowns in a Super Bowl game (2), record shared
1982	Byron White Humanitarian Award
1990	Inducted into Pro Football Hall of Fame

One of his most revealing statistics is the number of games he played during his career: 173. In thirteen years of NFL football Franco missed only nine games, making him one of the game's most durable players. That durability also allowed him to play in nine straight Pro Bowls from 1973-1981.

Pittsburgh released Franco after the 1983 season because of a contract dispute. Franco then signed with the Seattle Seahawks, but played only eight games before retiring. In January, 1990, he was inducted into the Pro Football Hall of Fame. He is remembered as one of professional football's most brilliant players.

Franco became the chief executive officer of Super Bakery. In 1996, Franco and his partner Lydell Mitchell, who was one of Franco's teammates at Penn State, bought Parks Sausages Company, which is located in Baltimore. Parks Sausages was the first African American-owned company in the United States to be publicly traded. Franco worked toward reviving the company, which was near bankruptcy, and making it economically competitive.

Summary

Franco Harris seemed destined for the Pro Football Hall of Fame. His exciting rookie year launched a sensational career that stands as one of the greatest. As he continued to play, he helped guide his team to four Super Bowl championships and eight AFC division championships. Franco's rushing records are among the most impressive accomplishments of any player's. While his numbers are outstanding, the most memorable point about Franco may be the crucial role he played in transforming the Pittsburgh Steelers into one of the most frequently victorious teams in pro football history.

William B. Roy

Additional Sources

Carroll, Bob. *Total Football: The Official Encyclopedia of the National Football League.* New York: HarperCollins, 1999.

McNeal, Stan. "The Third Degree with Franco Harris." *Sporting News* 228, no. 47 (November 22, 2004): 11.

Mendelson, Abby. *The Pittsburgh Steelers: The Official Team History.* Lanham, Md.: Taylor Trade, 2006.

Prato, Lou, and Scott Brown. *What It Means to Be a Nittany Lion: Joe Paterno and Penn State's Greatest Players.* Chicago: Triumph Books, 2006.

Marvin Harrison

Born: August 25, 1972
      Philadelphia, Pennsylvania
Also known as: Marvin Daniel Harrison (full name)

Early Life

Marvin Daniel Harrison was born on August 25, 1972, in Philadelphia, Pennsylvania. His father, Marvin, Sr., died when Marvin was two years old. His mother, Linda, moved the family around Philadelphia to find a good school and after-school club for Marvin. The family settled in Roxborough, Philadelphia. The town had a recognized recreational football program of which Marvin quickly became a part. Eventually, Marvin enrolled in Roman Catholic High School, a school that was known

for sending its athletes to college. Marvin was a dedicated student, missing only one day his entire four years of high school, and a hard worker, cutting the grass at the athletic fields. He was also a stellar athlete, playing basketball and football. After high school, he went to Syracuse University to play football.

The Road to Excellence

While at Syracuse, Marvin became a star quickly. He was a four-year letterman and three-year starter and set the all-time receiving record with 2,718 yards. He ranked second in touchdowns, with 20, and third in receptions, with 135. His 102.8 receiving yards per game led the Big East Conference, set a school record, and ranked eighth nationally.

Marvin also set a school record with a 96-yard touchdown reception versus West Virginia University. Surprisingly, Marvin was not chosen in the 1996 NFL draft until the Indianapolis Colts picked him near the end of the first round.

In his rookie season, Marvin led the Colts in receptions with 64, receiving yards with 836, and receiving touchdowns with 8. He ranked second in Colts history for receptions and yards in a rookie season. In 1997, Marvin again led the team in receptions, with 73; receiving yards, with 866; and receiving touchdowns, with 6. Though he started twelve games in 1998, he suffered a separated shoulder and sat out the remainder of the season. However, in 1999, he returned with an incredible season, finishing with 115 receptions, 1,663 yards, and 12 touchdowns. He finished first in the league in yards, was second in receptions, and tied for second in touchdowns. The season marked the beginning of an amazing era for Marvin: For each of the next seven seasons, he totaled more than 1,000 yards and scored at least 10 touchdowns.

The Emerging Champion

From 1999 to 2006, Marvin amassed awards and set numerous records. In 2002, he estab-

Marvin Harrison, who set numerous NFL records for wide receivers. (AP/Wide World Photos)

lished a new record for the most receptions in a single season with 143, surpassing the old record by 20 receptions. In 2005, he tied Steve Smith, of the Carolina Panthers, for the most receiving touchdowns that season with 12. Between 1999 and 2002, Marvin became the first NFL player to compile 100 or more receptions in four consecutive seasons. Furthermore, in 2002, he was the first receiver to catch at least eight passes in twelve different games. His three seasons—1999, 2001, and 2002—with at least 1,500 receiving yards ranked second behind only Jerry Rice, who had four. Marvin also was second to Rice with fifty-five career 100-yard receiving games; Rice had seventy-six. However, in 2006, Marvin surpassed one of Rice's records with eight consecutive seasons of at least 1,000 yards receiving and at least 10 receiving touchdowns.

The 2006 season marked another milestone for Marvin. During a game against the Jacksonville Jaguars, Marvin tallied his one-thousandth reception. Three other receivers had preceded Marvin to the one-thousand-catch plateau, but he was the fastest to accomplish the feat, doing so in 167 career games. Marvin led the Colts in receptions, yards, and touchdowns that season, and the team advanced to Super Bowl XLI, its first since relocating to Indianapolis. The Colts defeated the Chicago Bears, 29-17, to become the 2006 NFL champions.

NFL Record

Most receptions over eight seasons, 826 (1999-2006)

Most receptions in one season, 143

First player to have at least 100 receptions in four consecutive seasons

First player to have at least 50 receptions in first eleven seasons

Honors and Awards

1999	NFL Alumni wide receiver of the year
	Football Digest most improved player
1999-2006	NFL Pro Bowls
	NFL All-Pro
2003	*Sporting News* NFL all-pro team

Continuing the Story

In 2007, though Marvin injured his knee and played in only five regular-season games, he still broke records in abbreviated action. He and the Colts quarterback, Peyton Manning, established the record for the most receptions between a quarterback and a wide receiver, with 723, and the record for the most receiving touchdowns between a quarterback and wide receiver, with 107.

Marvin played in fifteen games during the 2008 season and caught 60 passes—his least productive full season as a pro. In February, 2009, he declined the Colts' request that he take a pay cut and was—by mutual agreement—given his full release. He left the team as the Colts' all-time leading receiver.

Summary

Marvin Harrison was known for his extreme commitment to the game, as well as his stoic on-field demeanor. However, regardless of how little attention he wished to receive for his accomplishments, his prowess as a wide receiver ranked him statistically among the top receivers in NFL history.

Lamia Nuseibeh Scherzinger

NFL Statistics

Season	GP	Rec.	Yds.	Avg.	TD
1996	16	64	836	13.1	8
1997	16	73	866	11.9	6
1998	12	59	776	13.2	7
1999	16	115	1,663	14.5	12
2000	16	102	1,413	13.9	14
2001	16	109	1,524	14.0	15
2002	16	143	1,722	12.0	11
2003	15	94	1,272	13.5	10
2004	16	86	1,113	12.9	15
2005	15	82	1,146	14.0	12
2006	16	95	1,366	14.4	12
2007	5	20	247	12.4	1
2008	15	60	636	10.6	5
Totals	190	1,102	14,580	13.2	128

Notes: GP = games played; Rec. = receptions; Yds. = yards; Avg. = average yards per reception; TD = touchdowns

Additional Sources

Chappell, Mike, Phil Richards, and Ted Marchibroda. *Tales from the Indianapolis Colts Sideline.* Champain, Ill.: Sports, 2004.

Demasio, Nunyo. "The Marvelous and Mysterious Marvin Harrison." *Sports Illustrated* 106, no. 1. (January 8, 2007): 41.

Jenkins, Sally. "Little Fanfare for an Uncommon Man." *Washington Post*, October 18, 2006, p. E1.

Ted Hendricks

Born: November 1, 1947
      Guatemala City, Guatemala
Also known as: Theodore Paul Hendricks (full name); the Mad Stork

Early Life
Theodore Paul Hendricks was born on November 1, 1947, in Guatemala City, Guatemala. His father, a mechanic and troubleshooter for Pan American Airlines, was from McAllen, Texas, but his mother was a native Guatemalan who also worked for Pan Am. While in Guatemala, Ted met his mother's family and learned to speak Spanish fluently, but the family soon came to the United States and settled in Hialeah, Florida, where Ted grew up.

At Hialeah High School, Ted chose football as his primary sport, despite the fact that his height and weight made him look more like a basketball prospect—but Ted's thin, tall frame was deceiving. He excelled in his position as defensive end, breaking into opposing backfields to sack quarterbacks or knock down their passes. Across town, in Coral Gables, football coaches at the University of Miami were eager to offer Ted a scholarship.

The Road to Excellence
Ted entered Miami as a physics major. At the time, Miami was not the perennial college football power that it became in the 1980's, but it fielded strong teams and scheduled tough competition. Ted confounded the opposition, just as he had in high school. Despite the fact that he was named all-American for three consecutive years, many scouts were still dubious about his professional football prospects. At 214 pounds he seemed too slight to play defensive end and much too tall to be a linebacker. When Ted was selected by the NFL's Baltimore Colts in the second round of the 1969 NFL draft many experts thought it was a gamble.

The Emerging Champion
Ted saw little action his first year with the Colts, playing mostly on special teams, but when

coach Don Shula revamped the linebacker corps, Ted landed a starting job as right outside linebacker. Ted, because of his great playing range and reach, played his position uniquely and effectively. His playing style at Miami had earned his famous nickname, "The Mad Stork."

As he had in college, Ted intimidated quarterbacks. He was one of the best pass rushers in the game, generally wreaking havoc in the enemy's backfield. His height allowed him to bat down passes or reach into defensive pockets and haul quarterbacks to the ground. When he was not blitzing, he was good at shallow pass coverage in the secondary and stopping sweeps to the right side. Ted

Ted Hendricks playing for the Raiders in 1983. (Al Messerschmidt/Getty Images)

NFL Record

Most safeties, 4 (record shared)

Honors and Awards

1966-68	College All-American
1968	Rockne Award
1972, 1981-84	NFL Pro Bowl Team
1980	Seagram's Seven Crowns of Sports Award
1987	Inducted into College Football Hall of Fame
1990	Inducted into Pro Football Hall of Fame
1994	NFL 75th Anniversary All-Time Team

soon proved that his gangly frame was not a detriment to his professional aspirations. In fact, in his entire career he never missed a game because of injuries. He was dependable and good, and fans everywhere knew it. Coaches and sportswriters knew it, too; he was chosen to play in the Pro Bowl five times.

Despite his success, Ted was not particularly happy playing for the Colts, and although his discontent did not affect his play, it made him hard to handle off the field. Although Ted could be a one-man wrecking crew, as he was in the Colts' 1971 victory over Dallas in Super Bowl V, in 1974, the Baltimore management decided to trade him to the Green Bay Packers. The next year, when Ted was a free agent, the Packers traded him to the Oakland Raiders, one of the most intimidating teams in the history of professional football.

Continuing the Story

Ted found a home with the Raiders. Ted, a free-spirited maverick, blended in with Oakland's misfits. The team's style suited him. As long as he played hard and well, the Oakland management let him do as he pleased. At Oakland, Ted made friends, especially with John Matuszak, his roommate. Like some other Raiders, Ted and Matuszak played hard and lived fast. They were proud of their bad-guy reputations. Ted was one of the team clowns, famous for crazy antics like riding a horse to the practice field or inviting an exotic dancer to a team meeting. After one of the Mad Stork's pranks, coach John Madden joked that "Ted's elevator doesn't go all the way to the top."

Clown or not, on the football field Ted was all business. His ferocious play and team dedication helped the Raiders to the Super Bowl in 1977, 1981, and 1984. After the 1984 Super Bowl, in which the Raiders humbled the Washington Redskins 38-9, Ted retired. Through most of the 1983 season, although he missed no games, Ted had been in agony, suffering from painful muscle pulls that made it hard for him even to get out of bed. He was thirty-six, and his hard style of life and play had finally caught up with him. His efforts, however, were eventually rewarded. In 1990, Ted was inducted into the Pro Football Hall of Fame. He was included in the NFL's seventy-fifth anniversary all-time team in 1994.

After he retired, Ted returned to Florida, where he has spent his time golfing, bowling, hunting, and fishing. A generous, warmhearted man, Ted has also devoted time to charitable appearances and fund-raising. He has also been a coach for the Special Olympics.

Summary

Spindly legged and thin, Ted Hendricks cut an unusual figure as an outside linebacker in professional football, but few if any pros ever played that position better. His height made it difficult to see past him, much less pass or kick over him. Among other career achievements, he blocked 25 place kicks, intercepted 26 passes, and scored 4 safeties. He was also extremely durable, and in his fifteen-year NFL career played in 215 consecutive games.

John W. Fiero

Additional Sources

Conner, Floyd. *Football's Most Wanted: The Top Ten Book of the Great Game's Outrageous Characters, Fortunate Fumbles, and Other Oddities.* Washington, D.C.: Brassey's, 2000.

Flores, Tom, and Matt Fulks. *Tom Flores' Tales from the Oakland Raiders.* Champaign, Ill.: Sports, 2007.

Martz, Jim. *Tales from the Miami Hurricanes Sideline.* Champaign, Ill.: Sports, 2004.

Newhouse, Dave. *The Ultimate Oakland Raiders Trivia Book.* Rochester, N.Y.: American Sports Media, 2001.

Gene Hickerson

Born: February 15, 1935
Trenton, Tennessee
Died: October 20, 2008
Olmsted Falls, Ohio
Also known as: Robert Eugene Hickerson (full name)

Early Life
Born in 1935, in Trenton in western Tennessee, Robert Eugene Hickerson grew up in the Memphis region. There he later became a friend of singer Elvis Presley, who was born in northern Mississippi only five weeks earlier. Because of his friendship with Gene, Presley later became a fan of the Cleveland Browns, for whom Gene played football.

Gene Hickerson. (Diamond Images/Getty Images)

Gene attended high school in Trezevant, a town near Memphis and Trenton, and played on the school's football team. An outstanding fullback, he was recruited by the University of Mississippi, which is not far from Memphis. At the university, he switched his position to offensive tackle and became one of the finest offensive linemen in Southeastern Conference history.

The Road to Excellence
In 1956, Gene played in the Cotton Bowl when Mississippi beat Texas Christian University. Paul Brown, the coach of the Cleveland Browns in the NFL, watched the game and was impressed by Gene's speed. He imagined Gene playing in the NFL as a pulling guard—an offensive lineman who specialized in protecting the quarterback and sometimes blocking downfield for running backs. His vision was prophetic, as Gene was to become one of the finest pulling guards in NFL history.

At that time, college players could not go into the NFL until their classes graduated, and Gene was still only a college junior. In the 1957 NFL draft, the Browns used their seventh-round pick to make Gene a future choice. The strategy of drafting him early, before he had caught the attention of other scouts, worked well for the Browns. Although the Canadian Football League offered Gene a three-year contract worth fifty thousand dollars—a huge sum in those days—Gene accepted the Browns' offer of ten thousand dollars for one year in addition to a one-thousand-dollar signing bonus after he graduated.

The Emerging Champion
In 1958, Gene started his professional playing career as one of Coach Brown's "messengers": guards, doing little more than alternating with another player to carry plays from the sideline to the huddle. During the 1961 season, his career was temporarily derailed when he twice broke his leg. However, after sitting out that season and two games in 1962, he

never missed another game during his professional career.

In 1963, after Paul Brown left the team, Blanton Collier took over as coach and immediately made Gene a full-time player. Gene's exemplary line play, particularly as lead blocker in the Browns' trademark end-sweep play, contributed to the great success of legendary running back Jim Brown. Brown retired at the end of the 1965 season to pursue an acting career. The fact that an eighth-round draft choice named Leroy Kelly continued his string of 1,000-yard rushing seasons attests to the stability and talent of the Browns' offensive line that Gene anchored.

The highlight of Gene's career was the great 1964 Browns team that won the NFL Championship game (before the creation of the Super Bowl), 27-0, against the heavily favored Baltimore Colts, led by Johnny Unitas. Jim Brown noted that Gene and tackle Dick Schafrath routinely blocked three players between them on one play. Offensive tackle Monte Clark called Gene the best pass blocker on the team. Gene rarely allowed defenders whom he blocked to reach his quarterback. A testament to Gene's versatility during that great season was the fact that he led the Browns' special teams in tackles.

After the 1964 season, Gene began receiving wider recognition. He was named an all-pro player five seasons in a row and was voted to six consecutive all-star games between 1965 and 1970. This recognition was well deserved. The Browns had 1,000-yard rushers during nine of the seasons in which Gene played and boasted the league top rusher in seven of them. The Browns also led the NFL in average yards per carry through most of those years. Three of the Browns' 1,000-yard runners—Brown, Bobby Mitchell, and Kelly—were later inducted in the Pro Football Hall of Fame. All of them maintained that their success would not have been possible without the linemen who blocked for them, and they all called for Gene's induction into the hall of fame. Gene was elected to the NFL's all-decade team for the 1960's, but his hall-of-fame call would wait for many years.

Continuing the Story

Variously described as a sensitive southern gentleman and a raucous practical joker, Gene was personable. During his playing years, his friends ranged from his teammates to business associates and included both Presley and members of the Cleveland Orchestra, whose concerts he attended. John Wooten, an African American player who held the other guard position while Gene was with the Browns, noted that the team maintained harmony during the racially turbulent 1960's in large part because of men like Gene. A white southerner, Gene exemplified the manner in which the team overcame possible divisiveness through their deep respect for one another. Gene himself, when asked to account for the success of the 1964 championship team, attributed it to the players' putting the team ahead of individual agendas.

Gene retired from football in 1973, at the age of thirty-seven, but was not inducted into the Pro Football Hall of Fame until more than thirty years later. The call finally came in 2007. By that time, he was seventy-two years old and suffered from Alzheimer's disease and dementia. He was unable to give an acceptance speech in the induction ceremony in Canton, Ohio, so Bobby Franklin, his best friend of fifty-two years and teammate at Ole Miss and Cleveland, introduced him. Gene's only son, Bob, delivered his acceptance speech. Also attending were his daughter Nancy, his grandchildren, and other family and friends. In the minds of his former teammates and the three great running backs who had followed his blocking into the hall of fame before him, the recognition was long overdue. In a symbolic gesture, Brown, Mitchell, and Kelly joined Gene on stage and pushed his wheelchair over to view his bronze bust as if he were leading yet another sweep with his running backs behind him.

Summary

Offensive linemen in football are typically unsung heroes who do not receive the attention enjoyed by ballhandling backs and defensive stars. However, Gene Hickerson's outstanding career bears witness to the importance of great linemen on successful teams. The Cleveland Browns never had a losing

Honors and Awards	
1957	All-Southeastern Conference
1964-70	NFL All-Pro
1965-70	NFL Pro Bowl
1970	NFL all-decade team (1960's)
1979	Inducted into Mississippi Sports Hall of Fame
1988	Inducted into "Ole Miss" Sports Hall of Fame
2007	Inducted into Pro Football Hall of Fame

season with Gene on the team. During a fifteen-year career in the NFL, he played in 202 games, helped catapult three great running backs into the Pro Football Hall of Fame, and helped lead his team to an NFL Championship.

William L. Howard

Additional Sources

Grossi, Tony. "Hickerson Pulls into Canton." *The Cleveland Plain Dealer,* August 5, 2007.

_____. *Tales from the Browns Sidelines.* Champaign, Ill.: Sports, 2004.

Natali, Alan. *Brown's Town: Twenty Famous Browns Talk Among Themselves.* Wilmington, Ohio: Orange Frazer Press, 2001.

Pluto, Terry. *Browns Town 1964: The Cleveland Browns and the 1964 Championship.* Cleveland: Gray, 1997.

Ross, Alan. *Browns Glory.* Nashville, Tenn.: Cumberland House, 2005.

Elroy "Crazylegs" Hirsch

Born: June 17, 1923
Wausau, Wisconsin
Died: January 28, 2004
Madison, Wisconsin
Also known as: Elroy Leon Hirsch (full name);
Crazylegs

Early Life

On June 17, 1923, Elroy Leon Hirsch was born in Wausau, Wisconsin, 150 miles north of Madison. When very young, he was adopted by his foster parents, Otto Peter and Mayme Sabena (Magnuson) Hirsch, both of Norwegian-German ancestry. Otto worked at the Wausau Iron Works for forty years. As a boy, Elroy was exceedingly quick on his feet. Before long, he discovered he had another talent: He was good at catching footballs, and he practiced a number of fancy catches. None of his friends could

Elroy "Crazylegs" Hirsch, who earned his nickname because of his unorthodox running style. (Courtesy of Amateur Athletic Foundation of Los Angeles)

do quite the same tricks. Soon, Elroy began practicing more remarkable feats.

In a park near town, he would run full speed at a tree, then shift the football at the last second, changing direction barely in time to miss the tree. He occasionally collided with the tree. At the time, Elroy weighed only 125 pounds and had been cut from the high school football squad because of his size. Consequently, his elusive running style helped his quest to play football. After a summer of dodging trees, he had built himself up an additional 40 pounds and even grown taller.

The Road to Excellence

Elroy made the football team that fall and played under coach Win Brockmeyer, who was to become Elroy's lifelong friend and an important influence on his football career. Eventually, Elroy named his son after Win. Brockmeyer taught Elroy that football must be played as an eleven-man game. He also helped him to develop a sense of values—trust, loyalty, courtesy, and the importance of cooperation—that stayed with him for life, on and off the football field.

At first, Elroy was only an average player, but by his senior year at Wausau High, he had turned into an excellent halfback. He scored 102 points to lead the Wisconsin Valley Conference. After his high school graduation, Elroy enrolled at the University of Wisconsin. Elroy made the university's varsity team as a sophomore and became an all-American halfback. He did the same the following year. In 1942, he led Wisconsin to the number-three ranking in the national polls with an 8-1-1 record. He also won letters in four major sports that year, to become the only letterman in Wisconsin history to earn four letters in a nine-month period.

In 1942, as a halfback, Elroy gained 226 yards receiving and 766 yards rushing. That year Elroy was nicknamed "Crazylegs" because of his extraordinary running style. He had a way of flip-flopping his legs while running, chopping at the air. It seemed no one could catch forward passes as he could, either. Running at full speed with his head turned back, he could vary speed, change direc-

NFL Statistics

Season	GP	Rushing Car.	Yds.	Avg.	TD	Receiving Rec.	Yds.	Avg.	TD
1946	14	87	226	2.6	1	27	347	12.9	3
1947	5	23	51	2.2	1	10	282	28.2	3
1948	5	23	93	4.0	0	7	101	14.4	1
1949	12	68	287	4.2	1	22	326	14.8	4
1950	12	2	19	9.5	0	42	687	16.4	7
1951	12	1	3	3.0	0	66	1,495	22.7	17
1952	10	—	—	—	—	25	590	23.6	4
1953	12	1	-6	-6.0	0	61	941	15.4	4
1954	12	1	6	6.0	0	35	720	20.6	3
1955	9	—	—	—	—	25	460	18.4	2
1956	12	—	—	—	—	35	603	17.2	6
1957	12	1	8	8.0	0	32	477	14.9	6
Totals	127	207	687	3.3	3	387	7,029	18.2	60

Notes: GP = games played; Car. = carries; Yds. = yards; Avg. = average yards per carry *or* average yards per reception; TD = touchdowns; Rec. = receptions

tion without turning his head, and fake and dodge opposing tacklers. Enemy defenders had a hard time stopping him. After only one season with the team, he was named the third-best football player in the Badgers' history. In his last year of college, Elroy helped to beat his future pro team, the Los Angeles Rams of the NFL, in the 1946 college all-star game and was named the game's most valuable player.

The Emerging Champion

Drafted by both the Chicago Rockets of the All-America Football Conference and the Rams, Elroy chose the Rockets because of his friendship with the team's coach. Unfortunately for him, his years with that team were a nightmare. First, he tore muscles in his knee and back and thought he might never run again. Then, he fractured his skull and spent a month in the hospital. When he emerged, he had lost some of his coordination. Gradually, Elroy retrained himself. Meanwhile, the Rockets skipped some payments, Elroy's contract expired, and the Rams hired him. The Rams even made a helmet specially designed to protect his injured head.

Still a halfback, Elroy was rarely used in his first year, and then mainly as a decoy on passes. Then, in 1950, things changed dramatically. The Rams' new coach decided to switch Crazylegs from halfback to end. At first Elroy did not do well, but after a season of hard work, he developed into a premier receiver.

Elroy had his greatest season ever in 1951. He topped the records of the league's all-time leading pass receivers. That year, he led the NFL with 102 points scored and 66 passes received. He set several NFL records, one for gaining 1,495 yards. He also tied Don Hutson's record of 17 touchdown receptions. Elroy was honored as NFL player of the year.

Continuing the Story

Fans loved Crazylegs for his elusiveness in the open field. Unlike other players who lost balance and slowed down when they caught a football, Elroy ran even faster. His ability to catch footballs over his head was a major asset. After proving to be the NFL's finest pass-catching end, Elroy retired after nine years with the Rams. He had 387 pass receptions, 7,029 yards, and 60 touchdowns in his short career. However, Elroy did not leave the football scene. He became the general manager of the Rams and worked as assistant to the team's president. Later on, Elroy tried his luck in Hollywood. The attractive and immensely popular former Ram made three movies: *Crazylegs* (1953)—in which he starred as himself— *Unchained* (1955), and *Zero Hour* (1957). Decades later, Elroy's nickname made headlines again when he sued against the makers of "Crazylegs" panty hose, claiming that he owned the rights to that name.

On June 27, 1946, Elroy married his childhood sweetheart, Ruth Stahmer. He and Ruth had a son, Win Stephen, and a daughter, Patricia Caroline. In

Honors and Awards

1946	Chicago College All-Star Game most valuable player
1951	NFL Player of the Year
	Sporting News NFL All-Star Team
1951, 1953	NFL All-Pro Team
1952-54	NFL Pro Bowl Team
1963	NFL All-Pro Team of the 1950's
1968	Inducted into Pro Football Hall of Fame
1969	All-First Fifty Years NFL Team
1974	Inducted into College Football Hall of Fame

1968, Elroy was inducted into the Pro Football Hall of Fame, in Canton, Ohio. The following year, the family moved to Wisconsin, and Elroy became the University of Wisconsin's athletic director. Not long after, he was named to the NFL's all-time team and to the National Football Foundation and College Football Hall of Fame. Elroy died in 2004.

Summary

Elroy "Crazylegs" Hirsch had a spectacular career as one of the most talented pass receivers ever to play in the NFL. He was known for his evasiveness while running and nicknamed for his unusual running style. While playing for the Rams, he was the first back to be made a flanker. As football's first flanker, he also helped popularize the long pass.

Nan White

Additional Sources

Carroll, Bob. *Total Football: The Official Encyclopedia of the National Football League.* New York: Harper-Collins, 1999.

Conner, Floyd. *Football's Most Wanted: The Top Ten Book of the Great Game's Outrageous Characters, Fortunate Fumbles, and Other Oddities.* Washington, D.C.: Brassey's, 2000.

Lazenby, Roland. *The Pictorial History of Football.* San Diego, Calif.: Thunder Bay Press, 2002.

Priest Holmes

Born: October 7, 1973
     Fort Smith, Arkansas
Also known as: Priest Anthony Holmes (full name)

Early Life

Priest Anthony Holmes was raised in San Antonio, Texas, by his mother, Norma, and his stepfather. His biological father, who died in 1989, was not active in his life. However, Priest was close to his stepfather, Herman Morris, who was a caring disciplinarian. He taught Priest to play chess, a game that Priest played throughout his childhood and continued to play as an adult.

Throughout his youth, Priest established a reputation as a hard worker who was quiet but attentive to his various jobs. Although his family was not wealthy, Priest made a little extra money by working. He especially enjoyed a summer job helping his grandfather with a lawn-care business in Detroit, Michigan.

Early on, Priest loved football and idolized Tony Dorsett, who played halfback for the Dallas Cowboys. Priest played the typical playground ball and established himself as a talented junior high school player as well.

The Road to Excellence

Priest attended John Marshall High School in San Antonio, where he proved to be highly successful on the football field. He led his team, the Rams, to the Class 5 state championship game. Although Priest played well against Odessa Permian High School (the subject of the movie *Friday Night Lights*), his team lost 27-14. He was named to the all-state team and finished his senior season with more than 2,000 rushing yards and 26 touchdowns.

Following high school, Priest was highly recruited by colleges around the country, despite his relatively small stature of 5 feet 9 inches. He signed with his favorite team, the University of Texas. While there, he played with future Heisman Trophy winner Ricky Williams, who overshadowed the smaller athlete.

Priest made a name for himself, too, though, and was a *USA Today* fabulous freshman honorable mention. He later gave a stellar performance in the 1997 Sun Bowl, rushing for 161 yards and 4 touchdowns. He was named the Sun Bowl's most valuable player after the Longhorns upset North Carolina, 35-19. Priest seemed destined for the NFL. However, during the 1995 season, he tore his anterior cruciate ligament in a scrimmage and was out for the season. His hopes for NFL stardom were rekindled during his senior year, when the Longhorns won the Big Twelve Conference Championship in an upset over the number-three-ranked University of Nebraska. Priest starred, with 120 rushing yards and 3 touchdowns in the game.

The Emerging Champion

Despite a promising college career, Priest was not drafted into the NFL. However, he did not quit on his dream of playing professional football. The Baltimore Ravens signed him as a free agent in 1997. While with the Ravens, Priest rushed for more than 1,000 yards in 1998 and helped his team win Super Bowl XXXV in 2001. Nevertheless, Priest was not satisfied with the amount of playing time he was given while with the Ravens, and after just four seasons, he looked elsewhere.

Priest was confident that Kansas City, the home of the Chiefs, was the place he could show his true talent for the game. After talking to head coach Dick Vermeil, he signed with the Chiefs in 2001. His was a good choice. In his first season, he carried the ball for 1,555 yards. In 2002, he was named the NFL's offensive player of the year by the

---

Honors and Awards

2001, 2002	Derrick Thomas Award (Chiefs most valuable player)
2001-2003	NFL Pro Bowl
	NFL All-Pro
2002	NFL offensive player of the year
	Kansas City Sports Commission special achievement award
2004	National Consortium for Academics and Sports civic leader award

Associated Press. For the second consecutive season, he was named to the all-pro team. He set team rushing records even though he missed the last two games of the season because of a hip injury. In his third year with the Chiefs, Priest scored 27 touchdowns, a career high and NFL-record at the time. Not surprisingly, he was again selected to the all-pro team.

NFL Statistics

		Rushing				Receiving			
Season	GP	Car.	Yds.	Avg.	TD	Rec.	Yds.	Avg.	TD
1997	7	0	0	0	0	0	0	0	0
1998	16	233	1,008	4.3	7	43	206	6.0	0
1999	9	89	506	5.7	1	13	104	8.0	1
2000	16	137	588	4.3	2	32	221	6.9	0
2001	16	327	1,555	4.8	8	62	916	9.9	2
2002	14	313	1,615	5.2	21	70	972	9.6	3
2003	16	320	1,420	4.4	27	74	690	9.3	0
2004	8	196	892	4.6	14	19	187	9.8	1
2005	7	119	451	3.8	6	21	197	9.4	1
2007	4	46	137	3.0	0	5	17	3.4	0
Totals	113	1,780	8,172	4.6	86	339	2,962	8.7	8

Notes: GP = games played; Car. = carries; Yds. = yards; Avg. = average yards per carry *or* average yards per reception; TD = touchdowns; Rec. = receptions

Continuing the Story

Priest's next two seasons with the Chiefs were marked by injuries, and he was not able to play in every game in 2004 or 2005. His injuries proved to be serious enough that he was unable to play a single game in 2006, and he ended his career with the Chiefs, having started sixty-one games in six seasons. Priest tried to make a comeback, but a neck injury had left him susceptible to paralysis if hit hard in a game. He left his mark on team history with ten different Chiefs career records, including rushing yards, 5,933; total touchdowns, 83; rushing touchdowns, 76; and 100-yard rushing games, 24.

Summary

Priest Holmes, though small by NFL standards and beset with injuries throughout his career, contributed to football both on national and team levels. His record of 27 rushing touchdowns in a season was later tied, by Shaun Alexander, and then broken, by LaDainian Tomlinson. As of 2008, Priest ranked third for most consecutive games scoring a rushing touchdown in NFL history. He rushed for touchdowns in eleven consecutive games in 2002.

He accomplished all of this despite a career cut short by injuries.

Priest contributed off the field as well, founding his own charitable organization called Team Priest. He is generous with his time and money for various causes and has a special interest in assisting underprivileged children. He spends a great deal of time with his own four children. In fact, he has declined lucrative endorsement deals to spend more time at home. Priest was often mentioned as one of the "good guys" in football based on his humble, hardworking attitude both on and off the field.

Valerie Brown

Additional Sources

Althaus, Bill. *Priest Holmes: From Sidelines to Center Stage.* Champaign, Ill.: Sports, 2003.

Chadlha, Jeffri. "A Small Miracle." *Sports Illustrated* 96, no. 21 (May 20, 2002).

Silver, Michael. "High Priest." *Sports Illustrated* 99, no. 12 (September 29, 2003).

Paul Hornung

Born: December 23, 1935
     Louisville, Kentucky
Also known as: Paul Vernon Hornung (full
    name); the Golden Boy

Early Life

Paul Vernon Hornung, later known as "the Golden Boy," was born on December 23, 1935, in Louisville, Kentucky. After Paul's parents divorced when he was four, his mother, Loretta, reared the boy in an Irish Louisville neighborhood. Paul and his mother struggled to achieve a normal family life. While Loretta worked long hours as an employment director for the United States Army, Paul surpassed the other boys at St. Patrick's Grammar School physically. Even though he came from a single-parent family, which was unusual in the 1940's, Paul always got a football or baseball glove, courtesy of his mother, whenever he needed one.

The Road to Excellence

Paul first played football at St. Patrick's, where his coach, noticing that he could throw and kick farther and run faster than the other boys, made him the team's quarterback. Baseball also appealed to Paul. At the age of thirteen, Paul became the starting second baseman on an American Legion team filled with eighteen-year-olds, and the team reached the national playoffs. Paul's true love was football, though. He passed, ran, and kicked Louisville's Flaget High School to the Kentucky state championship. During the spring of 1953, numerous college recruiters and coaches—including Kentucky's famous Paul "Bear" Bryant—sought Paul's services. Like thousands of other Catholic boys, though, Paul yearned to play for the University of Notre Dame and the legendary Frank Leahy, who eventually signed him.

Paul's early career at Notre Dame did not attract much notice. He spent his first season playing on the freshman squad and the second laboring behind all-American Ralph Guglielmi. Coach Terry Brennan, who replaced Leahy, developed Paul's versatility, playing him at fullback and defensive back before switching him to quarterback, where

he won all-American honors in his junior season. During his senior year, even though Notre Dame lost eight of its ten games, the nation's press dubbed Paul the Golden Boy and awarded him the Heisman Trophy, the highest honor in the collegiate ranks. The Green Bay Packers of the NFL drafted him.

The Emerging Champion

Paul's major problem in the professional ranks stemmed from the Packers' inability to apply his multiple skills to a sport increasingly dominated by specialists. Consequently, he spent his first two years rotating between fullback, halfback, and quar-

Paul Hornung, who played multiple positions for the Green Bay Packers during a nine-year NFL career. (Courtesy of Amateur Athletic Foundation of Los Angeles)

terback. In 1959, though, the Packers hired Vince Lombardi as coach. Lombardi, who had developed Frank Gifford into a great halfback at New York, saved Paul's career by converting him to left halfback. The conversion was a turning point in Paul's professional life. "Vince Lombardi exerted the greatest influence on my life," Paul remembered. "Without him I doubt if I would be in the league." Lombardi, perhaps realizing that he filled Paul's need for a father figure, stated that "his personality is such that he has to be the center of attention at all times."

Once Paul and Lombardi understood each other, the team came together and compiled its best record in fourteen years. Although other players such as Bart Starr and Jim Taylor received their share of headlines, only Paul could claim true superstar status during those early years. He was a unique player. He could run, pass, catch, and kick with accuracy and distance. In 1959, these skills enabled Paul to win his first NFL scoring championship with 94 points.

Other records followed quickly. In 1960, the Packers won the division, and Paul set a single-season scoring mark with 176 points in only twelve games. Although the Packers lost the championship that year, the team dominated the NFL in 1961. For the third consecutive year, Paul led the league in scoring and won the most valuable player award, even though he was unable to practice

while serving in the United States Army. To the amazement of the nation's football fans and sportswriters, Paul's army stint seemed to improve his gridiron performances, culminating with a record-setting 19-point outburst in Green Bay's 37-0 championship victory over the New York Giants.

Continuing the Story

Paul's career also had its low points. The press, which frequently criticized his "bad habits," publicized his activities with professional gamblers. In 1963, Paul received a one-year suspension from NFL commissioner Pete Rozelle. Although Paul was not accused of throwing any games, his identification with unsavory elements tarnished his image and delayed his admission to the Pro Football Hall of Fame.

The Packers, who lost the title during Paul's absence in 1963, never again depended on him in the same manner. Although he remained one of the team's leaders, his days of superstar sta-

Honors, Awards, and Records

1955-56	*Sporting News* College All-American
1956	Heisman Trophy
	Camp Award
	Citizens Savings College Football Player of the Year
1957	Overall first choice in the NFL draft
1960	NFL record for the most points in a season, 176
1960-61	NFL Pro Bowl Team
	NFL All-Pro Team
	Sporting News NFL Western Division All-Star Team
1961	Associated Press NFL Player of the Year
	United Press International NFL Player of the Year
	Newspaper Enterprise Association NFL Player of the Year
	Bert Bell Award
	Sporting News NFL Player of the Year
	National Football Association Championship Game most valuable player
	NFL record for the most points in a postseason game, 19 (record shared)
1970	NFL All-Pro Team of the 1960's
1985	Inducted into College Football Hall of Fame
1986	Inducted into Pro Football Hall of Fame

NFL Statistics

| Season | GP | Rushing | | | | Receiving | | | |
		Car.	Yds.	Avg.	TD	Rec.	Yds.	Avg.	TD
1957	12	60	319	5.3	3	6	34	5.7	0
1958	12	69	310	4.5	2	15	137	9.1	0
1959	12	152	681	4.5	7	15	113	7.5	0
1960	12	160	671	4.2	13	28	257	9.2	2
1961	12	127	597	4.7	8	15	145	9.7	2
1962	9	57	219	3.8	5	9	168	18.7	2
1964	14	103	415	4.0	5	9	96	10.9	0
1965	12	89	299	3.0	5	19	336	17.7	3
1966	9	76	200	3.0	2	14	192	13.7	3
Totals	**104**	**893**	**3,711**	**4.2**	**50**	**130**	**1,480**	**11.4**	**12**

Notes: GP = games played; Car. = carries; Yds. = yards; Avg. = average yards per carry *or* average yards per reception; TD = touchdowns; Rec. = receptions

tus ended with the suspension. In 1965, Paul enjoyed one more burst of glory on a foggy December afternoon, scoring five touchdowns in Green Bay's 42-27 victory over the Baltimore Colts. However, he could not better this performance during the entire 1966 season, when a pinched nerve forced him to the sidelines. When the Packers defeated the Kansas City Chiefs 35-12 in Super Bowl I, he watched helplessly as a spectator in uniform. Paul never played again.

Controversy continued to plague the "Golden Boy," even in retirement. In 1982, when the National Collegiate Athletic Association (NCAA) rejected him as a television announcer, Paul launched a successful $3 million lawsuit against the organization. When the court rendered a favorable verdict, both the college and professional football halls of fame finally admitted him. Paul served as the president of Paul Hornung Sports Showcase and Paul Hornung Enterprises. He was also vice-president of a real estate and investment company. In 2004, he authored his autobiography, appropriately entitled *Golden Boy*.

Summary

Paul Hornung may have been the finest all-purpose player ever to participate in professional football. His 1960 scoring record of 176 points included 15 touchdowns, 15 field goals, and 41 extra points in twelve games. Vince Lombardi, perhaps the game's greatest coach, described Paul as "what you try to make every one of your players—a true believer. He smelled the goal line."

J. Christopher Schnell

Additional Sources

Hornung, Paul, and William F. Reed. *Golden Boy*. New York: Simon & Schuster, 2004.

_____. *Lombardi and Me: Players, Coaches, and Colleagues Talk About the Man and the Myth*. Chicago: Triumph Books, 2006.

Pennington, Bill. *The Heisman: Great American Stories of the Men Who Won*. New York: ReganBooks, 2004.

Whittingham, Richard. *Sunday's Heroes: NFL Legends Talk About the Times of Their Lives*. Chicago: Triumph Books, 2004.

Ken Houston

Born: November 12, 1944
Lufkin, Texas
Also known as: Kenneth Ray Houston (full
name)

Early Life
Kenneth Ray Houston was born on November 12, 1944, in the tiny town of Lufkin on the Texas prairies. Ken's early life was a simple one. He dreamed of someday becoming a star basketball player but spent most of his time hunting, fishing, or swimming. Many times he liked nothing better than to walk through the woods and think.

The Road to Excellence
In high school, Ken was big and fast. He played center on the school's football team because he was the only man on the team quick enough to get outside to block on the sweeps, the plays where the running back is sent out wide of the defense. Ken also swam in high school and was a member of the track team, handling most of the field events, which involve jumping and throwing. Because he was such a talented athlete, Ken was pursued by college recruiters. He chose to accept a football scholarship to Prairie View A&M, a small all-black college in Texas.

When Ken arrived at Prairie View, he was almost kicked off the team because the coaches realized that, at only 6 feet 3 inches and 198 pounds, Ken was nowhere near big enough to play center in college football. Instead, Ken was switched to the defensive backfield and made all-American teams in each of his three varsity seasons. Despite all the honors Ken received, professional scouts were not sure how good the competition was at such a small school. The Houston Oilers of the now-defunct American Football League (AFL) decided to take a chance on Ken and used a late-round draft choice to claim him.

The Emerging Champion
It did not take Ken long to make an impression on the Oilers. By the third game of his rookie season, he was a starting defensive back. He intercepted

four passes that year, and five the next season, when he began his string of all-star appearances.

In 1971, Ken emerged as a star. He had always been a quiet man off the field, although on the field opposing ball carriers remembered him after crunching tackles. That season, though, everyone noticed Ken. He intercepted nine passes and set an NFL record by returning four of them for touchdowns. Never had a strong safety played so well. One of the people who noticed the budding star was Washington Redskins coach George Allen. Allen had just taken the Redskins to the Super Bowl and wanted to go back. Allen decided that Ken would fit in well with the Redskins, so he traded five players for Ken after the 1972 season.

The Oilers had never been very good while Ken

Ken Houston. (Lou Witt/NFL/Getty Images)

was there, but the Redskins were Super Bowl contenders. The team was often on television, and Ken continued to draw notice, although he still remained quiet and religious off the playing field, preferring to let others get credit for the team's success. Ken could not always avoid the spotlight, though. In 1974, he made one of the most famous plays ever on ABC's *Monday Night Football.* He stopped the Cowboys' Walt Garrison—a rodeo rider in the off-season—just short of the goal line on the last play of the game to preserve a victory for the Redskins.

Continuing the Story

Ken helped the Redskins reach the playoffs in three of his first four seasons with the team. He continued his career with the Redskins until his retirement in 1980. Every year, when the season was over, his fellow players named him to the Pro Bowl, professional football's all-star game. Every year, too, his teammates would marvel at his composure and leadership. As the years went by, Ken became more and more dangerous as a defensive player. Many quarterbacks refused to throw to his area of the field, fearing an interception. As a result, Ken expanded his role, roaming all over the field to make tackles or break up passes. He became known as a fierce tackler—a rare defensive back who could stop the run near the line of scrimmage or deflect a pass downfield.

Ken always seemed to play his best against the Dallas Cowboys, the Redskins' archrivals. He made the stop on Garrison to win the Monday night game, and the next year he returned a punt for a touchdown that was the difference in a 28-21 Redskins victory. On another occasion, he made a key interception to kill a promising Cowboys drive in a game the Redskins eventually won in overtime. Eventually, Ken became the Redskins' defensive signal-caller, setting up his teammates for the offensive play to come. His generosity and quiet confidence made him a favorite of Redskins fans, and he was always in demand as a public speaker.

Ken's leadership qualities and cool head served him well after his retirement. Ken decided to go into coaching, working for a year at the high school level before getting back into the NFL as an assis-

NFL Records
NFL Records
First to score 9 touchdowns on interceptions
First to score 4 touchdowns on interceptions in one season (1971)
First to score 2 touchdowns on interceptions in one game (1971)

Honors and Awards

1965-67	College All-American
1969-70	AFL All-Star Team
1971	*Sporting News* AFC All-Star Team
1971-80	NFL Pro Bowl Team
1973-76	*Sporting News* NFC All-Star Team
1974-76, 1978	NFL All-Pro Team
1980	NFL All-Pro Team of the 1970's
1986	Inducted into Pro Football Hall of Fame
1994	NFL 75th Anniversary All-Time Team

tant coach. After Ken left the coaching ranks he settled in Houston, Texas, and became a counselor at the Terrell Alternative School, for expelled students from the sixth through twelfth grades. Ken believes in working with children to get them to the level where they can achieve their dreams. He also works with the Texas Children's Hospital.

Summary

Football fans everywhere remember Ken Houston as a spectacular player. He hit hard, and he could turn an intercepted pass into a touchdown for his team as well as anyone in the game. Fans in Washington and Houston, though, recall Ken as a quiet man, someone very different from the hard-charging player on the field. Despite his heroics, he was never a man who really hungered for the spotlight.

John McNamara

Additional Sources

Attner, Paul, Sean Stewart, Phil Simms, and Dave Sloan. "Football's One Hundred Greatest Players: Better than all the Rest." *Sporting News* 223, no. 45 (November 8, 1999): 58-64.

Barber, Phil. "NFL: Football's One Hundred Greatest Players—The Hit Men." *The Sporting News* 223 (November 1, 1999): 12-16.

Carroll, Bob. *Total Football: The Official Encyclopedia of the National Football League.* New York: HarperCollins, 1999.

Sam Huff

Born: October 4, 1934
     Edna Gas, West Virginia
Also known as: Robert E. Lee Samuel Huff (full
  name)

Early Life

Robert E. Lee Samuel Huff was born on October 4, 1934, in Edna Gas, a coal mining town near Morgantown, in West Virginia. Sam's father worked in the coal mines. Sam was born in the middle of the Depression and money was tight. Sometimes Sam's father could get only one day's work in a week. The family—Sam and his five brothers and sisters— lived in a coal company house that had five rooms. With this background, Sam wanted to finish high school and do some type of work other than coal mining. He found football.

The Road to Excellence

Sam grew to become a 200-pound tackle for Farmington High School in West Virginia. He made the Class B all-state team, which was the smallest school classification for all-state teams. Coach Art

"Pappy" Lewis of West Virginia University (WVU) showed an interest in Sam and began dropping by the school to watch Sam play. Coach Lewis was so impressed that Sam was offered a full football scholarship to attend West Virginia University. In his senior year of high school, Sam married Mary Fletcher, his high school sweetheart and classmate. Many of Sam's friends began to work in the mines, but the new Mr. and Mrs. Huff left for Morgantown and WVU. Even though Sam had a full scholarship, he worked to earn extra money by waiting on tables while attending school.

The Emerging Champion

Sam had decided that he wanted to be a coach. He majored in physical education at WVU and maintained good grades. In 1955, his senior year, Sam and his good friend Bruce Bosley both were named all-Americans. Sam was the third draft choice of the New York Giants of the NFL that year.

The Giants tried Sam at defensive line and then at offensive guard, but he did not work well at either position. In the third game of the season, the Giants' middle linebacker was injured. Sam came in to finish the game at that position. The opportunity did not escape him; he became the Giants' middle linebacker for the next eight years.

Because Sam was an astute student of the game, he adapted to the complex system of blitzing linebackers and slanting linemen concocted by the Giants' defensive coach, Tom Landry. Landry's system had one goal—to funnel the play to the inside so that Sam could make the tackle. Many coaches held special meetings to plan ways to combat Sam. Many said that Sam had perfected the linebacker's position by hours and hours of study. He watched the offensive players for clues. He felt that if the center had his weight off the ball and was back on his haunches, the play would be a pass because he was getting ready to move back fast and block a charging linebacker. If the guards had their weight off their hands, Sam guessed the play would be a run around end,

Honors and Awards

1955	Consensus All-American
	Scholastic All-American
1956	Chicago College All-Star Game most valuable player
1959	NFL Most Valuable Defensive Player
	West Virginian of the Year
1959-62, 1965	NFL Pro Bowl Team
1961	NFL Pro Bowl Co-Player of the Game
1963	NFL All-Pro Team of the 1950's
1976	Inducted into West Virginia State Hall of Fame
1980	Inducted into College Football Hall of Fame
	Inducted into Washington Hall of Stars
1982	Inducted into Pro Football Hall of Fame
1988	Inducted into West Virginia University School of Physical Education Hall of Fame
1990	West Virginia University Alumni Association's Academy of Distinguished Alumni
	Inducted into New York Sports Museum and Hall of Fame

because the guards were already thinking about pulling and leading the play. A back that was coming straight ahead on a handoff would have more weight on his hand and be in a sprinter's position so he could move quickly into the line. These deductions, among others, allowed Sam to prepare himself for the other teams' plays. This was a new, scientific approach to the game. Defensive players had always used brute force, but Sam's approach included both intelligence and superior strength.

Sam glamorized defensive football for the first time in the game's history. Sam and his defensive crew inspired a fanatic band of followers who stood four deep in the mezzanine of Yankee Stadium to cheer for them. The Giants averaged more than 65,000 fans a game in the late 1950's, a tremendous increase in attendance. In 1959, Sam was named the most valuable defensive player in the NFL and was featured in the cover story of *Time* magazine's November, 1959, issue. He was also named West Virginian of the year. He had come a long way from the coal camp of Edna Gas.

Continuing the Story

In 1960, CBS Television News filmed a football documentary entitled "The Violent World of Sam Huff." A microphone was placed on Sam during a football game, and a camera followed his every move to give viewers a vivid sense of what NFL football was like for the players. The program was a big success, and Sam became one of the best-known athletes in the country.

In 1964, Sam moved to the Washington Redskins, where he played for the next five seasons. He played in Washington for the famous coach Vince Lombardi, who once said of Sam "It's uncanny the way Huff follows the ball. He ignores all the things you do to take him away from the play and comes

after the ball wherever it is thrown or wherever the run goes." Lombardi liked Sam so much that in 1969-1970 he made him a player/coach for the Redskins. In his career, Sam played in five Pro Bowl games and was named the game's most valuable player in 1961. After his retirement, Sam worked as a color analyst for the Redskins games on WMAL Radio in Washington, hosted a local Washington television football program, and worked as a vice president for the Marriott Hotels chain. He later became involved in horse breeding and racing. He settled in eastern West Virginia, near Washington, D.C. In 1982, he was inducted into the Pro Football Hall of Fame. In 2005, WVU retired his uniform number.

Summary

As one of the greatest linebackers in the history of the NFL, Sam Huff became a legend in his own time. He was an inspiration to many young athletes in his own state and across the country. West Virginians still proclaim Sam to be the greatest defensive football player to have played in the modern era.

Tom Kinder

Additional Sources

Hornung, Paul, and William F. Reed. *Lombardi and Me: Players, Coaches, and Colleagues Talk About the Man and the Myth.* Chicago: Triumph Books, 2006.

Huff, Sam. "A Hard Life." *Sports Illustrated* 99, no. 11 (September 22, 2003): 33.

McCullough, Bob. *My Greatest Day in Football: The Legends of Football Recount Their Greatest Moments.* New York: Thomas Dunne Books/St. Martin's Press, 2002.

Whittingham, Richard. *Illustrated History of the New York Giants.* Chicago: Triumph Books, 2005.

Don Hutson

Born: January 13, 1913
     Pine Bluff, Arkansas
Died: June 26, 1997
     Rancho Mirage, California
Also known as: Donald Montgomery Hutson (full name); the Alabama Antelope

Early Life

Donald Montgomery Hutson, one of the greatest pass receivers in football history, was born on January 13, 1913, in Pine Bluff, Arkansas. The son of a conductor on the Cotton Belt Railroad, Don was a thin and shy boy whose main interest was raising pet snakes. He enjoyed playing basketball and baseball, but Don's younger twin brothers, Raymond and Robert, were considered the better athletes in the Hutson family.

During Don's senior year in high school, a close friend, Bob Seawell, who starred on the football team, persuaded Don to try out for the football squad. Don did so, and began developing the skills that made him a great pass receiver. He excelled as a high school football player, but colleges were more interested in Seawell. Eventually, Seawell agreed to attend the University of Alabama, on the condition that Don came with him. As a result, Alabama gave Don a scholarship too.

The Road to Excellence

At Alabama, Don developed slowly. At first, he looked so frail at 160 pounds that he was almost ignored by the football coach. However, his blinding speed—he ran the 100-yard dash in 9.7 seconds—impressed the coach. He played little in his freshman and sophomore years, but in his junior year in 1933, Don made the starting team and played more frequently.

By his senior year, Don had blossomed as a player and had become known as the "Alabama Antelope." The Crimson Tide fielded a powerful team that year. Led by passer Millard "Dixie" Howell, the legendary Paul

"Bear" Bryant at one end, and Don at the other end, Alabama won all nine of its games. The Howell-to-Hutson duo became famous. The team reached its peak in the postseason Rose Bowl game by beating Stanford 29-13. The game was Don's finest hour as a collegiate player. He caught 6 passes for 165 yards and 2 touchdowns. He was chosen to the 1934 all-American team and is considered to this day to be one of Alabama's greatest players. Don also excelled in baseball and track at Alabama. There were times when he ran in a track meet and played baseball on the same day.

The year 1935 was a major one in Don's life. He graduated from Alabama, married his sweetheart Julia Richards, and signed contracts to play in two professional sports. Don signed with the football Green Bay Packers and the baseball Brooklyn Dodg-

Don Hutson making a leaping catch. (Getty Images)

216

NFL Statistics

Season	GP	Rec.	Yds.	Avg.	TD
1935	12	18	420	23.3	6
1936	11	34	536	15.8	8
1937	11	41	552	13.5	7
1938	10	32	548	17.1	9
1939	11	34	846	24.9	6
1940	11	45	664	14.8	7
1941	11	58	738	12.7	10
1942	11	74	1,211	16.4	17
1943	10	47	776	16.5	11
1944	10	58	866	14.9	9
1945	10	47	834	17.7	9
Totals	118	488	7,991	16.4	99

Notes: GP = games played; Rec. = receptions; Yds. = yards; Avg. = average yards per reception; TD = touchdowns

ers. Both contracts arrived in the office of NFL commissioner Joe Carr on the same day, but he upheld the Packers' contract because it was postmarked seventeen minutes earlier than that of the Dodgers.

The Emerging Champion

Many doubted that Don, at 6 feet 1 inch and 178 pounds, could stand the pounding of professional football, but Don soon silenced the doubters. On the first play of his first NFL game, he caught an 83-yard touchdown pass to lead the Packers to a 7-0 victory over Green Bay's archrivals the Chicago Bears. That was just the beginning. In his eleven seasons with the Packers, Don became one of the greatest pass receivers the game had ever seen.

Don outmaneuvered every defensive back who tried to cover him. Opposing teams assigned their fastest backs to cover him, but he seemed always to break free and catch a big pass. He was sometimes double- and triple-teamed, but again he would slip past the defense. George Halas, the coach of the Bears, once said that he conceded Don two touchdowns every time Chicago played the Packers.

Don led the NFL in receiving during eight of his eleven years. In all, he caught 488 passes for 7,991 yards and 99 touchdowns. A superb place-

kicker as well, he also led the league in scoring four times and finished with 823 career points. He was named to the all-NFL team an incredible nine times. Don also led the Packers to four Western Division titles and three NFL championships. His best year was 1942, when he caught 74 passes for 1,211 yards and 17 touchdowns.

Continuing the Story

With his big hands, great speed, and quick fakes, Don was a natural offensive end. He became football's first split end. During a game against Brooklyn, Don lined up against an old teammate from Alabama. To move away from him, Don moved farther away from the ball on the line of scrimmage. Thus the split end was born. Don invented many faking and cutting moves that receivers still use today. Former Philadelphia Eagles football coach Alfred "Greasy" Neale once said that Don was the only man he ever saw who could run in three directions at one time.

Don also introduced the catcher's squat for catching passes. He would run into the end zone, circle back just inside the goal line, and take a low pass from the quarterback. Another technique he used was to run toward the goalpost, grab it with one arm and swing himself around facing the play, and catch the ball with his other arm for a touchdown.

In addition to his offensive prowess, Don was a great defensive safety in the days when players played offense and defense. His coach, Curly Lam-

Honors and Awards

1934	Consensus All-American
1936, 1938-45	NFL All-Pro Team
1940 (two games), 1942 (two games)	NFL Pro Bowl Team
1941-42	Carr Trophy
1951	Inducted into College Football Hall of Fame
1963	NFL All-Pro Team of the 1930's
	Inducted into Pro Football Hall of Fame
1969	NFL All-Time Offensive End
	Sports Illustrated Silver Anniversary Team
	One Hundredth Anniversary of College Football All-Time Team
	Uniform number 14 retired by Green Bay Packers

beau, said that Don never missed a tackle and saved as many touchdowns as he made.

In 1945, Don retired from football at the age of thirty-two. After retiring, he purchased a Chevrolet and Cadillac automobile agency in Racine, Wisconsin. He and his wife, Julia, had three daughters. He was later voted into the National Football Foundation and College Hall of Fame and the Pro Football Hall of Fame. He was also chosen to several modern all-time all-American teams.

Summary

Don Hutson was the forerunner of the wide receivers of today. He made pass-catching an exciting art, and introduced faking and cutting techniques that receivers still use. In his career, he set nineteen NFL records. What he lacked in bulk and strength Don made up for in speed and agility, to become one of the all-time great wide receivers.

Nan White

Additional Sources

Gulbrandsen, Don. *The Green Bay Packers: The Complete Illustrated History.* St. Paul, Minn.: Motorbooks International, 2007.

Sugar, Burt R. *The One Hundred Greatest Athletes of All Time.* New York: Citadel Press, 1995.

Walsh, Christopher J. *Where Football Is King: A History of the SEC.* Lanham, Md.: Taylor Trade, 2006.

Yaeger, Don, Sam Cunningham, and John Papadakis. *Turning of the Tide: How One Game Changed the South.* New York: Center Street, 2006.

Michael Irvin

Born: March 5, 1966
     Fort Lauderdale, Florida
Also known as: Michael Jerome Irvin (full name);
    the Playmaker

Early Life

Michael Jerome Irvin was born the fifteenth of seventeen children on March 5, 1966, in Fort Lauderdale, Florida, to Walter and Pearl Irvin. The impoverished family lived in a two-bedroom home until Walter made more bedrooms out of the porch and garage. At the age of thirteen, while helping his father with his roofing business on a sultry Florida afternoon, Michael decided that football would be his way out of poverty.

Michael Irvin moments after scoring a touchdown in the 1996 National Football Conference Championship game. (AP/Wide World Photos)

The Road to Excellence

Trained by his brother Willie, Michael ran the miles to and from school. As a sophomore he made the Piper High School football team. During this time he discovered prejudice and that others were not as poor as he. Fired from Burger King for stealing food and later suspended from school for reasons he would not reveal, he enrolled at St. Thomas Aquinas Catholic school.

Piper High charged the school and Michael with "recruiting violations" and forced him to sit out his junior year. This allowed him to improve his academics and forge friendships with whites, since racial tensions were not as high at St. Thomas Aquinas. When his father died from cancer the same year, Michael blamed strenuous work for the death. He vowed to help his struggling family members financially by becoming a football star.

As a wide receiver at the University of Miami, he helped the team to an undefeated season in 1987, catching the winning touchdown pass to win the Orange Bowl. In three seasons as a starter he set records for catches (143), receiving yardage (2,423), and touchdown receptions (26).

In 1988, Michael was chosen in the first round by the Dallas Cowboys in the NFL's draft. With competitiveness and discipline learned as a child, he led the National Football Conference (NFC) in most yards per catch as a rookie (20.4). Michael was respectful and loyal to coach Jimmy Johnson. Extremely close to his teammates, especially running back Emmitt Smith, Michael asked Smith if he was all right after every play during an NFC Championship game in which Smith was injured.

The Emerging Champion

After suffering a season-ending knee injury in 1989, Michael's future in the

NFL Statistics

Season	GP	Rec.	Yds.	Avg.	TD
1988	14	32	654	20.4	5
1989	6	26	378	14.5	2
1990	12	20	413	20.7	5
1991	16	93	1,523	16.4	8
1992	16	78	1,396	17.9	7
1993	16	88	1,330	15.1	7
1994	16	79	1,241	15.7	6
1995	16	111	1,603	14.4	10
1996	11	64	962	15.0	2
1997	16	75	1,180	15.7	9
1998	16	74	1,057	14.3	1
1999	4	10	167	16.7	3
Totals	159	750	11,904	15.9	65

Notes: GP = games played; Rec. = receptions; Yds. = yards; Avg. = average yards per reception; TD = touchdowns

NFL was uncertain, but his spirit and drive brought him back. After missing the first four games of the 1990 season, his career exploded. He scored on every fourth catch and had a 20.7 yards-per-catch average that year.

In 1991, Michael had an outstanding year. He was the starting wide receiver and led the league in receiving yards. He had 93 receptions for 1,523 yards. He was chosen the NFL alumni wide receiver of the year and was the Pro Bowl most valuable player. In the Pro Bowl game he had 8 receptions for 125 yards and 1 touchdown. Against the Atlanta Falcons, he caught a career-high 10 passes for 169 yards. When the Cowboys defeated Super Bowl champion New York Giants, Michael caught 6 passes for 91 yards.

Michael was key to the Cowboys' Super Bowl win in 1992, with 6 receptions for 114 yards and 2 touchdowns. He finished the regular season second in the NFL in receiving yardage (1,396) and first in most yards per catch (17.9). By signing a $1.25 million contract with the Cowboys after the season, his dream of helping his family financially came true.

The 1993 season was another breakthrough year for Michael. He had a career-high 12 receptions against the San Francisco 49ers. He finished the season second in the NFL in receiving yardage (1,330) and third in receptions (88). He made the Pro Bowl for a third straight year and was key to the Cowboys' second consecutive Super Bowl victory, catching a 20-yard pass to get a first down on a

third-and-sixteen play, which led to a tying touchdown. He caught 2 more touchdown passes to beat the Buffalo Bills.

The next two seasons Michael set more records, and, in 1995, the Cowboys again won the Super Bowl. He received 192 yards during the 1994 NFC Championship game and, in 1995, had eleven 100-yard receiving games. That season he set a single-season record for receptions (111), receiving yardage (1,603), and consecutive 100-yard receiving games (7).

Continuing the Story

Michael has worked with children at football camps and with youth group organizations in Dallas. In 1996, his image was threatened, however, when he pled guilty for cocaine possession. He was suspended for the first five games of the season, put on four years of probation, and fined $10,000. In December of 1996, Michael was accused of holding a gun to a woman's head while a fellow teammate sexually assaulted her. He denied involvement in the incident and was cleared of all wrongdoing.

In 1996, Michael helped the Cowboys win the NFC Eastern Division Championship and broke Drew Pearson's record for most consecutive years as a team leader in receptions. By 1998, Michael was tenth in the NFL's all-time lists for receptions (740) and receiving yardage (11,737) and had led the Cowboys in receiving for eight consecutive years. He also had forty-six 100-yard receiving games to his career. A neck injury in 1999 contributed to his decision to retire from the NFL. He finished his career ninth on the NFL all-time leader board in receiving yardage (11,904) and tied for tenth in receptions (750).

After retiring from the NFL, Michael worked for the Entertainment and Sports Programming Net-

Honors and Achievements

1991	Pro Bowl most valuable player
	NFL Alumni Wide Receiver of the Year
	League leader in receiving yards
1992-93, 1995	Super Bowl championship team
2000	NFL All-Decade Team 1990's
2005	Inducted into Dallas Cowboys Ring of Honor
2007	Inducted into Pro Football Hall of Fame

work (ESPN) as a football analyst. His charismatic personality made him a popular and often controversial commentator. In 2007, he was inducted into the Pro Football Hall of Fame.

Summary

Michael Irvin was one of the greatest wide receivers in professional football. He was a hardworking, dedicated athlete. Off the field—although surrounded by controversy—he stayed loyal to his family, teammates, and coaches. He exemplifies the idea that with determination and hard work, dreams can come true.

Lori A. Petersen

Additional Sources

Bradley, Michael. *Big Games: College Football's Greatest Rivalries.* Washington, D.C.: Potomac Books, 2006.

Hitzges, Norm. *Greatest Team Ever: The Dallas Cowboys Dynasty of the 1990's.* Dallas, Tex.: Thomas Nelson, 2007.

Bo Jackson

Born: November 30, 1962
       Bessemer, Alabama
Also known as: Vincent Edward Jackson (birth name)
Other major sports: Baseball; track and field

Early Life

The son of Mrs. Florence Jackson Bond, Vincent Edward Jackson was born on November 30, 1962, in Bessemer, Alabama, a small steel town just southwest of Birmingham. His mother named him after Vincent Edwards, her favorite actor, television's Dr. Ben Casey. He was the eighth of ten children.

Two-sport athlete Bo Jackson of the Los Angeles Raiders in 1987. (Ron Vesely/Getty Images)

Growing up in a large family without much money required a special strength. Bo explained his tough childhood in his book *Bo Knows Bo* (1990):

> We never had enough food. But at least I could beat on other kids and steal their lunch money and buy myself something to eat. But I couldn't steal a father. I couldn't steal a father's hug when I needed one. I couldn't steal a father's whipping when I needed one.

There were times when Bo may have needed that whipping. His family remembers him as a rowdy child, one so rambunctious and high-spirited that he was described as wild as a "boarhog." The nickname by which the whole world now knows him is "Bo," an abbreviation of the slang expression "bo'hog." As a child, Bo developed a deep love for his family, in particular his mother, and a profound spirituality. When he was thirteen, he even planned on becoming a Baptist preacher. His Little League coaches, however, had other ideas about the future of this naturally gifted athlete.

The Road to Excellence

Bo played Little League baseball for only two weeks before the coaches, who thought him too rough and strong for the other players, bumped him up to the Pony League. Soon, he was playing in a semiprofessional men's league.

Football was a way for him to play games with other children his own age. By the time he was a ninth-grader at McAdory High School in McCalla, Alabama—a town not too far from Birmingham and Bessemer—Bo played both sports, and college recruiters began to take notice. They were not the only ones. Bo first received national attention in 1982 when the New York Yankees offered him a multiyear contract. Bo was still a senior in high school at the time. That year he had gained 1,173 yards on 108 carries and scored 17 touchdowns, set a high school record for home runs in a season—with 20 in only twenty-five games—and become a two-time state high school decathlon champion. Already some people were describing Bo as the "world's greatest athlete."

Bo was modest and downplayed comparisons to the legendary Jim Thorpe, who excelled in football and baseball shortly after the turn of the century. Even in high school, Bo was mild-mannered and, because of a speech impediment, appeared quiet and reflective. He thought a long time about accepting the Yankees' offer but turned it down to attend Auburn University in Auburn, Alabama.

The Emerging Champion

Bo's college was spectacular. He broke all of Auburn's football rushing records; in 1985, he set a school mark for the best single-season rushing performance (1,786 yards). He was the first Auburn back ever to rush in excess of 4,000 yards in a career, with a total of 4,303 yards. In his senior year, he rushed for more than 100 yards in a game eight times, giving him twenty-one 100-yard-plus performances. Bo capped off his collegiate football career by winning the fifty-first annual Heisman Trophy as the outstanding college football player in America.

As a freshman and as a sophomore, Bo lettered in track. In 1985, as the center fielder for the baseball team, he batted .401, with 17 home runs and 43 runs batted in. He was named to the all-district and all-region teams by the College Baseball Coaches Association and was considered one of the premier players in college baseball.

NFL Football Statistics

| Season | GP | Rushing | | | | Receiving | | | |
		Car.	Yds.	Avg.	TD	Rec.	Yds.	Avg.	TD
1987	7	81	554	6.8	4	16	136	8.5	2
1988	10	136	580	4.3	3	9	79	8.8	0
1989	11	173	950	5.5	4	9	69	7.7	0
1990	10	125	698	5.6	5	6	68	11.3	0
Totals	38	515	2,782	5.4	16	40	352	8.8	2

Notes: GP = games played; Car. = carries; Yds. = yards; Avg. = average yards per carry *or* average yards per reception; TD = touchdowns; Rec. = receptions

The Tampa Bay Buccaneers of the NFL offered Bo a five-year contract to play football. The Kansas City Royals of the Major League Baseball's American League countered by selecting him in the 1986 baseball draft. Bo surprised football fans by choosing a baseball career with Kansas City, but, in 1986, the Los Angeles Raiders asked him to reconsider football. This time he said that he would play both sports, if the Raiders could wait each year until after the baseball season for him to start playing football.

Few believed that Bo could succeed as a professional at both sports. Baseball and football have grueling schedules that overlap, and it seemed likely that eventually Bo would have to choose one or the other.

Continuing the Story

Bo thus became a man of two seasons, professional sports' first outfielder-tailback combination. Some fans were outraged at first, especially when Bo referred to football as a "hobby." He silenced the critics by distinguishing himself both as a Royal and as a Raider. He made all-star teams in both sports, a remarkable achievement for a man who played football for only half a season.

In early March, 1991, Bo's career as a two-sport professional athlete was derailed. On January 13, he had partially dislocated his left hip during a football game, severing the blood vessels that nourish the bones of the hip socket. Medical tests performed a month later disclosed that Bo was suffering from a degenera-

Major League Baseball Statistics

Season	GP	AB	Hits	2B	3B	HR	Runs	RBI	BA	SA
1986	25	82	17	2	1	2	9	9	.207	.329
1987	116	396	93	17	2	22	46	53	.235	.455
1988	124	439	108	16	4	25	63	68	.246	.472
1989	135	515	132	15	6	32	86	105	.256	.495
1990	111	405	110	16	1	28	74	78	.272	.523
1991	23	71	16	4	0	3	8	14	.225	.408
1993	85	284	66	9	0	16	32	45	.232	.433
1994	75	201	56	7	0	13	23	43	.279	.507
Totals	694	2,393	598	86	14	141	341	415	.250	.474

Notes: GP = games played; AB = at bats; 2B = doubles; 3B = triples; HR = home runs; RBI = runs batted in; BA = batting average; SA = slugging average

Honors and Awards

1982	*Football News* Freshman All-American
1983	Sugar Bowl game most valuable player
1983, 1985	Consensus All-American
1984	Liberty Bowl game most valuable player
1985	Heisman Trophy
	Sporting News College Player of the Year
	Sporting News College All-American
	College Baseball Coaches Association All-Region Team
	College Baseball Coaches Association All-District Team
1986	Overall first choice in the NFL draft
1989	Major League Baseball All-Star game most valuable player
1990	NFL All-Star Team
1993	American League comeback player of the year
	Received the Tony Conigliaro Award
1999	Inducted into College Football Hall of Fame

tive hip condition, and he was advised by doctors to discontinue playing sports. He was subsequently released by the Kansas City Royals on March 18, although he was signed to a one-year contract by the Chicago White Sox less than three weeks later. He did not play in any games for the Raiders during the 1991 season. Bo played only twenty-three games for Chicago in 1991 and missed all of the 1992 season. In 1993, he came back stronger, hitting 16 home runs in eighty-five games, including one in the division-clinching game against Seattle. The White Sox, however, decided to trade him to the California Angels for the 1994 season.

At 6 feet 1 inch and 225 pounds, with explosive speed and formidable strength, Bo electrified fans when he stepped to the plate. He may have struck out often, but the anticipation that Bo would perform an amazing athletic feat was always there. He became a household name through his numerous commercial endorsements. Even nonfans knew what the expression "Bo knows . . . " meant. At his

home, though, he has led a quiet life with his wife Linda, a child psychologist whom he met at Auburn, and his two sons, Garrett and Nicolas. Following his strike-shortened first season with the Angels, Bo decided to retire at the age of thirty-two in order to spend more time with his family and pursue a career outside of sports. In 1995, Bo completed his bachelor's degree at Auburn University in family and child development.

In 1999 Bo acquired the Birmingham, Alabama, franchise of the new Spring Football League (SFL), which hoped to serve as a training ground for young players to make the leap into the NFL. The same year, Bo was elected to the College Football Hall of Fame.

Summary

Bo Jackson was one of the best-known athletes in the United States. His skills and talent were awe-inspiring. As a baseball player or as a football running back, he carried the expectations of thousands of fans on his broad shoulders and rarely disappointed them.

William U. Eiland

Additional Sources

Devaney, John. *Bo Jackson: A Star for All Seasons.* New York: Walker, 1998.

Flores, Tom, and Matt Fulks. *Tom Flores' Tales from the Oakland Raiders.* Champaign, Ill.: Sports, 2007.

Gutman, Bill. *Bo Jackson: A Biography.* New York: Pocket Books, 1991.

Jackson, Bo, and Dick Schaap. *Bo Knows Bo: The Autobiography of a Ballplayer.* New York: Doubleday, 1990.

Thomas, Landon. *The SEC Team of the '80's: Auburn Football, 1980-1989.* Woodstock, Ga.: Tigers, 2004.

Keith Jackson

Born: April 19, 1965
Little Rock, Arkansas
Also known as: Keith Jerome Jackson (full name)

Early Life
Keith Jerome Jackson was born on April 19, 1965, in Little Rock, Arkansas. He was raised in a religious family. He began playing football at the age of nine. In high school, he was an outstanding athlete. He played on the varsity team in three different sports at Little Rock's Parkview High School, for whom he was twice named a high school all-American in football.

The Road to Excellence
Keith surprised many people by choosing to attend the University of Oklahoma. Because Oklahoma used the run-dominated wishbone offense, for Keith, who played tight end, pass-catching opportunities seemed limited. Despite this situation, he had a significant impact for the team, excelling as both a blocker and a receiver.

Keith started all four years at Oklahoma. He made the 1984 Big Eight Conference all-academic team his freshman year. In the following season, he became known for making big plays. Against second-ranked University of Nebraska, he had a spectacular 88-yard run for a touchdown, helping Oklahoma clinch the conference championship with a 27-7 victory. In the Orange Bowl, he caught a 71-yard touchdown pass in a 26-10 win over previously undefeated Penn State University, giving Oklahoma the national championship. He was named as a first-team all-Conference player.

In his junior year, Keith solidified his reputation as a playmaker. In 1986, despite having just 14 receptions, 5 catches were for touchdowns. Furthermore, he averaged an astonishing 28.8 yards per reception. Perhaps his two most important catches of the season came against traditional-power Nebraska. Keith caught a 17-yard touchdown pass to tie the score near the end of the game. Then, with 9 seconds remaining, he tipped a pass to himself, producing a 41-yard gain and setting up the game-winning field goal. Oklahoma's 20-17 victory

clinched the conference championship. Keith made both the all-Conference and all-American teams that year.

The Emerging Champion
In 1987, Keith had another impressive season. He was again named to the all-Conference and all-American teams, helping Oklahoma finish the regular season with an undefeated record. In his four years at Oklahoma, he had 62 catches for 1,470 yards, averaging more than 23 yards per reception. He also scored 14 touchdowns during his college years. As of 2008, he is one of only three players to start in four consecutive Orange Bowls. He also made the all-Conference academic team all four seasons. His individual performance contributed to the team's success. Oklahoma had a 42-5-1 record during this period, with four conference championships and a national title.

Keith's success at the college level made him attractive to NFL teams. In the 1988 draft, he was selected with the thirteenth pick by the Philadelphia Eagles. As a rookie, he caught 81 passes for 869 yards and 6 touchdowns. His number of receptions set a team, single-season record at the time and remained a franchise record for a rookie and tight end through 2007. In 1988, the league named him the offensive rookie of the year. During his four seasons with the Eagles, he made 242 catches for 2,756 yards and 20 touchdowns. He made the all-

NFL Statistics

Season	GP	Rec.	Yds.	Avg.	TD
1988	16	81	869	10.7	6
1989	14	63	648	10.3	3
1990	14	50	670	13.4	6
1991	16	48	569	11.9	5
1992	13	48	594	12.4	5
1993	15	39	613	15.7	6
1994	16	59	673	11.4	7
1995	9	13	142	10.9	1
1996	16	40	505	12.6	10
Totals	129	441	5,283	12.0	49

Notes: GP = games played; Rec. = receptions; Yds. = yards; Avg. = average yards per reception; TD = touchdowns

pro team in his first three seasons, from 1988 to 1990. His strong performance helped the Eagles become a winning team that made the playoffs in each of those three years.

Following the 1991 season, Keith became a free agent and joined the Miami Dolphins. In 1992, Miami won the division and advanced to the American Football Conference Championship game. In each of his first two seasons with the Dolphins, he made the Pro Bowl. After three strong years in Miami, he was traded to the Green Bay Packers prior to the 1995 season.

Continuing the Story

In Keith's first year with the Packers, the team won its first division title in more than two decades, eventually advancing to the National Football Conference Championship game. During the 1996 season, the Packers won the Super Bowl. Keith's performance played a key role in the team's success, as he made 40 receptions for 505 yards and a career-high 10 touchdowns. He retired after the championship season. In his nine-year professional career, he went to the Pro Bowl five times and was named first-team all-pro three times. He made 441 receptions for 5,283 yards and 49 touchdowns.

Immediately after retiring from playing football, Keith began a career in broadcasting. In 1997, he started his new profession as an expert commentator during NFL games for Turner Sports. Later, he took a job doing similar work for the University of Arkansas, where his son, Keith Jackson, Jr., was an outstanding football player. In addition

---

Honors and Awards

1988-90	NFL All-Pro first team
1988-90, 1992, 1996	NFL Pro Bowl Team
2001	Inducted into College Football Hall of Fame

---

to broadcasting, Keith, Sr., was active as a motivational speaker and philanthropist. He created an organization called Positive Atmosphere Reaches Kids, an after-school program for at-risk middle school and high school students. Keith's impressive performance as a football player was formally recognized following his retirement. In 2001, he was inducted into the National Football Foundation's College Football Hall of Fame.

Summary

Keith Jackson was one of the best tight ends in the history of football, as his assets included both blocking and receiving skills. His athleticism was unique: He combined size, strength, speed, and pass-catching abilities. He was one of the few athletes to win championships at all levels of his sport.

Kevin L. Brennan

Additional Sources

Didinger, Ray, and Robert Lyons. *The Eagles Encyclopedia.* Philadelphia: Temple University Press, 2005.

"Keith Jackson Heads to College Football Hall of Fame." *Pittsburgh Tribune-Review,* August 10, 2002.

Edgerrin James

Born: August 1, 1978
     Immokalee, Florida
Also known as: Edgerrin Tyree James (full
    name); the Edge

Early Life

Edgerrin James was born in Immokalee, Florida, a small farming community at the edge of the swampy Everglades. His mother, Julie, worked in a cafeteria. His father, Edward German, worked in the harvesting industry; his parents were not married. Edgerrin grew up in impoverished circumstances. Immokalee was dependent on the seasonal fruit and vegetable crop, and money was hard to earn in the off-season. The James family had to depend on food stamps to survive.

The frequent absence of his father was only one of the struggles with which Edgerrin dealt. His family was troubled by drug use and AIDS; violence and narcotics were ever-present in his immediate environment. He worked in the watermelon fields as a teenager, developing the physical strength he showed while playing Pop Warner football. His idol was the former Chicago Bears running back Walter Payton, and he tried to emulate Payton's approach to the game.

Edgerrin was not a diligent student in high school, but he showed his creativity by developing his own personal style. He wore his hair in dreadlocks and had his teeth capped in gold. Older family members cautioned him against appearing too rebellious, encouraging him to change his style and adopt a more conventional appearance. Edgerrin persisted in doing what he wanted, however. His personal style did not affect his football performance in high school. He became a star running back and was named a *Parade* All-American.

The Road to Excellence

Although many colleges tried to recruit Edgerrin, he felt most comfortable attending school close to home. The University of Miami had one of the nation's leading programs during the 1980's and 1990's. The Hurricanes' coach,

Butch Davis, took a personal interest in helping Edgerrin gain the academic qualifications to enter Miami, even though his standardized test scores were not high.

Edgerrin made the Miami starting lineup when he was a sophomore. In the 1997-1998 season, he rushed for more than 1,000 yards. He was an all-Big East selection his sophomore and junior years. He also became an effective secondary receiver, increasing his versatility. He was well known to local Florida fans and college football experts, but he was not a national figure at the time. He even had to share the running back position with teammates Najeh Davenport and James Jackson.

In December, 1998, Edgerrin, known as "the Edge," had the game of his life against the University of California at Los Angeles. He dominated the game, running for 299 yards on 39 carries and scoring 3 touchdowns. Suddenly the world of football

Arizona Cardinals running back Edgerrin James in 2007. (Ben Munn/CSM/Landov)

NFL Statistics

Season	GP	Rushing				Receiving			
		Car.	Yds.	Avg.	TD	Rec.	Yds.	Avg.	TD
1999	16	369	1,553	4.2	13	62	586	9.5	4
2000	16	387	1,709	4.4	13	63	594	9.4	5
2001	6	151	662	4.4	3	24	193	8.0	0
2002	14	277	989	3.6	2	61	354	5.8	1
2003	13	310	1,259	4.1	11	51	292	5.7	0
2004	16	334	1,548	4.6	9	51	483	9.5	0
2005	15	360	1,506	4.2	13	44	337	7.7	1
2006	16	337	1,159	3.4	6	38	217	5.7	0
2007	16	324	1,222	3.8	7	24	204	8.5	0
2008	13	133	514	4.2	3	12	85	7.1	0
Totals	141	2,982	12,121	4.1	80	430	3,345	7.8	11

Notes: GP = games played; Car. = carries; Yds. = yards; Avg. = average yards per carry *or* average yards per reception; TD = touchdowns; Rec. = receptions

focused on Edgerrin. Though Miami had not made a postseason appearance in his sophomore year, in 1998, the team appeared in the Micron PC Bowl, beating North Carolina State 46-23.

The Emerging Champion

The Miami program had produced numerous high draft picks over the previous two decades, but not all of them had become stars on the professional level. Despite Edgerrin's accomplishments, he was not considered the best player in the NFL draft. The Indianapolis Colts, with the fourth pick, were widely expected to take University of Texas running back Ricky Williams but gambled by picking Edgerrin. The Colts had earlier traded star running back Marshall Faulk to the St. Louis Rams, so Edgerrin was going to play in place of a legend. The pressure on him was tremendous. General manager Bill Polian and Coach Jim Mora were confident that Edgerrin could succeed.

Continuing the Story

Edgerrin's progress was momentarily impeded, though, when he and his agent were unable to agree with the Colts on a contract. Though he finally signed in August, he missed much of training camp. The Colts therefore did not feature him on offense during the first few weeks of the season. Soon, he became comfortable in the Colts' offense, which was led by quarterback Peyton Manning, a second-year player who had won the Heisman Trophy, and receiver Marvin Harrison. Displaying his ability

to catch the ball as well as run with it, often getting the crucial extra yard on the third down or gaining maximum yardage on first or second downs, Edgerrin stunned the league's defensive players.

The Colts stormed through the 1999-2000 season, finishing first in the American Football Conference (AFC) Eastern Division. Although some people thought the team was too young to flourish in postseason play, the Colts performed well in pressure situations. The team was favored to advance to the Super Bowl, a game in which the franchise had not played since its days in Baltimore. The team was poised to meet the St. Louis Rams and confront Faulk. However, the Tennessee Titans surprised the Colts in an AFC Divisional Championship, defeating them. There was a silver lining for Edgerrin, though, as he was named NFL rookie of the year for 1999-2000, led the league in rushing yards with 1,553, and was named to his first Pro Bowl.

The following year, Edgerrin led the league in rushing yards again with 1,709 and was named to his second consecutive Pro Bowl. However, in 2001, Edgerrin tore his anterior cruciate ligament six games into the season and did not return until the following year. The 2002 season was difficult for Edgerrin because he had undergone reconstructive knee surgery and suffered from numerous other injuries. The following season he returned for thirteen games and rushed for more than 1,200 yards, compiling 11 rushing touchdowns. In the 2004 season, he started all sixteen games for the Colts and earned his third Pro Bowl selection. He had a stellar season that year with 1,548 yards and 9 touchdowns. Then, in 2005, Edgerrin finished fifth in the NFL and second in the AFC in rushing yards with 1,506; he scored 13 rushing touchdowns.

Honors and Awards

1997-98	All-Big East team
1999	Associated Press NFL Offensive Rookie of the Year
	NFL All-Pro first team
1999-2000, 2004-05	NFL Pro Bowl Team

In 2006, the Colts traded Edgerrin to the Arizona Cardinals. He left Indianapolis as the Colts' all-time leading rusher with 9,226 yards. In 2006 and 2007, Edgerrin had solid seasons, rushing for 1,159 and 1,222 yards, respectively. He became the first Cardinals running back to rush for more than 1,000 yards in a season since Adrian Murrell in 1998. In 2006, he reached fifty 100-yard games faster than all but two other players in NFL history, doing so in 108 games. That season he became frustrated because he felt he was being underused. However, when the Cardinals went into postseason play, Edgerrin went into high gear. His strong running game in the playoffs helped carry the team to the Super Bowl. They lost to the Pittsburgh Steelers in a thriller that many people regard as the greatest game in Super Bowl history.

Summary

Edgerrin James proved wrong many who doubted his ability to succeed in professional football. He proved to people that he was a star, and he did so without losing his individuality or his own sense of style. In the 2008 season, he continued to climb the NFL's all-time rushing-yards list.

Nicholas Birns,
updated by Lamia Nuseibeh Scherzinger

Additional Sources

Attner, Paul. "Glory Be! With Edgerrin James On Board and a Dazzling Stadium Set to Be Open, the Sun Finally Appears to Be Shining on—and Not Just in—Arizona." *The Sporting News,* July 21, 2006.

Bagnato, Andrew. "Edgerrin James Says Birthday Won't Slow Him Down." *IndyStar,* July 28, 2008.

Bradley, John Ed. "Unaltered State." *Sports Illustrated* 91, no. 11 (September 20, 1999): 44-51.

Chappell, Mike, Phil Richards, and Ted Marchibroda. *Tales from the Indianapolis Colts Sideline.* Champaign, Ill.: Sports, 2004.

Pierce, Charles P. "The Magnificent Seven." *Esquire,* September, 2000, 208-217.

Jimmy Johnson

Born: March 31, 1938
       Dallas, Texas
Also known as: James Earl Johnson (full name)

Early Life

James Earl Johnson was born on March 31, 1938, in the Oak Cliff section of Dallas, Texas. Jimmy was one of six children. Oak Cliff was an African American neighborhood, and the Johnson family lived there for six years. His parents, Lewis Johnson and Alma Gibson Johnson, worked in the fields. Jimmy had two brothers, Rafer and Ed, and two sisters, Erma and Dolores. Rafer was the oldest of the six children, and he grew up to win the decathlon at the 1960 Summer Olympics.

In 1945, the Johnson family moved west to Kingsburg, California. The town is located in Central California's San Joaquin Valley. Jimmy's father had migrated to California the previous year in order to find work. Although Kingsburg had a population at the time of around twenty-five hundred, the Johnson family was the only black family in town. Rafer was the first of the Johnson children to attend Kingsburg High School. He was a star athlete there. Jimmy was inspired by his older brother. Jimmy was never very big, but he loved playing football. Encouraged by his coaches and other teammates, Jimmy worked hard and excelled at football. While at Kingsburg, Jimmy was captain of the football, baseball, and basketball teams.

The Road to Excellence

After graduating from Kingsburg High School, Jimmy attended Santa Monica City College. He only played football there for one year before he transferred to the University of California at Los Angeles (UCLA). Rafer also attended UCLA. Although weighing only 180 pounds, Jimmy proved to be a quality player in both wingback and defensive back positions. At UCLA he was an excellent receiver and running back and was considered the Bruins' best blocker and tackler. Jimmy also was a track star at UCLA. During both his junior and senior years there, he was an honors student. In 1961, the San Francisco 49ers of the NFL chose him in

the first round of the draft because of his speed, agility, and determination.

Jimmy began his professional football career with the 49ers as a defensive safety. During his rookie season, he had five interceptions playing safety. Because of his speed, he got a chance to play wide receiver in 1962. While injuries slowed Jimmy down for part of the season, he finished the year with thirty-four receptions and four touchdowns. As one of the primary targets of 49ers quarterback John Brodie, he averaged 18.4 yards per reception, which was the best on the team.

The Emerging Champion

Jimmy started the 1963 season as a wide receiver, but he soon was moved back to safety. A number of player injuries made it necessary for him to fill in

Cornerback Jimmy Johnson, who played sixteen seasons for the San Francisco 49ers. (Courtesy of Rafer Johnson)

Honors and Awards

1969, 1975	Len Eshmont Award
1969-72	All-Pro Team
1969-72, 1974	Pro Bowl
1971	George Halas Award
1977	Uniform number 37 retired by San Francisco 49ers
1994	Inducted into Pro Football Hall of Fame

---

wherever he was needed. The 49ers finished the season with a disappointing record of 2-12. In 1964, Jimmy was moved to left cornerback. He remained at the cornerback position for thirteen seasons. He earned the respect of teammates, coaches, and opponents alike for his blistering speed, quick reflexes, and ability to make solid tackles. Sadly, the 49ers were not a very strong team during the 1960's. In 1969, Jimmy was named to the Pro Bowl, made all-pro, and won the Len Eshmont Award.

The 49ers turned around from a 4-8-2 team in 1969 to a 10-3 team in 1970. The team captured the Western Division Championship, John Brodie was named NFL player of the year, and Jimmy was once again named to the Pro Bowl and selected as an all-pro. The 49ers also won the Western Division Championship again in 1971 and 1972. However, the team did not have another winning season until Jimmy's last year in 1976. During Jimmy's career, the 49ers played in only two NFL title games, and both times they were defeated by the Dallas Cowboys. While Jimmy could always be counted on to deliver a stellar performance on the field, the team's overall inconsistency prevented success.

Continuing the Story

After playing for sixteen years with the 49ers, Jimmy retired at the end of the 1976 season. During his career, he played in 212 games and had 47 interceptions. Because Jimmy was so good at his cornerback position, most quarterbacks in the NFL did not throw into his area. He was selected to play in five Pro Bowls and named all-pro on four occasions.

In 1971, he was given the George Halas Award for his courageous play. Jimmy was given the 49ers' most prestigious annual award, the Len Eshmont Award, twice (1969 and 1975). In 1977, his jersey number, 37, was retired by the 49ers. The ultimate honor finally came in 1994, when Jimmy was inducted into the Pro Football Hall of Fame. At the ceremonies held in Canton, Ohio, his brother Rafer introduced him. After retiring, Jimmy became active with the NFL Alumni chapter in Redwood City, California. He made public appearances in order to encourage young and old alike to be better people.

Summary

In addition to having outstanding speed, Jimmy Johnson had quiet determination and cool intensity. During his sixteen-year career with the San Francisco 49ers, he became one of the all-time great cornerbacks of professional football. Never outspoken, Jimmy let his skills on the playing field speak for him. Although he had a legend for an older brother, he did not let the comparisons get him down. A lesser man might have given up, but Jimmy was inspired by his brother's success. This inspiration helped Jimmy to a hall-of-fame career.

Jeffry Jensen

Additional Sources

MacCambridge, Michael. *America's Game: The Epic Story of How Pro Football Captured a Nation.* New York: Random House, 2004.

Massei, Craig. *Unofficial San Francisco 49ers Book of Lists.* Rochester, N.Y.: American Sports Media, 2002.

John Henry Johnson

Born: November 24, 1929
        Waterproof, Louisiana

Early Life

John Henry Johnson was born on November 24, 1929, in Waterproof, Louisiana, but his father, a Pullman porter, moved the family across the country to Pittsburg, California, near Oakland, when John Henry was still very young. John Henry was an

John Henry Johnson, who played in the NFL, the American Football League, and the Canadian Football League during a fourteen-year career. (Courtesy of Amateur Athletic Foundation of Los Angeles)

exceptional athlete at Pittsburg High School, earning twelve sports letters. In 1949, he set a California high school track and field record for the discus throw. In 1972, he was voted the East Bay Area High School Athlete of the Century by the *Oakland Tribune.*

As a football star, John Henry was recruited by many colleges, but he chose to stay close to home by attending St. Mary's College in nearby Moraga, California. St. Mary's was a small school, but the Gaels had a famous football heritage. The high point of John Henry's career there came in 1950, when his 84-yard kickoff return helped St. Mary's to tie the heavily favored University of Georgia. St. Mary's dropped its football program after the 1950 season. John Henry attended Modesto Junior College in California briefly and then entered Arizona State University, where he earned a degree in education in 1955. In 1952, his final year of football eligibility, he led all college players in punt returns.

The Road to Excellence

The Pittsburgh Steelers, perennial losers in the NFL, chose John Henry in the second round of the 1953 NFL draft, but he was unimpressed by either the team's record or contract offer. Instead, he accepted a considerably better offer of $11,000 from the Calgary Stampeders of the Canadian Football League (CFL). In 1953, as a rookie, John Henry earned the CFL most valuable player award. Although he led the league in no specific category, he rushed for 648 yards on 107 attempts, caught 33 passes for 365 yards, intercepted 5 passes, returned 47 punts and 20 kickoffs, completed 5 passes, and scored 8 touchdowns.

Impressed, the San Francisco 49ers of the NFL acquired the right to sign the young star. In 1954, John Henry joined the 49ers as the fourth man in a fabulous backfield. All four of the starters from that backfield have been enshrined in the Pro Football Hall of

Fame—fullback Joe Perry in 1969, halfback Hugh McElhenny in 1970, quarterback Y. A. Tittle in 1971, and John Henry in 1987.

John Henry rushed for 681 yards in his first year with San Francisco, but his primary duty was to block for the other three stars. Soon, he became known as the league's foremost blocking back, a reputation that continued throughout his career. At 6 feet 2 inches and 225 pounds, he was big enough to chop down hard-charging defensive ends, and his excellent speed allowed him to get out in front of his running mates to flatten downfield opponents. Good blocking takes more than size or speed, though. It takes an unselfish determination. John Henry enjoyed blocking for his teammates even more than he enjoyed running with the ball.

The Emerging Champion

Injuries spoiled John Henry's next two seasons. Additionally, like most NFL teams, the 49ers had gone to a backfield of only two runners with an extra pass receiver set wide; this reduced his playing time still further. In 1957, San Francisco traded John Henry to the Detroit Lions, who needed a strong fullback to protect quarterback Bobby Layne. The Lions and 49ers finished tied for the Western Division lead at season's end. John Henry was banged up and played only briefly in Detroit's playoff victory over San Francisco, but he was healthy for the NFL

Honors and Awards	
1953	Canadian Football League most valuable player
1955, 1963-65	NFL Pro Bowl Team
1987	Inducted into Pro Football Hall of Fame

Championship game and averaged five yards per carry as the Lions destroyed Cleveland, 59-14.

In both 1958 and 1959, John Henry was again slowed by injuries. Running backs are prone to injury, and, in general, their careers are shorter than those of other NFL players. The Lions, guessing John Henry was near the end, traded him away, but, in fact, his best years were still in front of him.

Continuing the Story

Ironically, John Henry was traded to Pittsburgh, the team he had refused to join in 1953. This time, the Steelers met his price. The Steelers of the early 1960's were never quite a championship team. During the six seasons John Henry played for them, they had only two winning seasons. Nevertheless, they were regarded around the league as a tough bunch of spoilers—the kind of team that always fought hard and left opponents bruised, if not beaten. Much of that distinction was the result of John Henry's fierce blocking and powerful running.

In 1962, he became the first Steeler and only the ninth NFL player to rush for more than 1,000 yards. Two years later, at the age of thirty-five, he again topped the 1,000-yard mark. No NFL runner past the age of thirty had ever gone more than 1,000 yards twice.

John Henry's best seasons came at a time when two other great fullbacks, Jim Brown of Cleveland and Jim Taylor of Green Bay, monopolized the all-NFL teams. Playing for a losing team like Pittsburgh, John Henry had no chance at those honors. However, he was recognized by his peers as a four-time Pro Bowl selection. After one last season with the Houston Oilers of the American Football League, in 1966, John Henry retired. At the time, he ranked as the fourth-leading all-time rusher in NFL history, with

NFL Statistics

		Rushing				Receiving			
Season	GP	Car.	Yds.	Avg.	TD	Rec.	Yds.	Avg.	TD
1954	12	129	681	5.3	9	28	183	6.5	0
1955	7	19	69	3.6	1	2	6	3.0	0
1956	12	80	301	3.8	2	8	90	11.3	0
1957	12	129	621	4.8	5	20	141	7.1	0
1958	9	56	254	4.5	0	7	60	8.6	0
1959	10	82	270	3.3	2	7	34	4.9	1
1960	12	118	621	5.3	2	12	112	9.3	1
1961	14	213	787	3.7	6	24	262	10.9	1
1962	14	251	1,141	4.5	7	32	226	7.1	2
1963	12	186	773	4.2	4	21	145	6.9	1
1964	14	235	1,048	4.5	7	17	69	4.1	1
1965	1	3	11	3.7	0	—	—	—	—
1966	14	70	226	3.2	3	8	150	18.8	0
Totals	143	1,571	6,803	4.2	48	186	1,478	8.2	7

Notes: GP = games played; Car. = carries; Yds. = yards; Avg. = average yards per carry *or* average yards per reception; TD = touchdowns; Rec. = receptions

7,451 yards. Although longer schedules and new rushing strategies have allowed many runners to move past him in the record books, John Henry did not drop off the "top 20" rushing list until the 1990 season.

Summary

After his retirement, John Henry Johnson worked in public relations and urban affairs in Pittsburgh, where he also founded an organization to aid disadvantaged youth, the John Henry Johnson Foundation. John Henry's rushing achievements are part of his statistical record and no doubt helped his election to the Pro Football Hall of Fame, but his unique ability as a blocker is what earned him the gratitude of his teammates and coaches. There are no statistics to show how many extra yards his fellow runners gained or how many sacks his quarterbacks were spared because of John Henry's mighty blocks.

Bob Carroll

Additional Sources

Carroll, Bob. *Total Football: The Official Encyclopedia of the National Football League.* New York: Harper-Collins, 1999.

McCullough, Bob. *My Greatest Day in Football: The Legends of Football Recount Their Greatest Moments.* New York: Thomas Dunne Books/St. Martin's Press, 2002.

Smith, Ron, and Dan Dierdorf. *Heroes of the Hall.* St. Louis: Sporting News, 2003.

Deacon Jones

Born: December 9, 1938
      Eatonville, Florida
Also known as: David D. Jones (full name);
  Secretary of Defense

Early Life
Mattie Jones gave birth to David D. Jones on December 9, 1938, in Eatonville, Florida. David grew up playing with his two brothers and five sisters. His father, Ishmael, worked as a carpenter and gardener at a time when such work was hard to find.

Deacon Jones, who is regarded as one of the finest defensive ends in NFL history. (Courtesy of Amateur Athletic Foundation of Los Angeles)

With so many children to feed, the family had a difficult time. However, all the Jones boys inherited their father's size and strength, and this came in handy on the football field, where all three boys became outstanding players. At Orlando Hungerford High School, David starred not only in football but also in basketball and track.

The Road to Excellence
After attending Mississippi Vocational College briefly, David enrolled in South Carolina State College. There he played football as a two-way tackle and picked up his nickname, "Deacon," for his habit of leading his football squad in prayer. Having achieved little fame in college football, Deacon did not appear to have much of a future as a professional player—especially since pro scouts rarely paid attention to black schools.

Luck was on Deacon's side, though. One day, two scouts from the Los Angeles Rams of the NFL were studying game films featuring two backs in whom they were interested. They noticed one big lineman who kept charging through to hinder the backs' progress—thus Deacon drew their attention. In 1961, the Rams drafted him in the 14th round and signed him without a bonus. Somehow, Deacon had made it to the NFL. Since the Rams had two talented ends already, Deacon played offensive tackle. In 1961, though, one of the ends, Gene Brito, came down with a fatal illness, so Deacon took over as defensive end.

Deacon got off to a slow start as a professional. When he arrived in Los Angeles, he was short on both skill and experience as a player. Once in the NFL, he found he often lacked stamina as well. To make things worse, he indulged his love of food and put on many extra pounds. By 1963, he weighed 290 pounds, and the Rams began to think of trading him. However, Deacon lost weight quickly, and his playing improved markedly. He also began to study old game films of the Baltimore Colts, watching the moves of the famous defensive end Gino Marchetti. Deacon was especially impressed by Marchetti's method of attack, and began to adopt that style in his own play.

The Emerging Champion

The result of Deacon's new style was superb. By 1964, he was in top form. He soon ranked with Marchetti as one of the greatest defensive ends in NFL history. In addition, Deacon had one skill Marchetti lacked: speed. In high school track, he had run the 100-yard dash in 9.7 seconds. With the Rams, he was so quick that it was hard for opponents to run around him, and his Marchetti-style attacks happened so fast that it was hard to block him. In fact, opposing teams resorted to assigning at least two men to him. Deacon also demonstrated his prowess at hard, clean tackling, and is credited with introducing the term "sack" to modern football. His prime asset was his pass rushing ability, which turned the Deacon into football's most feared defender. Soon he was playing alongside tackles Merlin Olsen and Rosey Grier and end Lamar Lundy as one of the Rams' "Fearsome Foursome"—one of pro football's greatest defensive lines ever. Together, the foursome brutalized opposing teams.

In the course of his eleven seasons with the Rams, the 6-foot 4-inch, 250-pound Deacon was named NFL defensive player of the year twice, in 1967 and 1968. He was also a unanimous all-NFL selection from 1965 to 1970. He played in 143 consecutive games for Los Angeles until he injured his leg in 1971. During those games, he compiled an impressive record, including his 1966 fifty-yard return of an intercepted pass. He also recovered at least twelve fumbles and scored safeties in 1965 and 1967. The Deacon, who was all-NFL from 1965-1970, played in eight Pro Bowls.

Continuing the Story

After his injury in 1971, Deacon was traded in a seven-player swap to the San Diego Chargers. After two years in San Diego, Deacon joined the Wash-

Honors and Awards	
1965-70	NFL All-Pro Team
1965-71, 1973	NFL Pro Bowl Team
1967-68	Halas Trophy
1968	Citizens Savings Southern California Athlete of the Year
1970	NFL All-Pro Team of the 1960's
1980	Inducted into Pro Football Hall of Fame
1985	*Los Angeles Times*' Most Valuable Ram of All Time
1991	Vince Lombardi Award
1994	NFL 75th Anniversary All-Time Team
1995	Inducted into the Black Sports Hall of Fame
1999	All-Madden Millennium Team
	Sports Illustrated's Defensive End of the Century
	Gale Sayers Lifetime Spirit Achievement Award
2000	NFL Millennium All-Time Team
2001	NFL Alumni Spirit Award
2005	*Pro Football Weekly*'s Greatest Ram of All Time

ington Redskins and played for the franchise until his retirement in 1974. Throughout his career, Deacon often played with injuries, sometimes hurting so badly that tears came to his eyes. While fans assumed that a big man like him did not suffer, he assured them that he did, and that he even cried at times. According to his wife, Iretha, Deacon was always an easy man to live with, pain or no pain—as long as his team won.

As Deacon's career was winding down, he started taking voice and acting lessons to prepare for an entertainment career. He cut several records and started a nightclub act called "Soul by a Pro, the Deacon Jones Revue." His greatest achievement, however, came in 1980, when he was inducted into the Pro Football Hall of Fame as one of the game's greatest defensive ends. He has received numerous other awards, including the Gale Sayers Lifetime Spirit Achievement Award (1999), the NFL Alumni Organization "Order of the Leather Helmet" (1999), and the Junior Seau Foundation Legend of the Year Award (2005).

Summary

Deacon Jones ranks with Gino Marchetti, Reggie White, and Bruce Smith, Carl Eller, and others as one of the greatest defensive ends in football history. Deacon teamed with other members of the Rams' "Fearsome Foursome" to form one of pro football's greatest defensive lines. Deacon's strength was his pass rushing ability, which made him one of football's most feared defenders.

Nicholas White

Additional Sources

Barber, Phil. "NFL: Football's One Hundred Greatest Players—The Hit Men." *The Sporting News* 223 (November 1, 1999): 12-16.

Conner, Floyd. *Football's Most Wanted: The Top Ten Book of the Great Game's Outrageous Charac... tunate Fumbles, and Other Oddities.* Washin... D.C.: Brassey's, 2000.

Jones, Deacon, and John Klawitter. *The Book of D... con: The Wit and Wisdom of Deacon Jones.* Sant... Ana, Calif.: Seven Locks Press, 2001.

Klawitter, John, and Deacon Jones. *Headslap: The Life and Times of Deacon Jones.* Amherst, N.Y.: Prometheus Books, 1996.

Lee Roy Jordan

Born: April 27, 1941
Excel, Alabama

Early Life

Lee Roy Jordan was shaped by his family and the community in which he lived. He was the last of four boys born to Walter and Cleo Jordan, who also had two daughters. Tragically, Lee Roy's parents lost one daughter to leukemia at the age of two. Lee Roy lived in the small, farming community of Excel, Alabama. According to Lee Roy, Excel was so small that the stoplights were replaced with a more energy-efficient blinking four-way light.

Lee Roy and his family lived on a farm outside of town that produced cotton, sugarcane, and vegetables. They also raised hogs, turkeys, cattle, and chickens for food and money. As a result, Lee Roy learned the value of hard work, like most children raised by parents who grew up during the Depression. The work ethic served him well on the football field. When Lee Roy was not doing his farm chores or riding steers for fun, he was watching his older brothers—Walter, Jr., Carl, and Ben—play football. Oftentimes, in order to have enough players with which to practice, he got to play with them.

The Road to Excellence

The practice time with his older brothers paid off when Lee Roy began playing football for the high school team. In fact, he started on the varsity squad while in the eighth grade. In his junior year of high school, when he grew 4 inches and added 30 pounds, college scouts began to notice, especially after he had a big game against a running back the University of Alabama was recruiting.

Lee Roy was excited about the prospect of playing with Paul "Bear" Bryant, the legendary Alabama football coach, who was known to be particularly adept at molding into champions "undersized" players who could hit and were not afraid to work hard. Lee Roy said football was like a day off compared to his hard work on the farm.

The Emerging Champion

Lee Roy began his career at the University of Alabama in 1959, as part of the second group of players recruited by Bryant. He played both center and linebacker for Alabama but enjoyed defense more than offense because he liked giving the hits rather than receiving them.

Freshman were not eligible to play, so Lee Roy did not take the field for the varsity until his sophomore year in 1960. He helped lead the Crimson Tide to an 8-2-1 record and a spot in the Bluebonnet Bowl. He was the most valuable player of that game, as Alabama and the University of Texas played to a 3-3 tie.

Then, in 1961, Lee Roy helped Alabama to an 11-0 record and a national championship. The team followed that season with a 10-1 record, losing to only Georgia Tech by a score of 7-6. At the end of that season, Alabama played the University of Oklahoma Sooners in the Orange Bowl, and Lee Roy had the biggest game of his outstanding collegiate career, making an unbelievable 31 tackles. Not surprisingly, he was named the most valuable player of the game.

As captain of the team, Lee Roy took part in the coin toss before the Orange Bowl game. President John F. Kennedy participated in the coin toss as well. Lee Roy kept the silver dollar as a memento of that game. He felt the contest had extra significance not

---

Dallas Cowboys Records

Most career tackles, 1,236
Most career solo tackles, 743

Honors and Awards

1960	Bluebonnet Bowl most valuable player
1963	First-team all-American
1966, 1968-69, 1973, 1975	NFL All-Pro
1967-69, 1973-74	NFL Pro Bowl
1980	Inducted into Alabama Sports Hall of Fame
1983	Inducted into College Football Hall of Fame
1988	Inducted into Senior Bowl Hall of Fame
1989	Inducted into Dallas Cowboys Ring of Honor

only because of the presence of the president but also because of the two storied football programs headed by two famous coaches, Bryant and Bud Wilkinson.

Lee Roy became one of the most decorated football players ever to play for the Crimson Tide of Alabama. He was an all-American for two years and placed fourth in the voting for the Heisman Trophy in 1962. He was named as Alabama's player of the decade for the 1960's and was also a member of its team of the century. He was elected to the National Football Foundation's College Football Hall of Fame and was chosen for ESPN's all-time college football team.

Bryant, in his autobiography, said he never had another player like Lee Roy. After Lee Roy left Alabama for the NFL, Coach Bryant began giving the "Lee Roy Jordan Headhunter Award" to the hardest hitter in spring practice.

Continuing the Story

Lee Roy continued to excel in the NFL. During his NFL career, he was a member of the Dallas Cowboys team that played in three Super Bowls, winning one in 1972, and five National Football Conference Championship games. He was a major part of the Cowboys' famed "Doomsday Defense" and an all-pro linebacker who played in five Pro Bowls. In 1976, he retired as the Cowboys' all-time leading tackler, a record that was not broken for twenty-seven years. He became the seventh member of the prestigious Dallas Cowboys Ring of Honor in 1989.

Gil Brandt, personnel director for the Dallas Cowboys, said he did not know of anyone more competitive than Lee Roy. Although Lee Roy was relatively small for his position at 6 feet 1 inch and 215 pounds, his competitiveness, intelligence, and tenacity compensated for his lack of size. He was also an excellent leader who demanded the most from himself and the people around him.

Summary

When he retired from playing football after fourteen seasons with the Cowboys, Lee Roy Jordan wanted to stay in football as a coach but discovered that the starting salary was not enough for someone who was raising a family. Instead of moving to the football sideline, he took his competitiveness and leadership into the business world. He purchased a lumber company in Dallas that he renamed the Lee Roy Jordan Lumber Company.

Many hardworking, successful folks have come from Excel, Alabama, but no one excelled on the football field like Lee Roy. He played for two of the most famous coaches of all time, Paul "Bear" Bryant and Tom Landry, and was a standout player on teams that won championships. As Coach Bryant said, "(Lee Roy) never had a bad day. He did everything an all-American football player should do, with class. He's one of the finest football players the world has ever seen."

Paul Finnicum

Additional Sources

Hicks, Tommy. *Game of My Life: Alabama—Memorable Stories of Crimson Tide Football.* Champaign, Ill.: Sports, 2006.

Scott, Richard. *Legends of Alabama Football.* Champaign, Ill.: Sports, 2004.

Taylor, Jean-Jacques. *Game of My Life: Dallas Cowboys—Memorable Stories of Cowboys Football.* Champaign, Ill.: Sports, 2006.

Sonny Jurgensen

Born: August 23, 1934
  Wilmington, North Carolina
Also known as: Christian Adolph Jurgensen III
  (full name)

Early Life

Christian Adolph "Sonny" Jurgensen III was born on August 23, 1934, in Wilmington, North Carolina, to Christian Adolph Jurgensen, Jr., and Lola Johnson Jurgensen. Sonny began playing sandlot football when he was in the sixth grade, but as a youth he excelled in all sports. He was both a football and basketball star at New Hanover High School in Wilmington, and he was considered by many to be the best high school basketball player in the state. He was also thought to be a Major League Baseball prospect as a catcher.

The Road to Excellence

Although Sonny was destined to become one of professional football's greatest passers, he threw the ball infrequently as a quarterback at Duke University, where he also played on the basketball team. Duke coach Bill Murray approved of passing only in third down and long yardage situations, and Sonny threw just six touchdown passes in three college seasons.

Although Sonny passed only fifty-nine times in his senior year, the Philadelphia Eagles of the NFL sent Charlie Ganer, an assistant coach, to Duke to assess Sonny's passing skills. After seeing Sonny throw for ten minutes, Ganer decided the Eagles should take a chance on the unproven quarterback, and Philadelphia picked him in the fourth round of the NFL draft. Sonny received a bachelor's degree in education from Duke in 1957.

Sonny shared the Eagles' quarterback duties with Bobby Thomason during his rookie season. Even though the team won three of the four games Sonny started, the Eagles decided to acquire a veteran quarterback, choosing Norm Van Brocklin from the Los Angeles Rams. Sonny's principal assignment for the next three years was holding the ball for the

placekicker. In 1960, the Eagles won the NFL championship, and Van Brocklin retired to become coach of the Minnesota Vikings.

The Emerging Champion

Finally given the chance to start in 1961, Sonny led the league in passes completed and touchdown passes, setting an NFL record for yards gained passing. The Eagles, however, finished second in the division that year and dropped to last place the next two seasons as Sonny and many of his teammates were hampered by injuries. Because the quarter-

Sonny Jurgensen, who passed for more than 30,000 yards in his career while playing for the Philadelphia Eagles and Washington Redskins. (Courtesy of Amateur Athletic Foundation of Los Angeles)

NFL Statistics

Season	GP	PA	PC	Pct.	Yds.	Avg.	TD	Int.
1957	10	70	33	.471	470	6.7	5	8
1958	2	22	12	.545	259	11.8	0	1
1959	1	5	3	.600	27	5.4	1	0
1960	5	44	24	.545	486	11.0	5	1
1961	14	416	235	.565	3,723	8.9	32	24
1962	14	366	196	.536	3,261	8.9	22	26
1963	9	184	99	.538	1,413	7.7	11	13
1964	14	385	207	.538	2,934	7.6	24	13
1965	13	356	190	.534	2,367	6.7	15	16
1966	14	436	254	.583	3,209	7.4	28	19
1967	14	508	288	.567	3,747	7.4	31	16
1968	12	292	167	.572	1,980	6.8	17	11
1969	14	442	274	.620	3,102	7.0	22	15
1970	14	337	202	.599	2,354	7.0	23	10
1971	3	28	16	.571	170	6.1	0	2
1972	4	59	39	.661	633	10.7	2	4
1973	8	145	87	.600	904	6.2	6	5
1974	7	167	107	.641	1,185	7.1	11	5
Totals	172	4,262	2,433	.571	32,224	7.8	255	189

Notes: GP = games played; PA = passes attempted; PC = passes completed; Pct. = percent completed; Yds. = yards; Avg. = average yards per attempt; TD = touchdowns; Int. = interceptions

candy bars and milk shakes and I like women and Scotch." NFL Commissioner Pete Rozelle fined Sonny $500 for that remark. With amazingly little speed and a potbelly, Sonny was an unathletic-looking quarterback. When asked about his weight, he replied that he threw with his arm, not his stomach.

In 1971, the Redskins' fortunes began to change when the defense-minded George Allen became coach. However, during Allen's tenure, Sonny was hampered by shoulder, knee, and Achilles tendon injuries. His wife joked that Sonny would not know what to do in January if he did not have to have another operation. Sonny's playing time was also limited by Allen's preference for the more balanced play of Sonny's close friend Billy Kilmer. When the Redskins lost to the Miami Dolphins 14-7 in Super Bowl VII following the 1972 season, Sonny watched from the sidelines with a ruptured tendon.

back had a reputation as a hard-drinking ladies' man, Sonny received much of the blame for his team's decline. In 1964, he was traded to the Washington Redskins for Norm Snead, a quarterback with a much quieter private life.

Sonny had some spectacular seasons with the Redskins. In 1967, he set NFL records—since broken—for passes attempted, passes completed, and yards gained passing, despite a painful calcium deposit in his throwing arm. The Redskins, with a weak running game and a mediocre defense, depended almost completely on Sonny's arm during his early years with the team.

Given the chance to play, Sonny proved that even as an aging, crippled quarterback he could still get the job done, as he completed more than 60 percent of his passes in each of his final three seasons. In 1974, his last year, forty-year-old Sonny came off the bench to complete twelve passes for two touchdowns in the fourth quarter of a come-from-behind victory over the Cincinnati Bengals. The next week, he completed six of seven passes in the closing minutes of a game against Miami to pull out another win.

Continuing the Story

In eighteen NFL seasons, Sonny played on only eight winning teams and was a full-time starter on only two of those. He had difficulty getting along with most of the eight coaches he played under because of his reputation as a playboy. This was especially true during the period between his divorce from his first wife in 1964 and his marriage to Margo Hunt in 1967. Of Otto Graham, the former great Cleveland Browns quarterback who coached Sonny at Washington from 1966 to 1968, Sonny said, "There's only one difference between Otto and me. He likes

After his retirement, Sonny worked as a sportscaster for CBS and for Washington, D.C., television and radio stations. He and Margo settled in Mount Vernon, Virginia. They have two sons, Erik and Gunnar, and Sonny has two older sons, Gregory and Scott, from his first marriage. Sonny later be-

Honors and Awards

1962, 1965, 1967-68, 1970	NFL Pro Bowl Team
1970	NFL All-Pro Team of the 1960's
1983	Inducted into Pro Football Hall of Fame

gan working alongside Sam Huff as a color commentator for Washington Redskins games' radio broadcasts in the Washington area.

Summary

Sonny Jurgensen led the NFL in passing yardage five times, in completions four times, in touchdown passes twice, and in percentage of passes completed once. He twice completed five touchdown passes in one game and passed for more than 400 yards in a game five times. More impressive than his statistics was his flamboyant, courageous, intelligent play. When reasonably healthy, Sonny knew no equal in combining accurate long and short passes, waiting until the last split second to release the ball, dissecting defenses, working against the clock, and rousing his team to play at its best. He was elected to the Pro Football Hall of Fame in 1983.

Michael Adams

Additional Sources

Hornung, Paul, and William F. Reed. *Lombardi and Me: Players, Coaches, and Colleagues Talk About the Man and the Myth.* Chicago: Triumph Books, 2006.

King, Peter. *Greatest Quarterbacks.* Des Moines, Iowa: Sports Illustrated Books, 1999.

Macnow, Glen, and Big Daddy Graham. *The Great Book of Philadelphia Sports Lists.* Philadelphia: Running Press, 2006.

Jim Kelly

Born: February 14, 1960
        Pittsburgh, Pennsylvania
Also known as: James Edward Kelly (full name)

Early Life

James Edward Kelly was born on February 14, 1960, in Pittsburgh, Pennsylvania, to Joe Kelly, a machinist, and his wife, Alice. Jim, the fourth of six boys, grew up in a close-knit and loving family. Though under constant financial duress, the sports-minded Kellys were hardly ever seen without bats, balls, or gloves.

Baseball was Jim's first passion. He was a Little League standout at the age of ten, and his strong arm inspired his father to dream that Jim would one day be a professional football player. During high school in his hometown of East Brady, a small Western Pennsylvania municipality, Jim starred in both football and basketball. Thanks to Jim's football talents, East Brady was undefeated from the middle of his sophomore year until his graduation. As a senior, Jim was named an all-conference punter, placekicker, safety, and quarterback and was chosen as league player of the year. Though heavily recruited by a number of major colleges, including such area powerhouses as the University of Pittsburgh and Pennsylvania State University, Jim decided to head south to the University of Miami.

The Road to Excellence

At Miami, Jim joined a losing program, but with new coach Howard Schnellenberger and quarterback coach Earl Morrall, a former NFL standout, Jim received first-class mentoring. He was soon guiding a resurgent Hurricane team that was winning with impressive consistency. In 1980, Jim helped Miami to the Peach Bowl. In his junior year, Jim paced the Hurricanes to a 9-2 season in which he completed 168 of 286 passes for 2,403 yards and 143 touchdowns. As a senior, although he spent much of the year on the bench with a separated shoulder, Jim was a Heisman Trophy candidate.

Upon his graduation with a degree in business management, Jim was a top NFL prospect. At 6 feet 3 inches and 215 pounds, with large hands, muscular legs, and a powerful arm, Jim was a near-perfect package in the quarterback-rich 1983 draft, which also included Dan Marino, John Elway, and Ken O'Brien. The NFL's Buffalo Bills made Jim the team's number-one draft selection. Jim was also the top choice of the Houston Gamblers of the United States Football League (USFL). Although Buffalo and the NFL were far more established, Jim opted for the Gamblers and its open-ended run-and-shoot offense.

The Emerging Champion

During an abbreviated two-year run, Jim and the Gamblers showcased breathtaking aerial displays.

Quarterback Jim Kelly lead the Buffalo Bills to four consecutive Super Bowls in the 1990's. (Tony Tomsic/NFL/ Getty Images)

In 1984, his first year, Jim threw for 5,219 yards and 44 touchdowns, both professional rookie records. On one afternoon in 1985, Jim led the Gamblers to a 34-33 triumph over the Los Angeles Express by passing for 5 touchdowns and 574 yards, thus surpassing Norm Van Brocklin's long-standing NFL mark of 554. In spite of missing the final four games of his second season as the result of injury, Jim led the USFL in passing yards, touchdowns, and completion percentage. In 1984, he was voted the USFL's most valuable player.

As the USFL's fiscal fate spun out of control, the debt-ridden Gamblers were amalgamated with Donald Trump's New Jersey Generals in 1986. Jim, though, never played a down as a General; in the summer of 1986, the USFL collapsed when it effectively lost its antimonopoly suit against the entrenched NFL. In the ensuing upheaval, Jim signed with the NFL's Buffalo Bills, who had drafted him in 1983. In contrast to a number of former USFL stars, Jim made the transition to the NFL with comparative ease. In 1986, his debut season with the Bills, Jim passed for 3,593 yards, the second-best mark in Buffalo history.

In 1987, 1988, and 1989, Jim continued to provide solid leadership for the stalwart Bills. With his working-class background, Jim proved to be a perfect fit for the blue-collar industrial town and its blue-collar football team. Like most great NFL quarterbacks, Jim also showed great self-confidence. Howard Schnellenberger, who coached Jim at Miami, once described the Buffalo signal-caller as cocky. Jim also proved that he was rugged, and his ability to absorb the poundings routinely meted out to professional quarterbacks earned him the respect of teammates, opponents, and fans alike.

Continuing the Story

With the acquisition of all-purpose running back Thurman Thomas in 1988, the Bills, a good team in the late 1980's, became a great team. Buffalo's no-huddle, run-and-gun offense soon emerged as one of the NFL's most feared attacks. In 1990, Jim became a member of the NFL's quarterbacking elite by leading the Bills to the Super Bowl, a game Buffalo lost to the New York Giants by the frustratingly slim margin of 20-19.

In 1991, Jim led the NFL with 33 touchdown passes, which, along with his 3,844 passing yards and six 300-yard games, earned him an all-pro selection. Although Buffalo won its second straight American Football Conference (AFC) championship, the Bills came up short again in the Super Bowl, losing to the Washington Redskins. In 1992, although his passing statistics slipped because of injuries, Jim nevertheless helped catapult Buffalo into its third consecutive Super Bowl, this time against the Dallas Cowboys. The loss was another disappointment, especially for Jim, who was forced to the sidelines in the second quarter with a sprained knee. In 1993, under the patient and steady guidance of head coach Marv Levy, Jim picked up the shattered dreams and paced Buffalo to its fourth consecutive AFC title. The Super Bowl result, though, was the same—a humiliating loss to the Cowboys, who repeated as Super Bowl champs.

During his last three seasons, 1994-1996, Jim passed for more than 9,000 yards. At the end of 1996, his last professional season, the Bills finished 10-6 and made the playoffs for the eighth time in nine seasons. They lost 30-27 to the Jacksonville Jaguars. Jim announced his retirement from professional football in January, 1997. Even though Jim and the Bills never won the Super Bowl, Jim had impressive post-season rankings. In the catego-

NFL Statistics

Season	GP	PA	PC	Pct.	Yds.	Avg.	TD	Int.
1986	16	480	285	59.4	3,593	7.49	22	17
1987	12	419	250	59.7	2,798	6.68	19	11
1988	16	452	269	59.5	3,380	7.48	15	17
1989	13	391	228	58.3	3,130	8.01	25	18
1990	14	346	219	63.3	2,829	8.18	24	9
1991	15	474	304	64.1	3,844	8.11	33	17
1992	16	462	269	58.2	3,457	7.48	23	19
1993	16	470	288	61.3	3,382	7.20	18	18
1994	14	448	285	63.6	3,114	6.95	22	17
1995	15	458	255	55.7	3,130	6.83	22	13
1996	13	379	222	58.6	2,810	7.41	14	19
Totals	160	4,779	2,874	60.1	35,467	7.42	237	175

Notes: GP = games played; PA = passes attempted; PC = passes completed; Pct. = percent completed; Yds. = yards; Avg. = average yards per attempt; TD = touchdowns; Int. = interceptions

ries of passing attempts (545), passing completions (322), and yards passing (3,863), Jim was second only to Joe Montana.

Through good times and bad, Jim remained remarkably poised, which was reflected in the fact that he was one of the few modern quarterbacks to call his own signals. An obvious vote of confidence by his coach, master strategist Marv Levy, such latitude was an indication of Jim's intelligence and grace under pressure.

Jim became the head of Kelly Enterprises, which has a diverse range of activities, including sports marketing in promotions, event management, and player representation. Jim's work includes the Kelly for Kids Foundation and Hunter's Hope, which have distributed more than $2 million for children's charities in Western New York. Hunter's Hope was founded because of Jim's son Hunter, who suffered from Krabbe disease and died in 2005. Jim also became involved with his noncontact instructional football camp, in which more than 7,500 campers have taken part. He was inducted into the Pro Football Hall of Fame in 2002.

Summary

Jim Kelly and the Buffalo Bills constituted one of the great yet vexing sagas of modern sports. They were winners who, paradoxically, were known as losers because of consecutive Super Bowl de-

Honors, Awards, and Milestones	
1984	*Sporting News* USFL Rookie of the Year
	USFL most valuable player
1985	*Sporting News* USFL All-Star Team
1987-88, 1990-92	NFL Pro Bowl Team
1991	NFL Pro Bowl most valuable player
1991-94	Only quarterback to start in both three-straight and four-straight Super Bowl games
2002	Inducted into Pro Football Hall of Fame
	Walter Camp Man of the Year Award
2007	Named an ACC Football Championship Legend

feats. However—like the stars of the old Brooklyn Dodgers, who so often came tantalizingly close to ultimate victory only to lose—Kelly and the Bills became folk heroes.

Chuck Berg

Additional Sources

Levy, Marv, and Jim Kelly. *Marv Levy: Where Else Would You Rather Be?* Champaign, Ill.: Sports, 2004.

Schultz, Randy. *Legends of the Buffalo Bills.* Champaign, Ill.: Sports, 2003.

Tasker, Steve, and Scott Pitoniak. *Steve Tasker's Tales from the Buffalo Bills.* Champaign, Ill.: Sports, 2006.

Nile Kinnick

Born: July 9, 1918
    Adel, Iowa
Died: June 2, 1943
    Gulf of Paria, near Venezuela
Also known as: Nile Clarke Kinnick, Jr. (full
    name); Ironman

Early Life
Nile Clarke Kinnick, Jr., began and ended his life during wartime. He was born in Adel, Iowa, on July 9, 1918, shortly before World War I ended; he died serving his country in World War II. He was the son of Nile Kinnick and Frances Clarke, farmers who were devoted to the teachings of Christian Science. His maternal grandfather, George W. Clarke, had

Nile Kinnick posing with his Heisman Trophy in 1939.
(AP/Wide World Photos)

served as governor of Iowa from 1912 to 1916. He had two younger brothers, Ben and George.

Nile began showing athletic prowess at a young age. When he was in the eighth grade, he caught balls thrown by a hard-throwing pitcher his own age from a neighboring town who was named Bob Feller—a future baseball hall of famer. As a sophomore at Adel High School, Nile led the football team to an unbeaten season and then scored 485 points for the basketball team. He was also, it became apparent to his family and friends, an unusually sensitive boy.

The Road to Excellence
Nile came of age during the tough Depression years of the 1930's, which hit midwestern farmers such as his parents especially hard. In 1934, deteriorating farm conditions forced his family off its farm and into nearby Omaha, Nebraska, where his father worked for the Federal Land Bank. Meanwhile, at Omaha's Benson High School, Nile earned all-state honors in both football and basketball and graduated as a straight-A student. He was a classic example of what would later be a scholar-athlete in college.

Torn between choosing the University of Iowa or the University of Minnesota after high school, he settled on Iowa. There he took up football, basketball, and baseball, but he eventually decided to concentrate on football and his studies. "The athlete," he wrote in his diary before his junior season,

> learns to evaluate—to evaluate between athletics and studies, between playing for fun and playing as a business, between playing clean and playing dirty, between being conventional and being true to one's convictions. He is facing the identical conditions which will confront him after college. . . . But how many football players realize this?

The Emerging Champion
When Nile joined Iowa's varsity football team in 1937, the school had won only six games in the Western Conference (later the Big Ten) since 1930. Under first-year coach Irl Tubbs, the 1937

squad failed to improve, winning only one of its eight games. Nile himself had an outstanding season, however, making the all-Western Conference team. He could run, pass, punt, and drop-kick field goals with facility.

During the 1938 season, he was hobbled with what was probably a broken ankle, and the team again finished with only 1 win, plus 1 tie and 7 losses. As a practicing Christian Scientist, he would not allow his ankle to be examined or treated by medical personnel. Only his teammates could see him wince in pain during each of his 41 punts. Despite his injury, his 41.1-yard average ranked him fourth in the nation in punting.

Continuing the Story

In 1939, everything finally came together for Nile on the football field, and he enjoyed a season that would later become legendary. Iowa's new coach, Eddie Anderson, had coached Holy Cross to a 47-7-4 record in six seasons, and he had been captain of Notre Dame's team under fabled coach Knute Rockne. Nile later recalled that Iowa had "lost so many games my first two years we just sort of got used to it. Dr. Anderson gave us that intensity we needed to win." Anderson also brought with him backfield coach Frank Carideo, an all-American quarterback under Rockne. Also skilled in punting and drop-kicking, Carideo worked with Nile on kicking before and after practices.

After sitting on the bench for part of Iowa's 41-0 opening-day win over South Dakota, Nile played all sixty minutes in every game that followed and became known as the Ironman. When Iowa defeated Notre Dame, 7-6, in 1939, he played a game that many consider his signature performance. After Nile switched to right halfback from his usual left halfback spot for one play, the sterling Notre Dame defense was caught unprepared, and he ran for Iowa's game-winning touchdown.

Iowa finished the 1939 season ranked ninth in the Associated Press poll with a 6-1-1 record. Nile had played a role in 16 of the team's 19 touchdowns, passing for 11 and rushing for 5. Thanks to his kicking chores, he had accounted for 107 of the team's 130 points on the season, and he played 402 of a possible 480 minutes.

In addition to his success on the grid-iron, Nile was elected senior-class president. When he graduated, his cumulative 3.4 grade-point average earned him membership in the Phi Beta Kappa honor fraternity, and he delivered the commencement speech for the class of 1940. Nile was the leading vote-getter in the nation for the annual college all-star game against the NFL champions. The Green Bay Packers won, 45-28, but Nile did not let down his fans, many of whom attended the game primarily because he was in it. He scored 2 touchdowns and drop-kicked 4 extra points. The all-stars scored all 4 touchdowns while he was in the game.

After the 1939 season, Nile won virtually every major award that intercollegiate football bestowed, including the Heisman Trophy, college football's most prestigious award. He also ruled over baseball's Joe DiMaggio, boxing great Joe Louis, and legendary golfer Byron Nelson as the Associated Press's male athlete of the year.

During the same 1939 autumn in which Nile excelled on the football field, Germany invaded Poland, launching World War II. After Nile graduated, he spent one year in law school and then enlisted in the Naval Air Reserve. On December 4, 1941, three days before Japan attacked Pearl Harbor, he was called to duty. He visited Adel one last time in 1942 and said goodbye to his greatest fan, his father, who would outlive both him and his athletic brother Ben by almost a half-century.

On June 2, 1943, Nile flew in a routine training flight from the deck of the carrier USS *Lexington*, which was sailing in the Caribbean Sea off the coast of Venezuela. Because his plane developed a serious oil leak, he was not allowed to land it on the carrier. Instead, he made what appeared to be a perfect, wheels-up landing in the water, as he was required to do. He appeared to exit his sinking

Honors and Awards

1939	Heisman Trophy
	Maxwell Award
	All-American
	Associated Press athlete of the year
1951	Inducted into Iowa Sports Hall of Fame
	Inducted into College Football Hall of Fame
1972	Nile Kinnick Stadium christened at University of Iowa
1989	Most valuable player, University of Iowa one hundredth anniversary team

plane safely, but the rescue party sent to the spot where his plane went done found no trace of him or his plane. He was never seen again.

Summary

Nile Kinnick, Jr., never played professional football, and he had only one truly great college season. Nevertheless, his name has become synonymous with greatness in college sports because of his versatility, drive, and stamina on the field and his all-around excellence in college life. An Iowa sportscaster summed up his accomplishments: "He proved that college sports could be beautiful. Everything that can be said that is good about college athletics he was. He did not represent it. He was it."

When the college football hall of fame formed in 1951, Nile was among its first inductees. In 1972, the University of Iowa renamed its football stadium after Nile in honor of its only Heisman Trophy winner. The face on the coin tossed by officials to start every Big Ten Conference game is that of Nile, who is also venerated for giving his life in the service of his country at a time when he could have chosen almost any future he desired.

Richard Hauer Costa

Additional Sources

Baender, Paul, ed. *A Hero Perished: The Diary and Selected Letters of Nile Kinnick.* Iowa City: University of Iowa Press, 1991.

Fimrite, Ron. "Nile Kinnick: An American Hero." *Sports Illustrated* (August 31, 1987): 116-125.

Pennington, Bill. *The Heisman: Great American Stories.* New York: ReganBooks, 2004.

Jerry Kramer

Born: January 23, 1926
    Jordan, Montana
Also known as: Gerald Louis Kramer (full name)

Early Life
Gerald Louis Kramer was born on January 23, 1926, in Jordan, Montana. His childhood was an unusually rough one; he injured himself often while playing or working on the farm. Once, while

Guard Jerry Kramer, who anchored the offensive line on a Green Bay Packers' team that won multiple NFL Championships and Super Bowls in the 1960's. (Courtesy of Amateur Athletic Foundation of Los Angeles)

hunting, his grandfather's shotgun accidentally discharged and wounded Jerry on his right side. For weeks no one knew if he would live. When he was five, he tried to chop wood, but somehow the heavy axe slipped and cut his chin and neck. Doctors had to work for hours to save his life.

Jerry had a remarkable talent for surviving. For much of his life, he tested this talent to the fullest. At the age of twelve, he fell out of a tree and badly hurt his back and arm. In high school, he backed into a woodworking lathe during a manual arts class. Jerry always recovered from his mishaps, though. Jerry's parents moved to Sand Point, Idaho, when he was a teenager. By then, he had grown into a burly, muscular boy.

The Road to Excellence
At Sand Point High School, Jerry became interested in playing football. For an accident-prone child, this might not have been the wisest choice of a sport to play. As if to spite his unlucky tendencies, Jerry became a star tackle for his team. Again, though, Jerry was severely injured, this time while chasing a calf during farmwork. He tripped on a board that cut him deeply in the groin and leg. Three weeks after the required surgery, the brave youngster was back on the field playing for his team. He continued to play so well that he was eventually named all-state tackle.

For this achievement, Jerry was offered a football scholarship by the University of Idaho, which he accepted. While at college, he excelled on the field, in spite of a neck injury that required more surgery. Then a 6-foot 3-inch player weighing 235 pounds, he became one of the finest collegiate linemen and kickers, earning renown as a superior guard on both offense and defense. When he graduated from college, Jerry had nowhere to go but up: into the perilous arena of big-league football. He believed in himself, and he did not listen to any advice about avoiding such a brutal career. When the NFL Green Bay Packers invited him to play for the team, he accepted.

The Emerging Champion

Jerry's first NFL season, 1958, was an extremely challenging one for him both physically and mentally, because his opponents were talented, powerful, and brutal. Somehow, Jerry withstood the blows and cruelty. He never quit, and he became a mighty blocker.

As a guard for the Green Bay Packers, Jerry was a powerful force. He was a strong blocker and a master at leading running plays through his opponents' defenses. In time, he also became the Packers' top kicker, setting a then Packers' kicking record: 16 field goals and 43 extra points, for a total of 91 points in one season. For twelve years, Jerry played triumphantly for the Packers, and helped them to six conference titles and five NFL championships. Furthermore, he was a crucial element in the Packers' triumphs in the first two Super Bowls.

Jerry's playing took its toll, though. By twenty-nine years of age, he had undergone a total of twenty-three operations, many of them for severe injuries. Jerry never let such things slow him down for long, though. While with the Packers, he had eight operations in one year alone. Once, he incurred a severe leg fracture that made physicians predict the end of his career, but Jerry had a bolt placed in his ankle to hold the bone in his broken leg in place. In that condition, he resumed his career as one of the fiercest offensive guards in pro football.

Continuing the Story

It seemed as though nothing could stop Jerry. Once, he suffered such a severe injury while playing with the Packers that he was close to death and was even pronounced dead on the operating table. The football world prepared to mourn him, but Jerry recovered and shocked everyone. Plans for his funeral were forgotten. Jerry went back on the field once again.

When he turned thirty-two years old, Jerry decided to quit professional football while he was still a winner. During the celebrations that marked his departure, a special tribute was made to him that

Honors and Awards	
1960, 1962-63, 1966-67	All-NFL Team
1963-64, 1968	NFL Pro Bowl Team
1970	NFL All-Pro Team of the 1960's

would have made any athlete envious: Jerry was heralded as the most courageous athlete who had ever played football, either collegiate or professional. Jerry left the game not only as a winner but also as an inspiration.

Later, he wrote the critically acclaimed books *Instant Replay: The Green Bay Diary of Jerry Kramer* (1968), which was rereleased in 2006, and *Distant Replay* (1985). He also edited *Lombardi: Winning Is the Only Thing* (1970). Two of his sons played football at the University of Idaho and one, Jordan, played in the NFL for the Tennessee Titans and the Atlanta Falcons.

Summary

Jerry Kramer was one of the finest offensive guards in football history. He led the Green Bay Packers to six conference titles, five NFL championships, and two Super Bowl victories. Because of his injury jinx, he was considered the most accident-prone player in football history, but because he never gave in or gave up, he was honored by many as football's most courageous player ever.

Nan White

Additional Sources

Hornung, Paul, and William F. Reed. *Lombardi and Me: Players, Coaches, and Colleagues Talk About the Man and the Myth.* Chicago: Triumph Books, 2006.

Kramer, Jerry. *Farewell to Football.* New York: Bantam, 1970.

_____. *Instant Replay: The Green Bay Diary of Jerry Kramer.* Reprint. New York: Doubleday, 2006.

MacCambridge, Michael. *America's Game: The Epic Story of How Pro Football Captured a Nation.* New York: Random House, 2004.

Jack Lambert

Born: July 8, 1952
     Mantua, Ohio
Also known as: John Harold Lambert (full name)

Early Life

John Harold Lambert was born on July 8, 1952, in Mantua, Ohio, thirty miles north of Canton, the home of the Pro Football Hall of Fame. Mantua was a town supported by small dairy farms and light industry. There, Jack grew up, spending his summers driving a tractor and baling hay on his grandfather's farm.

Jack was a blond and wide-shouldered youth who soon developed farm-boy strength. He was disgusted when one Easter his mother had him dress in a bunny outfit to help deliver flowers for her flower shop. Jack inherited his tough nature from his father, a store detective in Cleveland and a former boxer who fought under the name of Johnny Lemons. When Jack was two years old, though, his parents divorced, and from then on he spent only weekends with his father. However, much of their time together was spent playing ball.

The Road to Excellence

By the time Jack had graduated from Crestwood High School, he had earned nine letters in basketball, baseball, and football. He was an intense player, but somehow he never lost his temper. If a referee made a call he did not like, he never got mad, but rather became quiet, holding the ball an extra second before throwing it back to the referee.

Jack was also rather skinny for a football player. Nevertheless, when he enrolled at Kent State University, he was chosen to play defensive end as a freshman. In subsequent years, he played middle linebacker. He played well, too. As a junior in 1972, he was named Mid-American Conference (MAC) player of the year, as well as most valuable player in the postseason Tangerine Bowl. The following year, he played in both the North-South all-star game and the All-American Bowl. He was chosen to the all-

MAC first team in both his junior and senior years.

By then, Jack weighed 215 pounds and stood 6 feet 4 inches tall. He was a few pounds lighter than the ideal middle linebacker, but he made up for it with his vicious tackling and competitiveness—perfect qualities for the tough-guy position of middle linebacker. Still, Jack never played dirty as long as the other guy played fair.

The Emerging Champion

In 1974, the Pittsburgh Steelers selected Jack in the second round of the NFL draft. The Steelers had sized him up accurately: intense, great nose for the ball, needs to add weight. The team soon found out what an excellent choice it had made. In his first

Jack Lambert, who was one of the leaders for the Pittsburgh Steelers' "Steel Curtain" defense. (Michael Fabus, courtesy of Pittsburgh Steelers)

season, Jack made every NFL all-rookie team and was chosen as the NFL's defensive rookie of the year. At the Steelers' Super Bowl victory that year, Jack was the team's only rookie starter. The following year, Jack made unanimous all-NFL and was named to the Pro Bowl for the first of nine consecutive times.

When Jack joined the Steelers, the team was just reaching its peak of greatness. Jack played along with talented men like Jack Ham, Andy Russell, and Ray Nitschke, and before long he stood out as one of the top players at his position in the history of football. His techniques were perfect. He was an intelligent, businesslike leader, calling the defensive signals. His productivity and determination were exceptional, even when he was in considerable pain. What set Jack apart, however, was his remarkable ability to defend against the pass. That talent made him a central figure in the Pittsburgh Steelers' famous "Steel Curtain" defense of the 1970's. The Steel Curtain so dominated opponents that teams sometimes simply gave up trying to run the ball against Jack and his cohorts. Helped by a ferocious defense, the Steelers won four Super Bowl titles during Jack's career.

By 1983, Jack had earned more awards than any other linebacker of his era. He was the NFL's top defensive player in 1976 and 1979, and was named the Steelers' most valuable player in 1981. As the defensive captain for eight years, he led his team in tackles from 1974 to 1983.

Continuing the Story

Because he was somewhat small for a linebacker, Jack found that he had to work extra hard. His aggressive, hyperactive playing style soon gave him an image that did not appeal to him, however. Fans loved him as a gap-toothed, snarling guy who played mean. Certainly, rival quarterbacks were intimidated by Jack's menacing intensity, which often left them in pain. When he hit hard, he felt he was only playing aggressively, the way the game was meant to be played. He insisted he never played dirty—unless, of course, the other player did first. Nevertheless, he began to be known as "Count Dracula in cleats" and "the pro from Pittsburgh, Transylvania."

Off the field, Jack was quite the opposite: a quiet, private bachelor with a love for fishing and an avid bird-watcher who once worked as a deputy game warden. He settled in an exclusive Pittsburgh suburb on an eighty-five-acre farm forty miles from town in Armstrong County. When he retired in 1985 after severely injuring his big toe, he visited military bases in the Far East and Europe along with other NFL players. He got involved in charity work, including the Ronald McDonald House in Pittsburgh. He was named to the NFL's all-decade teams for both the 1970's and the 1980's. His alma mater Crestwood High School renamed its stadium in his honor.

Summary

Jack Lambert, one of football's finest linebackers, was a central figure in the Pittsburgh Steelers' famous "Steel Curtain" defense of the 1970's. Jack's on-field ferocity, coupled with his impressive physical skills, made him one of the top defenders in the NFL and helped to make his team perennial champions.

Nicholas White

Additional Sources

Chastain, Bill. *Steel Dynasty: The Team That Changed the NFL.* Chicago: Triumph Books, 2005.

Rand, Jonathan, and Mike Singletary. *Riddell Presents the Gridiron's Greatest Linebackers.* Champaign, Ill.: Sports, 2003.

Rotunno, Ron. *Jack Lambert, Tough as Steel: Arguably America's Best Middle-Linebacker Ever!* 2d ed. New Wilmington, Pa.: Son-Rise, 2002.

Smith, Ron, and Dan Dierdorf. *Heroes of the Hall.* St. Louis: Sporting News, 2003.

Honors and Awards

1973	Tangerine Bowl Game most valuable player
	Mid-American Conference Player of the Year
1973-74	All-Mid-American Conference Team
1974	North-South Bowl All-Star Team
	All-American Bowl All-Star Team
	NFL Defensive Rookie of the Year
	NFL All-Rookie Team
1974-84	NFL All-Pro Team
1975-76, 1978-79	*Sporting News* AFC All-Star Team
1976	Associated Press Defensive Player of the Year
	Seagram's Seven Crowns of Sports Award
1976-84	NFL Pro Bowl Team
1976, 1979	Halas Trophy (1976 corecipient)
1981, 1983	*Sporting News* NFL All-Star Team
1985	AFL-NFL 1960-84 All-Star Team
1990	Inducted into Pro Football Hall of Fame

Dick "Night Train" Lane

Born: April 16, 1928
   Austin, Texas
Died: January 29, 2002
   Austin, Texas
Also known as: Richard Lane (full name); Night Train

Early Life
Richard Lane was born on April 16, 1928, in Austin, the capital of Texas. Located in the center of the state, at that time Austin was a small city where

Cornerback Dick Lane, who set the record for most interceptions in a season, with 14, in 1952. (NFL/Getty Images)

oilmen, cattle ranchers, and politicians rubbed elbows with students from the University of Texas, which was located only a short distance from the capital.

Growing up in Austin during the 1930's was difficult for Dick because he was poor and black. During the Depression, finding work was difficult for African Americans in Texas. His mother left him with a foster mother when he was very young. Dick had to attend segregated black schools. While he dreamed of playing for the University of Texas Longhorns, the dream could not come true, because Texas did not allow black students to attend white colleges.

The Road to Excellence
When Dick began to play sports at Austin's Anderson High School, he was an immediate star on both the football and basketball teams. As an end in football, he led Anderson to the state football championship finals for black high schools and was named to the all-state team. Though only 6 feet 1 inch tall, he played center on the basketball team and was also named to the all-state basketball team.

When Dick's foster mother died following his junior year in high school, Dick moved to Scotts Bluff, Nebraska, to live with his biological mother. Instead of going to high school, Dick enrolled at Scotts Bluff Junior College, where he could finish high school and begin college at the same time. He played on the football team and was so successful that he was named to some 1947 junior college all-American teams. He had trouble at home with his mother, however, and at the end of the football season he joined the U.S. Army.

253

Honors, Awards, and Records

1947	Junior College All-American
1952	NFL record for the most interceptions in a season, 14
1955-57, 1959, 1961-63	NFL Pro Bowl Team
1956, 1960-63	NFL All-Pro Team
1963	NFL All-Pro Team of the 1950's
1969	All-Time NFL Team
1974	Inducted into Pro Football Hall of Fame

While in the U.S. Army, Dick played three seasons for the Fort Ord base team. In 1951, he caught eighteen touchdown passes for Ord against a schedule of army teams and some colleges.

The Emerging Champion

In the summer of 1952, Dick got a tryout with the NFL champion Los Angeles Rams. His chances of making the team were poor, because he was too small to play defensive end, and the Rams were loaded with such outstanding offensive ends as Tom Fears, Bob Carey, and Elroy "Crazylegs" Hirsch. Dick was tried at defensive back, where he was an immediate success because of his excellent pass-catching ability, his speed, and his toughness.

Dick got his nickname during the 1952 preseason camp. "Night Train," by Buddy Morrow, was a popular song that summer. The song was a favorite of Tom Fears, the great Ram end, to whom Dick often went for advice. Teammates began to associate Dick's constant visits to Fears's room, and the fact that he was African American, with the song. The name stuck. In a 1990 interview, Dick said he was unsure if he liked the name, adding,

> But in a preseason game against Washington we handled their star Charlie "Choo Choo" Justice pretty well. The next day a headline said something like "Night Train derails Choo Choo." After that I knew I had a name for life.

From the first game of the season, Night Train was the starting cornerback, but the Rams lost their first game 37-7 to the Cleveland Browns and proceeded to lose three of their first four games. Night Train took many chances early in the season and led the league in interceptions, but he also gave up many touchdowns.

The Rams turned the corner in the fifth game of the season. With the Rams ahead of the Chicago

Bears only 10-7, Night Train intercepted a Bear pass on the 35-yard line and returned it to the 4-yard line. The Rams scored easily and went on to beat the Bears 31-7.

The Rams then proceeded to win the next seven games to tie for the league championship with the Detroit Lions at nine wins and three losses. Night Train continued to intercept passes at a record rate. By the end of the season he had established a league record of fourteen interceptions. He had an unbelievable season for a rookie, particularly for someone who had played only one year of college football. In 1954, Night Train was traded to the Chicago Cardinals. He led the league again with ten interceptions.

Continuing the Story

After the 1954 season, Night Train never led the NFL in interceptions again. Most teams realized how strong he was at intercepting passes and would not throw in the area he covered. The Cardinals occasionally used Night Train on offense as a receiver; in 1955, he caught a ninety-seven-yard touchdown pass. The next year he caught one pass for a seventy-five-yard gain.

In 1960, at the age of thirty-two, Night Train was traded from the lowly Cardinals to the Detroit Lions, a power in the Western Conference. Defense was the Lions' strength. Night Train, with his excellent speed and size for a defensive back, helped make Detroit's pass defense solid. In addition, he was a good tackler, using the ring-neck tackle—tackling high around the neck and riding the ball carrier down.

From 1960 through 1962, the Lions, with players like Alex Karras, Roger Brown, Yale Lary, and Night Train Lane, had excellent teams, but each season they finished second in the NFL's Western Conference to the great Green Bay Packer teams coached by the legendary Vince Lombardi.

Night Train was named to the all-pro team and to the Pro Bowl game each of those seasons. After 1963, though, age and bad knees caught up with him, and he retired at the age of thirty-seven following the 1965 season. Night Train received many honors after his retirement, including selection to the NFL all-pro team of the 1950's. His highest honor, though, came in 1974, when he was inducted into the Pro Football Hall of Fame. Night

Train settled in Detroit after his retirement and worked as the executive director of the Detroit Police Athletic League. He died in 2002.

Summary

Despite childhood poverty and little college football experience, Dick "Night Train" Lane had an unbelievable rookie season with the Los Angeles Rams in 1952. He not only made the team but also established an NFL record of fourteen interceptions. He continued as a defensive star for fourteen seasons and had sixty-eight career interceptions.

Dick remains the player against whom other defensive backs are measured.

C. Robert Barnett

Additional Sources

Carroll, Bob. *Total Football: The Official Encyclopedia of the National Football League.* New York: HarperCollins, 1999.

Reynolds, Neil. *Pain Gang: Pro Football's Fifty Toughest Players.* Washington, D.C.: Potomac, 2006.

Sharp, Drew, and Terry Foster. *Great Detroit Sports Debates.* Champaign, Ill.: Sports, 2006.

Steve Largent

Born: September 28, 1954
Tulsa, Oklahoma
Also known as: Steven Michael Largent (full
name)

Early Life
Born on September 28, 1954, in Tulsa, Oklahoma,
Steven Michael Largent knew a childhood of hurt,
insecurity, and loss. When he was six years old, his
father, Jim, left the family and later divorced Steve's
mother, Sue. When Steve was nine, his mother remarried.

Steve's stepfather, John Cargill, was an electri-
cian with the Federal Aviation Administration, a
job that required him to move his new family of
four sons several times in the next two years. These
were years of turmoil and unhappiness for young
Steve and his brothers.

Steve got into some minor trouble in school,
and his mother and stepfather suggested that he
try out for the football team as a way of gaining
some discipline in his life. Not fast enough to be a
running back, he tried out as a wide receiver. His
coach at Putnam City High School in Oklahoma
City recognized that, with hard work, Steve could
become a good pass catcher.

Meanwhile, Steve's family life continued to get
worse. His stepfather drank heavily, and Steve's
mother called on Steve to be the peacemaker, quite
a responsibility for a tenth-grader. Eventually, his
mother and stepfather divorced, but by that time,
Steve had found real familial warmth at the home
of his girlfriend and future wife, Terry Bullock. She
became his biggest fan and his best friend, and he
credits her for providing him with the stability and
confidence he needed to turn his life around.

The Road to Excellence
On the football field, Steve proved himself willing
to dive for "uncatchable" balls and able somehow
to grab them before they hit the dirt. He developed
into an all-state football player. One of his high
school teammates was Pat Ryan, later a quarterback for the New York Jets. Steve was also an all-
state catcher for the Putnam High Pirates baseball
team, and was a teammate of pitcher Bob Shirley,
later a New York Yankee.

Even though he made all-state in two sports,
Steve did not attract a lot of attention from college
recruiters, most of whom considered him too short
at 5 feet 11 inches, too light at 190 pounds, and too
slow to make their teams. The University of Tulsa,
however, took a chance and offered him a football
scholarship; he started for the team in his freshman year. Tulsa was rewarded for its faith in Steve
when he led the nation in touchdown receptions in
both his junior and senior years. He was named a
second-team all-American by the Associated Press
in 1975 and was a two-time all-Missouri Valley Conference selection.

Steve pushed himself not only on the gridiron
but also in the classroom. There, too, he was successful. In 1976, Steve graduated with a degree in
biology and was chosen by the university's alumni
board as one of the school's top eight seniors.

The Emerging Champion
In spite of Steve's hard work, it seemed unlikely he
would be an early-round draft choice for the NFL.
No one realized just what a good prospect he was.
Steve was not chosen until the fourth round of the

NFL Statistics

Season	GP	Rec.	Yds.	Avg.	TD
1976	14	54	705	13.1	4
1977	14	33	643	19.5	10
1978	16	71	1,168	16.5	8
1979	15	66	1,237	18.7	9
1980	16	66	1,064	16.1	6
1981	16	75	1,224	16.3	9
1982	8	34	493	14.5	3
1983	15	72	1,074	14.9	11
1984	16	74	1,164	15.7	12
1985	16	79	1,287	16.3	6
1986	16	70	1,070	15.3	9
1987	13	58	912	15.7	8
1988	15	39	645	16.5	2
1989	10	28	403	14.4	3
Totals	200	819	13,089	16.0	100

Notes: GP = games played; Rec. = receptions; Yds. = yards; Avg. =
average yards per reception; TD = touchdowns

draft. The Houston Oilers drafted him but did not see Steve's potential. The Oilers waived him on August 24, 1976.

Jerry Rhome, a coach at Tulsa who had moved on to the Seattle Seahawks, urged the Seattle management to give Steve a real chance to prove himself. The Oilers recalled him so that they could trade him to the Seahawks for an eighth-round draft choice in 1977. These negotiations took just two days. The Oilers used that 1977 draft choice to select Steve Davis from the University of Georgia, while the Seahawks acquired a future all-pro and hall-of-famer.

Steve's first day at camp was not a good one. Overanxious and tired, he dropped nearly every ball that came his way. The next day, with his confidence given needed support by Coach Rhome, he showed his true worth, and two weeks later he came off the bench to make an almost miraculous catch.

Continuing the Story

Steve made miraculous catches for fourteen years with the Seahawks. In 1990, his brilliant career ended with a lengthy list of team and league records. Durable and tenacious, Steve missed only ten games in his career because of injury, including six in 1989 with a broken elbow. Other injuries to his knee, thumb, foot, and wrist kept him out of single games.

Always the overachiever, with average size and speed, Steve showed that hard work and intelligence can compensate for limited natural talent. For his first twelve seasons, Steve led the Seahawks in both receptions and yards. At the time of his retirement, he had played in more games (200) with more starts (197) than any other player in team history and finished second in career scoring with 100 touchdowns. As a mark of their respect for his annual accomplishments, his teammates voted him the Seahawks' most valuable player after the 1977, 1979, 1981, 1985, and 1987 seasons. In 1978, he became the first Seahawks player ever elected to the Pro Bowl and had five receptions, including one for a touchdown. He returned to the Pro Bowl six other times in his career.

NFL Records *(Since broken)*

Most touchdown catches, 100
Most catches, 819
Most seasons with at least 50 catches, 10
Most receiving yards, 13,089
Most seasons with at least 1,000 receiving yards, 8

Honors and Awards

1975	Associated Press All-American
1975-76	All-Missouri Valley Conference Team
1976	Associated Press All-Rookie Team
	United Press International All-Rookie Team
1978	*Sporting News* All-AFC Team
1978-79, 1985, 1987	Associated Press All-NFL Team
1978-82, 1984-87	United Press International All-AFC Team
1978, 1985-87	Newspaper Enterprise Association All-NFL Team
1979-80, 1982, 1985-88	NFL Pro Bowl Team
1979, 1985	*Sports Illustrated* All-NFL Team
1980-81, 1985	*College and Pro Football Weekly* All-AFC Team
1983	*Sporting News* All-NFL Team
1984	*Pro Football Weekly* All-Over 30 NFL Team
1985-87	Professional Football Writers of America All-NFL Team
	Football News All-AFC Team
1987	*Pro Football Weekly* All-AFC Team
1988	Traveler's NFL Man of the Year
	Bart Starr Award
1989	United States Jaycees Ten Outstanding Young Americans
1995	Inducted into Pro Football Hall of Fame

Although impressive, Steve's team statistics tell only half the story. The man many thought too fragile, too short, and too slow set six league career records: most receptions (819), yards (13,089), touchdowns (100), consecutive games with a reception (177), 50-catch seasons (10), and 1,000-yard seasons (8). Joining Green Bay's Don Hutson, Steve became only the second person in NFL history to have the career lead in receptions, yards, and touchdowns all at the same time. When he retired, he also ranked third of all time with forty career 100-yard games, sixth in total touchdowns with 100, and eighth in combined yards with 13,397. Accordingly, on July 29, 1995, Steve was inducted into the Pro Football Hall of Fame.

Along the way, Steve became a role model for youth and adults alike. Aside from his gridiron exploits, he is known for his commitment to the community and for his genuine concern for the ill and less fortunate. Active in the Fellowship of Christian

Athletes and Pro Athletes Outreach, Steve practices what he preaches. He has been involved with a number of charitable organizations, including the United Way, Children's Hospital, United Cerebral Palsy, the March of Dimes, and the Spina Bifida Foundation. In 1988, in recognition for his charitable work, he was voted Traveler's NFL man of the year and received the inaugural Bart Starr Award. In 1989, the United States Junior Chamber of Commerce (Jaycees) chose him as one of its Ten Outstanding Young Americans.

Steve was elected to Congress, representing the First Congressional District of Oklahoma, on November 1, 1994, and continued to serve for three terms. In 2002, he resigned from his Congressional position to run for Governor of Oklahoma. He lost narrowly to Brad Henry. Steve also served on the advisory board of the Tulsa area Salvation Army and on the board of trustees of Tulsa University. He and his wife, Terry, had a daughter, Casle, and three sons: Kyle, Kelly, and Kramer.

Summary

Steve Largent refused to believe the scouts and coaches who called his football skills lackluster, average, or insignificant. One of the best pass receivers ever to play the game, Steve was also one of its most popular players. At first glance, he may have appeared an unlikely superstar, but his career demonstrated that for a man with spirit and pride, there are no limits on potential.

William U. Eiland

Additional Sources

Cluff, Chris. *The Good, the Bad, and the Ugly Seattle Seahawks.* Chicago: Triumph Books, 2007.

McCullough, Bob. *My Greatest Day in Football: The Legends of Football Recount Their Greatest Moments.* New York: Thomas Dunne Books/St. Martin's Press, 2002.

Raible, Steve, and Mike Sando. *Steve Raible's Tales from the Seahawks Sideline.* Champaign, Ill.: Sports, 2004.

Bobby Layne

Born: December 19, 1926
   Santa Anna, Texas
Died: December 1, 1986
   Lubbock, Texas
Also known as: Robert Lawrence Layne (full
   name)

Early Life

Robert Lawrence Layne was born on December 19, 1926, in Santa Anna, Texas. He spent his early childhood playing in the streets of his small hometown. His life became difficult at a very early age. When he was six years old, his father died. Bobby was distraught. He was packed up and hurriedly sent off to live with an aunt and uncle in Fort Worth, Texas. Bobby hardly even knew them.

Eventually, Bobby and his new family moved to Dallas, Texas. In high school, he became a baseball pitcher. He practiced until he was so good that he won an athletic scholarship to the University of Texas. On the university's team, Bobby's was like a good luck charm: The team never lost a game while he was there. In fact, Bobby Layne pitched and won twenty-six games, including three no-hitters.

The Road to Excellence

When Bobby turned his attention seriously to football, he was successful almost from the start. The first team he played for was the University of Texas Longhorns. He led the Longhorns to twenty-eight victories out of thirty-four games he played. His rare quality of leadership came to the fore during those games. It seemed like any team that he directed would become a winner. Bobby was becoming a Texas hero.

However, Bobby had another side to his nature. He was known for partying and staying up late. His need for only five hours of sleep each night, and his controversial lifestyle caused some to nickname him the "Gadabout Gladiator."

After his stint with the Longhorns, Bobby was drafted by the Pittsburgh Steelers of the NFL and then was traded instantly to the Chicago Bears. Then the Bears decided that they did not need Bobby after all. When at last Bobby was sent off to

join the New York Bulldogs, a team with relatively low status in the hierarchy of professional football teams, he must have felt somewhat homeless and unwanted—the way he did when, at six years of age, he was sent to live with his relatives.

Bobby gave the Bulldogs everything he had as a player, but somehow the team rarely won a game. Before long, Bobby was so disheartened that he began to think of quitting football altogether.

The Emerging Champion

Bobby changed his mind when the Bulldogs suddenly traded him to the Detroit Lions. Even though the Lions were losing games steadily, and were yet to discover Bobby's potential, Bobby's spirits picked up. Finally he became the Lion's top quarterback. As a result, the team finished the season at the top of the division with a 9-3 record, tying with the Los Angeles Rams. The Lions beat the Rams 31-21 during the playoffs. Next, Detroit was matched against

Quarterback Bobby Layne, who played fifteen seasons in the NFL and set numerous passing records. (Courtesy of Amateur Athletic Foundation of Los Angeles)

Honors and Awards

1947	College All-American
1952-54, 1957, 1960	NFL Pro Bowl Team
1954, 1956, 1958	NFL All-Pro Team
1956	Inducted into College Football Hall of Fame
	Inducted into Michigan Sports Hall of Fame
1963	NFL All-Pro Team of the 1950's
1967	Inducted into Pro Football Hall of Fame
	Uniform number 22 retired by Detroit Lions

the seemingly invincible Cleveland Browns. Bobby led the Lions to a 17-7 victory—the first championship for the franchise in seventeen years.

The following year, Bobby's remarkable play-calling ability once more enabled his team to claim the conference championship. Again, the Lions faced the Browns in the title game and beat them. In all, the Texan quarterback led his team to three conference championships and two NFL titles.

Continuing the Story

The key to Bobby's success was his innate leadership ability. He believed that winning resulted when teammates believed in their leader. From his days of playing baseball through his professional career in football, Bobby made winners out of his teams.

The injuries Bobby had received over the years took their toll, though. In the late 1950's, he began to slow down. He was no longer his old triumphant self on the field. When he turned thirty-two, the Lions traded him to the Pittsburgh Steelers.

People wondered if Bobby would ever again play as he had earlier. When he joined the Steelers in 1958, they were already stuck in a losing streak. It took some time to turn things around, but Bobby called on his talents as a leader. Eventually he inspired his teammates to believe not only in him but also in themselves— as a result they won five consecutive games that season. It had been sixteen years since the Steelers had done so well.

Bobby played for the Steelers until 1962. Then, when he was thirty-five years old, he decided to retire to Lubbock, Texas. He was inducted into the Michigan and Pennsylvania Sports Halls of Fame, as well as the National Football Foundation's College Football Hall of Fame. In 1967, he was enshrined in the Pro Football Hall of Fame as one of the finest quarterbacks ever. Bobby's years of hard living exacted their price, though, and he died on December 1, 1986, in Lubbock.

Summary

Bobby Layne was a brilliant quarterback whose leadership guided the Detroit Lions to four conference titles and three NFL crowns. Bobby played in three Pro Bowls and was named to three all-pro teams. When he retired, he held many of the NFL's passing records, and he is remembered as one of the most spectacular quarterbacks of the 1950's.

Nan White

Additional Sources

King, Peter. *Greatest Quarterbacks*. Des Moines, Iowa: Sports Illustrated Books, 1999.

MacCambridge, Michael. *America's Game: The Epic Story of How Pro Football Captured a Nation*. New York: Random House, 2004.

St. John, Bob. *Heart of a Lion: The Wild and Woolly Life of Bobby Layne*. Dallas, Tex.: Taylor, 1991.

Smith, Ron, and Dan Dierdorf. *Heroes of the Hall*. St. Louis: Sporting News, 2003.

NFL Statistics

Season	GP	PA	PC	Pct.	Yds.	Avg.	TD	Int.
1948	11	52	16	.308	232	4.5	3	2
1949	12	299	155	.518	1,796	6.0	9	18
1950	12	336	152	.452	2,323	6.9	16	18
1951	12	332	152	.458	2,403	7.2	26	23
1952	12	287	139	.484	1,999	7.0	19	20
1953	12	273	125	.458	2,088	7.6	16	21
1954	12	246	135	.549	1,818	7.4	14	12
1955	12	270	143	.530	1,830	6.8	11	17
1956	12	244	129	.529	1,909	7.8	9	17
1957	11	179	87	.486	1,169	6.5	6	12
1958	12	294	145	.493	2,510	8.5	14	12
1959	12	297	142	.478	1,986	6.7	20	21
1960	12	209	103	.493	1,814	8.7	13	17
1961	8	149	75	.503	1,205	8.1	11	16
1962	13	233	116	.498	1,686	7.2	9	17
Totals	175	3,700	1,814	.490	26,768	7.2	196	243

Notes: GP = games played; PA = passes attempted; PC = passes completed; Pct. = percent completed; Yds. = yards; Avg. = average yards per attempt; TD = touchdowns; Int. = interceptions

Jamal Lewis

Born: August 26, 1979
Atlanta, Georgia
Also known as: Jamal Lafitte Lewis (full name);
the Beast

Early Life

Jamal Lafitte Lewis was born in Atlanta, Georgia, on August 26, 1979. His father, a former high school quarterback, began training Jamal and his

Running back Jamal Lewis high stepping Buffalo Bills defenders in a 2008 game. (John Kuntz/The Plain Dealer/Landov)

older brother, John, Jr., to excel at football from an early age. Jamal's brother was a star running back at Frederick Douglass High School. Jamal followed his brother to this high school and surpassed his achievements.

Jamal's combination of size, strength, and sprinting speed allowed him to become one of the greatest high school running backs in Georgia state history. He was the starting fullback for three years at Frederick Douglass High School, rushing for a school-record 4,879 yards and 68 touchdowns and averaging 9.7 yards per carry. His bruising running style earned him the nickname "The Beast." In his senior year, Jamal was named Class AAAA all-state and all-city and won most valuable player honors for his performance in the Georgia-Florida all-star game.

The Road to Excellence

Jamal was recruited by numerous schools and chose to attend the University of Tennessee. He became the leading freshman running back in the nation, tallying 1,364 rushing yards and averaging an impressive 5.9 yards per carry. He was a major contributor to his team's comeback victory over Auburn in the 1997 Southeastern Conference Championship game, gaining 127 yards. Jamal was named the *Sporting News* national freshman of the year.

Jamal began the 1998 season playing at a higher level than in his freshman year, rushing for 497 yards in his first four games, averaging 6.8 yards per carry, and scoring 3 touchdowns. In the fourth game of the season, against Auburn, he was having one of the best games of his career, with 140 yards on eighteen carries, including a 67-yard dash for a touchdown. However, during this game, he badly injured his right knee, ending his season.

Jamal's final season at Tennessee was marred by injuries. Still, he led the Volunteers in rushing, with 816 yards on 182 carries, and caught fifteen passes for 193 yards. Despite his injury problems, Jamal left Tennessee as the third all-time leading rusher in the university's history, with 2,677 yards. He was fourth in all-purpose yardage, with 3,161 yards.

The Emerging Champion

Because of Jamal's size—5 feet 11 inches and 245 pounds—and extraordinary speed, the Baltimore Ravens made Jamal the fifth overall pick in the 2000 NFL draft. As a rookie, he quickly earned the starting running-back position and had a stellar season: He rushed for 1,364 yards, caught 27 passes, and scored 6 touchdowns. He also contributed greatly to the Ravens' first championship, as he rushed for 103 yards and scored a touchdown in the team's victory in Super Bowl XXXV.

Entering the 2001 season, expectations were high for the Ravens and Jamal. However, Jamal suffered a torn anterior cruciate ligament in his left knee in the first week of training camp and missed the entire season. In 2002, Jamal dispelled any doubt about his ability to return from the knee injury. He rushed for 1,327 yards on 308 carries and was the Ravens' third leading receiver with 47 catches.

In 2003, Jamal had one of the greatest seasons in the history of the NFL. His 2,066 yards rushing was the second highest in league history, and his single-game total of 295 yards rushing against the Cleveland Browns set a record for most rushing yards

NFL Statistics

Season	GP	Rushing Car.	Yds.	Avg.	TD	Receiving Rec.	Yds.	Avg.	TD
2000	16	309	1,364	4.4	6	27	296	11.0	0
2002	16	308	1,327	4.3	6	47	442	9.4	1
2003	16	387	2,066	5.3	14	26	205	7.9	0
2004	12	235	1,006	4.3	7	10	116	11.6	0
2005	15	269	906	3.4	3	32	191	6.0	1
2006	16	314	1,132	3.6	9	18	115	6.4	0
2007	15	298	1,304	4.4	9	30	248	8.3	2
2008	16	279	1,002	3.6	4	23	178	7.7	0
Totals	122	2,399	10,107	4.2	58	213	1,791	8.4	4

Notes: GP = games played; Car. = carries; Yds. = yards; Avg. = average yards per carry or average yards per reception; TD = touchdowns; Rec. = receptions

ever gained in an NFL game. His record was broken by Adrian L. Peterson in 2007. Jamal was named to the NFL all-pro team and selected as the Associated Press offensive player of the year.

Continuing the Story

In 2004, Jamal's past caught up with him, as he was charged with using a cell phone to try to set up a drug deal in the year 2000. Jamal accepted a plea bargain and was sentenced to four months in a minimum-security prison and two months in an Atlanta halfway house. He served his time at the end of the 2004 season. Because of injuries and a two-game suspension for the drug conviction, Jamal played only twelve games in 2004. He still managed to amass 1,006 yards rushing with an average of 4.3 yards per carry.

The 2005 and 2006 seasons were disappointing for Jamal, as his yards-per-carry averages were an unimpressive 3.4 and 3.6, respectively. Because of his numerous past injuries and reduced production in these years, Jamal was released by the Ravens on February 28, 2007. Shortly thereafter, he signed a contract with the Cleveland Browns. He responded to Cleveland's faith with an outstanding 2007 campaign. Showing the same rare combination of sprinting speed and raw power that he had displayed his first four years in the league, he rushed for 1,304 yards in fifteen games—averaging 4.4 yards per carry—made 30 pass receptions, and scored 9 touchdowns. On February 21, 2008, Jamal agreed to terms on a three-year contract to stay with the Cleveland Browns. He rewarded

Awards and Milestones

1997	*Sporting News* first-team freshman all-American
	Associated Press second-team all-Southeastern Conference
2002	*Football Digest* comeback player of the year
2003	NFL Pro Bowl
	Associated Press NFL offensive player of the year
	Pro Football Writers Association NFL most valuable player
	Second most single-season rushing yards, 2,066
	Most rushing yards in a game, 295 (record broken)

the Browns by carrying the ball for more than 1,000 yards.

Summary

Jamal Lewis exemplified how determination and hard work can help an athlete counter youthful mistakes and multiple injuries. He overcame a serious knee injury to star for the Baltimore Ravens. Then, after another serious injury and drug conviction, he reestablished himself as one of the premier running backs in the NFL with the Cleveland Browns. Wanting to share with others, he founded the "Another Love for One Foundation" to help low-income people and promote understanding of diverse viewpoints.

Jerome L. Neapolitan

Additional Sources

Barra, Allen. *Big Play: Barra on Football.* Washington, D.C. : Brassey's, 2004.

King, Peter. "Jamal Lewis." *Sports Illustrated* 107, no. 5 (August 6, 2007).

Matte, Tom. *Tales from the Baltimore Ravens Sidelines.* Champaign, Ill.: Sports, 2004.

Ray Lewis

Born: May 15, 1975
　　　Bartow, Florida
Also known as: Ray Anthony Lewis (full name)

Early Life

Ray Anthony Lewis was born on May 15, 1975, in Bartow, Florida, to Ray Lewis, Sr., and Sunseria Keith. Ray never knew his biological father, who abandoned the family after Ray's birth. When he was a junior at Kathleen High School in Lakeland, Florida, his mother remarried and moved away. Thus, Ray moved in with his grandparents to continue playing football at Kathleen High School in Polk County, Florida. Ray was a standout in pee wee league football, and at Kathleen High School he starred in both football and wrestling.

The Road to Excellence

Ray was a multidimensional football star in high school, playing and excelling at linebacker, running back, and kick returner. He was named the team's most valuable player (MVP) in both his junior and senior years. In 2007, Ray was one of thirty-three players named to the Florida High

Linebacker Ray Lewis in 2009. (G. Newman Lowrance/Getty Images)

School Association all-century team. He was widely recruited and received a full scholarship to play at University of Miami.

Midway through his freshman year at Miami, Ray earned a position in the starting lineup as a linebacker. He was later named to the freshman all-American team. In his sophomore season, he led the Big East Conference in tackles and was named all-conference and all-American. In his junior year, he not only led the Big East Conference in tackles again but also had the second-highest number in University of Miami history. He was named all-American and was a runner-up for the Butkus Award as the nation's top linebacker. Forgoing his senior year to turn professional, Ray was drafted by the Baltimore Ravens in the first round, number twenty-six overall.

The Emerging Champion

Ray's impact in NFL was immediate: He was not only the Ravens' leading tackler in his rookie season but also emerged as the team's defensive leader. He was named to the 1996 *USA Today* all-rookie team. In his sophomore campaign he was even better. He led the league in tackles and was voted second-team all-pro. During the 1999-2000 campaign, he again led the league in tackles, was named first-team all-pro, and was widely regarded as the best linebacker in the NFL. He had become not only the best run stopper in the game but also a complete player who covered the entire field.

On January 31, 2000, Ray's career almost came to an end when Richard Lollar and Jacinth Baker were stabbed to death following a Super Bowl party in Atlanta, Georgia. Ray was at the scene of the crime and initially was charged with murder. He was later exonerated of involvement in the murders, but he pled

NFL Statistics

Season	GP	Tac.	Sacks	FF	FR	Int.
1996	14	110	2.5	—	—	1
1997	16	184	4.0	1	1	1
1998	14	120	3.0	1	0	2
1999	16	168	3.5	0	0	3
2000	16	137	3.0	0	3	2
2001	16	161	3.5	1	1	3
2002	5	57	0.0	1	1	2
2003	16	161	1.5	2	2	6
2004	15	146	1.0	1	2	0
2005	6	46	1.0	0	1	1
2006	14	103	5.0	1	1	2
2007	14	120	2.0	2	1	2
2008	16	117	3.5	0	0	3
Totals	**179**	**1,630**	**33.5**	**10**	**13**	**28**

Notes: GP = games played; Tac. = tackles; FF = forced fumbles; FR = fumble recoveries; Int. = interceptions

guilty to obstruction of justice and was sentenced to twelve months of probation.

Because of his ordeal, Ray heightened his focus and determination. He led the 2000-2001 Ravens to set the record for the fewest points allowed in a sixteen-game season. In the playoffs Ray played as though on a mission, making numerous tremendous and "clutch" plays. The Ravens easily beat the New York Giants 34-7 in Super Bowl XXXV, and Ray was named Super Bowl MVP. He was also named the NFL defensive player of the year.

Continuing the Story

Winning the Super Bowl did not reduce Ray's passion for the game, and in the following season, he again led the Ravens in tackles. The team's 10-6 record was good enough to make the playoffs, but the Ravens lost to the Pittsburgh Steelers in the second round. In the 2002 season, Ray missed eleven games because of a shoulder injury, and the team fell to a 7-9 record.

In 2003, Ray returned to have the finest year of his career. He had highs in tackles, 225, and interceptions, 6, and was named NFL defensive player of the year for the second time. Baltimore won the AFC North Division with a 10-6 record, but its offense struggled in a 20-17 playoff loss to the Tennessee Titans.

In 2004, Ray again led the NFL in tack-

les and was named first-team all-pro for the fifth time. The Ravens' 9-7 record was not good enough for the playoffs. Injuries caused Ray to miss the last ten games of the 2005 season, and without its leader, the Ravens fell to 6-10. In 2006, with Ray fully recovered, the Ravens returned to the playoffs with a 13-3 record but lost to the Indianapolis Colts. Despite playing with numerous injuries and missing two games, Ray again led the Ravens in tackles in 2007, but the team won only five games. The Ravens improved markedly in 2008 and made the playoffs. Ray's strong defensive play was one of the primary reasons for the team's success.

Summary

Ray Lewis will be remembered as one of greatest defensive players of all time. He was a Super Bowl MVP, two-time defensive player of the year, and seven-time all-pro. He led the NFL in tackles five times, and his 6 interceptions in 2003 set a record for the most ever by a middle linebacker. Ray planned to play into the second decade of the twenty-first century. Despite his brush with the law, Ray became a fine citizen. In 2005, he completed his degree at the University of Maryland University College. He started the Ray Lewis 52 Foundation, which provides personal and economic assistance to disadvantaged youth, and has pressed political, business, and philanthropic leaders to assist disability sports both in the United States and other countries.

Jerome L. Neapolitan

Additional Sources

Malinowski, Nicholas W. "Lewis, Ray." *Current Biography* 68, no. 1 (2007).

Matte, Tom, and Jeff Seibel. *Tom Matte's Tales from the Baltimore Ravens Sideline.* Champaign, Ill.: Sports, 2004.

Honors and Awards

1995	All-American
	All-Big East Conference
1996	*USA Today* all-rookie team
1997-2001, 2003-04, 2006-07	NFL Pro Bowl
1998-2001, 2003-04	NFL All-Pro
2000, 2003	Associated Press NFL defensive player of year
2001	Super Bowl most valuable player
2007	Florida High School Association all-century team

Bob Lilly

Born: July 26, 1939
   Olney, Texas
Also known as: Robert Lewis Lilly (full name);
   Mr. Cowboy

Early Life

Robert Lewis Lilly, destined to become one of football's most feared pass-rushers, was born on July 26, 1939, in Olney, Texas, to John and Margaret Louise (Redwine) Lilly. Bob and his family moved to Throckmorton, Texas, where John Lilly worked at various occupations. One day, when Bob was a junior at Throckmorton High School, his future in football was foreshadowed. He was playing volleyball when a line coach from Texas Christian University (TCU) watched him. Impressed with the boy's agility, the coach singled Bob out and asked about him. Nothing much came of the incident at the time, though; the Lilly family moved to Pendleton, Oregon, soon after, because a drought that year had caused Texas crops to fail.

The Road to Excellence

While at Pendleton High School, Bob became an excellent basketball player, averaging twenty-seven points per game. In addition, he excelled at the javelin throw at the state track meet. In football, however, he won highest honors: He was chosen as an all-American player.

Meanwhile, the coach from TCU heard about Bob again and decided to offer him a scholarship. Bob had received offers from several colleges, but he chose TCU because he missed Texas. Back in the state where football is king, Bob played tackle for TCU's team, the Horned Frogs, from 1958 to 1961.

In college, Bob enjoyed himself. For laughs, he would pick up Volkswagens and place them on the steps of campus buildings. He also had such a good time waterskiing that he nearly flunked out of school, but, just in time, he managed to pull up his grades. By his junior year, Bob was averaging eight tackles a game and recovering an average of seven fumbles; not surprisingly, he was elected to the all-Southwestern Conference team that year. At the

postseason Bluebonnet Bowl, he was named outstanding lineman, even though his team lost. By 1960, his senior year, Bob was so successful that he was chosen as a unanimous all-American.

The Emerging Champion

The following year, Bob was the number-one draft choice of the NFL's Dallas Cowboys; he was also the first player that team ever drafted. That same year he married his first wife, Katharine Waltman, by whom he eventually had three children. The couple divorced later, and Bob married Margaret Ann Threlkeld in 1972.

As a rookie, Bob played defensive end and was named to the NFL all-rookie team. In 1963, Bob was shifted from defensive end to defensive tackle and soon became one of football's finest linemen. Ernie Stautner, the Cowboy's defensive line coach, noticed that Bob seemed to avoid using such tactics as the forearm smash and the head slap out of fear of hurting other players. Stautner worked with Bob so he would use his hands more, thereby discouraging illegal holding and commanding more respect from offensive linemen. As a result, Bob became one of the most feared pass-rushers in the league.

Bob had remarkable speed, strength, and agility. Because he pursued his opponents with such intensity, they soon learned to run plays directly at him. That usually meant double- and triple-team blocking. Even so, the opposition rarely stopped Bob entirely. Because no one man could block him consistently, teams sent three men at him in an attempt to neutralize him; often he managed to get to the quarterback anyway. As a result, guards learned to do the only thing they could to slow Bob down: hang on to his jersey and be dragged by him. Throughout his career, Bob had to put up with this, because officials seldom called penalties for that kind of holding.

For fourteen seasons, Bob was the backbone of Dallas's "Doomsday Defense," playing in 196 consecutive regular-season games. Eight times he helped lead the Cowboys to the playoffs, and his team earned a Super Bowl victory in 1971. Bob was named to the Pro Bowl squad eleven times.

Continuing the Story

In addition to making all-NFL in 1966-1969 and all-NFC in 1970 and 1971, Bob was named to the AFL-NFL 1960-1984 all-star team. Later, he was elected to the Pro Football Hall of Fame and the National Football Foundation's College Football Hall of Fame. He was also the first player named to the Dallas Cowboys Ring of Honor. In 1994, Bob was selected to the NFL's Seventy-fifth Anniversary All-Time Team.

When he retired, Bob got involved in a number of businesses and worked for a beer distributorship in Waco, Texas. Over time, Bob made frequent television appearances, endorsing various products. In 1983, he cowrote a book about his football career entitled *Bob Lilly: Reflections.* In 1983, he sold his business and launched his landscape photography career. From 1984 to 1989, Bob lived in Las Cruces, New Mexico, where he opened a photo art gallery, complete with color and black-and-white darkrooms. In 1989, he moved back to Texas, settling in Graham, two hours west of Dallas. An interest in the need to retouch old pictures took him into the computer world of digital imaging. After a stellar NFL career, he became respected in the field of photography as well.

Summary

According to one of Bob Lilly's coaches, a player like Bob came along once in a coach's lifetime. He was an exceptional tackler whose primary talent was that no one man could contain him. He always

Honors and Awards

1959	All-Southwest Conference Team
1960	Bluebonnet Bowl Game Outstanding Lineman
	Consensus All-American
1961	Chicago College All-Star Team
	East-West All-Star Team
1962	NFL All-Rookie Team
1963, 1965-74	NFL Pro Bowl Team
1966-69	All-NFL Team
1970	NFL All-Pro Team of the 1960's
1970-71	All-NFC Team
1975	Inducted into Dallas Cowboys Ring of Honor
1980	Inducted into Pro Football Hall of Fame
1981	Inducted into College Football Hall of Fame
1985	AFL-NFL 1960-1984 All-Star Team
1986	NCAA Silver Anniversary Award
1994	NFL 75th Anniversary All-Time Team
2006	Inducted into East-West Shrine Game Hall of Fame

got past his first blocker and often made it through second and third blocks as well. He is remembered as one of the best pass-rushers in NFL history.

Nicholas White

Additional Sources

Barber, Phil. "NFL: Football's One Hundred Greatest Players—The Hit Men." *The Sporting News* 223 (November 1, 1999): 12-16.

Luksa, Frank. *Cowboys Essential: Everything You Need to Know to Be a Real Fan!* Chicago: Triumph Books, 2006.

Monk, Cody. *Legends of the Dallas Cowboys.* Champaign, Ill.: Sports, 2004.

Taylor, Jean-Jacques. *Game of My Life: Dallas Cowboys.* Champaign, Ill.: Sports, 2006.

Floyd Little

Born: July 4, 1942
       New Haven, Connecticut
Also known as: Floyd Douglas Little (full name);
   the Franchise

Early Life

Floyd Douglas Little was born on July 4, 1942, in New Haven, Connecticut, the son of Fred and Lula Little. Fred was a factory worker; he died in 1948, when Floyd was six years old. Floyd's mother worked as a clothes presser to support her family of six children. Floyd was shy and not always in good health during his early years. A speech problem made him withdraw even more, and for a number of years he refused to talk in class. As he got older, Floyd worked at odd jobs to help support the family. By the time he got to high school, he had proven that his running speed could make up for the lack of time he had to devote to football practice.

The Road to Excellence

At Hillhouse High School in New Haven, Floyd was a prep football all-American in 1962. He felt that he had not received a good education, so he enrolled in Bordertown Military Academy in New Jersey. He was the first African American student accepted at Bordertown. Floyd wanted to go to college, and he wanted to be able to succeed academically as well as play football. When he reached 5 feet 10 inches in height and weighed 196 pounds, and it was determined that he could handle college scholastically, he was recruited by a number of major colleges. Floyd narrowed down his choices to Notre Dame and Syracuse. Because of a personal appeal by running star Ernie Davis of Syracuse University, who at the time was dying from leukemia, Floyd decided that Syracuse was the college for him. After hearing that Davis had died,

he called the Syracuse football coach, Ben Schwartzwalder, and told him that he had chosen Syracuse. Floyd was given the privilege of wearing number 44, which had been worn not only by Ernie Davis but also by another former Syracuse football great, Jim Brown.

Floyd majored in both history and religion at Syracuse. During his college years, Floyd came into his own. His growing self-confidence and his athletic ability made him a popular player and a team

Denver Broncos running back Floyd Little, who ranks in the top ten for career rushing yards. (Courtesy of Denver Broncos)

AFL and NFL Statistics

Season	GP	Rushing Car.	Yds.	Avg.	TD	Receiving Rec.	Yds.	Avg.	TD
1967	13	130	381	2.9	1	7	11	1.6	0
1968	11	158	584	3.7	3	19	331	17.4	1
1969	9	146	729	5.0	6	19	218	11.5	1
1970	14	209	901	4.3	3	17	161	9.5	0
1971	14	284	1,133	4.0	6	26	255	9.8	0
1972	14	216	859	4.0	9	28	367	13.1	4
1973	14	256	979	3.8	12	41	423	10.3	1
1974	14	117	312	2.7	1	29	344	11.9	0
AFL Totals	33	434	1,694	3.9	10	45	560	12.4	2
NFL Totals	70	1,082	4,184	3.9	31	141	1,550	11.0	5

Notes: GP = games played; Car. = carries; Yds. = yards; Avg. = average yards per carry *or* average yards per reception; TD = touchdowns; Rec. = receptions

leader. Floyd made an immediate impact at Syracuse by scoring five touchdowns in his first college game, against the University of Kansas, the team of the amazing running back Gale Sayers.

The Emerging Champion

Floyd finished his sophomore year at Syracuse with a total of 12 touchdowns in 10 regular-season games. His junior season was his most productive; he scored 19 touchdowns, which led the nation in 1965. For the second year in a row, Floyd was named all-American. His senior year at Syracuse was no less spectacular—he led the Orangemen to the 1967 Gator Bowl. Floyd also became the first college football player since Doak Walker to be a three-time all-American.

During his career with the Syracuse Orangemen, Floyd scored 46 touchdowns and gained 5,529 total yards. Because of his outstanding college career, he was highly sought after by both the NFL and the American Football League (AFL). In 1967, Floyd was the number-one draft choice of the AFL's Denver Broncos.

Floyd was not sure that he or his wife, Joyce, would enjoy living in Denver, but he accepted the contract offered to him by the Bronco organization. The Littles were pleasantly surprised by the Denver environment, and Floyd looked forward to contributing to his new team. The Broncos also had a new coach, Lou Saban, for Floyd's rookie year. The 1967 season was difficult for Floyd. The Broncos were in a period of development, which meant that it was going to take time

before they could be considered a solid team. During his rookie year, Floyd gained only 381 yards rushing. The bright points of the season were that he led the AFL in punt returns and excelled at returning kickoffs.

Continuing the Story

As the Broncos improved over the next few seasons, so did Floyd's individual statistics. During the 1969 season, he gained 729 yards rushing in nine games and led the league in average yards per carry with 5.0. Floyd was a tough competitor. He distinguished between real injury and pain, and he did not let pain stop him from doing his best. Floyd wanted to help the team any way he could and, therefore, was willing to work harder and endure more so that his job would get done.

Floyd played for the Denver Broncos for eight seasons and was popular with the fans. In 1971, he led the league in rushing with 1,133 yards, and in 1973, he led the league in touchdowns with 12. During his career, Floyd was selected to *The Sporting News* all-star team on three occasions, played in the AFL all-star game twice, and played in the NFL Pro Bowl three times. In 1970, the AFL became known as the American Football Conference (AFC) when it merged with the NFL.

After Floyd retired from professional football in 1975, he earned a master's degree from the University of Denver School of Law and went into the Adolph Coors Company management training pro-

Honors and Awards

1964-66	College All-American
1969	*Sporting News* AFL All-Star Team
1969-70	AFL All-Star Team
1969-71	All-NFL Team
1970-71	*Sporting News* AFC All-Star Team
1971	Football Writers Association of America Outstanding Pro Back
1971-72, 1974	NFL Pro Bowl Team
	NFL All-Pro Team
1973	Brian Piccolo Award
1980	NFL All-Pro Team of the 1970's
1983	Inducted into College Football Hall of Fame
	Uniform number 44 retired by Denver Broncos
1984	Made inaugural member of Denver Broncos Ring of Fame

gram. Floyd had always been active in community service projects, including drug abuse programs and programs to help disadvantaged children. His wife, Joyce, whom he met at Syracuse, taught biology. Floyd was also a sportscaster for the National Broadcasting Company (NBC). After two years with NBC, he went to work for Ford Motor Company, and in 1979, he began to manage Lincoln/Mercury dealerships in California. Floyd continued to concentrate on business and charitable work, such as the Special Olympics, Boys and Girls Clubs, and the Leukemia Society.

Summary

Floyd Little's success in football is attributable to more than natural talent. He learned early in life that he would have to work hard to rise out of the poverty in which he lived. He knew that he needed an education and he fought to get one, even after he was told that he could not handle college classes. Floyd proved to himself and to those around him that he could excel both on and off the field. After his football career, Floyd gave to those who needed encouragement.

Jeffry Jensen

Additional Sources

Little, Floyd, and Tom Mackie. *Floyd Little's Tales from the Broncos Sideline.* Champaign, Ill.: Sports, 2006.

Pitoniak, Scott. *Syracuse University Football.* Charleston, S.C.: Arcadia, 2003.

Saccomano, Jim. *Game of My Life: Denver Broncos.* Champaign, Ill.: Sports, 2007.

Howie Long

Born: January 6, 1960
      Somerville, Massachusetts
Also known as: Howard Michael Long (full
    name)

Early Life
Howard Michael Long was born on January 6, 1960. His parents divorced when he was eleven, and he was left in the care of relatives. A large, shy, and awkward child, Howie lived with his grandmother in the Boston neighborhood of Charlestown, where he missed school regularly and was roughed up by thugs. Howie's uncle, a Boston Housing Authority employee, and aunt took him to live with them in Milford, Massachusetts, forty miles from Boston, where he discovered discipline, school, and football. At 6 feet 2 inches and 220 pounds, fifteen-year-old Howie was invited by the coach at Milford High School to play football. Howie participated and lettered in football, basketball, and track. As a senior, he made the *Scholastic Coach* All-American team. Eventually, he became a member of the Milford High School Hall of Fame.

The Road to Excellence
Rejecting an offer from Boston College, Howie accepted a football scholarship from Villanova University in Pennsylvania, where he received a degree in communications. A four-year football letterman, he also excelled in boxing, winning the title of northern collegiate champion. He led his Villanova team in sacks for two years and was chosen to play in the 1980 Blue-Gray Football Classic and was named the game's most valuable player (MVP). Following Howie's MVP performance, professional scouts took notice.

Howie was drafted in the second round of the 1981 NFL draft by the Oakland Raiders. He had been scouted by Raiders defensive-line coach Earl Leggett, who had challenged the team's other coaches to pick Howie. Leggett, who insisted that Howie play in a different position in each practice, developed Howie's strength and talents, helping him become a remarkably versatile defensive lineman. Howie credits Leggett for helping him realize his potential and maintain his position as a standout player with the Raiders for thirteen years.

The Emerging Champion
In his second year with the Raiders, Howie led the team with 5 sacks and was given a starting position in the fifth game of the season. In the following year, 1983, Howie boosted his record to 13 sacks, compiling five against the Washington Redskins in a single game. Howie played in the first of his eight Pro Bowl games. In 1984, the Raiders defeated the Washington Redskins in Super Bowl XVIII by a score of 38-9. Howie had a standout performance with 4 solo tackles and 1 assist. His accomplishments that year included 58 tackles and 12 sacks. Howie was designated by NFL Alumni as the NFL defensive lineman of the year. In 1985, he was named the NFL Players Association American Football Conference defensive lineman of the year. In addition, he was cited as the co-NFL defensive player of the year and was awarded the George S. Halas Trophy. Howie was chosen by John Madden to his all-Madden teams of 1984 and 1985 as well as Madden's tenth-anniversary team in 1994. In 2000,

Los Angeles Raiders defensive end Howie Long. (Ron Vesely/Getty Images)

he was enshrined in the Pro Football Hall of Fame and was introduced by an extremely proud Leggett.

One of the best defensive linemen to play in the NFL, Howie established a presence on the field that intimidated players on opposing teams. His size, 6 feet 5 inches and 275 pounds, combined with his strength and quickness, meant that he was double-teamed and often triple-teamed on the field, but he still found a way to dominate the game. His distinctive disruptive move was the "rip," a powerful upward-directed motion that was intended to break the grip of the opposing blocker.

Continuing the Story

Following his retirement at the end of the 1993 season, Howie became a Fox network NFL studio analyst. Impressive in preparation and delivery, he was awarded an Emmy in 1997 for outstanding TV personality/analyst. Also in 1994, Howie began hosting a TV series, *The World's Most Dangerous Stunts,* and later appeared on two episodes of *Married with Children* and in "Al Bundy Sports Spectacular" and "A Bundy Thanksgiving." In 1997, he hosted *Star Wars: The Myth and Magic* and appeared in two episodes of *Mad TV* and nine episodes of *ESPN Sports Century.* In 1998, he signed a contract with Twentieth Century Fox for three action films. He had a small part in John Woo's *Broken Arrow* (1996); the

---

Honors and Awards

1980	Blue-Gray game most valuable player
1983-85	NFL All-Pro
1983-87, 1989, 1992-93	NFL Pro Bowl
1984	NFL Players Association AFC defensive lineman of the year
1984-85	NFL Alumni defensive lineman of the year
1985	Raider Lineman's Club defensive lineman of the year
	George S. Halas Trophy (cowinner)
1986, 1989	Second-team all-pro
1990	NFL all-decade team (1980's)
2000	Inducted into Pro Football Hall of Fame
	Walter Camp Man of the Year

---

lead in *Firestorm* (1998), a movie which was almost universally panned; and a small role in Demian Lichtenstein's *3000 Miles to Graceland* (2001), a movie that was proclaimed "excruciating" by one critic. Howie made numerous commercials for companies including Pizza Hut, Nike, Coca-Cola, Pepsi, Coors Light, and Nabisco. He also became a spokesman for Radio Shack. He established a scholarship at Villanova to aid underprivileged children and hosted many athletic events in support of the scholarship. He donated much of his time to charity work, including Boys Town and Boys and Girls Clubs, and became a prominent spokesman for the American Cancer Society. Howie settled with his wife, Diane, and their three sons—Christopher, Kyle, and Howie—in Ivy, Virginia.

Summary

With guidance and discipline, Howie Long progressed from a troubled teen facing uncertain prospects to a confident and feared presence whose ability to perform on the field was legendary. Hounded by a fear of failure, Howie perfected his skills to become one of the best defensive ends ever to play football.

Mary Hurd

Additional Sources

Lombardo, John. *Raiders Forever: Stars of the NFL's Most Colorful Team Recall Their Glory Days.* Guilford, Conn.: Globe Pequot Press, 2003.

Long, Howie, and John Czarnecki. *Football for Dummies.* 3d ed. Hoboken, N.J.: John Wiley & Sons, 2007.

Zimmerman, Paul. "The Long Way Up: Howie Long Departed Boston's Streets for NFL Stardom." *Sports Illustrated,* January 23, 1989.

NFL Statistics

Season	GP	Sacks	FR	Int.
1981	16	0.0	0	0
1982	9	5.5	0	0
1983	26	13.0	2	0
1984	16	12.0	2	0
1985	16	10.0	0	0
1986	13	7.5	2	0
1987	14	4.0	2	0
1988	7	3.0	0	1
1989	14	5.0	1	0
1990	12	6.0	1	0
1991	14	3.0	0	1
1992	16	9.0	0	0
1993	16	6.0	0	0
Totals	**179**	**84.0**	**10**	**2**

Notes: GP = games played; Tac. = tackles; FF = forced fumbles; FR = fumble recoveries; Int. = interceptions

Ronnie Lott

Born: May 8, 1959
  Albuquerque, New Mexico
Also known as: Ronald Mandel Lott (full name);
  Intimidator

Early Life
Ronald Mandel Lott was born in Albuquerque, New Mexico, on May 8, 1959, the oldest of three children of Mary and Roy Lott. At the age of five, Ronnie and his family moved to Washington, D.C., when his father accepted an assignment in the U.S. Air Force. During his early years, Ronnie loved playing and watching all sports, but his favorite was basketball. His childhood in the inner city toughened him. At the age of nine, his family moved to San Bernardino, California, and a year later to Rialto, California.

Ronnie Lott, defensive back for the San Francisco 49ers, in 1990. (Al Messerschmidt/Getty Images)

The Road to Excellence
Ronnie attended Eisenhower High School in Rialto. While there, he made all-conference in baseball and basketball and in football for three consecutive years. Upon graduating from high school in 1977, he enrolled at the University of Southern California (USC) on a football scholarship as a free safety. During his sophomore year, USC won the Rose Bowl over Michigan and shared the number-one ranking in football with the University of Alabama.

During his sophomore season, Ronnie had eight interceptions, second in the nation. He was also elected to the all-American team two years in a row, and he was voted the USC Trojans' most valuable and inspirational player. While at USC, Ronnie also played as a reserve guard on the basketball team. In 1981, he was the eighth pick of the NFL draft, chosen by the San Francisco 49ers to play cornerback and safety.

The Emerging Champion
As a 6-foot, 203-pound defensive back, Ronnie made an immediate impression. On his first day of training camp, he became the starting left cornerback for the 49ers. During his first season in the NFL, Ronnie helped the 49ers win the Super Bowl in 1982. He also became the second rookie in the history of the NFL to return three interceptions for touchdowns. Along with Lawrence Taylor of the New York Giants, he received rookie of the year honors.

During his fourteen-year career in the NFL, Ronnie became known for his hard-hitting style. As a versatile defensive back he earned ten Pro Bowl invitations and played three different defensive positions: free safety, strong safety, and cornerback. By 1986, he was playing the position of free safety, a position that enabled him to cover the entire field.

Continuing the Story
Ronnie played his final season with the 49ers in 1990, and on March 25, 1991, he signed a two-year contract to play the position of strong

273

NFL Statistics

Season	Int.	Yds.	TD	Sacks
1981	7	117	3	0.0
1982	2	95	1	0.0
1983	4	22	0	1.0
1984	4	26	0	1.0
1985	6	68	0	1.5
1986	10	134	1	2.0
1987	5	62	0	0.0
1988	5	59	0	0.0
1989	5	34	0	0.0
1990	3	26	0	0.0
1991	8	52	0	1.0
1992	1	0	0	0.0
1993	3	35	0	1.0
1994	0	0	0	1.0
Totals	63	730	5	8.5

Notes: Int. = interceptions; Yds. = yards; TD = touchdowns

safety with the Los Angeles Raiders. In 1992, Ronnie led the team in tackles and was second in passes defended, with one interception; however, the Raiders lost nine games and did not make the playoffs.

In March, 1993, Ronnie signed a $3.1 million contract with the New York Jets. During his first year with the Jets, he was second on the team in interceptions with three. In his final year with the Jets, he took a $325,000 pay cut, which enabled the Jets to have more money under the salary cap. In 1995, he attempted to play for the Kansas City Chiefs, but injuries prevented him from continuing his career. He retired from the NFL before the start of the 1995 season.

On July 29, 2000, Ronnie was formally inducted into the Pro Football Hall of Fame in Canton, Ohio. This honor recognized the achievements he had made during his fourteen years with the league. During his career with the 49ers (1981-1990), Los Angeles Raiders (1991-1992), and the New York Jets (1993-1994) Ronnie had 63 career interceptions and twice led the league. He surpassed the 1,000-tackle mark in 1993 and had five seasons of at least 100 tackles. In Ronnie's ten seasons with the 49ers, the team won eight NFC Western Division titles and four Super Bowls. In twenty playoff contests, Ronnie recorded 9 interceptions, 89 tackles, 1 forced fumble, 1 fumble recovery, and 2 touchdowns.

Coach George Seifert called Ronnie football's greatest safety and the most committed football player he had ever known. Once, while playing in a NFL game, Ronnie smashed the tip of his little finger and chose to have it amputated because it would heal more quickly than it would have if he waited for a bone graft. Although he lost part of his little finger, he did not spend much time on the sidelines.

Ronnie owned his own sports marketing company, the Hitters Club. He also served as an analyst for the NFL. He settled in Cupertino, California, with his wife and their three children.

Summary

Ronnie Lott was one of the best defensive NFL players of all time. He played in four Super Bowl games and ten Pro Bowl games. He was named all-pro eight times, all-NFC six times, and all-AFC once and was enshrined into both the Pro Football Hall of Fame and the National Football Foundation's College Football Hall of Fame.

Lloyd Johnson

Additional Sources

Jacobs, Martin S. *San Francisco 49ers.* Charleston, S.C.: Arcadia, 2005.

Lott, Ronnie, and Jill Lieber. *Total Impact: Straight Talk from Football's Hardest Hitter.* New York: Doubleday, 1991.

Moore, Manfred, and Kevin Daniels. *Game Day USC Football: The Greatest Games, Players, Coaches and Teams in the Glorious Tradition of Trojan Football.* Chicago: Triumph Books, 2006.

Silver, Michael. "Together Forever." *Sports Illustrated* 93, no. 4 (July 24, 2000): 56-59.

Honors and Awards

1981	NFL Rookie of the Year
1981-84, 1986-91	NFL Pro Bowl Team
1981, 1983-84, 1986-91	NFL All-Pro
1980's, 1990's	NFL All-Decade Team
1994	NFL 75th Anniversary All-Time Team
2000	Inducted into Pro Football Hall of Fame
2002	Inducted into College Football Hall of Fame

Sid Luckman

Born: November 21, 1916
      Brooklyn, New York
Died: July 5, 1998
      Aventura, Florida
Also known as: Sidney Luckman (full name)

Early Life

Sidney Luckman, perhaps the most famous Jewish football player in American sports history, was born on November 21, 1916, in Brooklyn, New York. He was the son of Meyer Luckman, a Jewish immigrant. Growing up on the streets of New York, the short and stocky Sid liked playing football with his friends. No one had a ball, so they made one out of rags. When he was eight, his father bought him a football. The boys in his neighborhood talked constantly about their idol Red Grange, the great Illinois halfback. Young Sid's idol, however, was Benny Friedman, the Michigan quarterback.

The Road to Excellence

Sid attended Erasmus High School, where he developed his great skills as a passer and all-around player. He became the most publicized high school player in New York City. Sid's talent caught the eye of Lou Little, the head football coach of Columbia University. Coach Little persuaded Sid to attend Columbia even though he was offered scholarships from many other colleges. Sid worked his way through college washing dishes, running errands, and babysitting.

At Columbia, Sid's star shone even brighter. Under Little's guidance, he developed into one of the greatest quarterbacks in college football history. From 1936 through 1938, Sid started at tailback and was a true triple-threat player: a great passer, runner, and kicker. In fact, he once punted a ball 72 yards.

Although the Columbia team never had a winning season during these years, it did have some great moments. In his senior year, Sid led Columbia to a 20-18 victory over a powerful Army team. He completed 18 passes for 2 touchdowns and ran back a kickoff 85 yards for a third. He also kicked 2 extra points. Despite Columbia's losing record, Sid earned all-American honors in his senior year.

Sid's college play caught the attention of another great coach. George Halas, coach of the Chicago Bears, wanted Sid. Coach Halas traded for the

Chicago Bears quarterback Sid Luckman in 1945. (Nate Fine/NFL/ Getty Images)

first choice in the 1939 college draft and chose Sid. Sid was reluctant to play professional football after breaking his nose three times in college, but Halas's offer of ten thousand dollars persuaded him.

The Emerging Champion

Halas needed a smart athlete for the key position of quarterback in his new T-formation, and he knew that Sid was the man for the job. Sid quickly learned four hundred plays as well as all the quarterback strategies. He studied and mastered the T-formation. Halas later said that Sid never called a wrong play. By 1939, Sid became the first quarterback of the modern T-formation, a strategy that forever changed football.

The Bears had not won a championship since 1933. With Sid at the helm starting in 1939, the Bears achieved their glory years and won four championships in the next six years. The most memorable of these occurred in 1940, when the Bears crushed the powerful Washington Redskins 73-0. Led by Sid, the Bears achieved the most devastating victory of all time and scored the most points ever in an NFL game, a record that still stands.

Sid rivaled the Redskins' Sammy Baugh as the greatest quarterback of the 1940's. He was selected as an all-pro five times. Perhaps his greatest game was in 1943, against the New York Giants. The day of that game, Sid's friends had given him a two-thousand-dollar war bond in honor of "Sid Luckman Day." Sid responded by throwing a league-record 7 touchdown passes to lead the Bears to a 56-7 pounding of the Giants. During his twelve-year career, Sid threw 1,744 passes and completed 904, for 14,686 yards gained and 137 touchdowns.

Sid also served his country during World War II. In 1943, he enlisted in the U.S. Merchant Marines and played football during shore leave.

Continuing the Story

When the All-American Football Conference was formed in 1946, the Chicago Rockets offered Sid a job as player-coach for twenty-five thousand dollars a year. Sid turned it down out of loyalty to the Bears.

In 1950, Sid was replaced at quarterback, but Halas let him have one last chance to play. Sid managed to lead the team to a touchdown in a game against the Detroit Lions and left the field to a standing ovation. During that year, however, Sid suffered a shoulder injury that ended his career. He retired at the end of the 1950 season.

Following his retirement, Sid served as an assistant coach for the Bears, working closely with the quarterbacks. Halas always sent him a check at the end of the season for his work, but Sid would send it back. He felt he owed to the Bears the success he had achieved and was glad to help them in return. Sid later achieved success in the business world as an executive in a Chicago cellophane company. Sid's great career in college and professional football was capped with his selection to the National Football Foun-

NFL Statistics

Season	GP	PA	PC	Pct.	Yds.	Avg.	TD	Int.
1939	11	51	23	.451	636	12.5	5	4
1940	11	105	48	.457	941	8.9	4	9
1941	11	119	68	.571	1,181	9.9	9	6
1942	11	105	57	.543	1,024	9.8	10	13
1943	10	202	110	.545	2,194	10.9	28	12
1944	7	143	71	.497	1,018	7.1	11	12
1945	10	217	117	.539	1,727	8.0	14	10
1946	11	229	110	.480	1,826	8.0	17	16
1947	12	323	176	.545	2,712	8.4	24	31
1948	12	163	89	.546	1,047	6.4	13	14
1949	8	50	22	.440	200	4.0	1	3
1950	7	37	13	.351	180	4.9	1	2
Totals	**121**	**1,744**	**904**	**.518**	**14,686**	**8.4**	**137**	**132**

Notes: GP = games played; PA = passes attempted; PC = passes completed; Pct. = percent completed; Yds. = yards; Avg. = average yards per attempt; TD = touchdowns; Int. = interceptions

Honors, Awards, and Records

1938	College All-American
1940, 1942	NFL Pro Bowl Team
1941-44, 1947	NFL All-Pro Team
1943	Carr Trophy
	NFL record for the most touchdown passes in a game, 7 (record shared)
1960	Inducted into College Football Hall of Fame
1963	NFL All-Pro Team of the 1940's
1965	Inducted into Pro Football Hall of Fame
	Uniform number 42 retired by Chicago Bears

dation's College Football Hall of Fame and the Pro Football Hall of Fame.

Summary

Sid Luckman's combination of athletic skill and football contributed to the Chicago Bears' greatest years. He will be remembered not only as one of the greatest quarterbacks ever to play football but also as the first quarterback of the modern era. Sid played a key role in modernizing football.

Nan White

Additional Sources

King, Peter. *Greatest Quarterbacks.* Des Moines, Iowa: Sports Illustrated Books, 1999.

Luckman, Sid. *Luckman at Quarterback: Football as a Sport and a Career.* Chicago: Ziff-Davis, 1949.

Platt, Jim, and James Buckley. *Sports Immortals: Stories of Inspiration and Achievement.* Chicago: Triumph Books, 2002.

Whittingham, Richard. *What a Game They Played: An Inside Look at the Golden Era of Pro Football.* Lincoln: University of Nebraska Press, 2002.

Johnny Lujack

Born: January 4, 1925
      Connellsville, Pennsylvania
Also known as: John Christopher Lujack, Jr. (full
name)

Early Life

The youngest of four sons in a family of six children, John Christopher Lujack, Jr., was born on
January 4, 1925, in Connellsville, Pennsylvania.
Johnny's father worked as a boilermaker for the
railroad in Connellsville and was extremely sup-
portive of his son's athletic pursuits. Johnny grew
up in a town where the name "Lujack" was synonymous with athletic ability. With the exception of
two years, there was at least one Lujack brother on
the high school sports teams from 1928 to 1941.
Johnny was only fourteen when he was assigned the

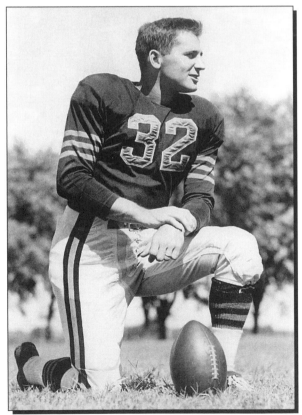

Heisman Trophy winner Johnny Lujack. (Courtesy of
Amateur Athletic Foundation of Los Angeles)

position of running back on the Connellsville high
school football team. He was a multisport talent
and went on to letter in baseball, basketball, and
track and field.

The Road to Excellence

By the time Johnny was a high school senior, he was
offered a contract by the Pittsburgh Pirates Major
League Baseball team. Johnny declined that offer,
as well as numerous college scholarships, and enrolled at the University of Notre Dame.

Johnny's first season with the Fighting Irish in
1943 fulfilled coach Frank Leahy's fondest expectations. In Johnny's first start against undefeated
Army, he completed 8 of 15 passes for 237 yards
and 2 touchdowns. Johnny plunged for a third
touchdown to give Notre Dame an astounding 26-0
upset victory. The Irish were named national champions that year.

In 1944, Johnny joined the U.S. Navy and served
on a submarine chaser in the Atlantic Ocean during World War II. Upon his honorable discharge
from the Navy in 1946, Johnny returned to Notre
Dame to guide its football team to further victories.

In 1946 and 1947, the Irish were named national
champions. Johnny was dubbed "coach on the
field" by Frank Leahy because of the leadership,
poise, and daring he displayed. In the three seasons
Johnny played for the Irish—all three of which
were national championship seasons—he completed
144 passes in 280 attempts for 2,080 yards. Among
the honors given to Johnny during his college
career were the Heisman Trophy (1947) and membership on the consensus all-American team in
1946 and 1947.

The Emerging Champion

Johnny was already a legend in the minds of many
people when he signed an $18,750 four-year con-
tract with the NFL Chicago Bears. Fresh in people's
memories were Johnny's amazing athletic feats,
both offensive and defensive, such as his jarring
open-field tackles in the historic scoreless tie with
Army in 1946.

As a defensive back for the Bears, Johnny's per-

Honors and Awards

1946-47	Consensus All-American
1947	Heisman Trophy
	Walter Camp Award
	Associated Press Male Athlete of the Year
1948, 1950	NFL All-Pro Team
1951-52	NFL Pro Bowl Team
1960	Inducted into College Football Hall of Fame

formances were stellar. He stalked the defensive backfield, frustrating the offensive effort of some of the best quarterbacks and running backs in the league. For his dominance, Johnny was named all-pro defensive back in 1948. The following year, however, Johnny resumed his role as quarterback. In a game against the Chicago Cardinals, the Bears' legendary quarterback, Sid Luckman, was injured. Johnny was called on as replacement.

In that game, Johnny broke Sammy Baugh's single-game record by passing for 468 yards and also threw 6 touchdown passes. The next year, he became the Bears' starting quarterback and was named all-pro at the season's end. By 1951, however, Johnny's arm had lost its accuracy and power, and he decided to retire. Johnny's career with the Chicago Bears had been remarkable. In four years, he completed 404 of 808 passes for 6,295 yards and 41 touchdowns.

Continuing the Story

After Johnny retired as a professional player at the age of twenty-six, he served as an assistant coach under Frank Leahy at Notre Dame. As a coach, Johnny was highly regarded by Leahy, who once said of Johnny, "He has everything it takes for success—brains, character, and personality. He can make a million dollars if he wants to."

Johnny never became a head coach, but he did make a million dollars. In 1954, he opened a successful automobile dealership in Davenport, Iowa, and also served as a television color announcer for college and professional football games. Johnny married Patricia Ann Schierbrock in 1948, and they had three children, Mary Jane, John Frances, and Carolyn Elizabeth.

Johnny never regretted turning down a career as a professional baseball player because he became one of the all-time great players on the University of Notre Dame's football team and an all-pro for the Chicago Bears. Asked what game he preferred, college or professional, Johnny said, "I would rather see one pro game than six played by top-ranking collegiate teams. The pros offer far more variety."

Nevertheless, Johnny is remembered most for his performances as a college player. Notre Dame historian Jim Beach said,

Johnny was the kind of quarterback who called runs when passes were expected, and passed on fourth down. He kept the defense in a state of confusion and his teammates on their toes. He knew the job of every man on every play.

For his achievements, Johnny was elected to the National Football Foundation's College Football Hall of Fame in 1960.

Summary

As a college athlete, Johnny Lujack quarterbacked Notre Dame to three national championships: 1943, 1946, and 1947. He was a consensus all-American in 1946 and 1947 and was awarded the Heisman Trophy as a senior. Picked first in the draft by the Chicago Bears in 1948, Johnny played four years, earning the distinction as an all-pro on both defense and offense. He won the acclaim of sportswriters and fans throughout the United States.

Rustin Larson

Additional Sources

Heisler, John. *Echoes of Notre Dame Football: The Greatest Stories Ever Told.* Chicago: Triumph Books, 2005.

King, Joe. *Inside Pro Football: For the TV Fan—A Special Section by Johnny Lujack, Tom Harmon, and Red Grange.* Englewood Cliffs, N.J.: Prentice-Hall, 1958.

Pennington, Bill. *The Heisman: Great American Stories of the Men Who Won.* New York: Regan-Books, 2004.

Prister, Tim. *What It Means to Be Fighting Irish: Ara Parseghian and Notre Dame's Greatest Players.* Chicago: Triumph Books, 2004.

John Lynch

Born: September 25, 1971
        Hinsdale, Illinois
Also known as: John Terrence Lynch (full name)

Early Life

John Terrence Lynch was born on September 25, 1971, in Hinsdale, Illinois. His father, John, Sr., who played football briefly for the Pittsburgh Steelers during the early 1970's, moved the family to San Diego, California, and began a rise to prominence in the radio industry. At Torrey Pines High School in Del Mar, California, John starred for both the baseball and football teams. Primarily, he was a pitcher in baseball and a quarterback and defensive back in football. As a junior and senior, he was captain of the football team. During his high school years, he met his future wife, tennis player Linda Allred. John and Linda grew closer during their years together at Stanford University, where both excelled academically as they pursued potential careers as professional athletes.

The Road to Excellence

At Stanford, John played both baseball and football. He gained a reputation as a hard-throwing right-handed pitcher and designated hitter for the baseball team and a hard-hitting safety for the football team. Although he contemplated leaving school after his junior year to concentrate on a baseball career, he decided to stay his senior year and play for head coach Bill Walsh. During that senior year, John recorded nine tackles, intercepted a pass, and forced a fumble in a 33-16 upset of Notre Dame.

In 1992, John was drafted in the second round by the Florida Marlins, at the time a new Major League Baseball franchise. On June 15 of that year, he threw the first pitch in the history of the Marlins' minor-league system. The cap he wore in that game was donated to the Na-

tional Baseball Hall of Fame in Cooperstown, New York. After a short season in the low minor leagues, John returned to Stanford for his final year of college football.

While John impressed NFL scouts with his hard-hitting ability on the field and his easygoing demeanor off the field, some were concerned that the 6-foot-2, 220-pound Californian would choose a career in baseball instead of football. All along, John insisted that his first love was football. The Tampa Bay Buccaneers, a franchise that had not made the NFL playoffs since 1982, took him at his word and drafted him in the third round in 1993.

John Lynch playing for the Denver Broncos in 2007. (Paul Spinelli/ Getty Images)

The Emerging Champion

John came to the Buccaneers when the franchise was on the verge of a major transition. There were three lean seasons under head coach Sam Wyche, but new team owner Malcolm Glazer hired Minnesota Vikings defensive coordinator Tony Dungy in 1996. The defensive scheme devised by Dungy and his defensive coordinator, Monte Kiffin, fit well with John's ability to intimidate potential pass receivers with his hitting ability and with his ability to stop the run from his strong-safety position. In the three seasons before Dungy arrived, John made a total of 65 tackles. In Dungy's first year, John made 103 tackles, 74 unassisted.

In 1997, Dungy's second year and John's fifth with the Buccaneers, Tampa Bay began the season 5-0 and eventually secured the National Football Conference (NFC) Central Division Championship, sending the team into the playoffs for the first time since 1982. John emerged as a key member of a dominant defense that included standout players such as linebackers Hardy Nickerson and Derrick Brooks, defensive tackle Warren Sapp, and cornerback Ronde Barber. During that season, John made a helmet-to-helmet hit on his brother-in-law, Chicago Bears tight end John Allred, giving Allred a mild concussion.

From 1999 to 2002, John reached the peak of his career. He was named to the NFL all-pro team four consecutive years. In 1999, he helped lead the Buc-

---

Milestone

As a minor-league baseball player, threw the first pitch in the history of the Florida Marlins organization

Honors and Awards

1997, 1999-2007	NFL Pro Bowl
1999-2000	*Sporting News* first-team all-NFL
1999-2002	Associated Press All-Pro

---

caneers into the NFC Championship game against the eventual Super Bowl champions, the St. Louis Rams. When Dungy was fired following the 2001 season, John and his teammates regrouped under new head coach Jon Gruden. The Buccaneers, playing in John's adopted hometown of San Diego, defeated the Oakland Raiders to win Super Bowl XXXVII in January, 2003.

Continuing the Story

In the year after the championship season, John experienced professional disappointment for the first time since his early years with the Buccaneers. While still considered to be among the best defensive backs in the NFL, he was limited by shoulder and neck injuries and missed two games of the 2003 season. He underwent surgery to repair the damage, but the Buccaneers cut ties with him after his eleventh NFL season in order to create payroll flexibility.

Disappointed not to get the chance to finish his career with the Buccaneers, but still believing he could play football at a high level, John considered signing with the New York Jets, where former Buccaneers defensive-backs coach Herm Edwards had become the head coach. John also considered joining Dungy with the Indianapolis Colts but finally settled on the Denver Broncos.

In Denver, John accepted a move from his long-time position of strong safety to free safety and continued to play as if he were in his prime. On October 3, 2004, he made an emotional return to Tampa to face his former teammates, a game the Broncos won, 16-13. He carried his off-field philanthropy to Denver, using his charitable organization, the John Lynch Foundation, to recognize and reward outstanding students in Tampa and Denver. In 2007, at the age of thirty-six and after injuries limited him to thirteen games, John consid-

---

NFL Statistics

Season	GP	Tac.	Sacks	FF	FR	Int.
1993	15	13	0.0	1	0	0
1994	16	15	0.0	0	0	0
1995	9	37	0.0	0	0	3
1996	16	103	1.0	2	1	3
1997	16	109	0.0	1	2	2
1998	15	85	2.0	1	1	2
1999	16	117	0.5	1	0	2
2000	16	85	1.0	0	2	3
2001	16	87	1.0	1	1	3
2002	15	64	0.0	0	0	3
2003	14	72	0.5	0	1	2
2004	15	64	2.0	3	0	1
2005	16	61	4.0	4	0	2
2006	16	83	0.0	2	1	0
2007	13	59	1.0	0	0	0
Totals	224	1,054	13.0	16	9	26

Notes: GP = games played; Tac. = tackles; FF = forced fumbles; FR = fumble recoveries; Int. = interceptions

ered retirement even though he was named to his ninth Pro Bowl team. In March, 2008, he agreed to a one-year contract to return to the Broncos for a final season.

Summary

John Lynch made his reputation in the NFL with his jarring hits and his natural leadership ability. Those qualities, coupled with his charismatic personality, made him an all-time fan favorite in two of the most passionate football towns in the United States. For nearly a decade, he defined the position

of strong safety in the NFL. Off the field, his generosity was noted in the two communities where he played.

Carter Gaddis

Additional Sources

Altobelli, Lisa. "First Person: John Lynch." *Sports Illustrated* 104, no. 3 (January 23, 2006): 35.

Bradley, Michael. *Football All-Stars: The NFL's Best.* New York: Rosen, 2003.

Harry, Chris, and Joey Johnston. *Tales From the Bucs Sideline.* Champaign, Ill.: Sports, 2004.

Hugh McElhenny

Born: December 31, 1928
      Los Angeles, California
Also known as: Hugh Edward McElhenny, Jr. (full name); the King; Slider

Early Life

Hugh Edward McElhenny, Jr., who would someday become one of football's best broken-field runners of all time, was born on December 31, 1928, in Los Angeles, California, to a petite mother and a wiry, 130-pound, 5-foot 4-inch father. When he was eleven years old, Hugh stepped on a broken milk bottle and severed all the tendons in one foot. Not only was he bedridden for five months and on crutches for seven, but also doctors proclaimed he would never walk again.

Hugh began a series of exercises that gradually strengthened his foot. Instead of having to use a cane for life, he was eventually able to join the

Hugh McElhenny (39) carrying the ball for the San Francisco 49ers in a 1952 game against the Dallas Texans. (Frank Rippon/Getty Images)

George Washington High School football team. He still had to take painkiller shots before each game, and he wore a steel plate in the sole of his shoe.

One other incident actually served to further Hugh's future career. When he was six, a man with a shotgun chased Hugh and his friends off a vacant lot. Hugh was shot in the back. From then on, he ran scared. Whenever he played football, he ran as fast as he could, imagining that man with the gun chasing him. At a high school track meet, he was clocked at 9.7 seconds for the 100-yard dash and he set the world's interscholastic 120-yard hurdles record of 14 seconds.

The Road to Excellence

Hugh's father, a prosperous coin machine operator, disliked football and refused to sign Hugh's permission slip to play the game in high school. His mother signed it, and Hugh made her proud by playing brilliantly. Consequently, forty colleges wooed him with scholarships. Hugh wanted to be near his childhood sweetheart Peggy Ogston, whom he later married, so he chose Compton Junior College.

Hugh, 6 feet 1 inch and 205 pounds, scored 23 touchdowns at Compton and led the school to the national junior college championship. Meanwhile, another sixty-three colleges courted Hugh, hoping to recruit him. Rumors were that he chose the University of Washington because the road there was "paved with twenty-dollar bills." Hugh's may have been the first celebrated recruiting case to come to public attention. While at the University of Washington, Hugh openly admitted to having three cars, $30,000 in the bank, two professional teams paying his way through school, and the promise of a lifetime job from four companies.

In his junior year, Hugh scored five touchdowns and gained 296 yards in a single game; he also set a Pacific Coast Conference single-season rushing record. The following year, he made all-American after scoring seventeen touchdowns and 125 total points.

The Emerging Champion
Hugh signed with the San Francisco 49ers after confidently asking them for $30,000. He soon agreed to a compromise—only $7,000—and became known as the first college star to take a cut in salary in order to play professionally.

As a rookie in 1952, Hugh led the league in rushing average with seven yards per carry. He scored sixty points. He was named all-pro and rookie of the year. Few NFL players have had a finer first season. That year and from then on, Hugh ran with the ball the way boys do in their happiest dreams: with speed, power, instinct, and a complete mastery of moves such as faking, sudden bursts, spinning, pivoting, and sidestepping. He also made full use of his keen intuition and wide-angle vision that told him where his opponents lurked. Sometimes he made instinctive plays like crisscrossing a field forty yards in order to gain five yards.

Because he was a superb pass receiver and an

Honors and Awards

1951	College All-American
1952-53	NFL All-Pro Team
1953-54, 1957-59, 1962	NFL Pro Bowl Team
1958	NFL Pro Bowl Co-Player of the Game
1963	NFL All-Pro Team of the 1950's
1970	Inducted into Pro Football Hall of Fame
1981	Inducted into College Football Hall of Fame
	Uniform number 39 retired by San Francisco 49ers

outstanding running back, Hugh was soon nicknamed "the King" by his teammates. At times, owing to his body rhythm and balance, the 49ers also referred to him as "Slider" because of his skill at sliding away from or eluding tacklers.

Hugh's best playing years were from 1952 to 1958, when he wore out six pairs of shoes a season. He played in six Pro Bowl games. His team never won a title during his tenure, however. In his short career with San Francisco, Hugh amassed 4,288 yards. He also made 264 pass receptions and 360 points.

Continuing the Story
In 1955, Hugh injured the same foot he had maimed as a child. Still, he managed to average 3.6 yards per carry. His playing began to go into a slump, however. After quarreling with his new coach, the tough taskmaster Red Hickey, Hugh asked to be traded.

Hugh continued with the Minnesota Vikings, where he was team captain and most valuable player in 1961. Soon, however, the years of twisting and turning the cartilage in his knees caught up with him. When he was traded to the New York Giants in 1963, he knew he had to prove he was not washed up. In striving to do his best, Hugh pulled a muscle in his thigh. Soon after helping the Giants win the Eastern Conference championship, he tired of the pain and retired to San Francisco.

There, Hugh worked for Al-

NFL Statistics

		Rushing				Receiving			
Season	GP	Car.	Yds.	Avg.	TD	Rec.	Yds.	Avg.	TD
1952	12	98	684	7.0	6	26	367	14.1	3
1953	12	112	503	4.5	3	30	474	15.8	2
1954	6	64	515	8.0	6	8	162	20.3	0
1955	12	90	327	3.6	4	11	203	18.5	2
1956	12	185	916	5.0	8	16	193	12.1	0
1957	12	102	478	4.7	1	37	458	12.4	2
1958	12	113	451	4.0	6	31	366	11.8	2
1959	10	18	67	3.7	1	22	329	15.0	3
1960	9	95	347	3.7	0	14	114	8.1	1
1961	13	120	570	4.8	3	37	283	7.6	3
1962	11	50	200	4.0	0	16	191	11.9	0
1963	14	55	175	3.2	0	11	91	8.3	2
1964	8	22	48	2.2	0	5	16	3.2	0
Totals	143	1,124	5,281	4.7	38	264	3,247	12.3	20

Notes: GP = games played; Car. = carries; Yds. = yards; Avg. = average yards per carry *or* average yards per reception; TD = touchdowns; Rec. = receptions

len and Darwood, an advertising agency, where he handled the NFL's merchandising account. He was inducted into the Pro Football Hall of Fame in 1970.

As the preeminent ball carrier of the 1950's, Hugh had what it took to be the best: dedication, speed, and size. Another reason the King was so successful was that he was the first of football's running specialists. He was the first running back able to concentrate exclusively on his strength, which was running with the ball. Before his time, backfield men played on both defense as well as offense. The era of the specialist began with Hugh, among others. By the time he retired in 1964, all players were able to specialize in what they did best.

Summary

Hugh McElhenny earned his nickname "the King" for his many royal qualities on the gridiron, enabling him to rank among the world's top running backs. His statistics show he was more than just a runner, for he caught 264 passes in his career. He retired with one of the best averages in yards per carry in pro football history.

Nicholas White

Additional Sources

Carroll, Bob. *Total Football: The Official Encyclopedia of the National Football League.* New York: HarperCollins, 1999.

Maiocco, Mat. *San Francisco 49ers: Where Have You Gone?* Champaign, Ill.: Sports, 2005.

Reggie McKenzie

Born: July 27, 1950
Detroit, Michigan
Also known as: Reginald McKenzie (full name)

Early Life

Reginald McKenzie was born on July 27, 1950, in Detroit, Michigan. His family's home, however, was just outside the city in Highland Park. Reggie was one of eight children of Nettie and Henry McKenzie. Like many in Highland Park, Reggie's family was poor, but Reggie's parents worked hard to see that their children made the most of their opportunities. They encouraged Reggie to be a positive part of his community by participating in such organized recreation as Little League and Boy Scout Troop 1286.

Scouting was an important part of Reggie's early life. Scout Master Sam Smith taught Reggie about leadership and stressed the importance of caring for others and believing in oneself. Reggie remained an active member of the Boy Scouts right through his years at Highland Park High School.

The Road to Excellence

At Highland Park High School, Reggie excelled as a two-way football star, playing both offensive and defensive tackle. He credits his line coach Jim Bobbitt with encouraging the kind of positive thinking and self-confidence needed to become a professional football star. That attitude helped Reggie deal with the disappointment he felt when a recruiter from Michigan State University told him

that he did not have what it took to be a major college football player. The University of Michigan disagreed, however, and soon afterward offered Reggie an athletic scholarship.

As an offensive guard on a Michigan Wolverines team that ran the ball often and with great success, Reggie gained considerable national attention. During his four years at Michigan, Reggie played on two Rose Bowl teams and was selected to play in the Hula Bowl and college all-star games. In 1972, after earning all-Big Ten honors as a junior and senior, Reggie was named a consensus all-American. Just as there were those who questioned his ability to play college football, there were a few professional scouts who wondered if Reggie's lack of pass-blocking experience at Michigan would limit him as a professional. The Buffalo Bills, however, never doubted his ability and drafted him in the second round of the 1972 NFL draft.

The Emerging Champion

When Reggie joined the Bills in 1972, the team was in desperate need of offensive-line help. Even though "the Juice," O. J. Simpson, one of the greatest running backs ever, was a member of the Bills backfield the previous three seasons, the team compiled disappointing 4-10, 3-10-1, and 1-13 records. That began to change when Reggie joined the team.

After his first professional game, a preseason match in Chicago against the Bears, Reggie realized his new team also needed a team leader. In that game, the Bills held a commanding 24-0 half-time lead, but the Bears rallied and ended up tying the game 24-24. In the locker room afterward, a disgusted Reggie announced that he would not be a part of a team that just quits. In his rookie season, Reggie not only became a starter but, by most accounts, the most solid performer on the offensive line. Although their 4-9-1 record in 1972 was not good, it was the best the team had done since 1966. That season, behind Reggie's lead blocks, Simpson led the NFL in rushing with 1,251 yards.

During the off-season, Reggie suggested to

Honors and Awards

1971-72	All-Big Ten Conference Team
1972	Chicago College All-Star Team
	Hula Bowl All-Star Team
	Consensus All-American
1973	Wisconsin Pro Football Writers NFL Top Blocking Lineman
	Associated Press All-NFL Team
	Sporting News All-AFC Team
	Professional Football Writers of America All-NFL Team
	Football News All-NFL Team
1973, 1980	United Press International All-AFC Team
1983	University of Michigan Second-Fifty-Year All-Time Team

Simpson that, because the offensive line blocked well enough in 1972 for him to gain 1,251 yards, they should be able to get him 2,000 yards in 1973. When training camp opened, Reggie told the rest of his teammates his new goal. Most, including Simpson, thought Reggie's dream was farfetched.

By the seventh game of the 1973 season, however, Simpson had already rushed for more than 1,000 yards. Suddenly, the Bills' players began to believe in Reggie's prediction. In the final game of the season, Simpson needed 197 yards to hit the 2,000-yard mark. Behind the blocking of Reggie and the rest of the offensive line, Simpson gained 200 yards and became the first running back to rush for more than 2,000 yards in a season. For his efforts, Reggie, in just his second professional season, was named all-NFL by the Associated Press (AP), Pro Football Writers of America (PFWA), and *Football News*.

Continuing the Story

A fixture in the Bills starting lineup from his first game of his rookie season, Reggie started in 140 consecutive games, a team record. His streak came to an end in 1981 only after a serious knee injury sidelined him for the season's final ten games.

In 1983, after eleven seasons in a Buffalo Bills uniform, Reggie was traded to the Seattle Seahawks, where he rejoined Chuck Knox, the former Bills head coach. Knox, who had coached the Bills from 1978 until 1982, was known for his successful run-oriented offenses. When he traded for Reggie, he knew he got a player who not only could demonstrate his "run-offense" first-hand but was a proven team leader as well.

Although injuries began to take their toll, Reggie managed to play twenty-four of a possible thirty-two games with the Seahawks. His inspirational play earned him respect and admiration from fans and players alike.

Summary

Although Reggie McKenzie retired as an active player after the 1984 season, he was quickly moved into a management position with the Seahawks as director of marketing and sales. Knowing the importance of positive role models and opportunities in education, Reggie founded and would continue to run the Reggie McKenzie Foundation, which tutors needy Detroit-area youngsters in reading and life skills so they too might someday realize their potential. The foundation has been successful and has received a number of awards for its work.

Joseph Horrigan

Additional Sources

Carroll, Bob. *Total Football: The Official Encyclopedia of the National Football League.* New York: HarperCollins, 1999.

Gauruder, Dana, and Rob Doster. *Game Day: Michigan Football—The Greatest Games, Players, Coaches, and Teams in the Glorious Tradition of Wolverine Football.* Chicago: Triumph Books, 2006.

Schultz, Randy. *Legends of the Buffalo Bills.* Champaign, Ill.: Sports, 2003.

Jim McMahon

Born: August 21, 1959
        Jersey City, New Jersey
Also known as: James Robert McMahon (full
    name)

Early Life

James Robert McMahon was born on August 21,
1959, to Roberta (Williams) McMahon and James
Francis McMahon in Jersey City, New Jersey. Jim
was the second of six children. Jim's mother, a Mor-
mon, and father, a Catholic, moved the family to
San Jose, California, when Jim was three years old.

When Jim was halfway through high school, the
McMahons moved again. Jim started his junior
year of high school in Roy, Utah, and he quickly
made a name for himself in his new town. Jim
lettered in three sports: baseball, basketball,
and football. In 1977, he was named all-state
most valuable player in football. As a Catholic,
Jim would have attended the University of Notre Dame if he had been recruited by the
school. He was not, however, and, based on the
pass-oriented offense at Brigham Young University (BYU), Jim decided to play college football as a quarterback in the Western Athletic
Conference (WAC).

The Road to Excellence

Jim was obviously a talented young athlete, and
his performance with the Cougars at BYU was
awesome. In 1978, his sophomore year, he
shared the quarterback position, yet he still
won all-WAC honors. In 1979, Jim shattered
college football records. In one season, Jim
passed for more than 4,000 yards and tied
two National Collegiate Athletic Association
(NCAA) records. He also set thirty-two NCAA
total-offense and season-passing records.

In 1980, Jim threw 47 touchdowns, gaining
a total of 4,627 yards with 4,571 yards passing.
He gained an average of 385.6 total yards per
game and threw for an average of 380.9 yards
per game. In the 1980 season, Jim passed for
more than 300 yards in eleven consecutive
games, averaging 10.7 yards per pass attempt.

He was chosen all-WAC for the second consecutive
year, and his passing totals were the best in the
country. He played most of the season with a
hyperextended knee that caused him to miss two
games, but he played in the July and Senior Bowls
and was selected a consensus all-American. At the
end of the season, Jim was honored as the country's
best quarterback with the first annual Davey
O'Brien National Quarterback Award. As the Cougars' full-time quarterback for two years, Jim threw
81 touchdowns, passing for 8,126 yards. Not surprisingly, the Cougars won WAC titles and Holiday
Bowl championships both years.

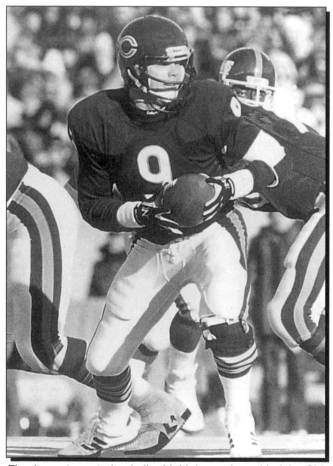

*Flamboyant quarterback Jim McMahon, who guided the Chi-
cago Bears to victory in Super Bowl XX in 1986.* (Courtesy of
Chicago Bears)

288

The Emerging Champion

In Jim's years at BYU, he set fifty-six NCAA records; this in itself was a record, as the previous highest total was only eighteen. He threw for 84 touchdowns with 9,723 total yards and 9,536 yards passing. His completion rate at BYU surpassed 64 percent, while his interception rate stayed at less than 3 percent.

In the first round of the 1982 NFL draft, Jim was picked fifth, the first choice of the Chicago Bears. His ability to throw repeatedly and accurately carried him through seven years with the Bears in which he threw for 67 touchdowns, completing 874 passes for 11,203 yards. In 1984, Jim received a high 97.8 rating as quarterback, but after nine games he was knocked out for the season with a lacerated kidney.

Jim was back in great form in 1985. The Bears compiled a 15-1 regular season record, and Jim threw for 15 touchdowns and 2,392 total yards, completing 56.9 percent of his 313 passes. In postseason play, both the New York Giants and the Los Angeles Rams lost to the unstoppable Bears, who dominated the New England Patriots in Super Bowl XX, winning 46-10. In the Super Bowl, Jim threw 2 touchdown passes, completing 12 of 20 passes for 256 yards. He became a national celebrity, as much for his trademark headbands and outrageous behavior as for his football talent. The Bears were compared to the greatest NFL teams ever, and it seemed that Jim and his teammates were on top of the world.

Continuing the Story

Jim's body, however, could not take much more. In 1986, he was out frequently with injuries, although

NFL Statistics

Season	GP	PA	PC	Pct.	Yds.	Avg.	TD	Int.
1982	8	210	120	57.1	1,501	7.15	9	7
1983	14	295	175	59.3	2,184	7.40	12	13
1984	9	143	85	59.4	1,146	8.01	8	2
1985	13	313	178	56.9	2,392	7.64	15	11
1986	6	150	77	51.3	995	6.63	5	8
1987	7	210	125	59.5	1,639	7.81	12	8
1988	9	192	114	59.4	1,346	7.01	6	7
1989	12	318	176	55.3	2,132	6.70	10	10
1990	5	9	6	66.7	63	7.00	0	0
1991	12	311	187	60.1	2,239	7.20	12	11
1992	4	43	22	51.2	279	6.49	1	2
1993	12	331	200	60.4	1,967	5.94	9	8
1994	3	43	23	53.5	219	5.09	1	3
1995	1	1	1	100.0	6	6.00	0	0
1996	5	4	3	75.0	39	9.75	0	0
Totals	120	2,573	1,492	58.0	18,147	7.05	100	90

Notes: GP = games played; PA = passes attempted; PC = passes completed; Pct. = percent completed; Yds. = yards; Avg. = average yards per attempt; TD = touchdowns; Int = interceptions

Honors and Awards

1981	Davey O'Brien National Quarterback Award
1982	United Press International NFC Rookie of the Year
1985	NFL Pro Bowl
1991	*Pro Football Weekly* Comeback Player of the Year
1999	Inducted into College Football Hall of Fame

he threw 5 touchdown passes in six games. The Bears, with an awesome Buddy Ryan-coached defense, hardly missed a beat in the regular season, going 14-2 and again winning the Central Division title. Jim, however, could not play in the postseason. After a December game against the Bears' old rivals, the Green Bay Packers, Jim's shoulder required surgery. The Bears were not the same without him and failed to repeat as Super Bowl champions.

In the next two seasons, Jim struggled to stay in the lineup. He showed flashes of brilliance, but his best days were clearly behind him. Moreover, he quarreled publicly with Bears coach Mike Ditka, and after the 1988 season he was traded to the San Diego Chargers.

After only one season as a starter at San Diego, he moved on to the Philadelphia Eagles and, after three seasons there, to the Minnesota Vikings. He had become primarily a backup quarterback; as his career wound down, he devoted more time to his family: In 1982, he had married Nancy Daines, and they had four children. Jim then spent one season, 1994, with Arizona and two more seasons, 1995-1996, with Green Bay. He retired from pro football at the end of the 1996 season.

In the next few years, Jim appeared in Sherwin Williams commercials presented during Super Bowls XXXIII and XXXIV and the Nike "Fun Police" commercials with Gary Payton. He also participated in several charitable events, including the Charity Golf Tournament in Arizona and the Children's Miracle Network activities. In 1999, he was elected to the National Football Foundation's College Football Hall of Fame. In 2006, he visited Iraq to encourage American troops stationed in the country.

Summary

Jim McMahon's determined career in football was perhaps best characterized by his tremendous spirit and athleticism. His natural athletic talent combined with his leadership skills, intelligence, and determination helped make him one of the great players of his era.

Alicia Neumann

Additional Sources

McGrath, Dan, and Bill Adee. *The '85 Bears: Still Chicago's Team.* Chicago: Triumph Books, 2005.

McMahon, Jim, and Dave Brown. *Jim McMahon's In-Your-Face Book of Pro Football Trivia.* Chicago: Contemporary Books, 2003.

McMahon, Jim, and Bob Verdi. *McMahon!* New York: Warner Books, 1987.

Taylor, Roy. *Chicago Bears History.* Charleston, S.C.: Arcadia, 2004.

Donovan McNabb

Born: November 25, 1976
   Chicago, Illinois
Also known as: Donovan Jamal McNabb (full
   name)

Early Life

Donovan Jamal McNabb was born the son of middle-class parents, Sam and Wilma McNabb, who taught him and his older brother Sean the value of hard work, humility, and honesty. In 1984, the McNabbs moved from the tough neighborhood of Southside Chicago to Dolton, a southern Chicago suburb, because they sought a safer environment for their sons. Their neighbors greeted the first African American family on the block with racial epithets and obscenities and vandalized their home. However, the McNabbs proved to be good neighbors, and Donovan—cheerful, intelligent, and friendly—became a popular student at school. Soon the community accepted the family.

Although Donovan was a gifted athlete, his incessant clowning left his junior high school coaches with the impression that he was not serious about sports. In the meantime, his brother became a high school star in football and basketball. Donovan idolized him and served as the basketball manager when his brother was on the team.

The Road to Excellence

In seventh grade Donovan played quarterback on a neighborhood team and continued in the position at Mt. Carmel, a Chicago Catholic high school. Like his brother, he excelled in both basketball and football. Donovan started as a junior and averaged more than 35 points per game. He was heavily recruited by colleges and chose Syracuse University, where he had the best opportunity to start as quarterback, play basketball, and

major in communications. Behind Donovan, in his first year of eligibility, the Syracuse Orangemen won nine out of ten games and earned a victory over Clemson University in the Gator Bowl.

In his second year, Donovan won Big East Conference player of the year award and led his team to a share of the Big East title and another bowl victory, this time at the Liberty Bowl. In his third season, he set a school record for total passing yards, with 2,488, and was again named Big East player of the year in both his junior and his senior years for an unprecedented three times. Donovan had hopes for the Heisman Trophy but lost to University of Texas running back Ricky Williams. Furthermore, despite Donovan's achievements, NFL scouts rated a number of other senior quarterbacks—such as Cade McNown, Dante Culpepper, and Tim Couch—higher. In the end, Donovan outplayed all of them in the NFL.

Donovan McNabb, who led the Philadelphia Eagles to the Super Bowl in 2005. (Tim Shaffer/Reuters/Landov)

The Emerging Champion

In the 1999 draft, Cleveland drew first and chose Couch. The Philadelphia Eagles picked next. Andy Reid, the team's new coach, was determined to select Donovan, but when the pick was announced, the vocal Philadelphia fans booed lustily, disappointed that the team did not pick the spectacular running back Ricky Williams. In the end, Reid was justified because Williams was plagued by off-field problems throughout his NFL career.

In 1999, Reid started Donovan in midseason. In 2000, with an outstanding defense and an improved offensive line, the team won eleven games under Donovan, who proved to be one of the league's bright young quarterbacks. The Eagles went to the playoffs for the first time in five years but fell to the New York Giants in the second round.

Over the following seven years, the Eagles, behind Donovan, made the playoffs five times, winning the division on four occasions. However, the team was unable to win the Super Bowl. The Eagles advanced to the championship game once, in 2005, but lost by three points to the New England

NFL Statistics

Season	GP	PA	PC	Pct.	Yds.	Avg.	TD	Int.
1999	12	216	106	49.1	948	4.4	8	7
2000	16	569	330	58.0	3,365	5.9	21	13
2001	16	493	285	57.8	3,233	6.6	25	12
2002	10	361	211	58.4	2,289	6.3	17	6
2003	16	478	275	57.5	3,216	6.7	16	11
2004	15	469	300	64.0	3,875	8.3	31	8
2005	9	357	211	59.1	2,507	7.0	16	9
2006	10	316	180	57.0	2,647	8.4	18	6
2007	14	473	291	61.5	3,324	7.0	19	7
2008	16	571	345	60.4	3,916	6.9	23	11
Totals	134	4,303	2,534	58.9	29,320	6.8	194	90

Notes: GP = games played; PA = passes attempted; PC = passes completed; Pct. = percent completed; Yds. = yards; Avg. = average yards per attempt; TD = touchdowns; Int. = interceptions

Patriots. Donovan continued to be followed by controversy. He was blamed for the team's poor time management in the last minutes of the Super Bowl. In three separate years, he was injured and had to miss long periods of the season. As the Eagles performed well behind Donovan's backups, critics said that he was not the reason for the team's success, pointing to the club's stellar defense.

Continuing the Story

In 2003, the controversial conservative radio personality Rush Limbaugh, who was a commentator for an ESPN football show at the time, said Donovan was overrated because the NFL wanted to promote black quarterbacks. Limbaugh's statement was quickly refuted by other pundits who pointed out that Donovan was comparable to any quarterback in the league, regardless of race.

Though 2004, in which Donovan passed for a career-high 31 touchdowns, was his strongest year statistically, he continued to display strong leadership qualities in the following seasons despite suffering through several injuries. In 2007, he started fourteen of his team's sixteen games, passed for more than 3,000 yards for the fifth time in his career, and completed better than 61 percent of his passes. That year, he was chosen as the quarterback on the Eagles' seventy-fifth anniversary team.

During the 2008 season, Donovan did even better in every statistical catagory. Once again,

Syracuse University Records

Most career touchdown passes, 77
Most career yards, 8,389
Highest career passing efficiency, 155.1
Most single-season touchdowns, 22

Big East Conference Records

Most career yards, 9,950
Most career passing yards, 8,389
Most career touchdown passes, 77

Honors and Awards

1990's	Big East Conference Offensive Player of the Decade
1996-98	Big East Conference Player of the Year
2000-04	NFL Pro Bowl
2002	Wanamaker Award
2004	NFC Offensive Player of the Year
2007	Quarterback of Philadelphia Eagles seventy-fifth anniversary team

he led the Eagles to the conference championship game, only to lose to the Arizona Cardinals in a thriller. During the team's 32-25 loss, Donovan threw for 375 yards and three touchdowns.

Summary

Donovan McNabb helped enhance the image of the African American quarterback in the NFL. Although he possessed great athleticism, he also became known for his character, intelligence, and leadership. Despite the impatience of the Philadelphia fans, who desired nothing less than a Super Bowl victory, Donovan's records established him as one the greatest quarterbacks in team history. At the end of the 2008 season, his career record of only 90 interceptions in 4,303 pass attempts stood as an NFL record for fewest interceptions per attempt (2.09 percent) in league history.

Frederick B. Chary

Additional Sources

Mattern, Joanne. *Donovan McNabb: The Story of a Football Player.* Hockessin, Del.: Mitchell Lane, 2005.

Robinson, Tom. *Donovan McNabb: Leader on and off the Field.* Berkeley Heights, N.J.: Enslow, 2007.

Steenkamer, Paul. *Donovan McNabb.* Berkeley Heights, N.J.: Enslow, 2003.

Steve McNair

Born: February 14, 1973
　　　Mount Olive, Mississippi
Died: July 4, 2009
　　　Nashville, Tennessee
Also known as: Steve LaTreal McNair (full name); Air McNair

Early Life

Steve LaTreal McNair was born in Mount Olive, Mississippi, in 1973. He was the fourth of five children born to Lucille McNair. He grew up in a cramped three-bedroom house. His mother gave him the nickname "Monk," short for monkey, because of his tendency to climb trees near his home.

Steve's older brother Fred was the heralded quarterback in the family and was considered the best athlete. Steve attended Mount Olive High School, where he excelled at football and participated in basketball and baseball. In ninth grade, he told his mother that he was disappointed that everyone always mentioned Fred and that he was going to be better than his brother. True to his word, he became Mount Olive's starting quarterback and led the team to a state title in 1989. He also played defensive end, tying a state record with 30 career interceptions, with 15 in his senior year alone. In his senior season, he was a high school all-American selection by *Prep* magazine and made the all-state team.

The Road to Excellence

At Alcorn State University, outside of Lorman, Mississippi, Steve really began to showcase his talents. While he had offers to play defensive back at other schools, he desired to play quarterback, and Alcorn State was the only university to give him that opportunity. Normally, a quarterback playing at a division I-AA, all-black school with an enrollment of approximately 3,300 would not garner serious national attention. However, Steve compiled eye-catching statistics.

As a freshman at Alcorn State in 1991, Steve rushed for 242 yards; passed for 2,895 yards; and had 30 touchdowns, 6 rushing and 24 passing. *Sports Illustrated* named him its offensive player of the year for all NCAA divisions. He was also named to the all-Southwestern Athletic Conference first team.

During the four years Steve played for Alcorn State, he displayed the full range of his football talents. By the time he was a senior, he had become the only player in NCAA history to gain more than 16,000 yards in total

Steve McNair. (AP/Wide World Photos)

NFL Statistics

Season	GP	PA	PC	Pct.	Yds.	Avg.	TD	Int.
1995	6	80	41	.512	569	7.11	3	1
1996	10	143	88	.615	1,197	8.37	6	4
1997	16	415	216	.520	2,665	6.42	14	13
1998	16	492	289	.587	3,228	6.56	15	10
1999	11	331	187	.565	2,179	6.58	12	8
2000	16	396	248	.626	2,847	7.19	15	13
2001	15	431	264	61.3	3,350	7.8	21	12
2002	16	492	301	61.2	3,387	6.9	22	15
2003	14	400	250	62.5	3,215	8.0	24	7
2004	8	215	129	60.0	1,343	6.2	8	9
2005	14	476	292	61.3	3,161	6.6	16	11
2006	16	468	295	63.0	3,050	6.5	16	12
2007	6	205	133	64.9	1,113	5.4	2	4
Totals	161	4,544	2,733	60.1	31,304	6.9	174	119

Notes: GP = games played; PA = passes attempted; PC = passes completed; Pct. = percent completed; Yds. = yards; Avg. = average yards per attempt; TD = touchdowns; Int. = interceptions

He rushed for an additional 169 yards on 31 carries with 2 touchdowns.

In 1997, the owner of the Oilers, Bud Adams, moved the team from Houston, Texas, to Nashville, Tennessee, and changed its name to the Tennessee Titans. Steve was the Titans' starting quarterback in sixteen games. He helped set a team record for the fewest interceptions, 13, in a single season. He also led the team in rushing touchdowns, 8, and ranked second in team rushing with 674 yards, the third most in NFL history by a quarterback.

offense during his career. Because of his incredible college passing statistics, he became known as "Air McNair." He also set a collegiate record by averaging 400.5 yards in total offense per game, and he threw for a total of 119 career touchdowns. He broke every Alcorn State game, season, and career passing and total-offense record.

In 1994, Steve made his fourth consecutive all-Southwestern Athletic Conference team and was a unanimous Associated Press all-American. He won the Walter Payton Award for the top NCAA Division I-AA player; was awarded the Eddie Robinson Trophy, for the top player at a black college; and finished third in the Heisman Trophy balloting.

The Emerging Champion

Some teams were reluctant to draft him because he played at a small school, and they wondered if he could compete in the NFL. However, the Houston Oilers drafted Steve third overall—which at the time was the highest position a black quarterback had ever been drafted. The Oilers developed him slowly, keeping him in the backup position and allowing him to adjust to the professional game. He played in four games—two as a starter—and passed for 569 total yards, with 3 touchdowns and 1 interception. He also rushed for 38 yards on 11 carries.

In 1996, Steve played in ten games and started four times. He completed 61.5 percent of his passes for 1,197 yards and 4 touchdowns.

Continuing the Story

In 1998, Steve set career highs in pass attempts, 492; completions, 289; yards, 3,228; and passing touchdowns, 15. He led all NFL quarterbacks in rushing, with 599 yards, for the second consecutive season and helped set a new team record for fewest interceptions with 10. Steve also gained a reputation as a "comeback player," as he led the team to several last-minute scores during the year.

In 1999, Steve missed five games because of back surgery. His backup, Neil O'Donnell, led the Titans so well in Steve's absence that some fans did not want Steve to return immediately as the starter. However, coach Jeff Fisher named Steve as the starter following his recovery, and he went on to win nine of his eleven starts. In fact, he led the team to the NFC Championship game, in which the Titans beat the Jacksonville Jaguars 33-14 to advance to the Super Bowl against the St. Louis Rams.

Honors and Awards

1991	*Sports Illustrated* NCAA football player of the year
1991-94	All-Southwestern Athletic Conference first team
1994	Associated Press All-American
	Walter Payton Award
	Eddie Robinson Trophy
2000, 2003, 2005	NFL Pro Bowl
2003	Associated Press NFL most valuable player
	NFL All-Pro Team

In the 2000 Super Bowl, Steve led his team to a remarkable comeback after trailing the Rams at halftime 16-0. Although he only threw for 214 yards, compared to Rams quarterback Kurt Warner's 414 yards, his performance on critical drives kept the Titans in the game until the last play. He set a Super Bowl record for quarterbacks when he rushed for 64 yards. However, Steve and the Titans were stopped one yard short of sending the game into overtime when Kevin Dyson was tackled by Rams linebacker Mike Jones to end the game.

Steve was never able to replicate his incredible statistics from college, but he was an excellent quarterback. For the 2003 season, he was named the most valuable player, sharing the honor along with Peyton Manning. He also showed amazing grit and determination.

In April 2006, Steve was traded to the Baltimore Ravens. He quickly became the team's starting quarterback but suffered through two injury-plagued seasons. Worn down by his recurring injuries, he announced his retirement from professional football in the spring of 2008. With a home and business interests in Nashville and a farm in Mississippi, Steve was still only thirty-five years old and appeared set to enjoy a busy life as an entrepreneur and philanthropist. Just over one year later, however, his life came to a sudden and shocking end. On July 4, 2009, he and a young woman friend were found shot to death in a Nashville condominium. Investigators concluded that the woman, with whom Steve had been having an affair, shot him several times while he was sleeping and then shot herself.

Summary

Despite the apparently sordid nature of his untimely death, Steve McNair will be remembered as one of football's great quarterbacks. From his spectacular college career through his years in the NFL, he was a double threat to defenses because he had a strong passing arm and was an explosive runner. He was also known as one of the NFL great "gamers"—a player who absorbed hard knocks without complaining and returned to the playing field, even in pain. He never won a Super Bowl, but he will also be remembered for the athletic skills and competitive nature with which he led the Tennessee Titans to one of the most exciting Super Bowl finishes of all time. Had receiver Kevin Dyson managed only one more yard on Steve's last Super Bowl pass play, Steve might now also be remembered as a Super Bowl MVP.

Tinker D. Murray, updated by P. Huston Ladner

Additional Sources

Collie, Ashley Jude. *Gridiron Greats: Eight of Today's Hottest NFL Stars.* New York: Rosen, 2003.

Legwold, Jeff. *Steve McNair: High-Flying Quarterback.* St. Charles, Mo.: GHB, 2001.

Pompei, Dan. "More Air for McNair." *The Sporting News,* August 7, 2000, 39.

Price, S. L. "Air McNair." *Sports Illustrated* 81, no. 13 (September 26, 1994): 40.

Stewart, Mark. *Steve McNair: Running and Gunning.* Brookfield, Conn.: Millbrook Press, 2001.

Archie Manning

Born: May 19, 1949
   Drew, Mississippi
Also known as: Elisha Archie Manning III (full
   name)

Early Life

Elisha Archie Manning III was born on May 19,
1949, in Drew, Mississippi, to Elisha Archie
"Buddy" Manning, Jr., and Jane "Sis" Manning.
Archie was an athletic youth who played baseball,
football, and basketball. He wanted to be a running back on the football team but was not considered fast enough; instead, he became a quarterback. His favorite sport was baseball, and he was a
gifted player who was recruited as a professional
when he finished high school. However, he had
been offered football scholarships to Tulane University, Mississippi State University, and the University of Mississippi. Archie decided to forgo baseball
and use his football scholarship at the University of
Mississippi in order to gain a college degree.

The Road to Excellence

Archie did not start his first year, 1967, at Mississippi, but he performed well on the freshman
squad. During the summer of 1968, Archie's father
committed suicide, and the young football player
was the first to discover the body. He initially
wanted to quit football and college in order to provide for his family, but his mother persuaded him
to return to Mississippi.

Archie became the starting quarterback his
sophomore year. He was a great passer who could
also run the ball. He remained the starter for three
years. He developed into a superb player; however,
the Mississippi team was mediocre. In 1969, in the
first prime-time televised college football game,
Archie passed for 436 yards and ran for 104 more in
a 33-32 loss to the University of Alabama. Archie's
540 yards tied a Southeastern Conference record.
That year, Archie placed fourth in voting for
the Heisman Trophy. He was third the following
year. During his college career, Archie accumulated 4,753 passing yards, had 823.5 running yards,
and scored 56 touchdowns. He was named a collegiate all-American and his jersey, number 18, was
retired by Mississippi after his graduation in 1971.
In 1970, Archie met his future wife, Olivia Williams. The two married in 1971 and had three children, Cooper, Peyton, and Eli.

The Emerging Champion

Archie was the second pick in the 1971 NFL draft
and was chosen by the New Orleans Saints. During
his first season, he shared quarterback responsibilities with Edd Hargett. Archie started ten games
and threw 6 touchdowns and 9 interceptions. He
also ran for 4 touchdowns. The Saints finished
the season with a record of four victories, eight defeats, and two ties. After his initial lackluster debut,
Archie emerged as one of the best quarterbacks in
the NFL. In his second year, his first as starter, he
led the NFL in both passing attempts
and completions, throwing for 2,781
yards and 18 touchdowns. Nonetheless,
the team struggled. That year, Archie
was sacked 43 times, a league high for
the year.

   In Archie's eleven years with the
Saints, the team never had a winning
record. New Orleans was plagued by a
poor defense and weaknesses in the offensive line and running game. Archie
also had some injuries to overcome, including a shoulder injury that prevented
him from playing during the 1976 sea-

NFL Statistics

Season	GP	PA	PC	Pct.	Yds.	Avg.	TD	Int.
1971	12	177	86	51.3	1,164	6.6	6	9
1972	14	448	230	48.6	2,781	6.2	18	21
1973	13	267	140	52.4	1,642	6.1	10	12
1974	11	261	134	51.3	1,429	5.5	6	16
1975	13	338	159	47.0	1,683	5.0	7	20
1977	10	205	113	55.1	1,284	6.3	8	9
1978	16	471	291	61.8	3,416	7.3	17	16
1979	16	420	252	60.0	3,169	7.5	15	20
1980	16	509	309	60.7	3,716	7.3	23	20
1981	12	232	134	57.8	1,447	6.2	5	11
1982	7	132	67	50.7	880	6.7	6	8
1983	5	88	44	50.0	755	8.6	2	8
1984	6	94	52	55.3	545	5.8	2	3
Totals	151	3,642	2,011	55.2	23,911	6.6	125	173

Notes: GP = games played; PA = passes attemped; PC = passes completed; Pct. = percent completed; Yds. = yards; Avg. = average yards per attempt; TD = touchdowns; Int. = interceptions

son. The following year, he started only nine games and threw for 1,284 yards, his lowest output since his rookie year. However, the following season, Archie threw for 3,416 yards and 17 touchdowns. He was selected to the NFL Pro Bowl and was named the league's most valuable player. The Saints finished the season with seven victories and nine defeats. Archie returned to the Pro Bowl the following year, while the team finished with an even record of eight wins and eight defeats. Archie's best season was 1980: He threw for 23 touchdowns and more than 3,700 yards. However, the Saints won only one game that year. A new coach, Bum Phillips, was hired, and he brought in Ken Stabler as quarterback. Archie started eleven games that season and was traded to the Houston Oilers the following year.

Continuing the Story

Archie played for Houston for one year before moving to the Minnesota Vikings, retiring after the 1984 season. In Houston, Archie started only three games, and in Minnesota only two. During his fourteen years in the NFL, Archie threw for 23,911 yards and ran for 2,197. He passed for 125 touchdowns and ran for 18. However, the teams for which he played had a record of just 47 wins, 139 losses, and 2 ties.

After retiring from the NFL, Archie became a football commentator for college and professional football. He also devoted himself to teaching his sons the intricacies of football. Cooper, the eldest, was an outstanding wide receiver at Mississippi, whose career was cut short when he was diagnosed with spinal stenosis. However, Archie's other two sons, Peyton and Eli, became star college quarterbacks and then played in the NFL. Peyton played for the Indianapolis Colts, where he set a number of league records and won the 2007 Super Bowl. Eli played for the New York Giants and won the Super Bowl the following year. Not only did both sons win Super Bowls in consecutive years, they were also named most valuable player in their respective Super Bowl games.

Summary

Archie Manning was a great quarterback who played for a weak team. His presence on the Saints carried the team through a period of significant adversity. He was the all-time passing leader for the Saints and his jersey was retired by the team. In 1989, he was named to both the Mississippi Sports Hall of Fame and the National Football Foundation's College Football Hall of Fame. Archie's greatest legacy, however, is the football dynasty carried on by his sons.

Tom Lansford

Additional Sources

Manning, Archie, Peyton Manning, and John Underwood. *Manning.* New York: Harper, 2001.

Serpas, Christian. *The New Orleans Saints: Twenty-five Years of Heroic Effort.* Layfayette, La.: Acadian House, 1992.

Worthington, J. A. *The Mannings: Football's First Family.* Bloomington, Minn.: Red Brick Learning, 2006.

Eli Manning

Born: January 3, 1981
New Orleans, Louisiana
Also known as: Elisha Nelson Manning (full
name)

Early Life

Eli Manning was born Elisha Nelson Manning on
January 3, 1981, in New Orleans, Louisiana, to
Archie and Olivia Manning. The youngest of three
boys, Eli, and his brothers Cooper and Peyton, exhibited athletic ability from a young age. Their
father, a quarterback, had a successful career as a
collegian at the University of Mississippi and as a
professional with the New Orleans Saints, the
Houston Oilers, and the Minnesota Vikings. Eli's
oldest brother Cooper was diagnosed with a cogni-
tive spinal disease and chose to retire from football
rather than risk paralysis. Eli's older brother Pey-

ton had a successful career playing for the University of Tennessee and the Indianapolis Colts.

When Eli was a child, his father traveled regularly. Cooper and Peyton dealt with their father's
absence, while Eli was more sensitive, spending a
good deal of time with his mother. Many attribute
his ability to remain calm under pressure on the
football field to the reassuring times he spent with
his mother. He excelled in baseball and basketball
but was noticed for his football abilities above all
else.

The Road to Excellence

Eli played for the prestigious Isidore Newman
High School in New Orleans, as did his brothers.
While in high school, Eli started three seasons,
throwing more than 7,000 yards and leading his
school to state championship with an 11-1 record.

His performance caught the attention of scouts across the country,
and he was heavily courted. While
Eli considered his options, former
University of Tennessee offensive
coordinator David Cutcliffe told Eli
that he had become the head coach
for the University of Mississippi. Cutcliffe had been instrumental in developing Peyton's career, so Eli decided to attend his father's alma
mater. He enrolled at Mississippi in
1999.

Eli sat out his first college season. During that semester he was
arrested for public drunkenness and
possession of alcohol by a minor.
Embarrassed by his mistakes, Eli returned to practice determined to
prove himself and was named the
Rebels starting quarterback in 2001.
Eli surpassed expectations during
his college career, compiling 10,119
passing yards, 81 touchdowns, and
a passer rating of 137.7. Furthermore, in 2003, he led the Rebels to
a 10-3 record and a victory in the

*Eli Manning holding the Vince Lombardi Trophy after leading the New York
Giants to an upset victory of the New England Patriots in Super Bowl XLII.*
(Mike Blake/Reuters/Landov)

Honors and Awards

2001, 2003	Conerly Trophy Winner
2003	Johnny Unitas Golden Arm Award
	Maxwell Award
	National Football Foundation and College Football Hall of Fame Scholar Athlete Award
	Southeastern Conference most valuable back
	Mississippi Sportsperson of the Year
	Mississippi Amateur Athlete of the Year
	Southeastern Conference Offensive Player of the Year
2004	Cotton Bowl offensive player of the game
2008	Super Bowl most valuable player

Cotton Bowl. That year, he was third in the running for the Heisman Trophy. He set fifty-four team records and received the Johnny Unitas Golden Arm Award, the Maxwell Award, the National Football Foundation and College Football Hall of Fame Scholar Athlete Award, as well as many others.

In 2004, Eli graduated with a degree in marketing and a grade point average of 3.44. Because of his impressive college career, Eli became the number-one NFL draft pick.

The Emerging Champion
The San Diego Chargers held the first pick in the 2004 draft. However, Eli stated that he would not play for the team. San Diego selected Eli and traded him within hours to the New York Giants for Phillip Rivers. Eli signed a six-year contract with the Giants for $74 million plus a $20 million signing bonus.

Eli began the 2004 season on the bench as Kurt Warner's backup. However, Eli started the last seven games of the season, winning only one. Warner voided his contract after 2004, and Eli became the official starting quarterback in 2005. In his second season, he fluctuated between moments of brilliance and monumental mistakes. He played with confidence and finished the season completing 294 of 557 passes for 3,762 yards, helping the team finish the season with an 11-5 record. He scored 24 touchdowns, 18 more than in his rookie year, but also threw 17

interceptions. Eli's third year resulted in similar numbers. In both seasons, he started strong and finished tired. In 2006, the team made the playoffs as a wild card but lost to the Philadelphia Eagles.

Continuing the Story
By 2007, Eli had become comfortable with his role and exuded confidence in his skills and those of his teammates. Despite suffering through injuries, the Giants finished strongly with a 10-6 record. In the 2007 playoffs, the Giants beat the Tampa Bay Buccaneers, the Dallas Cowboys, and the Green Bay Packers, securing them a trip to the championship game. The Giants played the New England Patriots in Super Bowl XLII, New York's first Super Bowl since 2000.

The New England Patriots entered the 2008 Super Bowl game undefeated and heavily favored to win. However, Eli threw two go-ahead fourth-quarter touchdowns, sealing a 17-14 victory over the Patriots. For his stellar performance, Eli was named the most valuable player (MVP) of Super Bowl XLII.

Many observers considered the Giants' 2008 Super Bowl victory something of a fluke, and few expected the Giants to be major contenders in the 2008 season. However, the Giants proved the doubters wrong after the new season started, and Eli had another strong passing year. Eli led the team to a 12-4 record, but the Giants were upset by the Eagles in their first playoff game.

Standing at 6 feet 4 inches and weighing an impressive 225 pounds, Eli possessed the build for a powerful quarterback. Furthermore, he had a powerful, quick, and accurate arm and an ability to maintain control of the ball. Coming from a football dynasty, he also possessed the discipline and

NFL Statistics

Season	GP	PA	PC	Pct.	Yds.	Avg.	TD	Int.
2004	9	197	95	48.2	1,043	5.3	6	9
2005	16	557	294	52.8	3,762	6.8	24	17
2006	16	522	301	57.7	3,244	6.2	24	18
2007	16	529	297	56.1	3,336	6.3	23	20
2008	16	479	289	60.3	3,238	6.8	21	10
Totals	73	2,284	1,276	55.9	14,623	6.4	98	74

Notes: GP = games played; PA = passes attempted; PC = passes completed; Pct. = percent completed; Yds. = yards; Avg. = average yards per attempt; TD = touchdowns; Int. = interceptions

the desire to become the best in his field. However, his ability to correctly read the opposing defense before the start of a play, to remain calm in stressful situations, and to process scenarios rapidly, made him an incredible quarterback.

After the Hurricane Katrina disaster in September of 2005, Louisiana natives Eli and Peyton coordinated relief efforts to help those in need. They collected and sent relief supplies to Baton Rouge to help families who had lost nearly everything.

Summary

Although Eli Manning comes from a family of successful football stars, his success has been due mostly to his own determination and abilities, not to his name. He earned his place in the Ole Miss Sports Hall of Fame for his efforts, not those of his father or brother, and he led the New York Giants to the Super Bowl championship—a feat the team had not accomplished since 1991. Eli and his brother Peyton not only became the first pair of brothers to quarterback Super Bowl teams, but also they are the first brothers to be named the game's MVPs. They accomplished the feat in consecutive years.

Sara Vidar

Additional Sources

Christopher, Matt. *On the Field with . . . Eli and Peyton Manning.* Boston: Little, Brown, 2008.

Coughlin, Tom, and Brian Curtis. *A Team to Believe In: Our Journey to the Super Bowl Championship.* New York: Ballantine Books, 2008.

Hudson, Hugh. *Back-to-Back: Super Bowl Champions Peyton and Eli Manning—An Unauthorized Biography.* New York: Price Stern Sloan, 2008.

Vacchiano, Ralph, and Ernie Accorsi. *Eli Manning: The Making of a Quarterback: The Incredible Rise of the New York Giants.* New York: Skyhorse, 2008.

Peyton Manning

Born: March 24, 1976
New Orleans, Louisiana
Also known as: Peyton Williams Manning (full name)

Early Life

Peyton Williams Manning was born to Olivia and Archie Manning on March 24, 1976, in New Orleans, Louisiana. Peyton's father had been a two-time all-American quarterback at the University of Mississippi and was picked second overall in the NFL by the New Orleans Saints in 1971. He played professionally for fourteen years, which undoubtedly had a huge influence on his three sons, Cooper, Peyton, and Eli. The boys went to their father's

Indianapolis Colts quarterback Peyton Manning calls to his team during a game against the San Diego Chargers in 2009. (Donald Miralle/Getty Images)

games, and Peyton listened to cassettes of radio broadcasts of Archie's college games. However, Peyton was not allowed to play organized football until the seventh grade, since his father felt the game was too dangerous to play at a younger age.

The Road to Excellence

Peyton was known as an intense athlete from the start. He practiced diligently, studied film, and set high expectations for himself. However, he did not emerge as a star until his sophomore year at Isidore Newman High School. In his three years as a starter, the team lost only five games. Peyton threw for 82 touchdowns and more than 7,000 yards and was named the 1993 Gatorade national player of the year. Though it seemed like an obvious choice to follow in the footsteps of his father and older brother by going to the University of Mississippi, Peyton chose the University of Tennessee.

Peyton stayed for his senior season at Tennessee, though many speculated he would forgo his final season of eligibility. In college, Peyton had a 39-6 record as a starting quarterback, set thirty-three school and eight Southeastern Conference records, and won numerous awards. However, he did not receive the Heisman Trophy, given to the nation's top collegiate athlete. Peyton set two National Collegiate Athletic Association records, for single-season and career interception percentages. He finished his college career with 89 touchdowns and 11,201 passing yards.

The Emerging Champion

In the 1998 NFL draft, the Indianapolis Colts chose Peyton as the number-one overall pick. Indianapolis made its decision not only based on Peyton's athletic ability but also because of his mental toughness and leadership qualities. In Peyton's first play in his first preseason start with the Colts, he threw a 48-yard scoring pass to wide receiver Marvin Harrison, signifying the start of a memorable quarterback-wide receiver combination. Eventually, Peyton and Harrison broke the NFL records for the most completions, yards, and touchdowns between a quarterback and wide receiver.

Though the Colts had a losing record, 3-13, during his rookie season, Peyton set team and NFL rookie records in completions, attempts, yards, touchdowns, and consecutive games with touchdown passes. In 1999, the Colts finished 13-3, the biggest one-season improvement in NFL history. Though the team lost to the Tennessee Titans in the American Football Conference (AFC) divisional playoffs, Peyton ended the season with 4,135 yards and 331 completions, a team record.

The following season, Peyton set the Colts single-season record for passing yards, completions, games with 300 or more yards, and touchdowns. Then, in 2001, Peyton and the Colts first displayed the team's now famous "no-huddle offense," in which the offense huddled either for a few seconds or not at all before lining up for the next play. This offensive strategy helped the Colts become known as a fast-acting team that put pressure on the opposing team's defense.

During the 2002 season, Peyton became the first quarterback in NFL history to have 4,000 or more passing yards in four consecutive seasons. In 2003, he continued the streak, passing for more than 4,000 yards for the fifth season in a row. Furthermore, he shared the NFL most valu-

able player (MVP) honor with Tennessee Titan quarterback Steve McNair. In 2004, Peyton had another record-setting season: He broke the then-record for touchdown passes in one season, with 49, and the passer rating, with a 121.1 rating. He was selected as both the NFL MVP and offensive player of the year. Despite the many awards and records Peyton had achieved since his rookie season, he had not yet won a Super Bowl, which many believed was the last important barrier to cross.

Continuing the Story

In 2006, Peyton amassed 4,397 passing yards and led the league with a passer rating of 101 and 31 touchdown passes. The Colts advanced to the AFC Championship game against the New England Patriots, a team that had eliminated the Colts from the

Honors and Awards

1992-93	Louisiana Class 2A most valuable player
1993	New Orleans Quarterback Club Player of the Year
	Gatorade High School Player of the Year
1994	Southeastern Conference Freshman of the Year
1995	First-Team All-Southeastern Conference
1997	Davey O'Brien National Quarterback Award
	Johnny Unitas Golden Arm Award
	Maxwell Award
	James E. Sullivan Award
	Southeastern Conference Championship most valuable player
	Citrus Bowl most valuable player
	First-Team All-American
	Southeastern Conference Player of the Year
	First-Team All-Southeastern Conference
1999-2000, 2002-07	NFL Pro Bowl
1999-2000, 2006	NFL All-Pro Second Team
2003-04	Bert Bell Award
2003-04, 2008	NFL most valuable player
2003-05	NFL All-Pro First Team
2004	American Football Conference Offensive Player of the Year
2005	Walter Payton Man of the Year Award
	Byron "Whizzer" White Humanitarian Award
	Pro Bowl most valuable player
2007	Super Bowl most valuable player

NFL Statistics

Season	GP	PA	PC	Pct.	Yds.	Avg.	TD	Int.
1998	16	575	326	.567	3,739	6.50	26	28
1999	16	533	331	.621	4,135	7.76	26	15
2000	16	571	357	.625	4,413	7.73	33	15
2001	16	547	343	62.7	4,131	7.6	26	23
2002	16	591	392	66.3	4,200	7.1	27	19
2003	16	566	379	67.0	4,267	7.5	29	10
2004	16	497	336	67.6	4,557	9.2	49	10
2005	16	453	305	67.3	3,747	8.3	28	10
2006	16	557	362	65.0	4,397	7.9	31	9
2007	16	515	337	65.4	4,040	7.8	31	14
2008	16	555	371	66.8	4,002	7.2	27	12
Totals	176	5,960	3,839	64.4	45,628	7.7	333	165

Notes: GP = games played; PA = passes attempted; PC = passes completed; Pct. = percent completed; Yds. = yards; Avg. = average yards per attempt; TD = touchdowns; Int. = interceptions

playoffs in the two previous seasons. Though the Colts trailed 21-3, Peyton led the team to a 38-34 victory, following a fourth-quarter, seven-play, 80-yard touchdown drive to take the lead with only one minute left in the game. This eighteen-point comeback was the largest deficit ever overcome in an NFL conference championship game. In the Super Bowl, the Colts defeated the Chicago Bears, 29-17. Peyton was named the Super Bowl MVP and finally overcame the perception that he was unable to win the big games.

In 2007, Peyton helped the Colts to a 13-3 season and a first-round bye in the playoffs. The team lost the divisional playoff game to the San Diego Chargers, 28-24. However, Peyton finished the season with more than 4,000 yards for the eighth time.

During the 2008 season, the Colts started badly. Peyton had had knee surgery shortly before the season began, and he sat out the entire preseason schedule. When the regular season began, it was clear that he was not up to his usual form, and the Colts finished the first half of the season with a 4-4 record. By then, Peyton was back to form. He led the Colts to eight-straight victories to finish the season. An upset loss to the Chargers ended the season in the first playoff game, but for his outstanding leadership, Peyton was again named league MVP.

Summary

Peyton Manning's success as a football player reflected his life of dedication to his sport. These qualities led him to rank near the top in numerous NFL categories, including career completions, career passing yards, and career touchdown passes. He was the first quarterback in NFL history to throw for more than 3,000 yards in the first nine seasons of his career and be named to eight Pro Bowls.

Lamia Nuseibeh Scherzinger

Additional Sources

Brenner, Richard J. *Kurt Warner and Peyton Manning.* Syosset, N.Y.: East End, 2000.

Christopher, Matt. *On the Field with . . . Eli and Peyton Manning.* Boston: Little, Brown, 2008.

Hudson, Hugh. *Back-to-Back Super Bowl Champions Peyton and Eli Manning: An Unauthorized Biography.* New York: Price Stern Sloan, 2008.

Hyams, Jimmy. *Peyton Manning: Primed and Ready.* Kansas City, Mo.: Addax, 1998.

Manning, Archie, Peyton Manning, and John Underwood. *Manning.* New York: HarperCollins, 2000.

Stewart, Mark. *Peyton Manning: Rising Son.* Brookfield, Conn.: The Millbrook Press, 2000.

Worthington, J. A. *The Mannings: Football's First Family.* Bloomington, Minn.: Red Brick Learning, 2006.